D1611205

RESEARCH IN SPECIAL EDUCATION

Third Edition

RESEARCH IN SPECIAL EDUCATION

Designs, Methods, and Applications

By

PHILLIP D. RUMRILL, Jr.

University of Kentucky
Human Development Institute

BRYAN G. COOK

University of Virginia
Department of Curriculum, Instruction and Special Education

NATHAN A. STEVENSON

Kent State University
School of Lifespan Development and Educational Sciences

CHARLES C THOMAS · PUBLISHER · LTD.
Springfield · Illinois · U.S.A.

Published and Distributed Throughout the World by

CHARLES C THOMAS • PUBLISHER, LTD.
2600 South First Street
Springfield, Illinois 62704

© 2020 by CHARLES C THOMAS • PUBLISHER, LTD.

ISBN 978-0-398-09316-7 (paper)
ISBN 978-0-398-09317-4 (ebook)

First Edition, 2001
Second Edition, 2011
Third Edition, 2020

Library of Congress Catalog Card Number: 2019045609

With THOMAS BOOKS *careful attention is given to all details of manufacturing
and design. It is the Publisher's desire to present books that are satisfactory as to their
physical qualities and artistic possibilities and appropriate for their particular use.*
THOMAS BOOKS *will be true to those laws of quality that assure a good name
and good will.*

Printed in the United States of America
MM-C-1

Library of Congress Cataloging-in-Publication Data

Names: Rumrill, Phillip D., Jr. editor. | Cook, Bryan G., editor. |
  Stevenson, Nathan A., editor.
Title: Research in special education: designs, methods, and applica-
  tions / By Phillip D. Rumrill, Jr., University of Kentucky, Human
  Development Institute, Bryan G. Cook, University of Virginia
  Department of Curriculum, Instruction, and Special Education and
  Nathan A. Stevenson, Kent State Univerity, School of Lifespan
  Develpment and Educational Sciences.
Description: Third edition. | Springfield; Illinois : Charles C Thomas,
  Publisher, Ltd., [2020] | Includes bibliographical references and
  index.
Identifiers: LCCN 2019045609 (print) | LCCN 2019045610 (ebook) |
  ISBN 9780398093167 (paperback) | ISBN 9780398093174 (ebook)
Subjects: LCSH: Special education—Research—United States—
  Handbooks, manuals, etc. | People with disabilities—Education—
  Research—United States—Handbooks, manuals, etc.
Classification: LCC LC3981 .RBS 2020 (print) | LCC LC3981 (ebook)
  | DDC 371.9/07/2—dc23
LC record available at https://lccn.loc.gov/2019045609
LC ebook record available at https://lccn.loc.gov/2019045610

CONTRIBUTORS

JIAN LI, PH.D.
Associate Professor
Kent State University
School of Foundations, Leadership, and Administration
Kent, OH

TRICIA NIESZ, PH.D.
Associate Professor
Kent State University, School of Foundations, Leadership, and Administration
Kent, Ohio

LYNN C. KOCH, PH.D.
Professor
University of Arkansas
Department of Rehabilitation, Human Resources, and Communication Disorders
Fayetteville, AR

MYKAL LESLIE, PH.D., CRC, LPC
Assistant Professor, Kent State University
School of Lifespan Development and Educational Sciences
Kent, OH

ZACHARY STRICKLER, M.ED.
Graduate Student
Kent State University
School of Lifespan Development and Educational Sciences
Kent, OH

STUART P. RUMRILL, M.S. CRC
Graduate Student
University of Wisconsin
Madison, Wisconsin

Research in Special Education

JENNIFER DAVENPORT, M.S.
Graduate Student
University of Arkansas
Fayetteville, Arkansas

MELISSA JONES WILKINS, M.S.
Graduate Student
University of Arkansas
Fayetteville, Arkansas

For Amy; Chad, Cassidy, Stuart, Doug, Nate, and Connor; Shirley and Phillip Sr.; and Rick and Brian . . . PDR

For Jean and Gary . . . BGC

For Jenny, Carter, and Lily . . . NAS

PREFACE

This third edition was written as a text and resource guide for graduate-level students, practitioners, and teachers in the fields of special education, disability studies, early intervention, school psychology, and child and family services. The primary purpose of the book is to offer a broad-based examination of the role of scientific inquiry in contemporary special education. As with the first two editions, which were published in 2001 and 2011, our aim was to provide a comprehensive overview of the philosophical, ethical, methodological, and analytical fundamentals of social science and educational research—as well as to specify aspects of special education research that distinguish it from scientific inquiry in other fields of education and human services. Foremost among these distinctions are the research beneficiaries, i.e., children with disabilities, their parents, and special educators; the availability of federal funds for research and demonstration projects that seek to improve educational outcomes for children with disabilities; and the historical, philosophical, and legislative bases for the profession of special education.

We are very pleased to add Dr. Nathan Stevenson of Kent State University as a coauthor of this third edition. This new edition represents a revision of more than 30 percent in comparison to the 2011 second edition. We added more than 250 new references and thoroughly updated every chapter with new developments in research topics, designs, and methods that have emerged over the past decade in the field of special education. We also added considerable text related to evidence-based practice, open science, and quality indicators for special education research in a design-specific context.

Like the 2001 and 2011 versions, this third edition is divided into ten chapters. Chapter 1 establishes the theoretical underpinnings of social scientific inquiry; provides a foundation in the philosophical, epistemological, and methodological considerations related to the design and execution of research in general and special education research in particular; and discusses the broad purposes of research in special education and disability studies. Chapter 2 addresses issues that are preparatory to designing and evaluating special education research, such as sources of research ideas, translating research ideas into research hypotheses, identifying variables, and sampling issues. Chapter 3 discusses key measurement and statistical concepts used in the quantitative research tradition, including reliability and validity of measurement instruments; the purposes of descriptive, inferential, and nonparametric statistics in analyzing numerical data; and selected methods of statistical analysis. Researchers will note an expanded and updated section on the psychometric properties of educational and psychological instruments as well as updated text devoted to nonparametric and multivariate statistics. Chapter 4 reviews ethical issues and guidelines for the design, implementation, and reporting of research in special education. Chapter 5 addresses key criteria for evaluating the quality of special education research, drawing valid inferences from results, and generalizing findings from the research sample to the target population.

Chapters 6, 7, and 8 review the wide range of quantitative, qualitative, and integrative approaches to conducting research in special education, and they feature examples of these designs that we drew from the contemporary educational and disability studies literature. All three of these chapters have been completely updated with new examples and new text describing topic areas and research methods that are most commonly seen in the special education literature. Chapter 6 addresses intervention/ stimulus, nonmanipulation relationship and group comparative, and descriptive studies in the quantitative paradigm. Chapter 7 discusses qualitative research methods as they apply to special education. Chapter 8 examines and categorizes a variety of narrative literature reviews according to their purposes. Chapter 9 presents a published research article section by section; annotates the components and composition of a research report; and provides a protocol that students, practitioners, and educators can use to evaluate the technical soundness and scientific merits of published research articles. The final chapter of this text addresses future trends in special education research as they apply to a variety of stakeholders (e.g., administrators, policymakers, educators, researchers, children with disabilities, parents, funding agencies, consumer advocates).

Because this book was written as an introductory text for graduate students and practitioners in special education, we focus much of the information contained herein on the role of the reader as a "professional consumer" of research. In so doing, we not only orient the student or practitioner to the fundamentals of research design, we also introduce him or her to the professional literature in this dynamic field of inquiry. Like the companion text written by Phillip Rumrill and James Bellini, *Research in Rehabilitation Counseling* (Charles C Thomas, Publisher, 2018), this book provides the "basics" that one would need to begin conducting a research investigation, but we would encourage that person to supplement this book with course-work in statistics and advanced research design before initiating an empirical study.

PHILLIP D. RUMRILL, JR.
BRYAN G. COOK
NATHAN A. STEVENSON

ACKNOWLEDGMENTS

We would like to express our sincere gratitude to the people who made this third edition possible. We begin by thanking our faculty mentors— Dr. Richard Roessler of the University of Arkansas, Dr. Mel Semmel of the University of California at Santa Barbara, and Dr. Cynthia Okolo of Michigan State University—who introduced us to research in disability studies, rehabilitation, and special education and whose work continues to inspire our teaching, research, and writing. We also express our gratitude to our friends and colleagues throughout the United States who have provided us with valuable opportunities to collaborate on research and writing projects: Dr. Kay Schriner of the University of Arkansas, Dr. Brian McMahon of Virginia Commonwealth University, Dr. Paul Wehman of Virginia Commonwealth University, Dr. James Bellini of Syracuse University, Dr. Michael Gerber of the University of California at Santa Barbara, Dr. Lynn Koch of the University of Arkansas, Dr. Mykal Leslie of Kent State University, Dr. Jian Li of Kent State University, Dr. Malachy Bishop of the University of Wisconsin, Dr. Fong Chan of the University of Wisconsin, Dr. Timothy Landrum of the University of Louisville, Dr. Melody Tankersley of Kent State University, Dr. Robert Fraser of the University of Washington, Dr. Shawn Fitzgerald of Antiock New England Graduate School, Dr. David Strauser of the University of Illinois, Dr. Chung-Yi Chiu of the University of Illinois, Dr. Timothy Tansey of the University of Wisconsin, and Dr. Deborah Reed of the University of Iowa.

We are indebted to Dr. Tricia Niesz of Kent State University, Dr. Lynn Koch of the University of Arkansas, Ms. Jennifer Davenport of the University of Arkansas, Mr. Stuart Rumrill of the University of Wisconsin-Madison, and Ms. Melissa Jones Wilkins of the University of Arkansas for contributing the chapter on qualitative research; to Dr. Jian Li of Kent State University for her contributions to the chapter on measurement and statistics; to Dr. Mykal Leslie and Mr. Zachary Strickler of Kent State University and Mr. Stuart Rumrill of the University of Wisconsin-Madison for their contributions to the chapter on research ethics; and to Dr. James Bellini of Syracuse University for allowing us to draw from his co-authored companion text to this book, *Research in Rehabilitation Counseling* (Charles C Thomas, 2018). For their editorial and clerical assistance, we thank Mr. Nathan Rumrill, Ms. Aundrea Gee Cormier, and Mr. Christopher Konieczko, all of Kent State University.

Last, but certainly not least, we extend our appreciation to Mr. Michael Payne Thomas of Charles C Thomas, Publisher for the opportunity to complete this third edition. We look forward to many more cooperative writing and publishing endeavors in the years to come.

CONTENTS

RESEARCH IN SPECIAL EDUCATION

Chapter 1

INTRODUCTION TO RESEARCH
IN SPECIAL EDUCATION

The purpose of this chapter is to establish practical and scientific bases for the special education research enterprise. We begin with an introduction to and overview of the professional practice of special education. We then discuss different ways that special education stakeholders come to know things, such as which instructional practices are effective and should be used, with special attention to the strength for using scientific research as a way of knowing. We then examine primary roles of research in special education, including building the professional literature base, theory building, and identifying effective practices; as well as consider challenges to research in special education.

THE PROFESSIONAL PRACTICE OF SPECIAL EDUCATION

Special education is a multifaceted and extensive service delivery system. The Thirty-Ninth Annual Report to Congress (U.S. Department of Education, 2017) documents that, in 2015, over seven-million American infants, toddlers, children, and youth with disabilities received early-intervention and special-education services (7,172,125 infants, toddlers, children, and youth with disabilities to be exact). Individuals receiving services range from 0 to 21 years in age and are identified as having autism, deaf-blindness, developmental delay, emotional disturbance, hearing impairment, intellectual disability, multiple disabilities, orthopedic impairment, other health impairment (including attention deficit hyperactivity disorder), specific learning disability, speech and language impairment, traumatic brain injury, and visual impairments. Because the characteristics of learners with disabilities vary dramatically, many different professionals are needed to provide special education services in many different settings. In 2014, approximately 380,000

full-time equivalent (FTE) special education teachers, 470,000 FTE parapro-
fessionals (including one-to-one tutors, instructional assistants, support
providers, and translators), and more than 200,000 FTE providers of related
services (e.g., speech-language pathologists, psychologists, occupational therapists, counselors, rehabilitation counselors, physical therapists, social work-
ers, medical/nursing service staff, physical education teachers, and recreation and therapeutic recreation specialists) were employed in the delivery
of special education services throughout the U.S. and outlying areas (U.S.
Department of Education, 2017). Special educators provide services in homes,
community-based settings, regular early childhood programs, separate early
childhood classes, service provider locations (e.g., speech clinician's office),
inclusive classrooms, resource rooms, separate special education classes in
public schools, special schools, residential facilities, private schools, hospitals, correctional facilities, and other settings.

Although the majority of students with disabilities in the United States
are now educated in inclusive settings in public schools, it is important to
remember that a history of advocacy, court cases, and legislation was necessary to provide children with disabilities, especially those with severe disabilities, access to an appropriate education (Yell, Rogers, & Rogers, 1998).
Historically, the common belief that people with disabilities are not capable
of learning kept them out of educational settings. However, it is now widely
recognized that students with disabilities can learn and are entitled to an
appropriate education. Thus, one of the central functions of special education involves the development, identification, and application of instructional practices to effectively educate learners with disabilities. Furthermore, as
Kauffman and Badar (2014) noted, the right to effective instruction is "an important civil and moral right of students with disabilities" (p. 13).

Enacted to provide an appropriate education for students with disabilities, the Individuals with Disabilities in Education Act (IDEA, originally the
Education for All Handicapped Children Act) mandates that an educational team formulate an Individualized Education Plan (IEP), which stipulates
the annual educational goals, services, and placements for each identified
student with a disability. However, there is no guarantee that the individuals
comprising a student's IEP team (e.g., general and special-education teachers, specialists such as speech therapists, school administrators, and parents)
will decide on goals, services, and placements that will produce optimal outcomes for the student. Further, IEPs serve only as a loose guide for day-to-
day student-teacher interactions. Teachers typically have a great deal of freedom in how they interact with and instruct their students. Thus, the determination of what instruction students with disabilities receive is largely made
by teachers who strive to do their best, but who often have not received sufficient training and do not have enough time or resources to optimally meet

the diverse needs of their students. Furthermore, especially since the advent of the internet, teachers are inundated with information regarding recommended, best, promising, and evidence-based practices (see Cook & Farley, 2019). Some of these practices have merit, some are well-intended but untested, and occasionally some come from individuals who intentionally mislead educators trying to make a buck. Unfortunately, most educators do not have the training to critically evaluate the research (or lack of research) supporting the effectiveness of recommended practices. It is little wonder, then, that interventions known to be effective are frequently not implemented, whereas some interventions that have been shown to be relatively ineffective are commonly used (i.e., the research-to-practice gap; Cook & Farley, 2019).

It is seldom a simple and straightforward process to determine what instructional practices are most likely to improve outcomes for learners with disabilities. Indeed, if selecting appropriate and effective teaching practices for students with unique and often problematic learning needs were simple, there would likely be little or no need for special education. Research is one way—we argue it is the most reliable and valid way—for determining the educational effectiveness of instructional practices. In fact, special education pioneers such as Jean Marc Gaspard Itard and Elizabeth Farrell have used research, in one form or another, to inform effective policy and practice since the inception of the field (Kode, 2002; Lane, 1979). The continued influence of research is evident in contemporary reforms such as evidence-based practice and data-based individualization. Despite the benefits of making decisions based on sound research, many educators lack the requisite knowledge and skills to critically evaluate the research base, and instead use other, less reliable, ways of knowing to determine which instructional practices to use. We hope the content of this text detailed in the following sections and chapters will enable special education stakeholders to use research as a means to better understand the enterprise of special education and identify effective instructional practices, with the ultimate goal of improving outcomes and quality of life for learners with disabilities.

WAYS OF KNOWING

Although science provides a relatively objective method for "knowing," it is not the preferred method of many policymakers and teachers for making decisions about what happens in special education classrooms. Many educators prefer "flying by the seat of their pants" (Landrum & Tankersley, 1999, p. 325) and relying on anecdotal information from colleagues and the internet (e.g., Hott et al., 2018; Landrum, Cook, Tankersley, & Fitzgerald,

2007) to using research findings as the basis for pedagogical decisions. We review three of the most prevalent methods that special educators use to make decisions regarding the effectiveness of instructional practices—personal experience, expert testimony, and science—in the following subsections.

Personal Experience

Personal experience involves relying on one's previous experiences or the experiences of others in a similar situation as the basis for one's beliefs. For example, if a teacher perceives that using a whole language approach resulted in improved reading for one student with a learning disability (LD), she may decide to use whole language techniques for all students with LD whom she has in her class in subsequent years, because she has come to believe that this practice works based on personal experience. Alternatively, if a teacher does not have relevant personal experience on an issue, she may talk with fellow teachers in the faculty lounge or read teachers' blogs on the internet in order to access the personal experiences of other teachers.

Use of personal experience has many advantages for educators. First, and most obviously, it is very easy to access; all one has to do is remember one's past or ask someone else with relevant experience. Similarly, the information provided is likely to be perceived as "usable" (see Carnine, 1997, for a discussion of the accessibility, usability, and trustworthiness of educational information). That is, if teachers themselves or their colleagues have already successfully used a practice, it is likely that the information can be readily used by others. Also, because the information derived from personal experience comes from sources typically perceived as "battle-tested" and reliable (Landrum, Cook, Tankersley, & Fitzgerald, 2002), it is likely that teachers consider the information to be trustworthy.

However, personal experience is highly fallible, and using it to determine what and how to teach may result in students receiving less than optimal instruction. For example, just because an intervention works with one student in one situation does not mean that it will work if implemented for other students in other contexts. Furthermore, human perceptions are prone to multiple biases, which can cause people to perceive situations inaccurately. For example, if a teacher strongly believes that a particular instructional practice is going to work, agrees with the philosophy or theory behind the practice, and has devoted a lot of time and energy to implementing the practice, he or she is likely to evaluate the practice as more effective than it actually has been (i.e., confirmation bias; Nickerson, 1998). Similarly, people often fail to perceive objects and events that are unexpected (e.g., inattentional blindness; Simons & Chabris, 1999). For example, if a teacher is not expecting an instructional practice to work, he or she may overlook indications of its effectiveness. In essence, it is easy for teachers, like all people, to fool themselves when they form beliefs based on their own experiences. It is not surprising, then, that popular beliefs derived from personal experience and observations (e.g., the belief that the earth is the center of the universe) have been disproven by science throughout history (Kauffman, 1999). Accordingly, basing one's knowledge of what works and making instructional decisions on personal experience can result in the use of ineffective teaching strategies.

Expert Testimony

Sometimes, educators believe they know a particular instructional practice works because an expert has said or written that it does. The use of expert testimony, or authority, as a way of knowing has certain advantages. First, expert recommendations are readily available. Education, like most fields, has no shortage of experts espousing their opinions. An astounding number of textbooks and professional journals publish the recommendations of experts on a wide variety of topics, and many experts use the internet to disseminate their material. Teachers also attend professional conferences and in-service trainings at which experts present their ideas. Moreover, the college courses that prospective teachers are required to take to gain licensure are taught by professors typically thought of as experts (at least by the professors themselves). Secondly, information from experts is often trustworthy. Expertise is associated with advanced levels of experience, training, and competence. As such, it is likely that experts know what they are talking about, and, in education, will promote instructional practices that are, in fact, effective.

However, it is becoming increasingly difficult to tell who is a bona fide and trustworthy expert. An individual who creates a website touting or selling instructional materials and techniques is not necessarily a true expert. More importantly, even people who are considered experts because of their experience, training, and titles are often wrong (Freedman, 2010). In short, expertise is no guarantee for being correct. Indeed, special education's history is rife with examples of so-called experts recommending practices that have become popular and widely implemented, only to be proven ineffective when scientifically examined. For example, in the 1990s, facilitated communication (a technique involving a facilitator supporting the arm of an individual with autism or other disability while the individual with a disability typed) was promoted by experts as a valid form of communication (Biklen, 1990). However, subsequent research studies showed that the individuals with disabilities were not authoring the typed communications; rather, the communications were being cued and directed by the facilitator (see Mostert,

2001). Facilitated communication not only squandered the time and hopes of many individuals with autism and their families, it tore some families apart when allegations of sexual abuse were made in the facilitated communications. Often, individuals promoting ineffective techniques hold doctorates and are portrayed as experts in their fields. By virtue of their titles, credentials, and reputations, these so-called experts may garner the trust of teachers and parents. However, without systematic and objective evaluation of a practice, we can never be sure that it is effective, regardless of support from those claiming to be experts.

Science

Science refers to "the methodologies of testing disconfirmable hypotheses and proofs through publicly verifiable data" (Kauffman, 1999, p. 265). Science has advanced and served as a common basis for knowledge in diverse academic disciplines by using the scientific method, in which theories ranging from the way the world works to the way children learn are tested by examining (i.e., observing, recording, and analyzing) observable phenomena. Merton (1968) posited that norms such as common ownership of information, cultivated disinterestedness, and organized skepticism underlie the conduct of successful science.

Common ownership of information means that no one person or entity possesses, in the traditional sense, the data used to investigate hypotheses and theories. There are at least two purposes to common ownership of information. First, it is important that other scientists be able to authenticate or check the findings of any given investigation. No study is perfect, and there are multiple sources of error in the research process. As such, research consumers should place limited trust in the findings of a single study, but instead be confident in findings only when multiple studies report converging findings. Indeed, science is unique among ways of knowing in that it has a built-in self-correction mechanism (i.e., other researchers directly replicating a study to test whether the findings are valid; Sagan, 1996; Travers, Cook, Therrien, & Coyne, 2016). Thus, how a study is conducted and the data from which study findings are derived should be available to anyone so that they can be reanalyzed and replicated.

Second, common ownership of information allows researchers to build on and extend each other's work. In this case, because information about how the research was conducted and who participated in the research is publicly available, it is possible for other researchers to indirectly replicate the study by systematically differing some aspects of the study but replicating other aspects. For example, a research investigation may examine whether an instructional practice shown by previous research to be effective for reading fluency for elementary students is also effective for middle school students or for improving reading comprehension. Common ownership of information allows researchers to replicate and vary specific aspects of previous work to investigate whether the findings from previous studies apply to new populations, outcomes, and contexts.

Common ownership of information is typically accomplished through the reporting of research approaches and findings in research reports (e.g., published articles). In the "Method" section of a research report, the authors report detailed information on the participants, research design, procedures, and analysis involved in the study (see Chapter 9). Contact information for the primary author of the research report is also provided so that readers with more in-depth questions about the study can direct their queries to the author. Additionally, it is becoming increasingly common for researchers to share publicly their data and materials on the internet in order to facilitate verification and replication (see Chapter 10).

Cultivated disinterestedness means that researchers should not have a vested interest in the results of their investigations. If researchers stand to gain in some way from showing that an intervention works, they might—consciously or unconsciously—bias aspects of the research (e.g., by engaging in questionable research practices such as trying multiple approaches to analyzing data until desired results are obtained, or failing to report aspects of studies that do not yield desired findings; see John, Loewenstein, & Prelec, 2012). The goal of scientific research, to confirm or disconfirm hypotheses through empirical observations, can only be accomplished meaningfully if investigators conduct research in a disinterested and objective manner. If the norm of cultivated disinterestedness is not adhered to, the findings from an investigation may be a result of investigators' biased research methods rather than allowing the data to "speak for themselves." Common ownership of information allows the scientific community in a field to investigate whether gross violations of the norm of cultivated disinterestedness have occurred.

Finally, science involves *organized skepticism,* which means individual scientists and the larger scientific community should be skeptical when examining new knowledge claims and evaluating the findings and implications of research studies. This is not to say that scientists should be pessimistic and never accept new or novel approaches. Instead, the norm of organized skepticism is intended to guard against uncritical acceptance of invalid ideas and methods (Shermer, 2002). This skeptical approach is especially important in special education, because acceptance of invalid knowledge claims can adversely affect the education and lives of millions of children with disabilities. Common ownership of information suggests that the scientific community should rigorously examine the methods used in any particular research study to determine whether the research was conducted without bias, as per the norm of cultivated disinterestedness. In that process, the scientific community skeptically assesses the interpretation of the researcher's findings to ensure that the stated implications of the research are warranted.

The skepticism embodied in science is probably best exemplified in the incremental approach of scientists in the generation and expansion of new knowledge. Even when a single study that generates new knowledge claims has been cautiously and rigorously examined, the new claim to knowledge is viewed in the context of other existing findings. Evidence generated from a single study is not, by itself, acceptable as a valid knowledge claim. Acceptance of a new knowledge claim (e.g., that an instructional practice results in improved reading achievement for students with LD) by the scientific community requires an accumulation of findings over time. In this way, science does not allow knowledge to be determined by a single study, which is likely to involve some degree of error. Instead, science skeptically guards against putting one's trust in invalid ideas or practices by only accepting knowledge claims that have been supported by multiple investigations—which have, themselves, each been subjected to rigorous, skeptical examination.

The use of science as a way of knowing in special education, however, is not a panacea; science in education has important limitations of which researchers and informed research consumers should be aware. Because of its skeptical nature, science is a slow and gradual process that may not give teachers or policymakers immediate answers to their questions. In addition, because knowledge claims are the product of an accumulation of research findings over time rather than the result of one particular study, people can and do interpret the same literature base differently. Many practitioners become frustrated that competing interpretations of the research literature base sometimes occur, thereby resulting in confusion over whether a particular practice actually should be used. Critics of the scientific method have also challenged the notion that researchers are, or can be, truly disinterested and objective (Gallagher, 2006). Indeed, in most research, investigators pose hypotheses or predictions regarding the outcomes of the study. Can someone who has publicly stated her or his beliefs about the results of an investigation really be disinterested? Probably not. Another issue is that most practitioners do not have the requisite knowledge of and facility with the principles of research design and analysis to meaningfully examine reports of research findings. Thus, research to many educators is simply another form of expert testimony. Moreover, science never guarantees that a particular practice or intervention will be successful all of the time with all learners. Science, as applied in special education, provides information on what works more often or more effectively than other techniques, but it cannot predict with certainty that any intervention will be completely successful with any specific student or group of students.

Despite these limitations, science provides the most reliable, objective, and meaningful approach for determining what works and what to use in special education. As Kauffman (1999) stated, "it [science] is a peerless tool for establishing common knowledge" (p. 266). Without science, special educators are left to make decisions about which practices and policies to implement through their own or others' experiences, the advice of so-called experts, or their own intuition. Science, even when adhering to the norms of common ownership of information, cultivated disinterestedness, and organized skepticism, is not perfect; but it does lead to a knowledge base that has been objectively verified and is less prone to producing invalid knowledge claims. Winston Churchill once said that democracy is the worst form of government, except for all the rest. The same might be said about science; although it is an imperfect way of knowing, it is less flawed than other approaches. The existence and application of a scientific knowledge base is a sign of a mature profession (Kauffman, 1999); the special education research base informs and facilitates effective instruction for learners with disabilities.

RESEARCH AND SPECIAL EDUCATION

Special education is considered, along with other disciplines such as sociology and psychology, to be a social science. In contrast to the hard sciences, such as physics and chemistry, social sciences investigate people and their interactions with one another. One of the interesting and sometimes frustrating aspects of conducting and consuming research in the social sciences is that people's behaviors are so complex and multifaceted that scientists cannot reasonably hope to fully explain the behaviors of any individual or group. Nonetheless, scientific exploration has helped to generate many empirically supported theories that explain a great deal of human behavior and can be used to improve the education of students with and without disabilities.

Research can be thought of as the process of applying science. Researchers in special education collect and analyze empirical data regarding how learners respond to specific educational interventions, how performance is affected by grouping students in different ways, how students interact under certain conditions, how characteristics of teachers influence student experiences and outcomes, and other issues to expand the professional knowledge base and, in turn, improve policy and practice. CEC (n.d.) viewed scientific research and its contributions toward improving the instruction of students as so vital that it listed the following as one of 12 ethical principles for professional special educators: "Using evidence, instructional data, research, and professional knowledge to inform practice."

Scientific research has been used as a tool for investigating the efficacy of policies, procedures, and interventions in special education since the inception of the field. The roots of special education can be traced to a scientist, Jean Marc Gaspard Itard, who employed the principles of scientific research in his attempts to educate "the Wild Boy of Aveyron" in France during the early 1800s (Lane, 1979). Although many questions in special education remain unanswered or partially answered after decades of focused research, researchers have provided direct guidance to special educators by, for example, discerning that certain educational practices are more effective than others for students with disabilities (Cook, Tankersley, & Landrum, 2009; Forness, Kavale, Blum, & Lloyd, 1997). Research has at least three related purposes in the field of special education: building the professional literature base, theory building, and identifying effective practices (Rumrill & Bellini, 2018).

Building the Professional Literature Base

The professional literature base of special education exists in an almost innumerable variety of journals, books, websites, and other sources. The existence of a reliable and valid literature base is important so that teachers, administrators, parents, advocates, and policymakers do not have to personally investigate the host of issues in special education that they encounter. For example, it would be not only impractical for individuals to examine such issues as the prevalence and characteristics of different disabilities, the perceptions and attitudes of teachers, the barriers to implementing school reform, and the effectiveness of instructional techniques; if limited to one's own personal experience and contacts, the results are likely to be misleading. Instead, by accessing the special education literature base, special educators are able to draw on a wealth of previously conducted studies to answer questions and inform policy and practice.

Furthermore, it is important that educational stakeholders review research in the context of the larger literature base, rather than focusing on individual studies. Research investigations often replicate or in some way build on previous research to more thoroughly investigate a practice or policy. The formation of a broad literature base allows educators to place the findings of one study in the context of numerous related findings. Although different studies may have divergent results, the effectiveness of a practice or policy tends to become clear over time once the professional literature base accumulates multiple, high-quality research studies investigating a topic. For example, if a teacher reads a single research study to understand how to better communicate with parents, that study might have involved only a small number of parents and teachers whose communication styles were atypical.

Therefore, the findings from this one study may not indicate a generally effective approach to improve teacher-parent communication. However, if the teacher reads the broader body of research literature on teacher-parent communication, she will identify common findings across multiple research studies that she can use with greater confidence.

The professional literature base in special education can be accessed through a variety of sources. For example, some textbooks are devoted to describing research-based practices in special education (Burns, Riley-Tillman, & Rathvon, 2017; Cook & Tankersley, 2013). Research is also reported and synthesized in a variety of monographs and reports. For example, two divisions of CEC, the Division for Learning Disabilities and the Division for Research, cosponsor the publication of a series of "Current Practice Alerts," which synthesize the research literature on the effectiveness of specific instructional techniques for students with LD (see https://www.teachingld.org/alerts). The most voluminous portion of the special education research literature base is contained in professional journals. Although nonempirical articles such as position papers and policy analyses are published in journals, the reporting of original research is a primary purpose of many professional journals. The scope of special education journals may be specific to a particular disability (e.g., *Learning Disability Quarterly, Behavioral Disorders, American Journal on Intellectual and Developmental Disabilities*), a range of related disabilities (e.g., *Focus on Autism and Other Developmental Disabilities, Journal of the Association for Persons with Severe Handicaps*), an age range (e.g., *Topics in Early Childhood Special Education, Journal of Early Intervention*), or teaching in special education (e.g., *Teacher Education and Special Education, Teaching Exceptional Children*). Other journals broadly target the entire spectrum of topics associated with special education (e.g., *Exceptional Children, Exceptionality, Journal of Special Education, Remedial and Special Education*).

Theory Building

Theory building is a critical but often overlooked aspect of research in special education. Theories in the social sciences are explanations about how and why people behave, perform, interact, and feel, based on conceptual logic and previous observations and research. Theory provides a rationale or purpose for conducting research studies. By applying relevant theory to the issue being examined, researchers generate logical predictions or hypotheses about what will happen in a study. That is, research is implemented to test theory-based predictions. Theory, in turn, is also used to explain the findings of research studies. If the results of a study accord with the theory-based predictions, the theory is supported; and the researcher is able to explain why things happened as they did. When theories have been validated by multiple studies, special educators can have confidence in the theory and apply it in their classrooms. Conversely, if research findings do not support a theory, researchers are forced to re-examine that theory and either abandon or refine it so that it corresponds with research findings. In this manner, "science incorporates a self-correcting mechanism in which theories that cannot be reconciled with empirical data are not accepted" (Mayer, 2000, p. 38). Theory provides the overarching framework by which scientists make sense of phenomena in the world around them, whereas research findings provide the specific evidence on which theories are (a) generated, and (b) confirmed or disconfirmed. Without theory, then, it is difficult for educators to understand why a practice being researched worked or did not work, and thereby to apply the research findings to their own lives and classrooms. Because theory helps guide how teachers are trained, which educational policies are mandated, and how instructional programs are developed and implemented, the role that scientific research plays in developing and refining theory is a critical one.

Identifying Effective Practices

In addition to building a professional literature base and theory, a fundamental purpose of research in special education is to identify effective practices that enable educators to more effectively instruct students with disabilities. Because the identification of effective instructional practices is such an important endeavor, it is imperative that special educators be careful and systematic when interpreting the research literature. As previously noted, individual research studies identify promising, or potentially effective, practices that become established as effective through subsequent and related research that molds theory and strengthens a knowledge claim as part of the professional literature base. However, even a practice that has been reported to work in multiple studies might not merit special educators' trust if those studies are not of high quality; are not designed to determine whether a practice is effective; or show small, unimportant effects on student outcomes. Thus, following the lead of the medical field, special educators have begun to systematically apply standards related to the quantity of studies, quality of the research, research design, and magnitude of effect to research bases, with the goal of establishing evidence-based practices (see Cook & Odom, 2013). Specifically, evidence-based practices are supported by multiple research studies that (a) are of high quality, (b) use appropriate (i.e., experimental) research designs to determine whether a practice works, and (c) demonstrate a meaningfully large effect on student outcomes. The U.S. Department of Education describes evidence-based practices and programs in general education and for some groups of learners with disabilities at the

What Works Clearinghouse (https://ies.ed.gov/ncee/wwc/). Researchers have also identified evidence-based practices for specific groups of students with disabilities (Cook, Cook, & Collins, 2016; Courtade, Test, & Cook, 2015; National Autism Center, 2015, Wong et al., 2015).

CHALLENGES TO RESEARCH IN SPECIAL EDUCATION

Despite its strengths and potential benefits, scientific research faces challenges and obstacles in special education, including (a) limited understanding of and regard for research among some stakeholders, and (b) insufficient replication in the literature base. Although researchers, practitioners, and individuals with disabilities and their family members share many goals (e.g., improving the opportunities and outcomes of children and youth with disabilities), these groups often differ in terms of their experiences, terminology, and values (Smith, Schmidt, Smith, & Cook, 2013). Whereas researchers tend to emphasize generating knowledge from controlled research studies (evidence-based practice), non-researchers (e.g., teachers, parents of children with disabilities) tend to value their own practical experiences and the real-life experiences of others in similar situations (practice-based evidence; Simons, Kushner, Jones, & James, 2003). Thus, many stakeholders do not value or prioritize research evidence (Boardman, Arguelles, Vaughn, Hughes, & Klingner, 2005).

It is important that researchers involve practitioners and individuals with disabilities and their families as partners in research. For example, special educators and children with disabilities and their families can be involved in research by identifying important, socially valid issues to be researched; selecting relevant, socially valid outcome measures to gauge the effects of instructional practices being researched; and providing their perceptions of the interventions used in studies and the outcomes achieved in research studies. Without involving practitioners and individuals with disabilities and their families as partners in research, research risks being a purely academic exercise with questionable relevance and minimal impact. Moreover, excluding non-researchers from the research process can result in disregard and mistrust of research among those who decide what and how to teach students with disabilities. It is our hope that the concepts in this book will enable all stakeholders to better understand the research enterprise and its important role in special education, and therefore be amenable to being involved in and applying the findings of research studies.

Another challenge to research in special education is publication bias and the scarcity of studies with null findings in the special-education research base. Publication bias occurs when studies with null findings (e.g., studies showing that an intervention did not cause improved learner outcomes) are published less frequently than studies with positive effects. Publication bias likely occurs because (a) researchers choose not to submit a study with null findings for publication, perhaps because they feel it is unlikely to be accepted for publication or because they do not want to publicize that a practice they support was ineffective, and (b) because journal editors may be less likely to accept studies with null results if and when they are submitted for publication. Similar to other fields, studies with null findings make up a small portion of the special education research base (Kittleman, Gion, Horner, Levin, & Kratochwill, 2018; Therrien & Cook, 2018), and evidence suggests that studies with null findings are less likely to be published than studies showing positive effects (Sham & Smith, 2014). Studies with null effects are critical not only for identifying generally ineffective practices, but also for identifying the boundaries of effectiveness for validated practices. That is, even effective practices do not work for all types of learners and for improving all outcomes. Therefore, just as researchers should seek to determine for whom and for what outcomes a practice works, it is important to examine for whom and for what outcomes a practice is ineffective. Accordingly, we hope that researchers will conduct and disseminate studies exploring the boundaries of effectiveness of practices, and that research consumers consider research with null effects when making instructional decisions.

SUMMARY

This chapter provides a brief overview of science and its role in special education. In addition to science, the use of personal experience and expert testimony as ways of knowing is discussed. Through norms of science, such as common ownership of information, cultivated disinterestedness, and organized skepticism, special education researchers have built a professional knowledge base, refined theory, and identified effective practices. It is our hope that, by reading the discussions of critical elements of special-education research presented throughout the next nine chapters of this book, special education stakeholders (e.g., practitioners, administrators, teacher-trainers, parents and family members, individuals with disabilities) will become active and critical consumers (and potentially, with additional training, producers) of research, leading to improved educational opportunities and outcomes for children and youth with disabilities.

Chapter 2

GETTING STARTED IN SPECIAL EDUCATION RESEARCH–VARIABLES, RESEARCH QUESTIONS, AND HYPOTHESES

INTRODUCTION

Research in the social sciences, including education, is rooted in conceptual frameworks or theories; that is, every scientifically sound research investigation begins with an idea or hypothesis, along with a thorough understanding of prior research. Both qualitative and quantitative research methods are characterized by the careful collection and analysis of data. More than anything else, making careful observations to confirm or disconfirm a hypothesis is the essence of scientific investigation. However, between the identification of a fruitful idea for research and the collection and analysis of data are several crucial steps in the research process. This chapter will address issues that are preparatory to designing and evaluating special education research. We include sections on sources of ideas for research, identifying and operationalizing research questions, statistical hypotheses, types of variables, and sampling issues.

SOURCES OF RESEARCH IDEAS

Ideas for research can come from a number of different sources. Individual curiosity, personal interests, past and current teaching experiences, service work with school districts and community agencies, and ongoing contact with children and youth with disabilities may provide inspiration for a special education research project (Rumrill, Cook, & Wiley, 2011). Research ideas can also be spurred by an interest in reexamining findings from prior research and filling gaps in the current scientific record.

In an effort to understand certain phenomena, researchers propose concepts, models, and theories to synthesize ideas, variables, and processes in an orderly fashion. The overarching purpose of scientific inquiry is to explain how phenomena relate to each other, which is accomplished using a wide variety of research methods (Goodwin & Goodwin, 2012; McMillan & Schumacher, 2009; Rumrill & Bellini, 2018). Theory is a particularly rich source of research ideas. Often, research is undertaken to test specific hypotheses suggested by theories or models. Moreover, there is an ongoing, reciprocal relationship between theory and research. Theory begins the process by suggesting possible fruitful avenues of research. The theory or model may specify the nature of the relationship among its concepts, elements, or processes that can be tested directly, or the researcher may deduce other hypotheses from theory. Research is then implemented to test the predicted relationship among the elements of the theory or model. If the researcher's hypothesis is supported by the data analysis, the validity of the theory is upheld and thereby strengthened. If the hypothesis is not supported, proponents of the theory need to critically examine the propositions of the theory that did not hold up in the empirical test. This process may lead to revision of the theory, new hypotheses, and subsequent tests of these hypotheses.

It is important to note that failure to confirm a hypothesis is not a failure of the scientific process but a natural byproduct of it. Understanding the limitations of theory and evidence is, arguably, as important as any other aspect of the research process. Researchers must not be fearful of abandoning or revising prior theory as new evidence comes to light.

Research efforts are often stimulated by the need to measure or operationalize various constructs. For example, special education researchers have long been interested in issues such as labeling, teacher attitudes toward children with disabilities, and peer acceptance—all of which have direct bearing on the way that educational services for children with disabilities are identified and implemented. At the level of the individual investigation, research is often precipitated by previous efforts in a given area. A substantial proportion of the published research in special education is directed toward building upon or expanding the results of previous studies. Therefore, it is vital for researchers to have a thorough knowledge of the literature in their area of research interest. This permits them to select a topic for research that is capable of yielding significant new knowledge and that builds on the previous efforts of others. In the discussion section of a research manuscript (see Chapter 9), the author will often include suggestions for future research efforts in the given area that are intended to build upon the findings presented in the paper, address ambiguities in the research findings, or illuminate areas not addressed directly in the paper. These suggestions provide valuable direction for subsequent researchers. In that regard, the hours spent reading the works of others (a habit that often begins in graduate school) constitute the best preparation for a researcher wishing to conduct a study of his or her own.

IDENTIFYING AND OPERATIONALIZING RESEARCH QUESTIONS

Identifying and Operationalizing Research Questions

Stated most simply, "research explores or examines the relationships among constructs" (Heppner, Wampold, Owen, Thompson, & Wang, 2015, p. 43). A construct is a concept that has no direct physical referent (e.g., intelligence, self-esteem, role, joy, sorrow). Because constructs refer to such characteristics as a person's mental state, capacities, or motivations that we cannot directly sense, we must infer their presence from behaviors and other consequences of their existence (Creswell, 2014). Most often, research questions in the social sciences express curiosity about the relationships between or among constructs (Heppner et al., 2015; Rumrill & Bellini, 2018).

Research Questions

As previously discussed, researchers generate ideas for their investigations from a number of sources, including personal experience, casual observation, existing theory, and previous investigations of the phenomena of interest. Whatever the original idea that provides the impetus for research, it must be described concretely so that it can be tested. The research question is usually stated in broad, abstract terms (McMillan & Schumacher, 2009). Often, the broad research question that motivates the research is not stated explicitly in the research article, but it can usually be deduced from a careful reading of the title, the abstract, and the purpose statement that typically concludes the introductory section of a published article (see Chapter 9). The following is a sampling of research questions drawn from recent issues of special education journals:

A. How independent are secondary students with learning disabilities (LD) in mathematics when using virtual manipulatives to complete multistep linear equations (Satsangi, Hammer, & Hogan, 2018, p. 229)?
B. Is there a direct relationship between self-determination and academic achievement for adolescents with intellectual disabilities (Gaumer Erickson, Noonan, Zheng, & Brussow, 2015, p. 46)?

C. What is the average size of the reading achievement gap between school-age students with and without disabilities in the United States (Gilmour, Fuchs, & Wehby, 2018, p. 5)?

D. Do students who identify with a disability or as LGBQ, or both, report higher levels of suicidal ideation than do students who do not identify with either identity (King, Merrin, Espelage, Grant, & Bub, 2018, p. 145)?

Drew (1980) identified three categories of research questions: descriptive, difference, and relationship questions. Descriptive questions ask what some phenomenon is like. Example A is a descriptive research question because the study sought to describe secondary students with LD in mathematics and their ability to use digital manipulatives to represent key mathematical concepts in algebra (Satsangi et al., 2018). Example B is a relationship question in that it seeks to identify and describe a potential relation between self-determination and academic achievement for students with intellectual disabilities (Gaumer Erickson et al., 2015). Examples C and D are difference questions. Difference questions ask if there are differences between groups of people as a function of one or more identified variables. In example C, Gilmour et al. (2018) sought to understand the difference in reading achievement between students with and students without disabilities. In example D, King and colleagues (2018) asked if there were differences in rates of suicidal ideation among groups distinguished by disability status and sexual orientation.

It is important to note that some research questions may seem to fit more than one of the categories described by Drew (1980). Many studies also examine multiple research questions in the same investigation. Nevertheless, crafting a precise research question is a critical component of any study. A well-crafted research question plays a large role in determining the research design and data that need to be collected.

Operational Definitions

Each of the research questions cited previously represents the fundamental research idea that motivated the given study. However, considerable work is needed to translate these broad research ideas into empirical research projects that can be executed. The concepts inherent in the broad research question must be formulated into operational definitions. Operational definitions refer to defining constructs on the basis of the specific activities and operations used to measure them in the investigation (Heppner et al., 2015). Particular measurement instruments are often used to operationalize the constructs inherent in the broad research question. For a knowledge claim to have merit, the manner in which the broad research question is translated into the specific operations of the investigation must make sense to others in the research community.

Operational definitions link the general ideas and concepts that motivate the study to the specific, measurable events that constitute the empirical test of the research question (Heppner et al., 2015; McMillan & Schumacher, 2009). It is an essential link in the chain of reasoning leading from formulating a research question to making a knowledge claim based on the results of a study. A weak link between research questions and research operations will reduce the credibility of the knowledge claim no matter how exemplary the investigation may be along other important dimensions (Goodwin & Goodwin, 2012). A second function of the operational definition is to permit replication of the research procedure by other researchers using similar and different samples (Cronbach, 1988).

In example A cited in the previous section on research questions, the research team operationally defined the independent and dependent variables so they would be easily interpretable and unambiguous to readers and other researchers seeking to replicate or expand this research. Researchers defined explicit instruction as, "the researcher providing each student instruction that incorporated repeated modeling, practice, and feedback on how to solve multistep linear equations" (Satsangi et al., 2018, p. 230).

In example B, self-determination of participants was measured during their final high school year on a 72-item self-report scale, the Arc Self-Determination Scale. The scale provided data relating to autonomy, self-regulation, psychological empowerment, and self-realization as well as an overall score for self-determination (Wehmeyer & Schwartz, 1997). Academic achievement was operationalized in math and reading through the use of the Woodcock-Johnson Research Edition (WJ-RE; Woodcock, McGrew, & Mather, 2007). WJ-RE is a shortened version of the Woodcock-Johnson III, which is a standardized and norm-referenced measure of achievement that has been psychometrically evaluated for reliability and validity.

In example D, Gilmour and colleagues (2018) examined the gap in reading achievement by synthesizing the current body of evidence in a unique approach to research called a meta-analysis. Meta-analyses attempt to make inferences about a phenomenon that has previously been studied on multiple occasions (see Chapter 6). In the case of example D, the research team operationalized the gap in reading achievement between students with disabilities and students without disabilities by the difference (as measured by standard deviations) in the pooled effect sizes from 23 different studies.

Although the previous examples represent quantitative research studies, it is important to note that operationalization of variables is not exclusive to quantitative investigations. Qualitative studies also translate key abstract concepts into specific research operations for the purpose of generating knowledge. For example, Bettini, Wang, Cumming, Kimerling, and Schutz (2018) utilized a qualitative method (semi-structured interviews) to investigate how teachers of students with emotional and behavioral disorders (EBD) in self-contained classes defined their roles. Clearly, how the research team defined the population of interest, interview questions, and constructs of interest (e.g., self-contained) influenced the research design and data collection. Through detailed systematic interrogation of the data, including mechanisms to ensure trustworthiness and reliability of analysis across investigators, the research team ultimately found numerous differences between teachers' perceived roles and the actual daily work they performed (Bettini et al., 2018).

Limitations of Operational Definitions

Operational definitions of constructs are essential to virtually every scientific investigation, and they serve to link the abstract conceptual foundation of a study to its concrete procedures. However, there are several limitations of operational definitions to keep in mind (Rumrill & Bellini, 2018):

1. An operational definition may be incomplete, may greatly simplify, or may bear little resemblance to the abstract construct of interest. For example, an important special education construct such as self-determination may be operationalized for the purpose of an investigation. In example B discussed in the previous section, Gaumer Erickson et al. (2015) drew on prior conceptions of self-determination as behaviors in which the primary causal agent is the individual exhibiting the behavior. This construct was further clarified to the exclusion of external factors as a causal factor in behavior. This distinct operational definition of self-determination was necessarily narrow to enable accurate, reliable, and replicable study. However, this definition left out environmental influences, which certainly influence decision-making and action in any social context.

2. Operational definitions may include features that are irrelevant or not central to the original construct. For example, an investigation of family adjustment issues associated with the onset of disability in children may be operationalized by including in the study families who have children with disabilities and who have sought support services. However, this operational definition of family adjustment problems includes elements that may be irrelevant and could influence the results of the study. Families may seek services for reasons unrelated to disability issues, such as poverty or illness. Also, seeking services is determined by many factors other than experiencing adjustment problems, including availability and expense of services, cultural attitudes to-

ward seeking professional help, and encouragement from others. Thus, there is always a concern that the methods used to define the construct of interest include components that are not related to the original construct but that influence the study findings in ways that the researcher may not anticipate.

3. Often, individual researchers will operationalize the same construct in different ways. Consider the construct of anxiety. Anxiety may be operationalized as a self-report (paper and pencil measure), as skin galvanic response (physiological measure), or as a behavioral rating by an observer. Use of discrepant operational definitions of the same constructs in different studies often leads to different empirical findings, thereby making it difficult to compare studies to each other or to evaluate the credibility of findings in an area of research. Also, utilizing different operational definitions for the same construct implies that the results of a study must be qualified or restricted to the specific operational definitions used. In other words, findings that are based on a particular operational definition of a key construct may not be generalizable to other, different approaches to measuring the same phenomenon. Fortunately, researchers and practitioners are not restricted to single studies in evaluating the status of knowledge in a given area. As research within a topic advances and becomes more complex, subsequent researchers incorporate the lessons of previous studies and operational definitions acquire greater specification as knowledge accumulates (Heppner et al., 2015).

4. The concept of a *latent variable* is used in research to reflect the idea that the same variables can be measured in different ways (Rumrill & Bellini, 2018). The specific measures that are used are referred to as observed variables, or *indicators* of the construct of interest, whereas the latent variable is unobserved. It is not possible to measure a variable in "pure" form, divorced from the method of measurement. Rather, scores on a measured variable are a mixture or combination of variation due to the trait or construct and variation associated with the specific method used to measure the variable (see Chapter 3). In that regard, scores are trait-method units (Campbell & Fiske, 1959). The notion of the operational definition implies that the findings of a study may be restricted (to some degree) to the specific methods used to measure variables, and that measurement, although essential for quantitative studies, also presents the possibility of a confounding influence. When a latent variable is measured in at least two different ways in a study, it is possible to separate the effects due to the construct from the effects due to the measurement method (Campbell & Fiske, 1959; Kazdin, 2002).

5. It is the (sometimes) weak connections between constructs and quantitative operational definitions (or, between latent variables and their measured indicators) that may underlie the characterization of social sciences as "soft," that is, less amenable to clear and convincing confirmation and disconfirmation by empirical tests than the "harder" physical sciences (Rumrill & Bellini, 2018).

Research Hypotheses and Statistical Hypotheses

Whereas research questions are stated in abstract, conceptual terms, research hypotheses are typically stated in terms of the expected relationships among the constructs in a study. They may also be stated in an if/then format that expresses the presumed causal relationship: If these specific conditions are met, then the following result is expected. For example, the research hypothesis tested in the Satsangi et al. (2018) study could be stated as, "there is a causal relation between use of virtual manipulatives with explicit instruction and improvement in students' ability to solve multistep linear equations for students with LD in mathematics." The research hypothesis tested in the Gaumer Erickson et al. (2015) study could be stated as, "there is a direct relationship between self-determination and academic achievement for adolescents with intellectual disabilities."

Statistical hypotheses refer to the specific operational definitions used to measure the variables of interest and the specific statistical approach used in the study. Typically, the statistical hypothesis is stated in its "null" form; in other words, it posits no significant differences on the variables of interest. This is because the logic of statistical tests, based on probability theory, is oriented toward *disconfirming* the hypothesis of no differences between experimental (the group which receives a treatment or intervention) and control (the group which receives no intervention or an intervention that is not relevant to the study purpose) groups (see Chapter 6). For example, Gaumer Erickson et al. (2018) could have addressed the following statistical hypotheses:

1. There is no positive linear correlation between scores on the Arc Self-Determination Scale and scores on the Woodcock-Johnson Research Edition.
2. The factor structure of the items in the Arc-Self Determination Scale are not best represented by a 3-factor model consisting of the subscales of autonomy, self-realization, and psychological empowerment.
3. The subscale of autonomy does not account for the largest proportion of variance in math achievement as measured by the math indicator of the Woodcock-Johnson Research Edition.

Research Questions, Research
Operations, and Knowledge Claims

Research questions are developed from a variety of sources including casual observations and particular interests of the researcher, existing theory that specifies how variables may be related, and previous research in a given area (Rumrill & Bellini, 2018). To test particular hypothesized relationships developed from observation, existing theory, and/or previous research, it is first necessary to operationalize these abstract concepts, that is, make them concrete through specific procedures and measurement operations. In this way, the hypothesis is tested using empirical data. The findings of the study are then delimited by the particular definitions and measures used to operationalize the constructs of interest and the specific conditions in which the constructs were investigated. However, after the investigation is concluded and the results are analyzed, the researcher typically wishes to make statements about the more abstract level of concepts that inform the particulars of the research situation. In other words, science seeks generalized knowledge rather than knowledge that is limited to a particular experimental situation (Rumrill & Bellini, 2018). The strength of a knowledge claim depends upon the quality of the operational definitions, measurement instruments, research design and implementation, the clarity or non-ambiguity of the findings, and how the results of a particular study contribute to the weight of empirical evidence in a given research area.

IDENTIFYING RESEARCH VARIABLES

Most simply stated, variables are "characteristics of persons or things that can take on two or more values" (Bolton & Parker, 1998, p. 444). Types of variables are distinguished by their measurement characteristics. *Categorical* variables are those whose values may include a limited number of discrete categories. Examples of categorical variables include gender, which usually takes on two values, female and male, and marital status, which can have a number of values such as married, single, separated, divorced, or widowed. In given individuals, categorical variables may take on only one of a limited range of possible values. *Continuous* variables are variables that may take any value along a continuum of scores. For example, age (for human beings) may take any value ranging from 0 to approximately 100 years. Intelligence, as expressed in terms of intelligence quotient scores, can take on any value between approximately 20 (below which intelligence is generally regarded as unmeasurable) and approximately 180.

Variables may be directly observable (e.g., eye color) or nonobservable (e.g., self-esteem). Many observable variables, such as movement of digital objects on a screen to represent mathematical operations as in example A (Satsangi et al., 2018), may need to be defined so that all members of the research team are sure to notice the same occurrences of the behaviors. However, in the social sciences in general, and special education research in particular, many key variables of interest are nonobservable (e.g., attitudes toward inclusion of students with disabilities, psychosocial adjustment). These nonobservable variables must be inferred from indirect sources of measurement, such as self-report questionnaires, psychometric tests, and the reports of significant others.

Independent and Dependent Variables and the Logic of Experimentation

Variables are also distinguished by their role in the research process. *Independent variables* are the variables that the researcher manipulates in an experiment, or the variables that are theorized to predict or explain the variation of other study variables in non-manipulation correlational and group-comparative studies (Rumrill & Bellini, 2018; See Chapter 6). Synonyms for independent variables include: input, cause, antecedent, predictor, process, and treatment variables (Bolton & Parker, 1998). In the logic of experimentation, the independent variable causes or produces changes in the *dependent variable*. Synonyms for dependent variables include: measured, consequent, criterion, outcome, and response variables (Bolton & Parker, 1998). In the King et al. (2018) study, the dependent variables were the measured outcomes that the researchers presumed to be influenced by membership in groups defined by disability status, LGBTQ status, or both.

The purpose of experimentation is to examine causal relationships among variables (Kazdin, 1998). In the logic of experimentation, a researcher attempts to examine causality by "systematically varying or altering one variable or set of variables and examining the resultant changes in or consequences for another variable or set of variables" (Heppner et al., 1992, p.40). The variable that is varied, altered, or manipulated in the study is the independent variable. Often, the independent variable is an intervention that is provided to one group but not to other groups. When the independent variable is an intervention, it is called a treatment or situational variable (Kazdin, 1998).

In experimentation, the term *manipulation* refers to the deliberate process of examining the effects of varying the value or level of an independent variable (Rumrill & Bellini, 2018). To examine these effects, resultant changes in the dependent variable (or set of variables) are observed. In the simplest experiment, this manipulation of the independent variable is accomplished by using two groups, a group which receives an intervention and a group which does not receive the intervention. If all preexisting differences between the two groups are minimized except for the difference in the value or level of the independent variable (an extremely difficult proposition to actualize), then the logic of experimental design permits the researcher to conclude that the measured differences between the two groups on the dependent variable (measured after the intervention is concluded) are the result of the independent variable.

In many, if not most, examples of special education research, it is not possible, due to ethical constraints or logical impossibility, to manipulate the independent variable. For example, it is not possible in the real world to randomly assign study participants to a disability status. Also, in "field" research (e.g., the classroom), it is often impossible to ensure that all preexisting differences between experimental and control groups are identified and controlled in the investigation. There are also ethical concerns that limit researchers' ability to cleanly distinguish treatment versus control groups. In some cases, it may be unethical to deny or withdraw a treatment that is needed for a research participant. Though the quest for scientific discovery in special education research is a good end in and of itself, the concerns of participants as people with inalienable human rights must always supersede the demands of research. In these cases, it is more difficult to infer causal relationships between independent and dependent variables based on the study findings (Cook & Campbell, 1979). It is the research design of a study, rather than the specific statistical analyses used in the investigation, which determines the inferential status, or strength of the causal inferences that can be made on the basis of a study's findings (Heppner et al., 2015). In its traditional meaning, independent variable refers to a variable that is amenable to experimental manipulation for the purpose of inferring causal connections.

Status or Individual Difference Variables

Variables that characterize or describe subjects but cannot be assigned or manipulated by the researcher are *status* or *individual difference variables* (Kazdin, 2002). These variables may be aspects of personality (e.g., self-esteem, locus of control, intelligence), aspects of a person's socioeconomic situation (e.g., education level, marital status, family income), or aspects of group membership (e.g., gender, race/ethnicity, sexual orientation). Characteristics of teachers, such as level and type of education, years of experience, and disability status are also examples of status or individual difference variables that have been studied in special education research.

Often, status variables are labeled as independent variables in the research literature and perform the same role as predictors in a statistical analysis. In these cases, making causal inferences based on observed results is problematic because the status variable has not been (and, in fact, cannot be) manipulated. The purpose of using status or individual difference variables in a statistical analysis is to detect *association* between the status and dependent variables, rather than to establish causal explanations. Also, we do not mean to suggest that causal explanation is impossible when the study does not include an experimental manipulation of independent variables. Causality can be inferred from the association between variables on the basis of logic, such as when the status variable logically occurs prior to the "effect," when the status variable covaries with the effect (i.e., changes in the status variable are associated with changes in the dependent variable), and when there is a mechanism of explanation that rationally links the variation of the status variable to its consequences (Creswell, 2014; Kazdin, 2002). Causality can also be inferred on the basis of the total evidence gathered from a series of investigations. For example, the well-established causal link between smoking and lung cancer is supported by a wealth of research evidence rather than the result of any single experimental study or small group of studies.

Moderator Variables

Moderator variables are status variables that influence (i.e., moderate) the effect of an independent or other status variable on a dependent variable. For example, a researcher wishing to compare attitudes toward the inclusion of students with disabilities between general and special education teachers finds that gender is also related to respondents' attitudes. In fact, women in this hypothetical study report more positive attitudes than men regardless of whether they are special education or general education teachers. In this example, gender serves to *moderate* the relationship between type of teaching setting and attitudes toward inclusion.

Moderator variables are often included in the design of a study when the researcher suspects that the relationship between an independent or status variable and a dependent variable is influenced by another status variable. Utilization of moderator variables in the design of investigations permits researchers to identify more precisely the nature of complex relationships among independent and dependent variables.

SAMPLING ISSUES

In conducting a research study, scientists would ideally investigate all people to whom they wish to generalize their findings. These people constitute a population, meaning that they make up the entire group of individuals having the characteristic or characteristics that interests the researcher. For example, researchers who are interested in how adolescents adjust to traumatic brain injury (TBI) in the United States would ideally include all Americans between the ages of 12 and 18 who have acquired TBI. However, the time and expense needed to include all members of this population would make the research infeasible. Therefore, researchers must content themselves with studying a *sample* of people who presumably represent the population of interest. A sample is a given number of subjects who are selected from a defined population and who are presumed to be representative of the population (Rumrill & Bellini, 2018).

Using a sample, subset of the population solves the problem of feasibility. However, a new problem is created for the researcher—whether he or she can generalize the results from the sample to the population of interest. In other words, it is possible that the results of the study may only be valid for the specific sample that is studied. The representativeness of a sample in relation to its population is a key issue in the conduct and evaluation of research investigations. The term *population validity* is defined as "the degree to which the sample of individuals in the study is representative of the population from which it was selected" (Borg & Gall, 1983, p. 99). The method of selecting a sample is vital to the entire research process. If research findings are not generalizable to some extent beyond the particular sample used in the study, the research does not provide us with new, practical knowledge. A study whose findings cannot be generalized to a population of interest may be considered a waste of time and effort.

Random and Systematic Sampling Error

Samples rarely have the exact same characteristics as the populations from which they are drawn. The differences between the characteristics of the sample and the characteristics of the population on the variables of interest are known as *sampling errors*. These may be of two types, random and systematic sampling error (Kalton, 1983).

Random sampling error refers to the "accidental" differences between sample and population characteristics that are likely to occur whenever a sample is drawn from a population of interest. The size of these errors (i.e., the magnitude of the differences between sample and population) tends to become smaller as one selects a larger random sample. Individuals who have characteristics that are unusual for the population will, if included in a small sample, have a larger effect on the average values for those characteristics. With a larger sample, more individuals will reflect the "average" value for the population on the given characteristic, whereas individuals with unusual characteristics will have a smaller effect on the average values of the characteristic. For this reason, researchers can be more confident in generalizing results from studies that employ large random samples than they can in generalizing results from studies with small random samples.

A sampling procedure is random if each member of the specified population has an *equal and independent chance* of being included in the sample. An important advantage of random sampling is that the degree to which the sample differs from the population can be reliably estimated using mathematical procedures. For example, when results of surveys are reported, a margin of error is often included. This is the mathematical estimation of the range of difference between sample and population.

Often, researchers in special education use nonrandom samples in conducting studies. When nonrandom samples are used, there is always the chance that *systematic sampling error* is present. Systematic sampling errors result from variables, not taken into account by the researcher, which nevertheless influence the results of sampling procedures. Systematic errors tend to be in a given direction and, unlike random sampling error, cannot be estimated by mathematical procedures. Systematic errors are more serious because they may distort research findings in ways that have not been anticipated and therefore may lead to false conclusions.

Types of Sampling

Random sampling is the best way of ensuring that the results of a study will generalize to the population of interest. Several distinct methods of random sampling may be used, depending upon the purpose of the research and the resources available to the investigator. Four common types of random sampling are simple random, systematic, stratified, and cluster sampling. Researchers may also use nonrandom sampling procedures in gathering data; however, when nonrandom sampling is used, the results of a study are less likely to generalize to the population of interest. Convenience, or volunteer, sampling is a nonrandom approach to sampling that is common in quantitative research investigations, and purposive sampling is a nonrandom method that has widespread application in qualitative research (see Chapter 7).

Simple Random Sampling

One of the most effective sampling procedures in conducting research is simple random sampling. In simple random sampling, each member of a population has an equal and independent chance of being included in the sample. In this context, "independent" means that the selection of one individual does not affect in any way the chances that other individuals may or may not be selected. It is an effective sampling technique because it yields research data that can be generalized to the population of interest within margins of error that can be specified statistically.

Systematic Sampling

Systematic sampling is similar to simple random sampling except that, in the former, there is an identifiable pattern to the process of participant selection. In systematic sampling, the first name is chosen from a list in random fashion, and then every third, eighth, or fifteenth name (for example) is selected, until the researcher has attained the sample size required for the study. Thus, after the first name is randomly chosen, all other members of the sample are automatically determined by their placement on the list. Systematic sampling is easier to accomplish than simple random sampling in cases where all members of the population are known, such as when the researcher has access to a directory of members of a professional organization. However, it is possible for systematic error to be introduced into a systematic sampling procedure if there exists some bias (unknown to the researcher) in how names are arranged on the list.

Stratified Sampling

Stratified sampling is a procedure for ensuring that members of the population who have certain characteristics are represented in the sample. The Federal government often uses stratified sampling to ensure that a sample is as close to the national population as possible on a number of identified characteristics, such as gender, race, education, and socioeconomic status. One approach to stratified sampling is to draw random samples of different sizes from identified sub-groups of a specified population so that the proportion of individuals in each group is the same as their proportion in the population. Consider research into the teaching strategies and job duties of special education teachers (Wehman, 2013). Researchers may know that the roles and functions of special education teachers differ on the basis of work setting, area of specialization, and level of education. Estimates (drawn from a registry) of the proportions of teachers at various levels of education and work settings may be available. It is therefore possible for researchers to use a sampling technique that stratifies the sample on the basis of education and work setting: specified proportions of teachers are drawn from private schools, public schools, residential programs, specific specialty areas (e.g., learning disabilities, multiple disabilities, deafness), and different educational levels (e.g., bachelor's, master's, and doctoral degrees). This approach would ensure that teachers of certain types are not overrepresented or underrepresented in the sample so that systematic error related to the stratification characteristics is not introduced into the study. By ensuring that the sample reflects the population on these key characteristics, the generalization of study results is enhanced (Borg & Gall, 1983).

Cluster Sampling

Cluster sampling is a procedure that is often utilized in educational research. Whereas in simple random, systematic, and stratified sampling the sampling unit is the individual, in cluster sampling the cluster (or preexisting group of individuals) is the sampling unit. A classic example of a cluster sampling unit is the school district. A researcher who is interested in comparing the performance of students in various school districts may well choose a cluster sampling procedure to accomplish the study. The researcher would randomly select the districts for inclusion in the study rather than randomly selecting students from all possible school districts. A key advantage of cluster sampling is that the resources needed to accomplish the study may be conserved by applying them more selectively; thus, fewer resources are needed to carry out the investigation. A key disadvantage of cluster sampling is the possibility that, unknown to the researcher, clusters may differ on variables that influence the study findings. Therefore, the educational researcher who compares the performance of students in various school districts would likely use a combination of stratified and cluster sampling procedures to take into account such well known influences as socioeconomic status of districts, student:teacher ratios, and dropout rates on school performance (Borg, Gall, & Gall, 1993).

Convenience Sampling

Research in any field is often limited by the availability of funds. Drawing large random samples can be very expensive and is therefore infeasible in most special education research investigations. Utilizing large samples in research is generally possible only when research makes few or minimal demands on individuals such as in public opinion or market research. Random sampling is also difficult in most social science research because researchers have the legal and ethical obligation to obtain informed consent from human subjects (and, when children are being studied, from their parents) before involving them in a research project (see Chapter 4). Individuals can refuse to participate for any reason, and without consequence, which often limits the recruitment of large samples.

For these reasons, most research in special education is conducted using volunteer or convenience samples. The main problem with convenience samples is the possibility of introducing systematic sampling error into the selection process. When systematic error is introduced, the sample will have characteristics different from the population from which it is drawn, potentially limiting the ability of the researcher to generalize the results of the study to the population of interest. In fact, classic research on volunteer subjects reviewed by Rosenthal and Rosnow (1969) indicates that people who volunteer for research tend to be different in a number of ways—including being better educated, of higher socioeconomic status, more intelligent, more sociable, and higher in need for social approval—from nonvolunteers.

The likelihood that systematic sampling error affects the results of a study that employs volunteer subjects can be evaluated by checking the ratio of individuals who agree to participate to individuals who are invited to participate, known as the response rate. It is common practice for researchers using questionnaires to report the percentage of participants who actually complete the questionnaire (Dillman, 2007). It is less likely that systematic sampling error is introduced when the response rate is high. If the researcher has access to additional data on the subjects invited to participate, he or she can provide a check on systematic sampling error by comparing participants with nonparticipants on selected characteristics that are presumed to be related to subjects' responses.

In evaluating the representativeness of a volunteer sample, the researcher and readers should consider the following questions: How likely is it that participants who volunteer for the study differ from the target population on selected characteristics? How relevant is this characteristic to the independent and dependent variables examined in the study? How would differences between the participants and the population on this characteristic be likely to influence the study results?

Because of the problems associated with volunteer samples and low response rates, skillful researchers work closely with personnel in the research setting, explain in full detail the nature of the research, solicit their ideas, and provide benefits to those who participate, all in an effort to increase the percentage of participants and reduce sampling bias (Dillman, 2007; McMillan & Schumacher, 2009).

Purposive Sampling

Qualitative researchers typically study only a few cases of individuals from a specified population (Rumrill & Bellini, 2018). Because the sample size in qualitative studies is often so small, the procedures used to select a sample in quantitative research are not applicable. For example, a qualitative researcher may select a respondent or setting to study because the individual or setting is an exemplary case of the phenomenon of interest, or a case from which the researcher feels he or she will learn the most (McReynolds & Koch, 1999). Purposive sampling refers to sampling decisions that are made in qualitative research based on theoretical and practical considerations relative to the research question. For example, a researcher wishing to conduct a qualitative study of language acquisition patterns among preschool children with hearing impairments might begin by soliciting interest from members of a parent advocacy group. She could identify children to participate in her study from the group, and she could ask group members to recommend other parents whose children meet the sampling criteria for the investigation. The purpose of this approach would be to draw a sample of children with similar characteristics, but the concepts of randomomization and representativeness that are essential concerns in quantitative research do not apply in qualitative investigations.

SUMMARY

This chapter has addressed several key issues that are preparatory to the design and evaluation of special education research. Ideas for research come from a number of sources—including curiosity about a phenomenon, personal interests, teaching practice, existing theory or models, and previous research efforts. The idea that motivates a research project is typically expressed in broad, abstract terms, often in the form of a research question. To translate a research question into an empirical research project, the constructs inherent in the research question must be formulated into operational definitions. Operational definitions specify constructs on the basis of the particular activities and operations used to measure the construct in the investigation. Statistical hypotheses are grounded in the specific operational definitions used to measure the constructs of interest and the specific statistical approach used in the study. Typically, the statistical hypothesis is stated in the "null" form that posits no significant differences on the (dependent) variables of interest.

Variables are characteristics of persons or things that can take on two or more values. Variables can be categorized by their measurement characteristics (i.e., categorical and continuous), or by their role in the research process (i.e., independent, dependent, status, and moderator). In special education research, it is often not possible to manipulate independent variables to evaluate their causal relationships to dependent variables. Therefore, much of special education research is concerned with the relationships between status variables and dependent variables.

Sampling is essential to the research process because researchers rarely have the resources to access all individuals who constitute a population of

sampling

interest. A sample is a given number of subjects who are selected from a defined population and who are representative of the population. The representativeness of a sample in relation to its population is a key issue in the reporting and evaluation of research findings. In simple random sampling, each member of a population has an equal and independent chance of being included in the sample. Simple random sampling is usually the preferred sampling strategy because sampling errors can be reliably estimated using statistical methods. Systematic sampling occurs when one member of a population is selected at random, then other subjects are selected based on uniform spacing on a list or registry. Stratified sampling may be used to enhance the representativeness of a sample in relation to population characteristics that are known. Cluster sampling employs the random selection of groups of subjects (e.g., school districts) with each member of the selected group taking part in the study. Convenience samples are used extensively in social science investigations including special education research. The key problem with using convenience samples is the possibility of introducing systematic sampling error into the selection process, which limits the ability of the researcher to generalize the results of the study to the population of interest. Purposive sampling, typically used in qualitative research, is based on theoretical and practical issues involved in implementing the investigation.

Chapter 3

MEASUREMENT AND STATISTICS IN SPECIAL EDUCATION RESEARCH

Co-Authored by Jian Li

INTRODUCTION

The purpose of this chapter is to discuss key measurement and statistical issues involved in designing and evaluating special education research. Quantitative researchers in special education use standardized and nonstandardized instruments to measure observable phenomena and translate them into numerical data for the purpose of analysis. Therefore, in the quantitative research tradition, measurement issues are central to the operationalization of research hypotheses and the interpretation of research findings. Measurement issues also have important implications for statistical analyses of research findings, because research conclusions are only as good or credible as the quantitative data on which they are based (Rumrill & Bellini, 2018).

Once a sample is identified, appropriate measurement instruments are chosen, and data are collected—analysis of the data is the next step in the research process. The term "statistics" comprises a branch of mathematical operations pertaining to analyzing numerical data. Statistical methods of data analysis are pivotal to all quantitative research. Having an adequate conceptual understanding of statistical methods and the role of statistics in interpreting research results is necessary for evaluating the contributions of particular research studies to the special education literature. After an overview of measurement issues in the first part of this chapter, the second half will address selected statistical concepts that are important for designing and evaluating special education research. We will not address the mathematical formulas that are used to calculate statistics as would be included in a basic statistics course; rather, we will focus on conceptual explanations of key statistical principles and on various approaches to statistical analysis of quantitative data.

MEASUREMENT ISSUES

Measurement involves the ascription of numbers to the responses of individuals, objects, or events according to specific rules (Power, 2013; Thorndike, 2005). For example, a self-report questionnaire typically requires a scoring key (or computer software program) that provides the rules for how to sum the separate items into a total score, which item responses need to be reverse scored (as is the procedure for scoring negatively phrased items), which items go together to form an interpretable scale, and so forth. Other rules associated with measurement include standards for (a) administering tests and inventories, and (b) interpreting test results (Thorndike, 2005).

Levels of Measurement

In the social sciences, there exists a four-level hierarchy of measurement scales that is largely differentiated by the type of mathematical manipulations (i.e., statistics) that can be performed on the numbers assigned to variable characteristics and the amount of information that can be gleaned from the numbers (Stevens, 1946; 1951). The four types of scales are nominal, ordinal, interval, and ratio (Thorndike, 2005).

Nominal Scale

The most basic type of measurement is known as the nominal scale. The nominal scale simply classifies characteristics of certain variables by assigning numbers to categories without consideration of a logical numerical ordering of the categories (Stevens, 1951); as the term "nominal" implies, variables are broken into categories on the basis of the names that are used for classification purposes. Eye color is an example of a nominally scaled variable, whereby those designated as having blue eyes would be grouped into one category, those with brown eyes into another, those with hazel eyes into another, and so forth. Anytime that categories need to be differentiated without one category representing more, higher frequencies, or greater value with respect to the variable of interest, the nominal scale is the appropriate choice. Variables such as gender (e.g., male, female, transgender, undifferentiated), type of educational placement (e.g., segregated special education classroom, inclusive classroom), and college major (e.g., psychology, English, nursing, education) are other examples of nominally categorized phenomena.

Returning to the eye color example, a researcher might codify all people with blue eyes in a study using a "1," all those with brown eyes using a "2," those with green eyes using a "3," and those with hazel eyes using a "4." Again, this would not imply that blue-eyed participants would have twice as much "eye color" as brown-eyed participants, or that participants with hazel-colored eyes are more important or accomplished than other participants. Rather, the numbers are simply used to differentiate the nominally derived categories of blue, brown, green, and hazel eye colorings. When variables are measured on the nominal scale, the researcher is restricted to simply determining how many (i.e., determining the frequency of) individuals, objects, or events have certain characteristics in common.

Ordinal Scale

When characteristics of a variable are categorized and follow a logical order (e.g., ranking of categories), the variable is considered to be measured on an ordinal scale. With ordinal measurement, the numerical values assigned to categories imply differences in the amount of the characteristic, and those values are assigned according to those amounts (Stevens, 1951). For example, the variable "life satisfaction" could be measured on an ordinal scale if research participants' levels of life satisfaction not only indicated different classifications of satisfaction toward life (i.e., satisfied/not satisfied), but were also ordered in some manner such that the degree or amount of life satisfaction (i.e., more or less satisfied) could be determined. Specifically, a measure of life satisfaction could be assessed using a five-point scale, whereby a 5 is assigned to the category "highly satisfied," a 4 to "somewhat satisfied," a 3 to "neither satisfied nor dissatisfied," a 2 to "somewhat dissatisfied," and a 1 to "highly dissatisfied." In this case, if an individual responding to this scale indicated that he or she was highly satisfied and another indicated that he or she was somewhat satisfied, not only could it be determined that these individuals differed in their life satisfaction, their amount or degree of life satisfaction could also be determined.

Unlike the nominal scale, the numbers assigned to ordinal measures imply that categories are lower, weaker, or worse than others. However, even though statements of "more" or "less" can be made regarding the characteristics of variables measured on an ordinal scale, it is not possible to determine "how much more" or "how much less" any characteristic of a variable is compared with another.

A good example of this distinction is the measurement of running performance using the order of finish as the (ordinal) scale. The measurement of performance in this case would clearly indicate which runner was better or worse than any other, but it would not be possible to determine how much better or worse any runner was compared with any other. That is, the first place runner could have preceded the second place runner to the finish line by several minutes or only by several seconds. The nature of the ordinal scale does not provide information regarding the magnitude of the difference between characteristics of a variable.

Interval Scale

The third level of measurement in the hierarchy is referred to as the interval scale. Variables measured on the interval scale are considered to have all the characteristics of the nominal and ordinal scales, plus one additional characteristic: the difference between any two points on an interval scale reflects an equal difference regardless of where on the scale the two points are located. Furthermore, because the difference between any two points on an interval scale is uniform throughout the scale, it is possible to determine the magnitude of differences between or among points (Stevens, 1951).

Ratio Scale

The highest scale of measurement is referred to as the ratio scale. In addition to the properties of the nominal, ordinal, and interval scales (i.e., classification, order or distances of equal intervals between points), the ratio scale has one additional property—a true zero point (Stevens, 1951). Age, time, and most physical measures such as height, weight, and length are examples of variables that are measured using this scale. The advantage of having a true zero point is that ratio comparisons can be made. For example, because time has a true zero point, it is possible to suggest that 10 minutes is twice as long as five minutes. For variables that are measured on an interval scale, these types of comparisons are not possible, because interval scales lack a true zero point. Take, for example, standardized intelligence tests, which are frequently used in educational and disability studies research. A score of zero on an intelligence test is theoretically not possible, because all people are assumed to have some degree of intelligence. In the social sciences, ratio levels of measurement are seldom used. In terms of statistical analysis, interval and ratio levels of measurement are often treated similarly (Goodwin & Goodwin, 2012; Wiersma, 2000).

THE PURPOSE OF MEASUREMENT
IN SPECIAL EDUCATION RESEARCH

Literally thousands of measurement instruments are used for the purposes of student assessment in special education, as well as for the design and implementation of special education research. These include measures of academic aptitude and achievement, peer acceptance, personality, emotional adjustment, medical and neurological functioning, speech and language capacities, hearing, vision, and vocational interests and values. Many of these instruments are available from commercial test developers, and other instruments are developed to measure selected constructs in the context of particular research projects. The first part of this chapter addresses several measurement concepts that are important for the design and evaluation of research, including standardization, reliability, and validity of measurement instruments.

Standardization

A measurement instrument is considered to be standardized if it has been carefully developed, its psychometric characteristics (e.g., reliability, validity) have been assessed and reported, and guidelines for administration have been provided—including minimum competency standards for those who administer, score, and interpret tests (Cronbach, 1990; Power, 2013; Thorndike, 2005). Standardized test manuals specify in detail the procedures used in instrument development, as well as the steps to be used in administering, scoring, and interpreting test data. Standardization is vital for ensuring consistency in the administration and interpretation of test data. Standardized tests typically provide tables of *norms,* such as the means and standard deviations for people to whom the test developers initially administered the instrument (i.e., the standardization sample or norm group) along with descriptions of the characteristics of the norm group. These data facilitate the application of the measurement instrument to other, similar samples of people. They also provide valuable benchmarks for interpretation of the scores of people who complete the test or inventory at a later time. Standardized tests and inventories provide evidence that the scores are consistent, that everyone takes the same test under similar conditions, and that scores are meaningfully related to other important educational and social outcomes. This enhances the applicability of test scores to the educational and helping professions.

It should be noted that many special education researchers and teachers use nonstandardized tests and inventories to measure variables of interest. These measures may provide important ecological information about individual students in particular settings, but they are less credible in a scientific sense because they do not offer evidence of psychometric characteristics such as reliability and validity.

Reliability

reliability - will it be the same every time?

Reliability refers to the consistency or precision of measurement and the extent to which measurement eliminates chance and other extraneous factors in resulting scores (Rumrill & Bellini, 2018; Hood & Johnson, 2002; Thorndike, 2005). Common synonyms for reliability include dependability, reproducibility, and stability. In classical test theory, the score that a person obtains on a test or inventory on a given occasion can be partitioned into two categories, a "true score" and an error component. A true score is a hypothetical concept that refers to the score the person would obtain under normal testing conditions. To grasp what is meant by true score, imagine that a student is administered a standardized intelligence test each day for 100 days. The individual would likely obtain a number of different scores (i.e., observed scores) over these occasions from which an average score (i.e., mean) could be computed. This mean score would approximate the person's true score around which the scores for all the testing occasions would vary (depending on the magnitude of the error component on each occasion). Thus, the person's true score remains the same on each testing occasion, but the observed score varies from occasion to occasion as a function of the magnitude of the error component for that occasion. Roughly stated, the error component is the difference between the person's true score and observed score on any given occasion (Rumrill & Bellini, 2018). The reliability of a measurement instrument is reflected in the approximate proportion of true score that is present in a person's observed score. In other words, the more reliable the test or instrument is, the smaller the error component will be. Fortunately, the conventional procedures used for estimating reliability usually make it unnecessary to subject a person to numerous administrations of the same test.

Where does error come from? Major sources of error in psychological and educational measurement include nonrepresentativeness of the instrument items; fluctuation in individual traits over time; lack of standardization in testing conditions; and subjective factors related to test performance such as stress, anxiety, depression, or annoyance (Power, 2013; Rumrill & Bellini, 2018; Thorndike, 2005). These are designated as errors because they influence observed scores yet are irrelevant to the purpose for which the test was designed (Hood & Johnson, 2002; Power, 2013). Thus, it is important to standardize testing conditions to reduce the incidence of extraneous errors and, thereby, to enhance the reliability or dependability of test scores.

Reliability, as applied to psychological and educational measures, is also a function of the relative stability of the personality trait being measured. All psychological traits are developed and expressed within specific contextual frameworks (e.g., family, friends, neighborhoods, schools, religious communities); we all act in different ways depending on the demands of the context. Yet, even for children, many psychological traits are relatively stable (e.g., extroversion, independence, tough-mindedness). Some traits, however, are more stable than others. For example, for most people there is considerable stability in the scores they obtain on intelligence tests at different times in their lives, whereas much less stability exists in scores obtained on a measure of depression, anxiety, or stress. Thus, the relative stability or instability of the source trait that the test or inventory purports to assess sets an upper limit for the stability of scores on a particular measure; a test can never be more stable (i.e., reliable) than the stability of the construct it measures (Thorndike, 2005).

Reliability of a test or inventory is reported in the form of a correlation coefficient. Reliability coefficients range from 0 to +1.0. Reliability coefficients at or greater than .80 are generally regarded as acceptable, because this means that at least 80 percent of the observed score represents true score according to classical test theory. However, what is considered to be acceptable reliability also depends on the purpose of measurement and the type of reliability. Reliability for instruments used in national testing programs (e.g., Graduate Record Examination, Stanford Achievement Tests) are typically greater than .90, whereas reliability coefficients for personality, interest, and attitudinal measures (which are usually less stable constructs than academic achievement) are often in the .70 to .90 range (Hood & Johnson, 1997; Rumrill & Bellini, 2018).

Types of Reliability

Reliability can be estimated in a number of ways, including test/retest, alternate forms of a test, internal consistency, and inter-rater reliability. Each of these approaches to reliability represents an estimation of the *stability* of scores.

TEST/RETEST RELIABILITY. Test/retest reliability is a measure of the stability of individuals' scores on a test or inventory over time. The basic procedure is as follows: A sample of people complete a measure at a given time and then return at a subsequent time to retake the same measure. The test/retest coefficient is an estimate of the magnitude of the relationship between the scores for test occasion 1 and test occasion 2, averaged across all people who comprise the test/retest sample. The magnitude of relationship between individuals' scores on the two occasions is related to at least two factors that are independent of the test itself: (a) the stability of the trait being assessed, and (b) the time interval between the two testing occasions. One would not expect a particularly high test/retest reliability coefficient for a measure of depression, mood, stress, or other traits that typically fluctuate over time. If the time interval between testing occasions is short and the test is performance oriented, the reliability estimate may be inflated by memory and practice effects. If the time interval between testing occasions is long (e.g., one year or more), a lower reliability estimate is expected because participants may have matured, learned, or otherwise changed their status with regard to the construct being measured. Test/retest is generally regarded as a conservative estimate of the true reliability of a test (Power, 2013; Rumrill & Bellini, 2018).

ALTERNATE FORM RELIABILITY. Alternate or parallel form reliability is a measure of the consistency of the same individuals' scores across comparable forms of a test. This approach is common in educational testing (e.g., Scholastic Aptitude Test, Graduate Record Examination, Stanford Achievement Tests) as a method of eliminating the influence of memory and practice effects on performance, especially when students are likely to take a test more than once. Alternate form reliability coefficients can be influenced by both (a) the stability of the construct being measured, and (b) the quality and equivalence of the items that comprise the test's alternate form.

INTERNAL CONSISTENCY RELIABILITY. Internal consistency reliability is a measure of the stability of scores across the items that compose a test or scale within a test. This type of reliability can be estimated in a variety of ways— of which two, split-half and inter-item, are most common. These are popular forms of reliability estimation because they can be obtained from a single administration of a test (Hood & Johnson, 1997). Split-half reliability is computed by dividing a test or inventory into two comparable halves (typically odd and even numbered items) and then assessing the magnitude of relationship (i.e., correlation) among scores on the two halves for all individuals who took the test. Dividing the test into odd and even items is the most common approach to ensuring comparability of the two halves, because this eliminates possible effects of fatigue and practice that are likely to vary from the beginning to the end of the test. The general weakness of split-half reliability estimation is related to a principle of sampling, which holds that, all other things being equal (e.g., adequate item coverage, elimination of errors related to the conditions of test administration), the more items that comprise a test, the more stable or reliable are the scores. Thus, splitting a test into halves has the consequence of decreasing the reliability estimate. The Spearman-Brown prophecy formula may be used to correct for the shortened length of split halves and provide an estimate of reliability for the full test (Bolton, 1979; Rumrill & Bellini, 2018).

Like split-half, inter-item reliability is obtained from a single administration of a test. Inter-item reliability differs from split-half in that it is computed by averaging all the intercorrelations among the items that compose the test or scale. Thus, inter-item reliability gauges the extent to which all items are related to each other, and it indicates the stability of scores across all items rather than across two halves. The Kuder-Richardson Formula 20 is used to estimate inter-item reliability when the test items require two-response answers (e.g., yes/no, true/false) and Cronbach's alpha coefficient is used when test items call for more than two response categories (Hood & Johnson, 1997). Inter-item reliability for most tests is often higher than reliability estimates using other methods (e.g., test/retest); hence, it should be considered a liberal (i.e., ceiling figure) estimate of reliability.

INTER-RATER RELIABILITY. Inter-rater reliability is used when the items that comprise a test or scale consist of ratings of individuals' behaviors that are made by an observer (e.g., special education teacher, school psychologist, parent, counselor). In these instances, it is important to have an estimate of the consistency of scores across a variety of observers or raters. Inter-rater reliability is computed by assessing the relationship (i.e., correlation) between ratings of two or more observers of the same individuals' behaviors. The consistency of observers' ratings can be improved by training the raters in the use of the test and by providing clear guidelines for assessment of the target behaviors before the estimation of reliability.

Standard Error of Measurement

As noted earlier in this chapter, reliability coefficients are estimates of the proportion of true score that is present in observed scores. Because we know that an individual's score on a test is composed of both true and error score components, it is useful to translate this knowledge to the interpretation of the observed score so as to compute a range of scores within which the person's true score likely falls (Rumrill & Bellini, 2018). The standard error of measurement (SEM) is an index of the estimated reliability of a test that is applied to an individual's test score. The SEM for an individual's score equals the standard deviation (for the standardization sample) multiplied by the square root of one minus the reliability of the test. Computing the SEM allows one to calculate from the observed score the approximate range of scores in which the person's true score probably falls. Thus, the SEM is useful in facilitating the interpretation of individuals' scores on measurement instruments as a probable range rather than as an absolute number. Consider the example of a student with an intellectual disability who receives a score of 70 on a standardized intelligence test. If the test's SEM is 3, the student's true score is most likely to fall between 67 and 73. Expressed in terms of probability, there is a 68 percent likelihood that an individual's true score is within one SEM unit above or below his or her observed score, a 95 percent likelihood that the true score falls within two SEM units, and a 99.9 percent likelihood that the true score exists within three SEM units of the observed score.

Validity

[handwritten: Validity - does it measure what it intended?]

Validity pertains to whether a test measures what it purports to measure, or "the soundness and relevance of a proposed interpretation" (Cronbach, 1990, p. 150). The term "validity" shares a common root with "value," and validity is a judgment of the value of the test. Whereas reliability is an estimate of the consistency or stability of scores, the issue of validity in measurement addresses questions such as: "What does the test measure?," "What do the test scores mean?," and "What types of decisions are appropriate to make on the basis of the test scores?" (Rumrill & Bellini, 2018).

The Joint Technical Standards for Educational and Psychological Testing (American Educational Research Association, American Psychological Association, & National Council on Measurement in Education, 1985) timelessly stated: "Validity is the most important consideration in test evaluation. The concept refers to the appropriateness, meaningfulness, and usefulness of the specific inferences made from test scores" (p. 9). In other words, validity concerns the appropriate uses of tests, the interpretability of test scores, and the social consequences associated with their uses.

Validity is always a matter of degree. Tests may be useful and defensible for some purposes and populations but less useful or defensible for other purposes or populations. No test is 100 percent valid for every purpose and every population of potential users. Moreover, use of a test for a population on which it has not been normed, or for a purpose whose consequences have not been investigated, may constitute misuse of the test data (American Psychological Association, 2013; Power, 2013). Validation of a measurement instrument is a process of inquiry into the meaning of test scores as well as the test's uses and consequences for specific purposes.

Types of Validity

Establishing the validity of a test involves three separate but interrelated lines of investigation: content, criterion, and construct validity (Rumrill & Bellini, 2018; Thorndike, 2005). All three aspects of validity are important for identifying the meaning and usefulness of a test. However, in evaluating the strengths and limitations of particular measurement instruments, the type of validity that is emphasized depends on the purposes and consequences of measurement.

CONTENT VALIDITY. As the term implies, content validity inquires into the content of the items of a test. The fundamental question in content validity is: Do the items adequately sample the content domain of the construct or constructs that the test purports to measure? (Rumrill & Bellini, 2018). Content validity is usually established by a careful examination of items by a panel of experts in a given field. For example, establishing the content validity of a measure of child intelligence would likely involve soliciting the judgment of experts (e.g., school psychologists, cognitive psychologists, learning and development specialists, teachers) regarding whether the items on the proposed test adequately sample the content domain of intellectual functioning within the developmental context of childhood.

CRITERION VALIDITY. Criterion validity inquires into the relationship (i.e., correlation) between scores on a test or inventory and other, external criteria to which the test or inventory is theoretically related. Criterion validity considerations involve the empirical basis for particular interpretations of test data. For example, because the Graduate Record Examination (GRE) was developed for use in selecting applicants for graduate schools, an important question related to this purpose is: Do GRE scores actually predict (and to what extent) academic performance in graduate school? The two types of criterion validity are concurrent and predictive validity.

Concurrent validity refers to the relationship between test scores and an external criterion that is measured at approximately the same time. For example, concurrent validation of a rating scale measuring aggressive behavior on the part of adolescents might involve comparing those ratings with psychologists' assessments (using different measures) of the same adolescents. The psychologists' assessments would be the external criterion against which the validity of the aggressive behavior scale is assessed. The size of the correlation coefficient between the two measures of aggressive behavior would indicate their degree of relationship, and it would therefore provide substantiation of the meaning and interpretability of scores on the aggressive behavior rating scale.

Predictive validity refers to the relationship between test scores and an external criterion that is measured sometime later. For example, one approach to investigating the predictive validity of the Strong Interest Inventory (SII) has involved assessing whether and to what degree individuals' scores on the SII predict subsequent career decisions. A number of long-term studies that assessed the relationships between individuals' scores on the SII and their subsequent career placements five to 20 years later have indicated that 55 percent to 70 percent of individuals who take the SII become employed in occupations congruent with their high scores on the SII Occupational Scales (Strauser, 2014). Those findings indicate that the SII may be a useful career planning tool for transition-age students with disabilities, especially as a means of identifying specific occupations that could be compatible with students' expressed interests.

Overall, validity coefficients are almost always lower than reliability coefficients (Rumrill & Bellini, 2018). However, this does not mean that test scores that have low correlations with external criteria are invalid. Whenever the relationship between a test score and an external criterion is assessed, the degree of relationship obtained is a function of the measurement characteristics (e.g., reliability, validity) of both instruments, the sources of error that enter into the measurement of each variable, the similarities or differences in the methods used to measure the variables, and many other factors. Thus, measuring a criterion variable for the purpose of evaluating the validity of a measurement instrument introduces numerous additional sources of error that usually serve to reduce the magnitude of the observed relationship between the test score and the criterion.

CONSTRUCT VALIDITY. Construct validation studies are concerned with understanding the underlying constructs, dimensions, or attributes being measured by means of a test or other instrument (Cronbach & Meehl, 1955; Messick, 1980). Construct validity pertains to the linkages between the theoretical construct and its measurement. For example, consider a measure of self-esteem. The construct self-esteem is generally viewed in terms of individuals' appraisals of their physical, cognitive, social, academic, and emotional status. To evaluate whether the instrument accurately measures what it purports to measure, it is first necessary to understand the meaning of the construct. Construct validity questions might include the following: In comparison to people with low self-esteem, how do people with high self-esteem act in this or that situation? What characteristics typify people with high and low self-esteem? How do they handle stress? For what activities do they exhibit preferences? The meanings of the construct need to be spelled out. Articulating the construct domain takes place during the process of instrument development, and evaluating the degree to which the appropriate content is covered by the items that comprise the instrument is an issue of content validity. However, in inquiring about the overall validity of the measure, it is also necessary to evaluate whether the intended construct meanings are reflected in the patterns observed in empirical data.

For example, do people who are indicated as having high self-esteem on the basis of the underlying theory of the construct actually report high scores on the self-esteem measure? In the absence of explanatory theory and empirical evidence, there is no way to judge the appropriateness, meaningfulness, and usefulness of test scores (Messick, 1988). Constructs are the building blocks of theories, and theories specify how particular constructs are related (Cronbach, 1990). Thus, construct validity involves a back-and-forth movement between scores observed on a test and the (implicit or explicit) theory within which the construct is embedded. Construct validity seeks the mutual verification of the measuring instrument and the theory of the construct that the instrument is intended to measure. The theoretical conception of the construct dictates the nature of the data used to verify the specific inferences that are warranted from scores on an instrument (Rumrill & Bellini, 2018). In turn, the scores on a test are used to validate, refute, or revise the theory itself. In this way, all the data (both conceptual and empirical) that flow from a theory and its application are useful in the process of construct validation (Cronbach & Meehl, 1955; Power, 2013). The emphasis placed on construct validity in contemporary approaches to test validation reflects a renewed focus on and appreciation for the role of explanatory theories, particularly testable theories, in the development of scientific knowledge.

Messick (1980; 1988) made the point that construct validity is the unifying force that integrates content and criterion validity considerations into a common framework for testing specific hypothetical relationships among the construct in question, other indicators of the construct, and distinct constructs. The construct meaning provides a rational basis for hypothesizing the concurrent and predictive relationships with other variables and for judging content relevance and representativeness. For an instrument to be construct valid, appropriate content is essential. Concurrent and predictive studies are also needed to demonstrate the empirical bases for construct meaning, which, in turn, provide the foundation for the interpretation of test scores. In the end, all validity becomes construct validity (Cronbach, 1990).

Relationship Between Reliability and Validity

It should now be clear that measurement instruments that are used for assessing children with disabilities and conducting special education research ideally have high reliability and validity. However, it is possible for a measurement instrument to have high reliability (i.e., scores are dependable, consistent, and stable) yet not be valid for specific purposes. For example, a broken watch that yields the same time reading no matter what the correct time happens to be would have perfect reliability, because the measure is 100 percent dependable. However, the watch would have no validity, because the reading is inaccurate on all but two brief occasions per day (i.e., the reading does not correspond to the actual time).

This simple analogy reflects the correspondence between the reliability and validity of measurement instruments. Measurements must be reliable to be valid, but they can be reliable without being valid. Therefore, at the risk of inducing flashbacks to readers' high school physical science courses, reliability is a *necessary but not sufficient* condition for validity. Reliability forms the upper limit for the validity of a test, because measurement must be dependable for it to be useful. However, validity is the single most important consideration in test use.

Looking at these concepts in another way, reliability is a general characteristic of test or inventory scores, whereas validity is specific to a particular purpose or use. For what purpose can the test be used and what are the consequences that flow from its use are the fundamental questions of validity.

Thus, one does not validate a test per se or even the scores yielded by a test. Rather, one validates the inferences that the user draws from the test scores and the decisions and actions that flow from those inferences. The emphasis on inferences and uses of test data firmly places the responsibility for validity on the test user (Angoff, 1988). Conversely, responsibility for the reliability of test scores belongs to the test developer (Rumrill & Bellini, 2018).

Sources of Information About Instruments

Most tests and inventories that are available in the United States are published by a few large publishers such as Consulting Psychologists Press, the Psychological Corporation, and Pro-Ed. Publishers of tests distribute catalogs each year from which manuals, scoring keys, and the tests themselves can be ordered. Often, these companies offer specimen kits that include a copy of the item booklet, the test manual, and a scoring key. The test manual should include information regarding the construction of the test; scores (norms) and characteristics of the standardization sample; directions for administering, scoring, and interpreting the test; reliability and standard error of measurement estimates; and validity studies.

The single best source of information about tests is the *Mental Measurements Yearbooks* (MMY) series, published by the Buros Institute of Mental Measurements at the University of Nebraska-Lincoln (Hood & Johnson, 2002; Rubin, Roessler, & Rumrill, 2016). The MMY series contains descriptive information about tests, including publishers, prices, and appropriate uses, as well as critical reviews of tests by one or more experts. Also, a complete list of published references pertaining to each test is included and updated with each new edition. *The Annual Mental Measurements Yearbook* contains information on more than 300 new or recently revised tests and inventories.

Tests in Print is also published by the Buros Institute and serves as a comprehensive bibliography to all known tests that are currently in the English language. This annual compendium includes information on test purpose, test publisher, intended test population, test authors, and publication dates for more than 4,000 testing instruments.

Tests and *Test Critiques* are published by Pro-Ed. *Tests* contains the latest information on more than 2,000 assessment instruments, organized into separate sections related to psychology, education, and business. The 14 volumes of *Test Critiques* provide in-depth evaluative reviews of more than 1,000 of the most widely used assessment instruments and include information on both technical aspects and practical applications of tests (Pro-Ed, 2015).

Special educators may also find information on assessment instruments, particularly reports about the development and use of particular instruments in research, in professional journals, including the *Journal of Special Education, Exceptional Children, Remedial and Special Education,* and *Teaching Exceptional Children.* Additionally, published research studies that use measurement instruments to operationally define constructs should document in the Methods section of the manuscript the reliability and validity evidence for these instruments (American Psychological Association, 2013).

STATISTICS: THE BASICS

Statistical methods consist of two types, descriptive and inferential. Descriptive statistics include methods of organizing, summarizing, and presenting data. Inferential statistics include procedures for reaching tentative conclusions, on the basis of probability theory, about population values from data that are derived from samples.

Descriptive Statistics

Descriptive statistics are concepts and tools that are useful in studying distributions of variables. As defined in Chapter 2, variables are "characteristics of persons or things that can take on two or more values" (Bolton & Parker, 1998, p. 444). A distribution is the "total set of values or scores for any variable" (Bolton, 1979, p. 15). Whenever quantitative data are collected in the course of a research investigation, these numerical scores are understood and described in terms of the characteristics of their distributions. Distributions are a natural starting point for understanding quantitative measurement and statistics because all statistical procedures are based on the distributions of variables.

Distributions

Whenever a continuous variable is measured, the total set of values obtained takes the form of a distribution of scores. For example, if a sample of male and female adults is weighed, the distribution of scores is likely to range between the values of 100 and 300 pounds, although more extreme scores may also be observed. A number of concepts are useful in describing the characteristics of distributions, including shape, central tendency, variability, and relationship.

As the term implies, a frequency distribution is a *distribution* of the *frequency* of scores' occurrence within a particular sample. The familiar bar graph, or histogram, is a graphic display of a distribution of scores for a sample along horizontal (score or variable value) and vertical (frequency of scores' occurrence) axes. In a bar graph, the length of each bar reflects the frequency of the associated score in the sample. In a frequency polygon, the frequency of each score is plotted as a single point rather than a bar, and these points are then connected to achieve a simple representation of the shape of the distribution.

Shape

When a large sample of individuals is measured on a continuous variable (e.g., weight, height, intelligence, age), it is likely that the distribution of the sample's scores will approximate a *normal distribution*. A normal distribution looks like the familiar bell-shaped curve, with one high point in the center, where most scores are clustered, and tapering "tails" at either end, where fewer scores are distributed (Rumrill & Bellini, 2018). Although many physical and mental characteristics tend to be normally distributed, it is important to understand that no measurable characteristic is precisely normally distributed. The bell-shaped curve is a mathematical concept that appears to closely approximate the distribution of many variables in nature, but it is not a fact of nature and, therefore, is unlikely to represent the distribution of a given sample of scores. Non-normal distributions may have two or more "humps," (i.e., bimodal or multimodal distributions) rather than the familiar one, or the single hump may be off-center rather than in the middle of the distribution of scores (i.e., asymmetrical distribution). A distribution is said to be *skewed* when most scores occur at the low or high end of the score value range rather than in the center of the range as in a symmetrical, normal distribution.

The normal distribution is the foundation for descriptive and inferential statistics (Bolton, 1979). Most inferential statistical tests require an assumption that the variables to be analyzed are distributed normally, known as the normality assumption. Fortunately, many statistical tests are not severely influenced by violations of the assumption of normality and then can be applied with reasonable confidence to distributions that are nonnormal (see the subsection on nonparametric statistics later in this chapter). Hays (1988) and Stevens (1992) provided thorough discussions of the theoretical assumptions that underlie particular statistical procedures and the various ways that violations of the normality assumption affect the interpretation of statistical significance tests.

Measures of Central Tendency

Measures of central tendency are used to describe the typical or average performance of a group on a measured characteristic. The *mode* is the numerical value or score that occurs most frequently in a distribution. If a distribution has two or more scores that occur most frequently, the distribution is said to be bimodal or multimodal. The mode is an appropriate measure of central tendency for both categorical (e.g., type of disability) and continuous variables (e.g., intelligence). The *median* is the middle-most score, or the score that divides the distribution in half, with 50 percent of scores falling below the median and 50 percent above the median. The median is an appropriate measure of central tendency when scores are rank-ordered or given percentile equivalents (e.g., scores on standardized achievement tests). The *mean* is the arithmetic average score. It is the most common measure of central tendency used to describe the distributions of continuous variables, and it is the basis for most inferential statistics. However, the mean score of a distribution is affected by extreme scores; a few extremely low scores will move the mean score downward, whereas a few extremely high scores will move the mean higher. For example, because the distribution of income in the United States indicates a small percentage of individuals with extremely high incomes, government agencies and the media report national income in terms of the median income rather than the mean. In distributions with extreme values, the median is a more accurate measure of central tendency because it is not as strongly influenced by the presence of extreme scores as the mean is. In the event that a distribution were precisely normal (which is a hypothetical, rather than actual, phenomenon), the mean, median, and mode would be identical.

Measures of Variability

Measures of variability provide information about the dispersion or spread of scores in a distribution. Whereas central tendency measures tell the researcher where the typical or average scores fall in a distribution, variability measures provide insight into the distribution as a whole. The *range* is a rough measure of how compact or extended a distribution of scores is. It is computed by subtracting the lowest score from the highest score and adding 1 to the difference. For example, a distribution of scores on a 100-point geography test wherein the low score is 32 and the high score is 84 would have a range of 53 (84 − 32 + 1). Although the range is easy to compute, it is not particularly useful in describing the variability of scores in a distribution, because a single extreme score at the lower or higher end inflates the range yet may not accurately reflect the pattern of variability in the distribution.

Variance is a statistic that provides more accurate information than the range regarding how widely spread scores are from the mean score. The variance is a single index that reflects the average deviation (or distance) of scores from the mean score in a distribution. The *standard deviation* is the most useful and most commonly reported measure of the variability of a distribution. The *standard deviation* is the square root of the variance and, like variance, reflects the average deviation of scores from the mean score. The usefulness of the standard deviation as a measure of variability is that it is expressed in the same units as the mean score. When a mean and standard deviation for a variable are reported, it permits the reader to understand both the average value of scores and the average variability of scores around the mean value.

By definition, when a variable is normally distributed, 68 percent of scores will fall within one standard deviation of (above and below) the mean value, 95 percent of scores will fall within two standard deviations of the mean, and 99.9 percent of scores will fall within three standard deviations of the mean. For example, for most standardized intelligence quotient (IQ) tests, the mean score is approximately 100 and the standard deviation is around 15. This means that 68 percent of scores on any IQ test are likely to fall between 85 and 115, 95 percent are likely to fall between 70 and 130, and almost all (99.9%) scores are likely to fall between 55 and 145. The characteristic variability of scores in a normal distribution (which is approximated in IQ scores) is the foundation for most inferential statistics.

Measures of Relationship

The correlation statistic is a measure of the linear relationship of two distributions of variables, or whether they covary. Bolton (1979) stated, "correlation indicates the extent to which persons are ordered in the same way on two different measures" (p. 20). The correlation statistic contains information about both the *magnitude* (or strength) and *direction* of the relationship between two variables. A correlation coefficient can range from +1.0 to - 1.0. A correlation of +1.0 means that there is a perfect, positive relationship between two variables. As the values of one variable increase, the values of the second value also increase in perfect proportion. However, there is rarely such perfect correspondence between two variables. In fact, a perfect correlation may be said to represent a tautology-two ways of expressing the same phenomenon. An example of a perfect correlation is the correspondence between weight in pounds and weight in kilograms.

Indeed, correlation coefficients are most informative when they are not perfect, that is, when they provide meaningful information about the relationship between two distinct variables. Consider measurements of height and shoe size. Most of the time, individuals who are taller also have larger feet. However, some tall individuals have small feet, and some short individuals wear larger shoes. The observed correlation between height and shoe size is approximately .85, a less-than-perfect but very strong linear relationship. A zero correlation between two variables means that they are not related in linear fashion; as one variable increases, the other may increase, decrease, or remain constant with no identifiable order to the relationship. Two variables whose correlation would approximate zero are the height of children and the number of pets they have at home; these variables likely coexist in random fashion, with no discernible relationship being evident. A negative correlation means that as the value of one variable increases, the value of the second variable decreases. For example, there is a relatively stable negative correlation between days absent from school and academic achievement. As absenteeism increases, academic achievement tends to decrease.

The Pearson product moment correlation coefficient is the most commonly reported correlation statistic and is appropriate as a measure of linear relationship when the two variables are continuous. Other measures of relationship are appropriate when different combinations of continuous, categorical, and dichotomous (i.e., having only two values) variables are the focus of analysis. Regardless of the type of correlational statistic used, a coefficient of zero always means that there is no discernible relationship between variables, and the closer the coefficient is to -1 or +1, the stronger the relationship. A table of different correlation statistics and their appropriate application to variables with given measurement characteristics is found in Gay and Airasian (2003, p. 318).

Inferential Statistics

As Drummond (2004) stated, "One of the major roles of statistics is to provide an inferential measuring tool, to state our degree of confidence in the accuracy (for a population) of certain measurements (of a sample) (p. 52). Inferential statistical methods consist of a family of techniques for translating empirical data into probability statements that are used as the primary basis for reaching decisions about research hypotheses. The purpose of inferential statistics is to make warranted *inferences,* based on probability theory, about the nature of the relationships between variables *in a population of interest based on the relationships between these variables that are observed in the sample.* In other words, the purpose of statistical significance tests is to determine the likelihood that the findings obtained in the sample are also reflected in the population from which the sample is drawn. The statistical significance test is used to determine whether the statistical hypothesis, stated in its null form (see Chapter 2), is likely to be true in the population.

It is important to understand that significance tests focus on the confirmation or disconfirmation of the null hypothesis, not the confirmation or disconfirmation of the research question or hypothesis. In other words, the strategy of statistical significance testing is to nullify the null hypothesis and thereby provisionally support the research hypothesis (Cohen, 1990). If the null hypothesis is rejected, based on the significance test, it means that it is unlikely, at a specified level of probability, that the results obtained could be due to chance alone. Tentative confirmation of a research hypothesis by disconfirming, at a specified level of probability, its null inverse is the most that statistical significance tests can accomplish. The test does not confirm that the positive research hypothesis is true. Nor does a statistically significant result in a given sample ensure that a similar result will be obtained if the study is replicated with a different sample (Cohen, 1990). These caveats underscore the tentative nature of all research conclusions based on statistical significance tests and the tentative connection between results obtained in a particular research investigation and the actual state of affairs that exists in the population.

Statistical Significance and Probability Values

What is the basis for determining that a statistically significant result exists in the population based on the sample data? The behavioral sciences (including special education) have adopted *by convention* a benchmark (or decision rule) for determining when a result is statistically significant. The conventional benchmark is the probability value, or *p-value, $p \leq .05$*. When a p-value less than or equal to .05 is obtained in hypothesis testing, it is interpreted to mean that there is likely to be a statistically significant relationship between the variables in the population of interest. When a p-value greater than .05 is obtained, it is interpreted to mean that it is likely that there is no statistically significant relationship between the variables in the population.

In the logic of statistics, a statistically significant result in a sample at the $p \leq .05$ level means that there is a 95 percent probability that the decision of statistical significance obtained in the sample data accurately reflects a true, significant relationship between the variables in the population. It also means that 5 percent of the time it is likely that a decision of statistical significance may be obtained in the sample when no actual significant relationship between the variables exists in the population. In other words, when a $p \leq .05$ is adopted as the benchmark of statistical significance, the researcher is willing to have the significance test be wrong approximately 5 percent of the time. As noted previously, the $p \leq .05$ benchmark is only a convention that has been adopted among social scientists. Other benchmarks could be adopted by individual researchers which provide a more or less stringent decision rule for the statistical test, such as $p \leq .01$ for a more stringent test, or $p \leq .10$ for a less stringent test. A more stringent benchmark enables the researcher to be more confident that the results obtained in a sample are true for the population, but the more stringent decision rule also requires a stronger relationship among variables to infer statistical significance. Conversely, a less stringent benchmark provides less confidence that the results for the sample are true for the population, but the relationship among variables need not be as strong to infer statistical significance.

The value of the statistical significance tests is that it provides the researcher with a decision rule for identifying potentially nonchance results at a specified level of confidence. Statistical significance does not guarantee that results are meaningful, but it can identify results that are likely due to chance factors rather than the factors under investigation.

Type I and Type II Errors

Two types of "errors" or false conclusions—when the statistical hypothesis test provides conclusions that do not correspond to the actual state of affairs in the population—are possible in hypothesis testing. The first type of error—*Type I error*—occurs when the researcher finds a statistically significant relationship between variables in the sample, but no actual significant relationship between these variables exists in the population of interest. It means that the null hypothesis (i.e., no significant differences between the variables in the population) is rejected, based on the statistical significance test, when the null hypothesis is actually true for the population. The Type I error rate that the researcher is willing to accept is expressed as the Alpha level (_) that is selected prior to conducting the statistical analysis. As noted previously, by convention most researchers in the social sciences set the Alpha level at .05.

The second type of error—*Type II error*—occurs when the researcher finds that there is no significant relationship between the variables in the sample, but a significant relationship between the variables exists in the population. A Type II error means that the null hypothesis is accepted, based on the statistical significance test, when the null hypothesis is actually false in the population. Type I errors occur when the statistical test is overly sensitive to statistical differences, and it picks up statistical "noise" that is misinterpreted as a significant effect (or "signal"). Type II errors result when the statistical test is not sensitive enough to accurately detect true differences between the variables, hence, the researcher concludes erroneously that no significant differences exist in the population. In other words, a Type I error represents a "false positive" conclusion, and a Type II error represents a "false negative" conclusion. The Type II error rate for an investigation is known as Beta (_).

It is important to reiterate that the basis for statistical significance tests is probability theory. Statistical significance tests yield only probability statements about the nature of a relationship between variables in a population based on the observed relationship in a sample. The only way to know for certain the actual nature of the relationship between these variables in the population of interest is to sample every member of the population, an impossible task in nearly every instance of research. Therefore, it is effectively impossible to know for certain when a Type I or Type II error has occurred in a statistical analysis. However, some conditions of the research situation and statistical analysis have been identified that make it more or less likely that a Type I or Type II error is responsible for the obtained results.

Conditions That Make Type I and Type II Errors More Likely

Using a higher (less stringent) benchmark for the statistical significance test—$p \leq .10$ or $p \leq .20$—makes it more likely that a researcher will find a statistically significant result in the sample when no true significant relationship between the variables exists in the population. Also, Type I errors are more likely when the researcher performs a large number of separate and independent statistical significance tests within a research study.

The principal condition that makes Type II errors more likely is when statistical significance tests are based on a small sample of subjects. The actual size of the sample needed to reduce the likelihood of Type II errors depends on the type of statistical analysis performed. The reason that quantitative analyses of small samples are more likely to result in Type II errors is that statistical significance tests are known to be highly sensitive to sample size: The larger the sample, the more sensitive the statistical test is for identifying significant relationships between variables (Cohen, 1990; Keith, 2006). As an example, consider two investigations, one using a sample of $N=10$ and the other using a sample of $N=100$. Analyses of these two data sets obtain the same magnitude of correlation between two variables, $r=.25$. In the case of the smaller sample, the correlation is found to not be statistically significant ($p>.05$), whereas in the second case the correlation is found to be statistically significant ($p<.05$). However, the magnitude of the correlation ($r=.25$) between the two variables is the same! Because the first study is based on a very small sample, and statistical tests are highly sensitive to sample size, it is likely that in this study the test was not sufficiently sensitive, or powerful enough, to detect a true significant relationship that exists between the variables in the population. The concept of power (Cohen, 1988) refers to the sensitivity of a statistical test to detect true relationships or differences. Given the different results of statistical significance testing in the two studies, it is likely that a Type II error occurred in the former study. In the second study ($N=100$), the test was sufficiently powerful and a statistically significant result was obtained. Low statistical power has been found to be a pervasive problem in social science research, including education and disability studies (Rumrill & Bellini, 2018). We will return to the issue of power in Chapter

5 when we address the statistical conclusion validity of research investigations.

Limitations of Statistical Significance Testing

Statistical significance tests are useful tools for identifying when results based on sample data are probably due to chance, or when the variable relationships indicated in a study likely reflect true variable relationships in the population of interest. The statistical significance test provides a dichotomous decision rule within specified levels of probability: yes, the variables are probably related, or no, the variables are probably not related. However, the goals of science are not limited to providing insight into whether or not variables are related. A more ambitious goal of science is to provide an understanding of causality, that is, the nature, magnitude, and mechanisms of variable relationships. Statistical significance testing yields information about whether variables are related, but not about the magnitude of the variable relationships that are identified. Statistical significance tests play an important but limited role in the advancement of human knowledge. As Cohen (1994) observed, the significance test "does not tell us what we want to know, and we want so much to know that, out of desperation, we nevertheless believe that it does" (p. 997).

As a practical matter, statistical significance tests are known to be highly sensitive to sample size, such that very small correlations between two variables or very small differences in the mean values for two groups are likely to be statistically significant (i.e., not likely due to chance) given a large enough sample. This characteristic of statistical significance tests has contributed to considerable confusion and some inaccurate conclusions about the veracity of numerous findings in social science research (Cohen, 1990; Heppner, Wampold, Owen, Thompson, & Wang, 2015).

Effect Size

The limitations of using statistical significance tests as the primary benchmark for determining when research results are important has led to a focus on alternate measures of experimental effects, known as effect size measures, to complement statistical tests. *Effect size* is the proportion of variance in one variable or a set of variables that is accounted for by another variable or set of variables (Cohen, 1988). Consistent with the consensus in the social sciences on the importance of effect size measures in reporting research findings, the 2013 American Psychological Association (*APA*) *Publication Manual* emphasized that:

It is almost always necessary to include some index of effect size or strength of relationship. . . . The general principle to be followed . . . is to provide the reader not only with information about statistical significance tests but also with enough information to assess the magnitude of the observed effect or relationship. (APA, 2013, pp. 28–29)

Guidelines of most major journals in the social sciences also require that authors report effect sizes associated with statistical analyses in published research, so that readers can assess the magnitude and practical value of the variable relationships identified. Readers should also keep in mind that, like the mean and standard deviation, effect size is a summary statistic, that is, an average value for the data set as a whole. This means that, within a given data set, there are likely to be subsets of participants for whom the effect size will be larger and subsets for whom the effect size will be smaller.

There are three major classes of effect size measures that may be reported based on the type of research design and statistical analysis used in a study: standardized difference effect sizes, variance accounted for effect sizes, and corrected effect sizes (Vacha-Haase & Thompson, 2004).

Standardized difference effect sizes are computed for statistical analyses that involve testing mean differences on a relevant outcome variable across two groups. Standardized differences are computed by the generic formula:

$$(MT - MC) \div SD$$

where MT is the posttest sample mean of the experimental or treatment group, MC is the posttest mean of the control group, and SD is some estimate of the population standard deviation (Vacha-Haase & Thompson, 2004). As the formula indicates, standardized difference effect sizes express the differences in mean values for two groups in standard deviation units. Hence, an effect size of .5 indicates that the experimental group mean for an outcome variable is one-half of a standard deviation higher than the mean for the control group, whereas an effect size of –1 indicates that the control group mean is one standard deviation unit higher on the outcome variable than the experimental group.

In practice, the standard deviation that is used to calculate effect size can be estimated in different ways, depending on the assumptions of the researcher. Glass (1976) proposed *delta* as a measure of standardized differences, which divides the sample mean difference by the sample standard deviation of the control group. This approach is preferred when the researcher suspects that the intervention that is being tested may increase (or decrease) both the mean level of the outcome variable and the variance of the distribution. In these cases, the standard deviation of the control group is likely to more accurately reflect the population variance and, hence, lead to a more accurate estimate of the effect size. Alternately, Cohen (1969) proposed *d,* which uses a standard deviation estimate that is averaged (pooled) across the intervention and control groups. In most cases, these different approaches to estimating mean difference effect sizes will yield similar results.

Variance accounted for indices are effect size measures that indicate the amount of variation in a dependent variable or set of dependent variables that is explained by a predictor variable or set of predictor variables, as a ratio of the total variation of the dependent variable(s). The square of the correlation coefficient (r^2) and multiple correlation coefficient (R^2) are the most common effect size measures used in published research. If the correlation between a predictor and an outcome variable is .7, then $r^2=.49$, indicating that 49 percent of the variation of the outcome variable is shared with the predictor variable.

The most commonly used statistical analyses are part of a single analytic family, known as the general linear model (GLM; Cohen, 1969; Miles & Shevlin, 2001). All GLM analyses (e.g., t-tests, analysis of variance [ANOVA] and covariance [ANCOVA], multiple regression, factor analysis) are essentially correlational methods. An r^2-type effect size can be computed from any of these statistical methods, though the manner of computation may differ. In all cases, the computed variance accounted for index represents the amount of variation of the dependent variable that is explained by the "model" (i.e., the independent or predictor variable or set of variables) as a ratio of the total variation of the dependent variable(s). In the context of ANOVA/ANCOVA, this index is known as the *correlation ratio* or *eta squared* (η^2) (Vacha-Haase & Thompson, 2004).

Corrected effect size measures are estimated population effect indices that adjust the sample effect size by removing the influence of sampling error variance (Vacha-Haase & Thompson, 2004). Every sample that is drawn from a population of interest has its own uniqueness or personality (i.e., sampling error variance), and some samples have more sampling error variance than others. Also, GLM procedures utilize mathematical procedures that maximize the effect size for the sample data. Therefore, the effect size for a sample tends to overestimate the effect size in the population and in future samples. Corrected effect size measures are generally more accurate estimates of population effects (Snyder & Lawson, 1993). Adjusted R^2 is a commonly reported corrected effect size index in the context of multiple regression, and *omega squared* (w^2) is used in the context of ANOVA/ANCOVA. Correction formulae are also available for most multivariate analyses (Vacha-Haase & Thompson, 2004).

A key advantage of computing and reporting effect size in published research is that it allows a direct evaluation of various investigations within a research domain that use samples of different size and different outcome measures. In particular, standardized difference measures of effect size (i.e., *delta* or *d*) are used extensively in meta-analysis (see Chapter 6) for analyzing, summarizing, and interpreting findings from large research programs so that global conclusions are accurate and cumulative.

Methods of Statistical Analysis

This section introduces a number of statistical techniques by which data are analyzed. The examples presented here are relatively common in special education research. These methods are tools, and statistical analyses are meaningful only when they are applied within an appropriately designed study and interpreted within the theoretical context of the research question. As Pedhazur (1997) stated, "Data do not speak for themselves but through the medium of the analytic techniques applied to them. Analytical techniques not only set limits to the scope and nature of the answers one may obtain from data, but also affect the type of questions a researcher asks and the manner in which the questions are formulated" (p. 4).

The T-Test

A number of different inferential statistical tests are used to analyze quantitative data in the social sciences. The simplest statistical test is known as the t-test, or test of mean differences between two samples (typically a treatment group and a comparison group). Consider the following example:

> A researcher has developed a psychosocial intervention designed to enhance the self-esteem of children with visual impairments. She wishes to know whether the intervention is effective. She identifies a sample of children with visual impairments from several local school districts and negotiates the support of the districts (and consent of the participants and their parents) in implementing the investigation. She randomly assigns the participants to two groups, a group that receives the intervention and a group that does not receive the intervention. Then, she implements the intervention. After the intervention is concluded, she administers a self-report measure of self-esteem to both groups. She expects that the mean scores on self-esteem for the intervention group will be greater than the mean scores on self-esteem for the comparison group; this will signify that the intervention was effective in enhancing self-esteem.

But, how can the researcher determine whether a mean difference is large enough to be noteworthy or indicative of a treatment effect, rather than the spurious result of chance sampling fluctuations? The t-test is used in this case to make warranted inferences about treatment effects (e.g., receipt or nonreceipt of an intervention) for a population (e.g., children with visual impairments) on the basis of between-group differences in the distribution of a dependent variable (e.g., performance on a measure of self-esteem). The researcher anticipates that, as a function of the psychosocial intervention, the mean score on the measure of self-esteem for the treatment group will be higher than the mean score for the comparison group. Thus, in a t-test, the effect of the intervention is reflected in *between group differences* on the dependent variable. The researcher also knows, however, that individuals within each group will obtain different scores from each other on the self esteem measure. The differences between the individuals within each group are known as *within group differences,* and they reflect the natural variability of individuals within a sample or subsample on any characteristic. The t- test is computed as a ratio of between-group differences to within-group differences on the dependent variable (Hinkle et al., 2003; Rumrill & Bellini, 2018). If the ratio of between-group differences to within-group differences is large enough, the difference between the two group means is statistically significant; on the other hand, if the ratio of between-group differences to within-group differences is not large enough, the difference between the two group means will not be statistically significant. Simply stated, statistical significance is a function of three factors: the potency of the treatment (the between-group difference on the outcome variable), the amount of variability within each group (within-group difference), and the size of the sample. Thus, the researcher is likely to be rewarded with a statistically significant result when the treatment effect is relatively large (e.g., the intervention results in substantial differences between groups on self-esteem scores), when the variability of individuals' scores within each group is relatively small, and when a large sample is used.

In the language of inferential statistics, the treatment effect is known as systematic variance or variance in scores that results from a known condition or intervention (Bolton, 1979; Rumrill & Bellini, 2018). Variation that is due to other, unmeasured factors on which the two groups may differ *and* that affects scores on the dependent variable is known as error variance. Error variance may also reflect sampling fluctuations (i.e., sampling error) that occur whenever a sample is drawn from a population. The *t*-test is a statistical method for partitioning the variation of scores into systematic and error variance. It is then converted into a probability value that indicates the likelihood that differences between two groups of a specific magnitude are due to chance or due to the efficacy of the intervention being tested. The *t*-test is the appropriate inferential statistical test when comparing the mean scores of two groups on an outcome variable.

Analysis of Variance

Analysis of variance (ANOVA) is the appropriate statistical strategy when more than two groups (a categorical variable with more than two "levels") are compared on an outcome variable. For example, the researcher may wish to compare the effectiveness of two distinct instructional interventions to increase mathematics achievement and compare both to a group that received no intervention. Like the t-test, ANOVA partitions the variation of the dependent variable in the three groups into systematic and error variance. A ratio of systematic to error variance is computed, known as the F-ratio, and it is converted into a probability value. The F-ratio for ANOVA provides the information needed to determine whether the means on the outcome variable (e.g., mathematics achievement for the three groups) are significantly different. Because, in this example, the goal of the researcher was to compare the efficacy of two different interventions with a nonintervention group, it is necessary to evaluate the mean differences of the three groups using "post hoc" (i.e., after the fact) tests. The post hoc test is used to determine whether the mean differences of each of three pairs of groups are statistically significant: group A is compared with group B; group A with group C; and group B with group C. Post-hoc tests can only be used when an ANOVA reveals that statistically significant differences exist between some combination of groups; they specify the groups between which differences occur.

Factorial ANOVA permits researchers to examine the separate and interactive effects of two or more categorical variables (typically an independent variable and a status variable) on an outcome variable. The separate effects of the independent and status variables on the outcome variable are known as main effects, and the moderating effects of combinations of independent and status variables are known as interactive effects. Factorial ANOVA provides a technique for partitioning the variation in the outcome variable into variance caused by the separate main effects, variance caused by interactive effects, and variance caused by error.

For example, a researcher wishes to compare reading achievement scores for a sample of special education students according to differences in disability category and type of placement. In this example, disability category (e.g., learning disability or behavioral disorder) would be considered a status variable, type of placement (e.g., inclusive classroom or segregated classroom) would be the independent variable, and reading achievement (e.g., scores on a standardized measure of reading performance) would be the dependent variable. The first two issues in the factorial ANOVA concern main effects: Does reading achievement differ as a function of disability category, and does it differ as a function of placement type? The researcher finds no significant main effects for disability category or type of placement; children with learning disabilities recorded reading scores that were not significantly different from those recorded by children with behavioral disorders, and scores were also similar for children in inclusive and segregated classrooms. Next, the researcher turns her attention to possible interaction effects between the status and independent variables on the dependent variable. Results indicated that children with learning disabilities who were placed in inclusive classrooms fared significantly better on the reading test than did their segregated counterparts with learning disabilities. Conversely, students with behavioral disorders placed in segregated classrooms achieved at a higher level on the reading measure than did their counterparts who were included. Therefore, a significant disability category by placement type interaction was observed.

Multiple Regression

Multiple regression analysis is a method of analyzing "the collective and separate effects of two or more independent (and/or status) variables on a dependent (or outcome) variable" (Pedhazur, 1997, p. 6). Akin to the factorial ANOVA technique, multiple regression provides a way to (a) assess the collective contribution of two or more variables to the variation in the dependent variable, and (b) partition the variation in the dependent variable into variance explained by each separate independent variable and error variance (Keith, 2015). Multiple regression is an extension of the simple correlation. Whereas correlation assesses the relationship between two variables, multiple regression assesses the relationship, or multiple correlation, between a set of independent or status variables and one dependent variable. Multiple regression analysis has two primary purposes, prediction and causal explanation. These different purposes are distinguished not by different statistical procedures but, rather, by the role of theory in guiding the decisions of the researcher and the interpretation of the data.

Multiple regression has been widely used in special education research to predict a variety of educational and social outcomes. For example, Heiman and Margalit (1998) examined the multiple relationships among loneliness, depression, peer acceptance, social skills, and demographic variables such as age and gender for a sample of 320 students with intellectual disabilities who were placed in self-contained special education classrooms (in public schools) and in special schools. Two separate multiple regression equations were computed to predict the dependent variable of loneliness, which was measured by scores on the Loneliness and Social Dissatisfaction Questionnaire (Asher, Parkhurst, Hymel, & Williams, 1990); one for students in self-contained special education classrooms and one for students in special schools. Independent, or predictor, variables were depression, social skills, peer acceptance, age, and gender. The combination of independent variables explained a significant proportion of variance in participants' loneliness scores for both groups of students.

Multiple regression is a highly flexible analytic technique (Pedhazur, 1997). It can be used with multiple continuous independent or status variables or a mixed set of dichotomous, categorical, and continuous independent or status variables. Typically, the dependent variable in a regression analysis is a continuous variable, but variations of regression (e.g., logistic regression, multinomial logistic regression) are used to predict dichotomous or categorical dependent variables. Output statistics from regression analysis include measures of effect size (i.e., multiple R for the multiple correlation and R^2 for the variance explained in the dependent variable by the set of independent variables), as well as statistical significance tests for the contribution of each independent variable to the prediction of the dependent variable.

Multivariate Analysis

Multivariate analysis consists of a family of statistical techniques that are used to examine the effects of one or a set of independent or status variables on a *set* of continuous dependent variables (Spicer, 2005). The term multivariate analysis is typically reserved for statistical analyses that use multiple, correlated outcome variables. Similar to multiple regression, the different multivariate approaches generate one or more equations that combine the set of predictor variables to best predict the outcome variables. These equations include different weights assigned to each predictor variable to maximize the prediction of the outcomes for the sample data, although the weights or multipliers are given different names in the different types of analysis (e.g., discriminant function coefficients in multiple discriminant analysis, path coefficients in path analysis). Multivariate analysis was relatively rare prior to the era of the personal computer (when the complex and time-consuming calculations were done by hand), but it is much more common in special education research since user-friendly statistical programs have become available.

There are also substantive reasons why multivariate analysis is preferred over other, less sophisticated approaches to data analysis. Rumrill and Bellini (2018) advocated for a multivariate approach to research design and analysis to enhance causal explanation of key processes (a primary goal of science) given the impossibility of randomly assigning treatment conditions to assess the effects of independent variables in most social science research. Also, these more complex approaches to modeling social or psychological processes or outcomes better reflect the nature of the phenomena that are the focus of research in the social sciences. In this view, social reality is multivariate, and most social science is research "in which the researcher cares about multiple outcomes, in which most outcomes have multiple causes, and in which most causes have multiple effects" (Thompson, 1986, p. 9). Parker (1990) advanced a more cautious view of the appropriateness of multivariate procedures for social science research, stating that sophisticated statistical analyses are no substitute for attention to the quality of the data and well-conceived and executed research designs.

Selected multivariate techniques include multivariate analysis of variance (MANOVA) and covariance (MANCOVA), multivariate multiple regression, multiple discriminant analysis (MDA), path analysis, canonical correlation analysis, multilevel modeling (MLM), factor analysis, and structural equation modeling. MANOVA and MANCOVA are extensions of ANOVA and ANCOVA, respectively, and they permit the evaluation of a set of predictor variables on a set of correlated outcome variables. Similarly, multivariate multiple regression is an extension of multiple regression in which a set of predictor variables is used to predict a set of correlated outcome variables. MDA is similar to multiple regression in that multiple predictor variables are included; however, in MDA the criterion is a categorical variable with at least three levels, and the purpose of the analysis is to predict group separation (Tacq, 1997). Path analysis is an extension of multiple regression that permits the evaluation of models of social phenomena, wherein a variable may be an outcome in one phase of a process model and a predictor variable in subsequent phases (Klem, 1995). Canonical correlation analysis is used to evaluate the degree of covariation or overlap between two theoretically related sets of variables, without consideration of priority or causality. MLM permits the analysis of data that are "nested" or hierarchically-ordered to include more than one level (e.g., teacher characteristics and student characteristics when both are relevant to explaining student outcomes, or student-level, teacher-level, and school-level data when all three levels of data are relevant to explaining student achievement). MLM is used to assess the separate and combined effects of these different "levels" of data on selected outcomes.

Factor analysis is utilized extensively in the development and validation of psychometric instruments (Power, 2013). Factor analysis differs from the other techniques discussed to this point in that the goal of factor analysis is to identify sources of covariation that are *internal* to a set of variables or items, rather than to identify the sources of covariation in an outcome variable or set of outcome variables using one or more independent or predictor variables (Tacq, 1997). In other words, the purpose of factor analysis is to identify the latent (i.e., underlying) structure of a set of correlated variables. Although these variables are most often items of a test or inventory, factor analysis may also be used to operationalize a construct using multiple indicators. Finally, structural equation modeling is an advanced multivariate technique that permits investigators to use sample data to evaluate both how *well* selected indicators (i.e., measured variables) of constructs represent their source latent variables *and* the nature of the relationships among the latent variables (Schumacker & Lomax, 2015; Merchant, Li, Karpinski, & Rumrill, 2013).

These different multivariate strategies differ in purpose and in the methods used to calculate composite variables. However, these techniques are not qualitatively different from the simpler analytic strategies such as the t-test or ANOVA. Rather, all of these statistical strategies are fundamentally similar in that they (a) assess the linear relationships among variables, and (b) provide methods for partitioning the variation of dependent variables into systematic (i.e., covariance) and residual variation. The systematic variance of the dependent variables is further partitioned into its different sources, that is, the unique contribution of each predictor variable to the observed variation in the dependent variable(s).

Nonparametric Statistics

All of the statistical methods described to this point in the chapter are known as parametric statistics. For conclusions or inferences to be defensible (i.e., valid), most standard parametric statistical significance tests also require that certain assumptions about the data are met. One key assumption is that the dependent variables under study are approximately normally distributed in the population. A second key assumption is that the variance of the dependent variable is consistent across the different values of the independent variable distribution, known as the homogeneity of variance assumption (Cohen et al., 2003; Miles & Shevlin, 2001). Finally, it is assumed that the measurement of the dependent variable is interval-level or higher. When these assumptions of the data are not met, the statistical analysis that is based on the data will not be as valid or credible.

When a dependent variable is not normally distributed, and/or when groups do not exhibit equal or proportional variance, *nonparametric* statistics are required to make warranted inferences on the basis of the sample under study. Commonly applied nonparametric statistics in special education research include the median test, chi square, Mann-Whitney U test, Kruskal-Wallis one-way analysis of variance, and the Wilcoxon matched-pairs signed-rank test. It is worth noting that nonparametric methods are also not "assumption-free," they simply have the benefit of requiring fewer assumptions than parametric methods. Table 3.1 lists the variety of parametric and nonparametric (i.e., inferential) statistical techniques discussed in this and earlier sections, the measurement characteristics of variables that are most appropriate for each procedure, and relevant research purposes for each technique.

Table 3.1
TYPES OF STATISTICAL ANALYSES

Type of Analysis	Variables	Purpose of Analysis
Correlation	Two (may be any combination of continuous, dichotomous, or categorical)	Assesses the linear relationship of two variables
t-Test	One categorical independent, one continuous dependent	Tests mean differences between two groups
ANOVA	One or more categorical independent and/or status, one continuous dependent	Tests mean differences for more than two groups
ANCOVA	One or more categorical independent and/or status, one or more continuous moderator, one continuous dependent	Tests mean differences for two or more groups while holding moderator variable constant across groups
Multiple regression	Two or more categorical and/or continuous independent and/or status, one continuous dependent	Assesses collective and separate correlation of multiple predictor variables to single outcome
Multiple discriminant analysis	One categorical independent or status, a set of continuous dependent	Assesses the differences among two or more groups on a set of dependent variables
Logistic regression	Two or more categorical and/or continuous independent and/or status, one dichotomous dependent	Assesses the probability or odds of the group membership in the outcome based on combination of values taken by the independent variables
Multivariate multiple regression	Two or more categorical and/or continuous independent and/or status, two or more continuous dependent	Assesses collective and separate correlation of multiple predictor variables to two or more outcome variables
MANOVA	Two or more categorical independent and/or status variables, two or more continuous dependent	Tests mean differences on two or more outcomes for two or more groups

continued

Table 3.1—*Continued*

Type of Analysis	Variables	Purpose of Analysis
Canonical correlation	Two or more sets of continuous variables	Assesses the relationships among two or more variable sets
Factor analysis	Set of continuous observed variables	Assesses the underlying dimensionality of a set of continuous variables
Cluster analysis	Set of continuous and/or categorical variables	Separates subjects/objects into groups in such a way that the subjects/objects in the same luster are more similar to each other than to those in other clusters
Path analysis	Set of observed variables	Uses correlation coefficients and regression analysis to assess the directed dependencies among two or more observed variables simultaneously that have complex relationships
Structural equation models	Set of observed and unobserved (latent) variables	Simultaneously assesses multiple relationships among observed variables and latent constructs that are hypothesized to be related in a certain way
Mann-Whitney	Independent variable is nominal outcome variable that has 2 levels	Assess differences in ordinal outcome
Kruskal-Wallis test	Independent variable is nominal outcome variable with more than 2 levels	Assess differences in ordinal outcome
Wilcoxon Test	Independent variable is nominal	Assesses differences in outcome variable that cannot be assumed to be normally distributed
Chi-square test	Independent variable is nominal	Assesses differences in nominal outcome variable with any number of levels

Practical Versus Statistical Significance

Statistical significance is a useful benchmark for determining when a research finding is likely to be the result of nonchance factors (e.g., treatment effects). However, statistical significance is not a useful criterion for determining when a research finding is likely to be relevant to practitioners. Given the known relationship between sample size and the probability of identifying statistically significant relationships among variables, the research consumer (i.e., reader) should always attend to the actual differences among means (when group comparisons are made) or other indicators of the magnitude of relationship that are independent of sample size (e.g., d, R2) when assessing the practical significance of a research finding.

Evaluating the practical significance of research findings also involves reassessing the status of the theoretical proposition after the empirical test, as well as the heuristic and practical value of the theoretical proposition relative to the goals, activities, and procedures of the particular agency or school. As Goodwin and Goodwin (2012), Rumrill and Bellini (2018), Serlin (1987), and Tracey (1991) all noted, research conclusions rarely apply directly to practice. Instead, research findings confirm or disconfirm particular theoretical propositions or models that, in turn, potentially enhance their credibility and usefulness for professional practice.

Notes on Samples, Populations, and Hypothesis Testing

As we have established, the ultimate purpose of inferential statistics is to make warranted inferences, on the basis of probability theory, about the nature of the relationships between or among variables in a population of interest on the basis of the relationships between or among these variables that are observed in a given sample. Once an inference about the relationships between or among variables in a population is made (on the basis of statistical analysis), a second inferential step—from the population of interest to the general hypothesis that was tested—is necessary to ensure the meaningfulness and generality of research propositions (Serlin, 1987). Whereas the inferential leap from sample to population is based on mathematical principles (i.e., statistics), the inferential leap from the population to the research hypothesis is based on the plausibility of the theory that provides an explanation for the results. It is the plausibility of theory that is supported by particular research findings and that, in turn, substantiates the contribution of research findings (Rumrill & Bellini, 2018). As applied to statistical procedures, the linkages among samples, populations, and hypotheses imply that theoretical considerations should guide the design, analysis, and interpretation of empirical results.

SUMMARY

In quantitative research, measurement issues are central to the operationalization of research hypotheses and the interpretation of findings. Three important characteristics by which researchers evaluate measurement instruments are standardization, reliability, and validity. Standardized tests provide evidence that scores are both consistent and meaningfully related to other important social outcomes. Reliability refers to the stability of scores, the extent to which measurement eliminates chance and other extraneous factors, and the approximate proportion of true score that is present in an obtained score. Several different strategies may be used to estimate reliability, including test/retest, alternate forms, internal consistency, and inter-rater. In aggregate, these methods assess to the stability of scores over time, across comparable forms of a test, across items of a test, and across different raters, respectively.

Validity is a judgment of the value of a test, or the appropriateness, interpretability, and social consequences of particular uses of a test. Three types of validity investigations are content, criterion, and construct validity. Content validity refers to whether the items of a test adequately sample the appropriate content domain. Criterion validity pertains to the relationships between test scores and other, external criteria. Construct validity deals with understanding the underlying constructs, dimensions, or attributes being measured by a test. Validity is the single most important consideration in test evaluation. Reliability is a necessary, but insufficient, condition for test validity; a test must be reliable to be valid, but not all reliable tests are valid.

Statistical methods of data analysis are used in quantitative research. Descriptive statistics are methods of organizing, summarizing, and presenting data. A number of concepts are useful in describing distributions of variables, including shape, measures of central tendency (i.e., mean, median, and mode), measures of variability (i.e., range, variance, and standard deviation), and measures of relationship (i.e., correlation). The normal distribution is the basis for both descriptive and inferential statistical methods. Measures of central tendency describe the typical performance of a group on a measured variable. Measures of variability provide information about the spread of scores in a given distribution. Measures of relationship furnish information about the magnitude and direction of the linear association of two variables.

Inferential statistics provide a basis for making inferences about the relationships among variables in a population based on the relationships that are observed in a sample. The probability value, $p < .05$, is the conventional benchmark for determining whether a research finding is statistically significant. However, two types of errors, type I and type II, are possible in hypothesis testing. A type I error occurs when the null hypothesis (i.e., no significant differences on the outcome variable) is rejected but is actually true in the population. A type II error occurs when the null hypothesis is accepted but is actually false in the population. Several conditions that make these errors more likely were identified. Given that statistical significance tests are highly sensitive to sample size, it is also important to evaluate research findings on the basis of effect size, which is the proportion of variance in one variable that is explained by a second variable, or the mean differences between two groups. Measures of effect size permit a direct evaluation of research findings across different studies.

A number of different inferential statistical techniques are used in special education research, including the *t*-test, analysis of variance, multiple regression, and multivariate analysis. When researchers are not able to meet the assumptions inherent in the parametric statistical paradigm (e.g., normal distribution, equivalent between-groups variance), they may use nonparametric statistics as data analytic tools. Table 3.1 presents the types of variables and research purposes associated with different inferential statistical approaches, both parametric and nonparametric. Practical significance of findings is a central issue in the evaluation of a research study. In assessing the practical significance of a study, the research consumer should attend to the actual differences among means when group comparisons are made or to other measures of the magnitude of relationships that are independent of sample size. Evaluating the practical significance of research findings also involves assessing the pragmatic value of the theoretical proposition that was tested relative to the goals, activities, and methods of the school or agency to which the research consumer seeks to generalize. It is the practical value of the theoretical proposition, confirmed by the empirical test, that substantiates the contribution of research to special education practice.

Chapter 4

ETHICAL ISSUES AND GUIDELINES FOR SPECIAL EDUCATION RESEARCH

Co-Authored by

Mykal Leslie
Zachary Strickler
Stuart Rumrill

INTRODUCTION

Ethics are a set of rules or guidelines regarding what is "right" or appropriate conduct (Corey, Corey, & Callanan, 2011; Rumrill & Bellini, 2018). Although we all maintain our own core ethics that guide us in our everyday lives, most professions set forth ethical guidelines, or codes, that specify how people should conduct themselves as representatives of those professions. For example, the Code of Ethics and Standards for Professional Practice for Special Education (Council for Exceptional Children, 2015) provides a structure for professional conduct with respect to such issues as instructional responsibilities, management of behavior, parent relationships, advocacy, professional employment, and interactions with other professionals.

Given the applied emphasis of research in special education, as described in Chapter 1 of this text, as well as the close contact that special education researchers have with children with disabilities, ethical issues are of paramount importance in the design, implementation, and dissemination of research in our field. To be sure, the special education researcher has obligations to several constituency groups that have vested interests in ensuring that empirical studies are carried out under the highest ethical standards and circumstances. Specifically, researchers in special education have ethical obligations to participants in their research, to the parents of research participants, to other researchers collaborating on investigations, to their employers, to the agencies that fund research projects, to professional consumers (i.e., readers) of research results, and to professional organizations with which they are affiliated.

The purpose of this chapter is to describe the considerations and standards that shape "right" or appropriate conduct in scientific inquiry as they apply to special education. The chapter begins with an overview of ethical principles that underlie all aspects of special education, then follows with standards concerning the treatment of human subjects in educational and social scientific research. The chapter concludes with a discussion of ethics as they apply to the process of reporting and publishing special education research.

UNDERLYING ETHICAL PRINCIPLES OF SPECIAL EDUCATION

Before the special education researcher begins to conceptualize and design a study, he or she must become familiar with the abiding ethical provisions that guide all educational interactions with children with disabilities and their parents. The Code of Ethics and Standards of Professional Practice for Special Education (Council for Exceptional Children, 2015) can be retrieved online at http://www.cec.sped.org. In addition to the ethical guidelines set forth by the Council for Exceptional Children to shape professional conduct in special education, medical and social science professions share an overarching set of precepts that serves to define what constitutes right and appropriate conduct in numerous settings and circumstances (including research). Specifically, non-maleficence, beneficence, autonomy, justice, and fidelity have been identified, by various ethicists, as hallmarks of professional behavior in human services (Beauchamp & Childress, 1979; Rubin, Roessler, & Rumrill, 2016). The following paragraphs define and explain these concepts as they apply to all aspects of special education practice and research.

Nonmaleficence

"First, do no harm." Known as nonmaleficence, the "do no harm" maxim in applied education and psychology means that researchers must take every precaution to ensure that participants are not subject to danger or negative consequences (Goodwin & Goodwin, 2012; Heppner et al., 2015; McMillan & Schumacher, 2009; Rumrill & Bellini, 2018). Most social science ethicists agree that nonmaleficence is the most basic and important guideline for the conduct of researchers and practitioners (Heppner et al., 2015; Rubin et al., 2016).

"Doing no harm" requires the special education researcher to do more than simply avoid inflicting intentional harm. Researchers must also minimize unintended risks to every extent possible, inform participants of any risks that cannot be controlled, and maintain vigilance in assessing any potentially harmful situations that might arise during the conduct of a study. Furthermore, nonmaleficence is seen as even more important than the ideal of providing benefit to (i.e., helping) the student, consumer, or participant. When a special education researcher is considering an intervention or procedure that could benefit one participant while potentially harming another, ethical standards dictate that he or she should not apply that intervention until the potential risks have been minimized and explained to the participant who may be subject to harm.

Beneficence

If nonmaleficence—the act or process of "doing no harm"—constitutes the most basic ethical obligation of the special education researcher, then beneficence—acting in a manner that promotes the well-being of others (Rubin et al., 2016)—must be viewed as the core principle that defines the purpose of any educational or human service relationship. It should be noted that beneficence applies to the well-being of both research participants and other professionals.

For example, the applied special education researcher who demonstrates an intervention to enhance the self-determination skills of children with cerebral palsy upholds the principle of beneficence in two ways. Not only is a direct benefit provided to participants in the investigation (especially to those who report improvements in self-determination after completing the intervention), readers of the research report or published article who incorporate the researcher's strategies into their own practices stand to enhance their students' prospects for successful psychological adjustment and other positive outcomes. In other words, beneficence in special education research can be observed in terms of both direct benefits to participants in particular studies and the contributions that published research makes to the professional knowledge base.

Implicit in the principle of beneficence is the notion of competence. Teachers have an ethical obligation to ensure that they receive appropriate continuing education and possess sufficient skills to help their students develop academic, social, vocational, and daily living skills (Council for Exceptional Children [CEC], 2015). This also means that teachers must realistically appraise the limitations of their training and experience and not attempt to exceed their qualifications by providing services that would be the more appropriate purview of another professional. This self-assessment process is equally important for the beneficent special education researcher. When applying the designs and techniques described in subsequent chapters of this book, researchers must ensure that their methods and analyses are compatible with their current levels of proficiency. In that vein, beneficence includes not only the desire or intention to contribute to the well-being of children with disabilities by means of special education research, but also the ability to carry out a responsible and scientifically sound investigation.

Autonomy

The concept of autonomy, defined by Kitchener (1984, p. 46) as "respect for the freedoms of choice and action of the individual to the extent that those freedoms do not conflict with similar freedoms of others," is a cornerstone of American laws, politics, and culture. The freedom to choose and act in accordance with one's own values, interests, and ambitions is among the most important liberties, and ethical standards in medical and social science research are imbued with the rights of subjects to participate (or not participate) of their own volition and without negative consequences.

Since the Nuremberg trials after World War II, the principle of autonomy has received steadily increasing attention from research ethicists (Heppner et al., 2015). Anyone who has conducted a research investigation at a college, university, or hospital during the past 35 years is familiar with the notion of informed consent, a mainstay requirement of ethical research practice, which holds that potential research participants must be informed about the nature and purpose of the investigation before their voluntary enrollment in the study.

As it applies to special education research, autonomy encompasses more than soliciting and securing informed consent from potential participants and their parents. The researcher must ensure that delivering an intervention or collecting data does not intrude any more than is absolutely necessary on participants' other pursuits (Rumrill & Bellini, 2018). In the event that an investigation requires or is intended to result in a particular course of action, participants must be granted assurances that the ultimate locus of control for their choices rests with them and/or their guardians. Even if the study involves activities that appear to be inherently helpful as per the principle of beneficence (e.g., communication skills training, instruction to improve reading comprehension, community-based work experiences), participants must retain absolute prerogative regarding whether, when, and to what extent they engage in the investigation.

Justice

In any field or sector of society wherein limited resources do not allow decision-makers to provide for all of the needs of all people, difficult choices must be made regarding "who gets what and why" (Howie et al., 1992, p. 49). Such is certainly the case in special education. In making decisions concerning who gets what and why, the principle of justice often serves as the ethical benchmark (Heppner et al., 2015; Rubin et al., 2016; Rumrill, Cook, & Wiley, 2011).

In education and other areas of human services, justice implies that resources and services are disbursed fairly and not on the basis of "advantaging" or "disadvantaging" characteristics (Howie et al., 1992, p. 50). In other words, just distribution of resources means that people who occupy a status of advantagement do not receive a disproportionate share of goods or services. It also means that people whose status is one of disadvantagement are not disproportionately excluded from accessing benefits or resources. Koch and Rumrill (2017) noted that justice in disability policy is not simply a matter of dividing resources evenly among all people who have a need or claim; rather, they asserted the age-old maxim that the purpose of social services (including special education) is to "level the playing field" for people to access certain benefits or amenities of society. In that regard, however, Bellini, Bolton, and Neath (1998) noted that justice or equity for one person often results in injustice or inequity for another. For example, a medical researcher conducting a study with an experimental drug to treat attention deficit disorder limits her investigation to 18 children because of limited funding for the project. The nineteenth and subsequent children who enroll in the study are not provided with the treatment; rather, they form a "services as usual" comparison group. The treatment turns out to be highly successful, which is, of course, beneficial to the participants who received the intervention. One could make the point, however, that the comparison group incurred an injustice, albeit an unavoidable one given the fiscal constraints of the study, by not having the opportunity to receive the experimental drug. As a means of more justly allocating the benefits of the intervention, the researcher might decide to administer the experimental drug to the comparison group sometime after the study has concluded.

Justice is a key principle in the delivery of special education services, and it poses key considerations for special education researchers as they design investigations, select participants, and apply consistent standards in determining "who gets what and why." By establishing a clear scheme and rationale for determining how research studies are justly and fairly carried out, special education researchers can add to the knowledge base in a manner that reflects the full spirit of ethical conduct in all social science disciplines.

Fidelity

The principle of fidelity is a core element of any effective helping or educational relationship. Fidelity means faithfulness, keeping promises and honoring agreements, and loyalty (Heppner et al., 2015). Being honest, not engaging in undue deception, and maintaining confidentiality are commonly accepted ways of manifesting fidelity in such relationships as supervisor/worker, teacher/student, counselor/client, and researcher/participant. Being viewed as trustworthy, credible, and honest provides an essential foundation on which special education researchers design and implement investigations that are imbued with the ideals of nonmaleficence, beneficence, autonomy, and justice. In perhaps the most fundamental sense, the principle of fidelity serves as a building block of ethical practice and effective relationships in all aspects of scientific inquiry in our field.

TREATMENT OF HUMAN SUBJECTS IN SPECIAL EDUCATION AND SOCIAL SCIENCE RESEARCH

As should be clear from reading the preceding text, protecting the welfare of research participants is an absolute priority for all social science researchers. Implicit in any investigation wherein researchers collect data from human subjects (and especially children) is the assurance that participants have not been coerced and that they (and their parents) have made informed choices on the basis of the risks and benefits associated with participation. Key ethical issues related to the treatment of human subjects include protecting participants from harm, institutional review procedures, informed consent, privacy and confidentiality, deception and debriefing, and considerations related to applying and withholding treatment.

Protecting Participants from Harm

The principle of autonomy implies that research participants should have the freedom to choose whether and to what extent they will be involved in a study—even in one where some degree of risk can be foreseen. However, the superseding nonmaleficence requirement dictates that researchers take precautions to ensure that potential risks have been minimized before inviting participants to join an investigation. Ary, Jacobs, and Razavieh (1985, p. 382) offered the following time-tested guidelines for educational researchers to use in developing studies that involve potential risk to participants:

A. Only when a problem is of scientific significance and it is not practical to investigate it in any other way is the psychologist (researcher) justified in exposing research subjects, whether children or adults, to physical or emotional stress as part of an investigation.

B. When a reasonable possibility of injurious aftereffects exists, research is conducted only when the subjects or their reasonable agents are fully informed of this possibility and agree to participate, nevertheless.

C. The psychologist (researcher) seriously considers the possibility of harmful aftereffects and avoids them, or removes them as soon as permitted by the design of the experiment.

It is important for readers to understand that harm can take many forms in special education research and that it cannot always be easily foreseen. Harm includes such obviously negative consequences as physical injury and death, but it may be more likely to take the form of embarrassment, irritation, anger, physical and emotional stress, loss of self-esteem, exacerbation of stress, delay of treatment, sleep deprivation, loss of respect from others, negative labeling, invasion of privacy, damage to personal dignity, loss of employment, and civil or criminal liabilities (Heppner et al., 2015). Harm can also emerge as either a direct consequence or an indirect result of participation in a research study. Direct harm is often seen in medical research in the form of unintended side effects of medication or treatments. Although more subtle, indirect harmful consequences of research can be just as serious. For example, a transition researcher who wishes to test the effectiveness of a job placement intervention for young adults with learning disabilities includes in her intervention several prompts to direct participants to obtain employment. What she fails to account for is the fact that participants who are receiving Supplemental Social Security Income benefits (which often include medical insurance coverage) could incur the risk of having their income and insurance benefits cut if they maintain full-time employment for an extended period of time (which is the goal of the placement intervention). In this hypothetical study, the desired outcome of employment brings with it the risk of indirect harm, namely, the loss of Social Security benefits. To address this possibility of indirect harm, the researcher may wish to provide a debriefing session for participants in which she informs them of work incentives in the Social Security Administration's programs that allow some beneficiaries to maintain employment without compromising their benefits (Strauser, 2014).

Institutional Review Procedures

The National Research Act of 1974 requires institutions receiving Federal funds (e.g., colleges and universities, research centers, hospitals, public schools) to review the ethical and legal soundness of proposals for research to be conducted at those institutions. The primary target of this statute is research that involves human subjects. As a means of proactively protecting such rights of participants as privacy, dignity, freedom from harm, choice, consentual participation, and withdrawal without consequence, most institutions covered by the National Research Act convene Institutional Review Boards (IRBs) to evaluate research proposals and to monitor the execution of those studies (Hepner et al., 2015; McMillan & Schumacher, 2009). In most cases, these institutions do not allow the researcher to initiate a study without first receiving official clearance from the IRB. An example of the form that is used to consider research proposals involving human subjects is provided in Table 4.1. Many institutions also require researchers to submit progress reports to the IRB at specified points throughout studies and to develop final reports after the conclusion of investigations.

Informed Consent

One of the most important issues that IRBs consider is informed consent. Informed consent is typically achieved by providing potential participants with a description of the purposes of the investigation, a statement of potential risks and benefits, an option not to participate without consequence, and the opportunity to withdraw from the study at any time and for any reason. Consent is officiated by asking participants (or parents/guardians of minors) to sign a form indicating that they understand their rights as human subjects and that they have agreed to participate voluntarily and without coercion. In the case of working with individuals unable to legally consent to participating in a research study (e.g., minors), the researcher must assure that assent, the agreement of someone not able to give legal consent, is obtained in addition to consent from parents/guardians. Table 4.2 presents an example of an informed consent document.

It is important to note that obtaining informed consent from participants is not necessary in all research investigations involving human subjects. Studies that examine extant data (i.e., data that have already been collected for another purpose) provide only summary data to the researcher(s) without linking individual participants' information with their names and/or require participants to provide anonymous information may not compel the researcher(s) to secure informed consent from each participant. An exception to the informed consent rule is also commonly invoked in legal research that interprets information that is a matter of public record.

Privacy and Confidentiality

As is specified in the informed consent document presented in Appendix C, research participants have the right to privacy with respect to information that they provide in a study. Researchers must keep personally identifying information about particular participants in strict confidence unless participants expressly waive their rights to confidentiality. McMillan and Schumacher (2009) identified several ways of safeguarding research participants' rights to privacy, including (a) collecting and coding data anonymously without ever knowing the participants' names; (b) using numerical or alphabetical coding systems to link data to participants' names, then destroying the system at the end of the investigation; (c) retaining a third party who links names to data and then provides the researcher with anonymous results; (d) using aliases or code numbers (e.g., a portion of one's Social Security number) in linking personally identifying information; and (e) reporting only summary or aggregate results for the entire sample or particular groups, rather than reporting information garnered from individual participants' responses.

Another level of safeguarding participants' rights to privacy is often used in investigations that involve case studies (Roessler et al., 2017). A common design in epidemiological medical research and in qualitative investigations in various fields, the case study approach involves gathering in-depth information about a relatively small number of individuals. Although aliases are almost always used in reporting these studies, the level of specificity in the information reported is such that participants may be recognizable to some readers. To minimize the prospects of unwanted recognition, researchers often send copies of the manuscript or research report for participants'(and their parents' in the case of children) review before the paper is submitted for publication. This gives the participant an opportunity to check the report for accuracy and to change any representations of his or her personal experiences that are objectionable.

Deception and Debriefing

The principle of fidelity implies honesty and trustworthiness, as noted in a previous section of this chapter. Fidelity does not, however, mean that a special education researcher must fully disclose all aspects of an investigation to participants at the inception of the study. In fact, to fully disclose all aspects of a particular study often biases the results or outcomes. The researcher should inform participants of the general purposes of the study, but degrees of deception are seen as necessary aspects of many, if not most, investigations. Deception can include withholding specific details of a study, not informing members of a control or comparison group what intervention or stimulus other participants will be exposed to, collecting data under some auspice other than a research study, and out-and-out lying to participants (Heppner et al., 2015; McMillan & Schumacher, 2009).

Of course, how much deception is too much from an ethical standpoint is always a matter of situational judgment. IRBs examine the level of deception that a researcher intends to use, with the primary consideration being how necessary deception is to the conduct of the study. McMillan and Schumacher (2009) asserted that deception should only be used in cases in which (a) the potential significance of the results is greater than the projected effects of lying; (b) deception is the only way to carry out the study; and (c) appropriate debriefing, in which the researcher informs the participants of the nature of and reasons for the deception after the study is completed, is used.

Most research ethicists agree that, regardless of whether or how much deception was used in a study, participants have the right to a full disclosure of the purpose, methods, and findings of an investigation after it is completed. Some researchers provide a summary report of the study to all participants as a matter of routine, whereas others prefer to hold in-person debriefing meetings with participants.

Applying and Withholding Treatment

In studies that involve the application of a treatment or intervention, the principle of beneficence often comes into conflict with limitations associated with resources, time, and scientific controls. Researchers are often faced with the difficult decision of choosing who will participate in an intervention and who will be excluded.

The ethics of applying and/or withholding treatment are almost always complicated, and they interact with some of the foundational principles of scientific inquiry. On one hand, it would seem that any researcher would want as many people as possible to benefit from a successful intervention. On the other hand, constraints of time and money often necessitate limiting an intervention or stimulus to a specified number of participants. Moreover, "good science" in experimental design (Creswell, 2014; Goodwin & Goodwin, 2012; Heppner et al., 2015) dictates that a group receiving an intervention or treatment should be compared with a control group that did not participate in the intervention. In addition, the principle of statistical power (as was described in Chapter 3) implies that researchers need not exceed certain thresholds of sample size to effectively gauge the impact of their interventions or treatments.

So, because overall sample and intrasample group sizes are limited by time, money, and scientific protocol, the "who gets what and why?" question reemerges as per the principle of justice. Many researchers provide abbreviated versions (e.g., written informational packets, self-help brochures) of interventions to participants who are not assigned to an experimental condition (Rumrill & Bellini, 2018). Other researchers place such participants on a waiting list and provide the treatment or training to them at a later date. For example, Palmer (1998) demonstrated an effective model for training college students with disabilities to request classroom accommodations from their instructors. Social scientific protocol dictated that he withhold the intervention from a number of interested participants who formed a comparison group. However, because the intervention presented useful information and resulted in valuable skill acquisition for those (randomly) selected to participate in the training, Palmer's study (as it was initially designed) effectively excluded half of the sample. Noting the inherent injustice in his original design, the researcher decided to provide the training to the comparison group after he had gathered baseline data from them concerning the hypothesized effects of the intervention.

ETHICAL CONSIDERATIONS INVOLVED IN REPORTING AND PUBLISHING SPECIAL EDUCATION RESEARCH

The role of ethics in special education research clearly and rightfully centers on the treatment of subjects or participants. Not only is the special education researcher responsible for upholding the fundamental ethical principles that underlie the profession and practice of special education (i.e., nonmaleficence, beneficence, autonomy, justice, fidelity), he or she must ensure that defined ethical standards related to scientific inquiry and the treatment of human subjects (e.g., confidentiality, informed consent, institutional review) are followed. However, the ethical special education researcher's obligation is not completely fulfilled by virtue of ethical conduct in the execution of a study. There are also ethical considerations to be made in the process of reporting and publishing research results. Synthesizing ethical provisions promulgated by the American Psychological Association and the Council for Exceptional Children, Rumrill and Bellini (2018) set forth a number of recommended standards for ethical practice in publishing social science research. These standards address such issues as relationships with research participants, authorship credit, the roles of editors and peer reviewers, acknowledgment of contributions, plagiarism, and copyright laws.

Relationships with Research Participants

In many published research articles, the investigators document how they adhered to the ethical standards of their home institutions in conducting particular investigations. They must describe how informed consent was obtained, and the "Method" section of a published research article should include a description of the manner in which participants were recruited for the study. The article should also include only information that cannot be linked to a participant's name or other identifying characteristics. It is important to remember that research participants considered to be at greater risk for harm, because of disadvantaging characteristics (e.g., children, people with disabilities, prisoners), are afforded a higher degree of protection under the National Research Act than are participants considered to be at less risk.

Data Collection, Analysis, and Reporting

Special education researchers must report data as they were collected. Tampering with, fabricating, and exaggerating results are considered unethical conduct (American Psychological Association [APA], 2013; CEC, 2015; Rumrill & Bellini, 2018). Also, the norm of common ownership of information (Merton, 1968; Rumrill & Bellini, 2018) requires that all data presented in a research article are essential to the full and accurate reporting of an investigation's results. Extraneous information may serve to distract the reader from the true meaning of the study and, therefore, should not be reported. Conversely, providing too little information in a research report or article renders it difficult for other researchers to replicate the investigation

The procedures that were used to analyze data must not mislead the reader, distort findings, or exaggerate the impact or meaning of research results. Many authors include a description of the scientific limitations of their studies in the "Discussion" sections of published articles. This serves as a means of accurately characterizing the overall contributions of their research, as well as a forum to honestly report the parameters in which research validity conclusions about a study can be drawn.

Procedures for Correcting Errors

If the author notices an error of fact or omission in a published article, he or she should make reasonable effort to notify readers by submitting a correction or retraction to be included in the next issue of the journal (APA, 2013). To prevent foreseeable errors from appearing in print, many journals provide authors with "galley" page proofs just before the finalized publication of each issue. These proofs provide a likeness of how the article will appear in print, and they afford authors the opportunity to make any final changes to the article before the journal's printing.

Citation and Acknowledgement Procedures

When citing facts, findings, or ideas that are not their own, authors must afford credit to the originator(s) of previously published work. Short direct quotes should be attributed to the page number of their original published source. Longer direct quotes or reprinting of an entire article usually requires the permission of the author(s) and/or publisher of the original work. Failure to obtain an original author's consent or offer appropriate acknowledgment may be viewed as plagiarism and a violation of copyright law (APA, 2013). Most journals in special education and disability studies adhere to the APA's (2013) guidelines for citing and acknowledging the works of other authors.

The concept of plagiarism needs additional attention here. Plagiarism can range from unintentional omissions of necessary citations to willful theft of another author's words in an attempt to make them one's own. The issue of giving credit where credit is due becomes complicated in circumstances related to the origin of ideas. Given that a discipline's knowledge base is built in small increments with each advance serving as an extension of the one before it (Creswell, 2014; Heppner et al., 2015), it is sometimes confusing to authors (and readers) who originated a particular concept and who extended or amplified it. How much one must extend an existing theory or model before claiming a new one is not provided in current ethical guidelines, nor is any allowance for the possibility that two or more authors could independently develop similar ideas at approximately the same time. Given that plagiarism almost always amounts to a situational judgment call, the best advice for special education authors is that they take every step possible to credit others for the work that others have done and be sure that claims of original ideas are qualified by acknowledging authors whose works contributed to the development of new knowledge.

Authorship Credit

To be granted authorship credit for a published article, an individual must have made an appropriate, substantive contribution to the manuscript (APA, 2013). According to Winston (1985), scholarly contributions to a research article that could merit publication credit include conceptualizing and refining research ideas, literature search, developing a research design, instrument selection, instrument construction/questionnaire design, selection of statistical analyses, collection and preparation of data, performing statistical analyses, interpreting statistical analyses, drafting manuscripts, and editing the manuscript. Individuals who do not warrant authorship credit but who contributed to an article in a minor way are often credited in an "Acknowledgments" or "Author Note" section at the end of the article. Heppner et al. (2015) identified several activities as minor contributions that do not usually warrant authorship credit: providing editorial feedback, consulting on design or statistical questions, serving as raters or judges, administering an intervention, providing (even extensive) clerical services, and generating conceptual ideas relevant to the study without contributing to the writing of the manuscript.

Rumrill and Bellini (2018) opined that authorship also implies that the person has not had a role in the editorial process or peer review of that article. In the event that an editor of a journal submits a paper for review and possible publication in that journal, he or she should defer all editorial decisions to a coeditor or editorial board member.

In terms of the institutional affiliations of authors, these should be accredited to the institutions at which authors were employed or affiliated at the time work on the article was completed. If an author changes his or her institutional affiliation during the editorial or publication processes, he or she may elect to add the new affiliation to the former one. In that event, the author credits bear both institutional affiliations.

Ordering of Authors

If an article was written by two or more authors (which is the case in most articles published in special education journals), the first author listed should be the one who has made the most significant contributions to the development of the article. Secondary authors' names should be listed in descending order of their contributions, unless otherwise indicated in an Author Note. When two or more authors contribute equally to a coauthored article or book, it is common for authors to be listed in alphabetical or reverse alphabetical order, accompanied by a statement that the publication represents an evenly distributed collaborative effort. In those cases, senior or principal authorship is shared by all contributors.

Publications Resulting from Dissertations or Theses

When an article with more than one author is the product of a student's dissertation or thesis, the student should usually be listed as the first author (APA, 2013; Rumrill & Bellini, 2018). Regardless of the student's institutional affiliation at the time of the article's publication, the institution that sponsored his or her study (where he or she earned the degree that was culminated by the dissertation or thesis) should also be included in the author credits.

Most experts agree that the student should be the first author of articles resulting from his or her dissertation, but whether and how the student's dissertation supervisor and committee members are accorded authorship credit can be complicated decisions. Opinions vary regarding whether including dissertation supervisors and committee members as coauthors on articles resulting from dissertations should be obligatory, but experts generally agree that anyone who is cited as a coauthor on a published article should have made a substantive contribution to the composition of the article (Heppner et al., 2015; Rumrill & Bellini, 2018).

Ethics Regarding Dual Submission and Re-Publication

Submitting a paper for review by a journal implies that the paper is not under current consideration by any other journal. Authors may not publish the same article in two different journals without tacit agreement from both journals' editors that a reprint is warranted and permissible. Authors also must not publish multiple articles from the same data set or within the same content area unless they have (a) secured necessary releases from the publishers of previous work, and/or (b) included (in the article) an explanation of how the new study differs in terms of purpose, research questions, and/or hypotheses.

Verification and Re-Analysis of Data

To every extent possible, authors should make their data available to other researchers who wish to reanalyze and/or verify the results of a published study. This does not mean that requests for verification must be honored in all cases. Issues such as participants' rights to privacy, proprietorship, and the motives and/or competence of the researcher seeking to certify or reanalyze findings may preclude authors from sharing their data with others.

Accordance of Results with Research Questions and Hypotheses

Researchers must report all findings that are relevant to their research questions and hypotheses, not only those that are statistically significant or that support a particular perspective. Exaggerating some results while ignoring others as a means of supporting a particular point of view or prediction is ethically unacceptable and should be avoided at all times.

Editorial and Peer Review Processes

Special education professionals who serve as journal editors, editorial board members, or reviewers for grant competitions must protect the confidentiality of authors who submit their work for peer review. Moreover, editors and reviewers may not use information contained in prepublished work without expressed consent from the originating author(s). We also believe that an editor or reviewer should not be added to a list of authors during the review or publication process if he or she did not appear in the original manuscript's author credits—even if he or she makes substantial contributions in an editorial role.

SUMMARY

The special education researcher is subject to a number of ethical considerations in the design, implementation, evaluation, and reporting of empirical research. First, the researcher must conform to the rules of "right" conduct as they apply to the ethical principles that underlie the field of special education. Nonmaleficence, perhaps the most basic tenet of any helping or human service profession, sets a priority on doing no harm to students or participants in research projects. Beneficence, a concept that serves to define the ultimate purpose of our field, implies that teachers and researchers should strive to help people in a way that improves their independence and quality of life. Autonomy provides a basis for absolute deference to individuals' (and their parents') rights to choose whether and to what extent they will participate in a service program or research investigation. Justice connotes fair and equal treatment of all participants without offering undue advantages to one participant or disadvantaging another. Fidelity in special education research means that the researcher is honest, trustworthy, and credible.

In addition to the overarching ethical considerations that special education researchers must make as representatives of the profession, it is important to abide by current ethical standards regarding the treatment of human subjects. Issues of informed consent, the use of deception, withholding treatment from a comparison or control group, and confidentiality are paramount concerns for responsible special education researchers, and most institutions have review boards that oversee how research participants are treated.

Finally, because the special education researcher seeks to disseminate his or her findings in professional journal articles, he or she is subject to rules of conduct associated with the publication process. In this chapter, we discussed such ethical concerns as authorship credit, plagiarism, copyright law, acknowledgment of contributions, and the roles of editors and peer reviewers.

Given the myriad of ethical issues that special education researchers face as they design, implement, evaluate, and disseminate their studies, it is essential to become familiar with the standards set forth by sponsoring institutions and professional associations. By maintaining vigilance in applying the highest standards of right and appropriate conduct in all interactions with research participants, one another, and those who review their work, special education researchers can continue a long tradition of responsible research practices whose ultimate purpose is to understand and improve the life experiences of children with disabilities.

Table 4.1
SAMPLE INSTITUTIONAL REVIEW BOARD DOCUMENT

**APPLICATION TO THE INSTITUTIONAL REVIEW BOARD
FOR THE PROTECTION OF HUMAN RESEARCH SUBJECTS**

ANSWERS MUST BE TYPED

DATE SUBMITTED:_____ IRB#_____ (The above to be completed by IRB Secretary)

SUBMITTED BY: (NOTE: If this application is submitted by a student, it must also have the name of the faculty member who will assume responsibility for seeing that the research is carried out in accordance with regulations.)

_____ Dept. _____ Phone _____
(Faculty Member)

_____ Dept. _____ Phone _____
(Student)

Undergraduate _____ Graduate _____ Program of Study _____

TITLE OF PROPOSAL:_____

CHECK APPROPRIATE REPLY:

A. Will the research be submitted as a grant or contract proposal?

Yes _____ No _____

continued

_____

Note: From *Research in Rehabilitation Counseling,* by P. Rumrill and J. Bellini, 2018, Springfield, IL: Charles C Thomas • Publisher, LTD. Copyright 2018 by Charles C Thomas • Publisher, LTD. Reprinted by permission.

Table 4.1—*Continued*

If the answer is Yes, who is the proposed sponsor?

Submission Deadline _____

B. Is the research currently being funded, in part or in whole?

Yes _____ No _____

State _____ Federal _____ University _____ Other (specify) _____

C. Has the research been reviewed before the IRB?

Yes _____ No _____

If yes, please give the date of the review _____ and the IRB# (if known) _____

D. Is this research to be performed for a master's thesis?

Yes _____ No _____

Is this research to be performed for a doctoral dissertation?

Yes _____ No _____

Is this research to be performed as part of a course requirement?

Yes _____ No _____

Is this research to be performed as an honor's thesis?

Yes _____ No _____

Other (explain) _____

**PLEASE READ INSTRUCTIONS BEFORE
COMPLETING THIS FORM**

To avoid delays, all questions must be answered. Incomplete forms will be returned to the investigator for additional information.

1. Summary of proposal. In concise, nontechnical language, describe the rationale and methods (experimental tests and procedures) to be used. **(DO NOT USE JARGON)** State clearly what the subjects will be required to do or be subjected to in the experiment. Use the space below. Applications without a summary in the space allotted will not be considered by the Board.

continued

Table 4.1—*Continued*

A. Rationale

B. Methods
(The source of questionnaires and surveys should be indicated, whether published, adapted, or newly formulated.)

2. Who will have direct contact with the subjects? Who will administer tests, conduct interviews, etc.? State their qualifications specifically with regard to the procedures to be used in this study.

3. Characteristics of subjects.

A. Sex M _____ F _____ Other _____

B. Age _____ Any subjects under age 18? Yes _____ No _____

C. Special ethnic group _____

D. Institutionalized Yes _____ No _____ (See item #4 below.)

E. General state of health _____ ("unknown" unless you will obtain health data on subjects prior to beginning the study.)

F. Source of subjects _____

G. How will subjects be identified and recruited? _____

NOTE: *If the research is conducted at an off-campus institution (e.g., a school, hospital, etc.), attach a statement signed by an appropriate official authorizing access to subjects (e.g., school district superintendent), or current approval from that institution's review committee. Full approval cannot be given without this authorization.*

4. Special groups—If subjects are either (1) **children**, (2) **mentally incompetent**, or (3) **legally restricted** (i.e., institutionalized), please explain the necessity for using this particular group. *Proposals using subjects from any of these groups cannot be given expedited review, but must go to the full Board.*

Yes _____ No _____ If yes, please attach memo explaining who and why.

continued

Table 4.1—*Continued*

---

5. Type of consent to be obtained. Informed consent requires that subjects be informed of and understand, by oral or written form, the procedures to be used in the research, and that they may refuse to participate or withdraw from the investigation at any time without prejudice. If oral consent is used, the investigator must explain to the subjects all of the points as required on a written consent form. A written version of what will be said when requesting oral consent must be attached to this application. **If written consent is used, the procedures must be clearly stated on the form signed by the subject. A copy of the written consent must be included as the last page of this application. MI consent forms must be on university letterhead unless exempted by the IRB. APPROVAL WILL NOT BE GRANTED WITHOUT A COPY OF THE CONSENT FORM!**

A. Oral Written Obtained and explained by whom _____

B. From whom will consent be obtained and by what means for minors (minors or children aged 7 and older must be asked for ASSENT) or the mentally incompetent?

6. Confidentiality

A. What precautions will be taken to insure the privacy and anonymity of the subjects, and the confidentiality of the data, both in your possession and in reports and publications?

B. Will audio, video or film recording be used? Yes _____ No _____

Specify which _____. If yes, what will be the description of the records when the research is complete? (All tapes, audio or video, MUST BE DESTROYED.)

7. Risk to Subjects
NOTE: *Investigators should complete this portion as succinctly as possible. If the Board has to request additional clarification or explanation, approval may be delayed a full month until the next meeting.*

A. Describe in detail any possible physical, social, political, legal, economic, or other risks to the subjects, either immediate or long range. Estimate the seriousness and extent of the risk. *Risk may be minimal but never totally absent. Do not say "No Risk."*

B. Describe what procedures will be used to minimize the risk you have stated above.

8. Benefits
Assess the benefits of research to:

A. The subjects

continued

Table 4.1—*Continued*

B. Society at large

C. Explain how the benefits outweigh the risks involved.

9. Signatures

A. Faculty

This is to certify that the procedures involved in this study are appropriate for minimizing risks to the subjects and acknowledges that I take full responsibility for the conduct of the research.

Signed _____ Date _____ (Faculty member)

Name typed _____

Campus phone _____ Campus address _____

B. Student**

Signed _____ Date _____

Graduate _____ Undergraduate _____

Name typed _____

Campus phone _____ Campus address _____

Please note: *If this study is being conducted by a student, a faculty member must sign in the space provided. A form without a faculty member's approval will be returned for signature.*

Table 4.2
SAMPLE INFORMED CONSENT FORM

Purpose

The Center for Disability Studies conducts research on the lived experiences of people with disabilities. This research is conducted to learn more about how to improve educational and employment outcomes for people with disabilities. Information from participants is maintained by the Center and will be used for research purposes only.

Agreement

By signing this form, I agree to participate in research conducted by the Center as described below:

A Study of Accommodation Needs and Activities

I agree to participate in a study of my experiences in requesting and using reasonable accommodations in the high school classroom and in the workplace. The study will involve no more than two personal visits of less than one hour each with a trained interviewer. The interviewer will request information on my perceptions of barriers in education and employment as well as possible reasonable accommodations. I will also provide information regarding my background and personal views of my current life and situation in no more than two telephone contacts with the interviewer.

I understand that the Center may provide research data to qualified persons and/or research centers subject to ethical restrictions. If such information is shared with qualified persons or organizations, I understand that it will not be possible to connect my name with the information that I provide. Information from this investigation may be published anonymously in a case study format. I have the right to approve any information developed for publication. I also understand that I have the option of withdrawing this consent and release of information and withdrawing my participation in this research process at any time. Should I withdraw, I understand that this will not affect my participation in any service program.

Signature of Participant _____ Date _____

Participant's Age _____

Parent's or Guardian's Signature (if participant is under the age of 18)

_____

Participant's Mailing Address _____

E-Mail Address _____

Daytime Phone Number _____

Chapter 5

RESEARCH VALIDITY

INTRODUCTION

This chapter examiens the criteria by which quantitative research investigations are evaluated and applies the concept of research validity to the methods that social scientists use to make warranted knowledge claims. Throughout this chapter, it is important to remember that the designs researchers use to ensure validity (e.g., experimental, single-subject, survey, correlational) are determined primarily by the research question or problem being addressed. No approach to empirical research is inherently better than any other, but each contributes in different ways to the development of scientific knowledge.

The purpose of all research is to generate warranted, or valid, conclusions about the relationships among variables (Kazdin, 2017; Rumrill & Bellini, 2018). Whereas test validity (as discussed in Chapter 3) refers to knowledge claims related to measurements or observations, the terms validity and invalidity as applied to research design refer to "the best available approximation of the truth or falsity of propositions, including propositions about cause" (Cook & Campbell, 1979, p. 37). Thus, validity in research pertains to the warrant for a knowledge claim on the basis of the characteristics of the entire study, including the quality of sampling procedures, measurement, research design, statistical analysis, and conclusions drawn from the findings (Creswell, 2014).

A research investigation may result in a weak knowledge claim if the types of inferences the investigator wishes to draw are not substantiated adequately in the design and implementation of the study. From the standpoint of methodology, the better the design and implementation of an investigation, the more implausible it makes alternative explanations for the results, and the stronger, or more valid, the knowledge claim of the investigator therefore becomes (Cook & Campbell, 1979). With that in mind, an exemplary research design is one in which the researcher's explanation for the findings is buttressed by the elimination, or falsification, of rival, alternative explanations (Popper, 1959). The falsificationist approach to evaluating knowledge claims underlies quantitative hypothesis testing and emphasizes the difficulty inherent in definitively confirming causal hypotheses. Moreover, it encourages a modest, incremental approach to the development of scientific knowledge, which (over time) enhances the stability and credibility of a particular profession (Rumrill & Bellini, 2018).

TYPES OF RESEARCH VALIDITY

The four major types of research validity are internal, external, construct, and statistical conclusion validity (Rumrill & Bellini, 2018). Together, these issues form the set of considerations that researchers address when they design a research investigation (Kazdin, 2002, 2017). Awareness of the various threats to valid inference and the methods of minimizing these threats is central to designing and evaluating special education research.

Internal Validity

Internal validity refers to the approximate certainty with which researchers infer that a relationship between two variables is causal (Cook & Campbell, 1979) or the extent to which an investigation rules out alternative explanations for the results (Kazdin, 2002). Possible causal factors other than the independent variable(s) that are not accounted for in the research design but that may also explain the results are called threats to internal validity (Cook & Rumrill, 2005). Overall, random assignment of research participants to experimental and control groups provides the best protection against threats to internal validity, because random assignment reduces the possibility of systematic group differences that may influence scores on the dependent measures. We will discuss the major threats to internal validity, including history, maturation, instrumentation, selection, attrition, and ambiguity about the direction of causal influence. Readers interested in a more comprehensive discussion of these issues should consult timeless texts authored by Cook and Campbell (1979) and Kazdin (2002).

History

History as a threat to internal validity refers to (a) historical events that are common to all research participants in their everyday lives, or (b) unplanned events occurring during the process of implementing an experimental procedure that plausibly represent rival explanations for the results

(Kazdin, 2002). For history to be a threat, the event must impinge on the experimental situation in some way and influence scores on the dependent variable.

Consider the example of a researcher who uses a posttest-only experimental design (see Chapter 6) to test whether an intervention improves the attitudes of school principals toward the inclusion of children with disabilities. She recruits 50 principals and assigns them at random to two groups, a treatment group and a control group. The researcher implements a number of activities to enhance the sensitivity of treatment group members to disability issues. The control group receives a lecture on strategies to prevent school violence, a topic unrelated to the treatment condition. After these separate activities, the principals in both groups complete a standardized measure of attitudes toward inclusion. The researcher hopes to demonstrate that the intervention is effective in improving the attitudes of treatment group members, as indicated by higher scores on the attitude measure by the treatment group compared with the control group. However, in the interim between completion of the two interventions and administration of the posttest, a highly publicized Supreme Court decision mandates substantial changes in the way that public schools arrange educational placements for children with disabilities. Because this ruling requires members of the study sample (i.e., school principals) to make changes in the way children with disabilities are served, the researcher has no way of knowing whether changes in participants' attitudes toward inclusion are the result of her intervention or the Supreme Court's verdict. Thus, history represents a rival explanation for the results of the investigation, which undermines the study's internal validity.

Maturation

Maturation is a threat to internal validity when an observed effect may be due to respondents' growing older, wiser, stronger or weaker, or better or more poorly adjusted during the course of the study, when this maturational process is not the target of the investigation. Maturation is most likely to represent a rival explanation for results when there is a long time period between pretest and posttest. For example, consider a hypothetical intervention designed to increase the expressive language capacities of preschool children (ages three to four) with mild hearing loss. The treatment, a language-rich preschool curriculum and training for parents of the children in speech-enhancement strategies, is implemented over a nine-month period. In this case, posttest expressive language scores, which are intended to measure the effect of the intervention, may instead reflect normal, childhood maturational processes (which, even without an intervention, could dramatically increase a young child's language facility over a nine-month period). Thus, the researcher's conclusion that the language-based intervention increased the treatment group's expressive language scores may be challenged on the basis of the rival explanation of maturation.

Instrumentation

Instrumentation is a threat to causal inference when an effect, as measured on the dependent variable, is due to systematic changes in the measuring instrument from pretest to posttest. This threat is most likely to occur when the dependent variable consists of observers' ratings of others' behaviors (e.g., sociability, aggression) and the raters either (a) become more experienced, more strict, or more lenient over the course of the data collection efforts or (b) otherwise apply ratings criteria inconsistently from pretest to posttest. In either event, observed changes in ratings from pretest to posttest may be attributable to changes in raters' performance rather than to the treatment or intervention that is the focus of the research. The rival explanation of instrumentation is particularly problematic in single-subject [also known as small-N] and applied behavior analysis research (see Chapter 6).

For example, a researcher conducts a classroom-based experiment to determine the effect of a token economy reinforcement system on the aggression of several children with behavioral disorders. In evaluating the dependent variable of aggression, he on several occasions makes a subjective interpretation of different children's physical contact with other children; a slap on the back is recorded as aggression in one instance but not in another, even though the researcher's operational definition of an aggressive act is any physical contact with another child. In this example, instrumentation becomes a threat to internal validity because the researcher cannot rule out the possibility that changes in aggression are attributable, at least in part, to his inconsistent (i.e., unreliable) measurement of the dependent variable.

Selection

The effect of an intervention can only be unambiguously attributed to the independent variable when the researcher is assured that treatment and control groups do not systematically differ on other variables that may influence the dependent measure. Random assignment to treatment and control groups provides the best safeguard against selection biases (Cook & Rumrill, 2005; Creswell, 2014; Rumrill & Bellini, 2018). We want to emphasize, however, that random assignment of participants to groups does not ensure that treatment and control groups are equal or matched.

The threat of selection as an alternate explanation for results often occurs in educational research when intact groups (reflecting unknown and possibly systematic biases) are used rather than groups composed of randomly assigned individuals. A common mode of inquiry in education is to assess the effects of an intervention by applying it to one classroom of students while withholding it from another. The problem with this "intact group" approach is that the reasons why particular children were placed in each class, often unknown to the researcher, could influence students' performance on outcome measures irrespective of the intervention. Selection may also be an issue when participants are selected for treatment and control groups on the basis of severity of presenting issues (e.g., degree of intellectual disability), because severity may systematically influence group means on the outcome variable (Kazdin, 2017).

Attrition

Attrition (also termed mortality) is a potential threat to causal inference when the effect of an intervention (i.e., differences between treatment and control groups on a posttest) may be attributable to systematic differences associated with the characteristics of individuals who withdrew during the course of the experiment. Attrition may result in a selection bias even when groups are initially chosen by random assignment, because, as a function of differential mortality, the treatment and control groups at posttest consist of different kinds of people (Cook & Rumrill, 2005).

Let us suppose that a school district wishes to test a rigorous standards reform program in which high school students must pass a difficult performance examination before advancing to the next grade. Half of the high schools in the district take part in the initiative (i.e., treatment group), whereas the remaining high schools proceed as usual (i.e., control group). After the first year of implementing this initiative, the superintendent pridefully announces to the school board that schools assigned to the treatment group reported a 17 percent increase in the rate of students who were promoted to the next grade. He adds that this increase is significantly higher than the 1 percent increase reported by schools assigned to the control group. What this administrator did not report was the fact that treatment schools observed a significantly higher dropout rate than did control schools, and that those students who dropped out did not, of course, take the year-end examination. Therefore, it is impossible to attribute higher promotion rates to the standards reform program because differential attrition (of students who, presumably, would not have done well on the examination) is a plausible, alternative explanation for the findings.

Ambiguity About the Direction of Causal Inference

Sometimes, it is not possible to determine with certainty whether variable A causes variable B or variable B causes variable A. For example, a researcher may hypothesize that the increased stress often associated with acquiring diabetes mellitus in childhood causes increased depression. The data analysis reveals a significant relationship (i.e., correlation) between stress and depression within a sample of children with Type I (i.e., insulin-dependent) diabetes. He has also ruled out other threats to internal validity on the basis of research design features and logic, which strengthens the warrant for the claim that the relationship between the variables is causal. However, the possibility remains that the direction of causal influence is reversed, that having higher levels of depression results in greater susceptibility to stress. Lack of certainty with respect to the direction of causal influence is most likely to be a problem in correlational studies in which the conceptual foundation of the investigation is unclear or provides insufficient direction (Rumrill & Bellini, 2018).

External Validity

A fundamental purpose of research in all social sciences is to establish valid knowledge that transcends the particular context of a given investigation. External validity addresses this issue of generalization—the extent to which an observed relationship among variables can be generalized beyond the conditions of the investigation to other populations, settings, and conditions (Creswell, 2014). External validity is a particularly important issue for practitioners who wish to use research findings in teaching practice and, therefore, need to evaluate whether the findings associated with a particular sample, procedure, and research setting will generalize to their own schools and classrooms. Whereas random assignment to experimental groups provides the best protection against threats to the internal validity of findings, *random selection* of research participants from the population of interest affords the strongest likelihood that results will generalize to other individuals in that population (Rumrill & Bellini, 2018). However, random selection does not ensure that findings will generalize to different populations, settings, or conditions. The most persuasive demonstration of generalization (i.e., external validity) occurs when empirical findings of several studies are consistent across various types of subjects (e.g., children of different ages and different disability statuses), settings (e.g., classroom, laboratory, and diverse community settings), and other conditions (e.g., different researchers, diverse cultures).

Potential threats to the generalization of research findings include those associated with the specific sample, stimulus, context, and assessment procedures used (Goodwin & Goodwin, 2012). Many of these threats can be excluded or minimized on the basis of common sense considerations. It is important for consumers of research to consider the context and findings of an investigation, as well as how a particular threat may restrict the applicability of observed results. If a particular threat does plausibly apply, caution in generalizing findings should be exercised.

Sample Characteristics

One vital question in assessing generalization is the extent to which findings may apply to people who vary in age, race, ethnic background, education, or other salient characteristics from those who constituted the research sample. For example, a services coordinator in a transition program for adolescents with autism spectrum disorders (ASD) has read an article on a social skills training program that was found to be highly effective for a sample of young adults with labels of learning disabilities. How generalizable are the findings for adolescents with ASD? External validity may be undermined as a direct function of the differences between the study sample (people with learning disabilities) and the population to which findings are sought to be generalized (people with ASD). The two groups in this example are likely to be quite different, which means that findings reported for one group may not generalize to the other.

Stimulus Characteristics

Stimulus characteristics refer to the specific features of a given treatment or intervention that may restrict generalization of experimental findings. These features include the characteristics of the setting, experimenters, or interviewers—or how the stimuli are presented in an experiment. The external validity concern is that the specific stimulus conditions of an experiment may restrict the validity of findings to those conditions only. Experimental features that could limit external validity include using only one experimenter to implement an intervention, showing only one videotaped vignette to illustrate the experimental condition, and using a specific setting that may have different characteristics and conditions than are found in other settings. For example, a researcher wishing to demonstrate a self-advocacy training program for college students with disabilities uses a videotaped "model"—a person with a spinal cord injury who demonstrates appropriate self-advocacy in discussing her classroom accommodation needs with a "model" history professor. Even if the training appears to have a significant impact on the treatment group's self-advocacy skills, there is no way to separate the content of the training from the specific examples used to illustrate the content. In other words, the training may be interpreted by participants not as self-advocacy training in general, but as training on how people with spinal cord injuries request accommodations in history courses. One way to reduce this threat to external validity would be to present model self-advocates with several different disabling conditions and/or to vary the subject matter of the class settings depicted in the vignettes.

Contextual Characteristics

The specific conditions in which an intervention is embedded and/or the arrangements that are key to implementing an investigation may restrict findings to those conditions or arrangements only. The responses of participants who are aware of the fact that they are participating in a research study or correctly guess the purpose of the investigation may be influenced by this knowledge. In other words, study participants may react to the specific investigative arrangements in ways that influence their responses. Participants who correctly guess the purpose of the study may also seek to please investigators by (a) avoiding responses that they believe will result in negative evaluation, or (b) providing "correct" responses. The external validity concern is: Would these same results be obtained if the subjects did not know they were being studied or did not correctly guess the purpose of the investigation? If it is plausible that subjects' responses were affected by their knowledge of the study purpose, then results should be restricted to the specific conditions of the study.

For example, a university professor wishes to survey preservice special education teachers regarding their attitudes toward inclusion. She uses cluster sampling, whereby students in three classes are selected to participate. This professor is well known to students in the special education program as a zealous advocate of full inclusion, and one of the classes selected to participate in the survey is her own course, "Inclusion and Human Rights in Education." Given this professor's strong opinions regarding inclusion, it is impossible to determine whether respondents (especially those students in her class) are expressing their own perspectives on the issue or reflecting what they think the professor would like them to report.

Another potential threat to external validity related to contextual characteristics of a study concerns multiple treatment interference. In some research contexts (particularly in real world settings), subjects may be exposed to several different treatments in addition to the intervention that is the target of the investigation. For example, children with attention deficit disorder (ADD) or attention deficit hyperactivity disorder (ADHD) may be receiving drug therapy and psychological counseling at the same time that they are participating in a social skills training program. *Multiple treatment interference* refers to the difficulty of drawing warranted conclusions about the target intervention when it is being evaluated in the context of other treatments (Goodwin & Goodwin, 2012; Kazdin, 2002). In these cases, the generalization of findings may be restricted to those conditions in which multiple treatments are administered. Bringing back our ADD/ADHD example, the impact of the social skills intervention could not be isolated because participants (almost invariably) would be receiving other treatments. Therefore, findings could only be generalized to settings in which children with ADD/ADHD are receiving other treatments in addition to social skills training.

Assessment Characteristics

The method of assessing the dependent variable in an investigation may also influence participants' responses and therefore restrict the generalization of findings to similar conditions of assessment. Many research investigations in special education and disability studies use self-report measures to assess change in the dependent variable of interest. When self-report instruments are used, participants are typically aware that their performance is being evaluated, and what is being assessed is often made obvious by the nature of the specific items that comprise the instrument. These assessment characteristics can alter subjects' responses from what they would be under different conditions. When subjects are aware that they are being assessed, the evaluation is said to be *obtrusive.* When this awareness affects subjects' responses, the measures are said to be *reactive* (Kazdin, 2002). Use of obtrusive and reactive measures may restrict the findings to those specific data collection conditions.

Assessment can also lead to subjects becoming sensitized to the constructs that are the target of the investigation, particularly when self-report assessments are administered before the implementation of an experimental intervention to measure participants' baseline status. When a pretest causes subjects to become more sensitive to the construct that is the focus of the intervention, it can alter both the effect of the intervention and subjects' responses to the intervention at posttest from what would be obtained under different conditions (i.e., real world conditions in which sensitization does not take place). Posttest sensitization is a threat to the generalization of findings because it raises the question of whether results can be extended to those situations in which prior sensitization to the construct of interest does not take place.

Construct Validity

Internal validity is an evaluation of the status of the observed relationship between independent and dependent variables or whether change (as measured by the dependent variable) can be attributed to an intervention

(the independent variable) rather than to other factors (e.g., history, maturation, selection). Construct validity of research operations focuses on the specific causal factors or mechanisms that are responsible for the observed
change in the dependent variable.

As explained in Chapter 2, empirical research depends on translating
key abstract concepts into specific research operations for the purpose of
generating knowledge. Operational definitions form the essential linkage
between the abstract, conceptual definition of a construct and the concrete
procedures that comprise the study. For example, the construct intelligence,
which can be defined in abstract terms as a person's ability to learn, might
be operationalized in a research study by students' standard scores on an
established intelligence test such as the Weschler Intelligence Scale for
Children. Once data are analyzed, researchers typically wish to induce general conclusions from the specific case that was the focus of the investigation.
The process of scientific investigation, then, is a circular movement from
abstract constructs (research planning and conceptualization phase) to concrete exemplars of these constructs (implementation of procedures, data
gathering, and data analysis phases) and back to the conceptual level (interpretation of findings phase). Two linkages in this circular movement are vital
in the generation of valid scientific knowledge: (a) the linkage between the
abstract constructs and the concrete research procedures, and (b) the return
linkage between concrete procedures and the conceptual interpretations that
are made on the basis of the findings (Rumrill & Bellini, 2018). Construct
validity pertains to both of these linkages. On one hand (linkage between
conceptual foundations and research operations), construct validity pertains
to the "fit" between (a) the operational definitions and research procedures,
and (b) the hypothetical constructs that are assumed to underlie them
(Kazdin, 2002). On the other hand (linkage between specific findings and
conceptual conclusions), construct validity is the approximate validity of the
generalizations about the higher order constructs that the researcher makes
on the basis of the concrete research operations (Cook & Campbell, 1979).
Taking both linkages into account, construct validity of research is an evaluation of the specific nature of the relationships that are demonstrated within a quantitative study. The threats to construct validity are confounds that
call into question the researcher's interpretation regarding the specific factors
that account for the study findings (Rumrill & Bellini, 2018).

A number of aspects of a study's design and procedures may make it difficult to accurately attribute the causal relationships indicated by the results
to the constructs of interest. Threats to the construct validity of research conclusions include inadequate explication and operationalization of constructs,
single operations and narrow stimulus sampling, experimenter expectancies,
and cues associated with the experimental situation.

Inadequate Explication and Operationalization of Constructs

One key consideration in construct validity pertains to the "fit" between (a) the conceptual and operational definitions used by the investigator, and (b) how the construct is typically defined in the literature and operationalized in research. If there is a poor match between the commonly accepted definition and the researcher's definition, this is likely to raise questions about the warrant for specific interpretations that the researcher makes regarding the relationship between variables. For example, the construct of achievement, as it is defined in most literature, is the extent to which students learned what they have been taught. Yet, most standardized achievement tests (e.g., Peabody Individual Achievement Test, Woodcock-Johnson Test of Achievement, Wide Range Achievement Test) do not necessarily correspond to the instruction that students receive in school classrooms. In other words, the content of these tests may more closely reflect constructs such as general knowledge or test-taking ability than the actual content of grade-level curriculum.

Single Operations and Narrow Stimulus Sampling

The definition of achievement cited in the previous paragraph raises questions about the advisability of using a single measure taken at one point in time as a sole indicator of the construct. The use of a single indicator to operationalize a construct is a problem because indicators underrepresent constructs and contain irrelevant variation that is mixed with the variation that is due to the construct of interest (Rumrill & Bellini, 2018). Method of measurement may represent one major source of irrelevant variation in a measured variable (see Chapter 3). Using two or more indicators that represent different methods of measurement allows the investigator to triangulate the construct, that is, separate the variation that is due to the construct from the variation associated with the method of measurement (Cook & Campbell, 1979; Rumrill & Bellini, 2018). When a construct is confounded with a second, irrelevant construct (e.g., achievement and test-taking ability), the researcher can eliminate the effect of the confounding construct on the dependent variable by (a) including a standard measure of the confounding construct in the investigation, and then (b) correlating this variable with the target construct to estimate the variation that can be attributed solely to the construct of interest.

Construct validity may also be limited by the use of a single exemplar or stimulus to operationalize a treatment of interest. For example, a researcher wishing to evaluate possible differences in case management practices between male and female special education supervisors presents participants with one case study of an 11-year-old female student who is profoundly deaf. Examining how special education supervisors would engage this student in case planning and service delivery activities provides limited insight into special education case management practice. Would respondents react differently to a 14-year-old boy with asthma and a specific learning disability, irrespective of gender differences in case management practices? With only one stimulus being presented to the supervisors, the researcher cannot answer that question, or others related to the representativeness of the case example vis a vis other students with disabilities. Therefore, respondents' reports of case management practices (the dependent variable) do not fully represent the construct of case management practice, because those reports pertain only to the single case study presented during the investigation.

Construct validity may also be limited by the use of a single individual to implement a treatment or intervention. Even if the treatment proves effective compared with a no-treatment control or comparison group, a reader who is conversant with construct validity issues may raise an alternative explanation to the findings, specifically, that the special character of the instructor may be responsible for the observed change in the dependent variable rather than the intervention itself (Rumrill & Bellini, 2018).

Experimenter Expectancies

In research situations where the principal investigator-or someone else knowledgeable about the study's purpose-directly implements a treatment, the researcher's expectations regarding the intervention may confound the interpretation of findings (Kazdin, 2017). For example, a researcher who is enthusiastic about the effects of a token economy in decreasing the disruptive behavior of adolescents with severe behavioral disorders may wish to contrast it with an alternate approach (e.g., behavioral contracts). However, the experimenter's enthusiasm for the preferred strategy, coupled with her intention to demonstrate its efficacy, could lead to differences in how she implements the different interventions. The construct validity issue in this case highlights the possibility that the experimenter's expectations and enthusiastic implementation of the token economy intervention provide a plausible, alternate explanation for the causal mechanism responsible for the observed change in the dependent variable of disruptive behavior.

Cues Associated with the Experimental Situation

Research participants may inadvertently receive cues, such as rumors about the experiment or information provided during the recruitment phase, that are incidental to the experimental treatment but that may contribute to the study results (Rumrill & Bellini, 2018). Hypothesis guessing by subjects–

the basis of the Hawthorne Effect—may lead to enhanced motivation on the part of the experimental group (and alter their performance) to please the researcher. Incidental contact between members of the treatment and comparison groups may also lead to (a) compensatory rivalry, whereby comparison group members are especially motivated to perform as well as or better than the treatment group on the outcome variables; or (b) demoralization, when cues of the experimental situation result in lower than normal motivation on the part of the comparison group and adversely affect their standing on the outcome variables. Each of these situations may be a threat to construct validity, because they represent plausible, alternative explanations for the causal mechanisms that are presumed to account for the experimental findings. Depending on the specific context of the investigation, these threats to construct validity can be minimized by providing fewer cues that permit participants to guess the precise nature of the research hypotheses, reducing the incidental contact between treatment and comparison groups, and providing a "treatment" to the comparison group that is valued and, hence, less likely to result in demoralization.

Statistical Conclusion Validity

Covariation between an independent and dependent variable is a necessary first step in establishing that their relationship is causal. Statistical conclusion validity pertains to the approximate validity of conclusions about the covariation of variables on the basis of the specific research operations and statistical tests used in an investigation (Goodwin & Goodwin, 2012; Kazdin, 2002, 2017). When research conditions or statistical tests are not sufficiently rigorous, the conclusions that are based on those procedures may be erroneous. Common threats to statistical conclusion validity include low statistical power, violated statistical assumptions, "fishing" and error rate problems, low reliability of dependent measures, and low reliability of treatment implementation.

Low Statistical Power

As defined in Chapter 3, the power of a statistical test is the probability of detecting a significant relationship between two variables in a sample when the variables are related in the population. Power is a function of the interaction of three characteristics of a study: sample size, the size of the "effect" (i.e., the size of mean differences between groups on the variables of interest or the magnitude of variable relationships), and the researcher's preset alpha level or benchmark of statistical significance (Cohen, 1990). Low statistical power is most likely to result when the sample size and effect size are small and the preset alpha level is conservative (Rumrill & Bellini, 2018). Low power may result in an invalid statistical decision (type II error), whereby the investigator concludes that two variables do not covary (e.g., a decision of no statistical significance) for the sample when, in fact, the two variables are significantly related in the population. Poor statistical conclusion validity resulting from low statistical power is a common problem in social science research in general (Goodwin & Goodwin, 2012) and special education and disability studies research in particular (Rumrill, Cook, & Wiley, 2011). However, low power is a problem that researchers can minimize by (a) using larger samples in their research, (b) enhancing the size of the "effect" between groups, and/or (c) choosing (before the statistical analysis) a less rigorous Alpha level as the benchmark of statistical significance (e.g., $p < .10$ rather than $p < .05$). Also, researchers are encouraged to perform a power analysis before their main analyses to estimate the likelihood that their statistical conclusions will be valid (Cohen, 1990; Creswell, 2014; Rumrill et al., 2011).

Violated Statistical Assumptions

The conclusion validity of most tests of statistical significance requires that certain statistical assumptions are met. When these assumptions cannot be made for the sample data, the statistical test is less accurate and the interpretations based on the analyses are less valid. For example, a key assumption for most mean comparisons between groups (e.g., t- tests, ANOVA, MANOVA) is that groups represent separate samples from the same population and, therefore, have roughly equal variance as indicated by the standard deviation of dependent variables. Specific assumptions for various statistical tests can be found in most introductory statistics textbooks (e.g., Gravetter, Wallnau, & Forzano, 2017).

We believe that the extent to which statistical assumptions have been met is one of the most underaddressed issues in special education research. Rarely do published research articles in our field specify the underlying assumptions of the statistical tests used by the author(s) or whether the distribution of study variables adheres to those assumptions. The danger inherent in this omission is that readers often find it difficult to discern whether the researcher(s) chose the correct statistical procedures to answer the research questions. Ambiguity concerning the appropriateness of selected statistical tests creates a threat to validity, because study findings can be only as meaningful as the precision of the researcher's data analytical techniques.

"Fishing" and Error Rate Problem

When multiple statistical tests are performed on a single data set, each comparison may be evaluated at a given, preset alpha level (e.g., p < .05), but the alpha level for the investigation as a whole (i.e., investigation-wise alpha) is the sum of all comparisons made. Therefore, performing multiple statistical tests without correcting for the number of comparisons increases the probability of concluding that covariation exists in the sample when, in fact, no covariation exists in the population from which the sample was drawn. In that event, the statistical test yields a false-positive result or type I error. The fishing and error rate problem refers to the situation in which the investigator goes "fishing" for statistically significant differences among variables in a data set and makes all possible comparisons among variables, which increases the likelihood that the statistical tests will yield false-positive results. When making multiple comparisons, the researcher can reduce the likelihood of false-positive results by applying a more rigorous alpha level for each separate test. For example, if five separate t- tests (comparing five separate dependent variables for two groups) are each evaluated at the p < .01 level of significance, then the p < .05 level of significance is maintained for the study as a whole, and the investigator can be reasonably assured (within a 5 percent margin of error) that a false-positive result has been avoided (Gravetter et al., 2017; Rumrill & Bellini, 2018). The researcher can also reduce the likelihood of type I errors by making a few, carefully planned statistical comparisons that are guided by theory rather than making all possible comparisons.

Reliability of Measures

Because measurement instruments with low reliability have a larger component of error as part of the observed score, they cannot be depended on to register true changes in the dependent variable. Using measures with low reliability as the basis for statistical tests can result in both type I and type II errors (Creswell, 2014; Goodwin & Goodwin, 2014). Thus, a large error component in the measurement of the dependent variable may increase the likelihood that (a) an insignificant mean difference between treatment and control groups does not reflect true differences in the population, or (b) an observed significant relationship between two variables is not a true relationship. In the case of correlational studies, low reliability in the measurement of independent and/or dependent variables may attenuate or exaggerate the magnitude of variable relationships.

Reliability of Treatment Implementation

When different people or agencies are responsible for implementing an investigation, a lack of standardization in the execution of the study may result. For example, one critique of the "efficacy" studies, which attempted to determine the relative efficacy of segregated special education placements and inclusive placements, is that the treatments were not reliably implemented. In other words, the instruction and environment associated with one segregated special classroom does not necessarily occur in other segregated special classes. There may also be differences from occasion to occasion even when the same person implements the treatment or intervention. This lack of standardization—both within and across persons and schools—can inflate the error variance in the dependent variable and decrease the accuracy of the statistical inference to the population of interest. As Cook and Campbell (1979) noted, this threat is pervasive in field research in which the researcher may be unable to control the quality of implementation of the intervention. The investigator should use all available means (e.g., extensive training of individuals and organizations) to ensure that the intervention is as standard as possible across individuals, settings, and occasions.

RELATION AMONG THE FOUR TYPES OF RESEARCH VALIDITY

Although each type of research validity is important in its own right, and the warrant for a knowledge claim is based, in part, on how well the researcher addresses these issues in an investigation, there is a logical order of consideration (Cook & Campbell, 1979; Rumrill & Bellini, 2018; Rumrill et al., 2011). Before it can be shown that two variables have a causal relationship, it is first necessary to establish that they covary. Hence, statistical conclusion validity, or the demonstration that two variables are related statistically, is the initial criterion by which a knowledge claim is evaluated in quantitative research. Internal validity is the second issue in research, which is to determine whether a causal link between two related variables can be inferred. The third issue of research, construct validity, is to determine the particular constructs or mechanisms that are involved in the demonstrated causal relationship between variables. External validity, the final issue in research, involves the question: How generalizable is the relationship and causal mechanism to other populations, settings, and conditions? Each dimension of research validity contributes to causal explanation, which is the ultimate goal of scientific inquiry.

At the risk of being redundant, we want to remind readers here that no single research investigation can address each of these validity issues equally well. Limited resources often require an investigator to make compromises in designing research, which is why the growth of scientific knowledge in any profession or discipline is measured by tentative steps of incremental progress. The specific procedures that strengthen the internal validity of an investigation (i.e., experimental control) may unavoidably serve to reduce the generalizability of findings to real world settings (i.e., external validity) (Cook & Campbell, 1979). Ideally, the types of validity that the researcher chooses to emphasize in designing a particular investigation are a function of the global research context-that is, the totality of relevant studies in the given area, the degree to which relationships among variables have been established in previous research, and the extent to which generalizability of findings has been investigated. When the specific relationships among variables are not well understood, the research focus should be placed on statistical conclusion validity and internal validity: Do the targeted variables covary, and can a causal relationship be demonstrated? Once the warrant for these conclusions has been established, the research program moves on to address issues of construct and external validity: What is the specific causal mechanism at work, and do results generalize to other populations, settings, and conditions? The variety and complexity of research validity issues cannot be addressed in a single study or even a small group of related studies. Rather, valid scientific knowledge can only be established through multiple investigations carried out by many researchers spanning a long period of time (Rumrill et al., 2011).

SUMMARY

In this chapter, we discussed the four types of research validity as criteria for establishing the warrant for scientific knowledge claims in the quantitative research paradigm. Each type of validity—internal, external, construct, and statistical conclusion—addresses a different aspect of the knowledge claim. Internal validity pertains to the strength of the inference that the relationship between two variables is causal. Threats to the internal validity of an investigation are rival explanations for the results that are not ruled out on the basis of the research design. External validity is the degree to which research findings can be generalized to other populations, settings, and conditions. Threats to external validity are those aspects of the study that could restrict findings to the specific circumstances of the investigation. Construct validity pertains to the specific causal mechanisms that are theorized to underlie the study findings. Threats to construct validity are those aspects of research design and procedures that make it difficult to accurately attribute the causal relationships indicated by the results to the constructs of interest.

Statistical conclusion validity is the approximate certainty of conclusions about the covariation of variables on the basis of the specific research operations and statistical tests used in an investigation. Threats to statistical conclusion validity are aspects of research design and implementation that may result in erroneous interpretations of observed findings.

Taken together, the four types of research validity form the basis for building a scientifically oriented professional knowledge base. By understanding how internal, external, construct, and statistical conclusion validity interact, as well as how they sometimes interfere with one another, readers will be better informed consumers of the empirical research that is printed in special education journals.

Chapter 6

QUANTITATIVE RESEARCH DESIGNS

INTRODUCTION

As noted in the first chapter of this book, the research paradigm that comprises quantitative designs features the numeric expression of information for purposes of summarization, classification, interpretation, and generalization. Rooted within the quantitative paradigm are fundamental precepts of scientific inquiry including sampling and population issues, validity and scientific control, probability and statistics, power, significance, and generalizability (see Chapters 1, 2, 3, and 5). Quantitative research approaches share in common the transcription of words and observations into numbers, but there is great variance within the paradigm in terms of how researchers address their questions and hypotheses.

We have organized this chapter around three broad categories of quantitative studies: intervention/stimulus studies, nonmanipulation studies, and descriptive studies. Primarily, these categories are differentiated based upon the purpose or reason for a particular investigation—not on the basis of the methodological or analytic techniques that are used in each study. The foremost consideration in determining the suitability of a particular design or set of methods is the researcher's curiosity, that is, the question or problem the research is devised to address (Creswell, 2014). As discussed elsewhere in this text, high-quality scientific research is driven by a process in which the methods are fit to address the research question and not the other way around.

INTERVENTION/STIMULUS STUDIES

One key purpose of research in all social science disciplines is to gauge the effects that interventions and stimuli have on individuals' behaviors, knowledge, attitudes, and emotions. Whether assessing the effects of particular teaching strategies on children with disabilities, evaluating the impact of school placements on children and teachers, or determining the effectiveness of school-to-work transition programs for youth with disabilities, special education researchers have a long history of intervention/stimulus studies that attempt to answer the question, What happens when . . . ? Including such approaches as true experiments, quasi-experimental designs, analogue studies, and single-subject designs, intervention/stimulus studies have played an important role in shaping preservice training, instructional practice, and policy initiatives in the field of education. This section describes each design subcategory, illustrated with examples from the special education and disability studies literature.

Experimental Designs

Although relatively rarely employed in contemporary special education research, true experiments constitute the most readily apparent images that people bring to mind when they think of scientific inquiry in the social and physical sciences. Indeed, the quantitative research paradigm is deeply ingrained in experimental design, to the extent that experiments are often viewed as the highest form of investigation into new knowledge (Heppner et al., 2015). We believe that researchers should not view designs in hierarchical, this one is better than that one fashion; nevertheless, true experiments provide the strongest warrant for claims to knowledge because of the systematic ways in which the effects of an intervention are isolated, other influences are controlled, and alternative causal explanations are reduced or eliminated. We have divided quantitative designs into three major categories—intervention/stimulus studies, nonmanipulation studies, and descriptive studies—but many experts categorize all research as either experimental or nonexperimental. This dichotomy does not permit one to fully appreciate the breadth of approaches that are used within the overarching umbrella of quantitative methodology, but it does provide a useful rubric for explaining what experimental design is and what it is not.

The logical structure for experimental research is relatively simple. One hypothesizes: If X, then Y; if therapy, then wellness, for example, or if quality education, then graduation. Usually related to the tenets of a particular body of knowledge (theory), the researcher uses some method to manipulate or measure X (the independent variable) and then observe Y (the dependent variable) to see if concomitant variation occurs (Heppner et al., 2015; McMillan & Schumacher, 2009). Concomitant variation is the amount of variation in Y that is attributable to (or caused by) variation in X. If sufficient concomitant variation (sufficient as determined by (a) the magnitude of relationship between X and Y and (b) the size of the sample [i.e., a test for statistical significance]), the If X, then Y proposition is evidenced to be valid.

In that scenario, the control or manipulation (variation) of X accounts for, or causes, variation in Y.

In nonexperimental research, Y is observed, and an X (or a number of Xs) is also observed before, after, or at the same time as Y. No attempt is made to control or manipulate X (Creswell, 2014; Goodwin & Goodwin, 2012). This does not mean that the If X, then Y hypothesis is not tested in nonexperimental research. Researchers use a number of nonexperimental techniques to ascribe *logical* validity to a variety of propositions. For example, high scores on the Graduate Record Examination (GRE) are generally considered to predict academic performance in graduate school. There is a positive correlation between GRE scores and grades in advanced degree programs; as GRE scores increase, so does the likelihood that the student will do well. It follows logically, then, that Y (grades in graduate school) is a partial function of X (GRE scores), even though both X and Y were observed as they occur without any manipulation or control of X. In terms of *empirical validity*, however, the warrant for new knowledge based on the linear relationship of two variables as in the GRE example is not as strong as it would be in the event that there is a cause and effect relationship between them. The primary reason for the limited empirical validity of nonexperimental research, as exemplified above, is that it does not account for alternative explanations for variation in the outcome (Y) variable. The linear relationship between GRE scores and graduate school grades does not account for other factors that might be attributable to (i.e., cause) grades in advanced degree programs (e.g., study habits, undergraduate grades, resources). Therefore, the design suggests a relationship between GRE scores and graduate school grades but does not enable researchers to make any causal inference.

To make the strongest warrant for a cause and effect relationship between the independent and dependent variables, the researcher must systematically control or manipulate the independent variable *and* do so using random procedures (Heppner et al., 2015; Kazdin, 2017). In a typical true experiment, X is manipulated across groups of people who are randomly chosen to receive varying degrees of the independent variable. The simplest example is the two-group experiment, wherein one randomly constituted group of participants receives an intervention (treatment group) and one randomly constituted group does not (control group). Random assignment to the two groups ensures that the two groups are more-or-less equal along demographic, psychological, and functional dimensions (i.e., status variables), or that any preexisting differences between the groups are attributable to chance rather than systematic factors (Goodwin & Goodwin, 2012; McMillan & Schumacher, 2009). Then, sometime after the treatment group has completed the intervention, the researcher compares the two groups on whatever outcome (i.e., dependent) variables theory dictates should result from the intervention. The If X then Y proposition may be supported if the treatment group performs at a higher level than the control group on outcome or dependent measures; in that event, the treatment group's superior outcome performance may be viewed as the result of the intervention (Rumrill & Bellini, 2018). The degree of certainty of the treatment effect is dependent on a number of factors including group size, magnitude of difference between experimental and control groups, variability of outcome measures, and several others previously discussed in Chapter 3.

Once experimental researchers have identified their independent and dependent variables based upon existing theory, they face several key issues in designing experiments so as to highlight the causal relationships among variables. The first issue involves how to manipulate the independent variable. One approach is to compare an active intervention to a group that completes the assessments at the same time as the treatment group, but otherwise does not receive an intervention (i.e., a pure control group). Although this design provides the simplest comparison for the impact of an intervention, it does have potential problems. One problem is that control group participants, without any formal intervention, may improve on an outcome due to maturation or other natural processes (Kazdin, 2017).

It is also possible that the treatment group improves on an outcome at the conclusion of the intervention, but it may be unclear whether improvement is due to the intervention activities or the result of researcher attention, contact with participants, or expectancies for change on the part of the participants. These issues are incidental to the intervention and do not prevent the researcher from concluding that the intervention was responsible for the change. However, they may present difficulties in drawing valid conclusions about the specific aspects of the intervention that were responsible for the change (Goodwin & Goodwin, 2012; Kazdin, 2017). The power of expectancies to influence outcomes is known as the *placebo effect*. Placebo effects result from factors other than the active ingredients in the intervention itself, such as the belief of the participants that the treatment is efficacious. To draw valid conclusions about what specific features of an intervention are responsible for the change, researchers may opt to include a nonspecific treatment group in the design. A nonspecific treatment group—also known as an *attention-placebo control group*—is designed to control for common factors that are associated with participation in a treatment. The inclusion of a nonspecific treatment group in the experimental design permits the researcher to eliminate the plausible explanation that the results of the treatment were due to factors other than the specific ingredients of the intervention.

Researchers may also design an experimental study to assess the impact of two or more treatment conditions on an outcome variable (or set of variables), with or without the addition of a control group. *Multigroup experiments* have the benefit of comparing different treatment modalities or intervention strategies within the same study (Heppner et al., 2015). The treatment conditions may involve different levels of the same intervention (e.g., a written how-to informational packet to one group as compared to a complete training program for another group) or two or more different interventions (e.g., supported employment services delivered in an integrated community setting and vocational services delivered in a nonintegrated workshop setting for adolescents with developmental disabilities). Multigroup experimental studies are often used in medical, psychological, and educational studies in which it would be unethical to deny an individual a potentially beneficial treatment simply for research purposes. This multigroup design allows the researcher to assess whether Intervention A is better (more effective) than Intervention B, and the inclusion of a control group permits an assessment of whether either Intervention A or B is better than nothing. However, it is also reasonable that the mean differences (i.e., effect size) on an outcome measure in a study that compares two active treatments will be smaller than the mean differences on an outcome in a study that compares an active treatment to no treatment. Thus, the nature of the comparisons made in a study has important implications for the various types of research validity, including statistical conclusion validity. In the event that a researcher wishes to compare two active treatments, and given that smaller effect sizes are likely in this comparison, the researcher could opt to increase statistical power to identify smaller mean differences across the groups by including more subjects or by using a more liberal Alpha value (e.g., .10 rather than .05) for the statistical benchmark.

Experimental researchers also face the issue of how outcomes will be assessed. Pretests are often used to establish a baseline for each participant's performance that is measured at some point before an intervention is begun. Then, sometime after the intervention has concluded, the researcher takes the same measures from all participants in a posttest. The established baseline gives the researcher an opportunity to gauge the degree to which participants have benefited from the intervention, as indicated by the average differences between pretest and posttest for treatment and control groups. Kazdin (2017) noted that the use of a pretest also yields statistical advantages for the data analysis. By using a pretest, within-group variability is reduced and more powerful statistical tests (e.g., analysis of covariance or repeated measures analysis of variance) may be used, potentially resulting in greater statistical power for the analysis and stronger statistical conclusion validity for the study.

Pretest-posttest experimental designs have the advantage of comparing individual participants' scores and group means at different points in time and then comparing progress on outcome measures across groups, permitting the researcher to make specific statements about change. The primary weakness in using a pretest-posttest design pertains to the possibility that administration of a pretest sensitizes the participants to the intervention, known as the *pretest sensitization effect*. A plausible pretest sensitization effect means that the results of a study can be generalized only to subjects who received a pretest. Pretest sensitization is most likely when the pretest and intervention are close together in time and in the perception of research participants (Kazdin, 2017).

To eliminate this possible pretest bias, the researcher may opt for a *posttest only experimental design*. In this design, participants are randomly assigned to two or more groups, an intervention is provided, and posttest measures are taken. Given random assignment to treatment and control groups and manipulation of the independent variable, the researcher can assume that any characteristics that could influence performance on the posttest are randomly distributed across the two groups. Furthermore, given the fact that participants were assessed on the outcome measure only after the conclusion of the intervention, the researcher can eliminate pretest sensitization as a rival explanation for the findings. However, the posttest only design does not allow the researcher to establish a baseline on the outcome variable for the participants, nor assess the degree to which participants improved as a result of the intervention. The posttest-only design does enable the researcher to answer the question, "Did individuals who received the treatment have higher (or lower) scores on the outcome variable than participants who did not receive the intervention?" The lack of a pretest also raises the discomforting possibility that the group differences on the outcome variable assessed at the conclusion of the intervention may actually be the result of preexisting group differences. Although the use of random assignment in the posttest only design allows for the assumption that all preexisting differences are randomized across the groups, in practice this is more likely to be true when the study includes a large number of subjects. Hence, selection may be a plausible threat to internal validity in the case of posttest only experimental designs that use smaller numbers of subjects.

The scenarios described above illustrate the difficulty researchers face in designing experimental research that yields inferences about a group to the exclusion of other potential explanations. Despite the underlying simplicity of quantitative design, there are numerous factors that must be carefully negotiated in the design, implementation, and analysis of any study. Researchers must be mindful of the benefits and drawbacks of each design element and use such elements strategically to produce the best possible design in service of the research questions.

A number of studies in the existing special education and disability studies literature have used different variations of experimental designs. For example, Sinclair, Christenson, and Thurlow (2005) investigated the effects of a "check-and-connect" intervention designed to keep adolescents with emotional or behavioral disabilities in school. It was hypothesized that receiving the intervention for a prolonged period of time would result in improved outcomes (e.g., attending school with greater persistence, decreased mobility, staying in school, completing school, having a developed transition plan as part of their IEP). The "check" component of the intervention consisted of daily monitoring of students' absenteeism, tardiness, behavioral referrals, suspensions, and accrual of credits. The "connect" component included problem-solving, providing timely and individualized supports to students, building relationships between adult monitors and students, following students when they changed schools, family outreach, and regularly discussing the importance of staying in school. The researchers were able to include 85 percent of all ninth grade students receiving special education for emotional or behavioral disabilities in a large urban school district. The participating students were randomly assigned to treatment ($n = 85$) or control ($n = 79$) groups. Students in the treatment group received the check-and-connect intervention over a period of four years.

At the end of the study (posttest only experimental design), results indicated that students in the treatment group, as compared with the control group, were significantly less likely to drop out of school, were significantly more likely to attend school with greater consistency, were significantly more likely to stay in one educational setting over the course of a year, and were significantly more likely to participate in their IEPs and to have a developed transition plan. However, students in the treatment group did not differ from control students in four-year school completion rates or parental participation in IEP meetings. The authors concluded that use of the extended "check-and-connect" intervention is likely to reduce the dropout rate and improve the educational experiences of students with emotional and behavioral disabilities. They also suggested that the intervention will be most successful when used in conjunction with "universal interventions oriented toward the promotion of students' engagement with school, such as positive behavioral supports and small learning communities" (Sinclair et al., 2005, p. 479).

Using a pretest/posttest experimental design, Vaughn and colleagues (2015) investigated the effects of a multicomponent reading intervention designed to improve high school students' reading skills necessary for successful learning in high school science and social studies courses. It was hypothesized that receiving the intervention would result in improved outcomes (e.g., vocabulary, reading achievement measures, course grades). The intervention consisted of systematic instruction in vocabulary and comprehension strategy instruction through modeling, scaffolded support, and practice opportunities with teacher feedback. Instruction was delivered in small groups using texts that aligned with the content of 9th and 10th grade science and social studies courses.

Researchers were able to include 66 students (17% of the sample) who were receiving special education services in the participating school district. Overall, the participating students were randomly assigned to treatment (*n* = 170) or control (*n* = 205) groups. Students in the treatment group received the multicomponent reading intervention over 2 years.

At the end of the study (pretest/posttest experimental design), results indicated that students in the treatment group showed greater gains in reading comprehension compared to the business-as-usual control group. The resulting difference was statistically significant. Results also showed the reading intervention was associated with improved grades in social studies. There were no significant correlations between science performance and improved reading ability. The authors concluded that use of the reading intervention is beneficial to the reading comprehension for at-risk learners and may have ancillary benefits on content area social studies coursework. However, even with moderate measurable effects students in the treatment group "continued to read at levels well below average, suggesting ongoing challenges with the complex text they are likely to encounter in high school" (Vaughn et al., 2015, p. 555).

Quasi-Experimental Designs

The protocol and logical structure of the true experiment is what permits the researcher to limit the effects of extraneous variables and ascribe causation to the independent variable (Rumrill et al., 2011). True experiments are characterized by random assignment of subjects to groups. Sometimes, however, it is not possible to gather all potential participants at the inception of an intervention study and randomly assign them to experimental conditions. When researchers test If X, then Y hypotheses by comparing two or more groups that are not randomly constituted, they do so using quasi-experimental methods.

As in experimental studies, quasi-experiments involve one or more treatment groups and a comparison (the nonrandom correlate for control) group who are subjected to varying levels of the independent variable. The same issues related to how the independent variable will be manipulated and how to assess outcomes that apply to experimental design also pertain to quasi-experiments. However, nonrandom assignment to groups affords less protection against the various threats to causal inference (i.e., internal validity; see Chapter 5). This means that alternate explanations for results (e.g., history, maturation, selection) cannot be ruled out as readily in quasi-experimental designs.

For example, Schaller and Parker (1997) conducted a quasi-experiment to determine the effects of graduate-level research instruction on perceived research anxiety, perceived utility of research for professional practice, and confidence in research skills of a sample (N=23) of masters-level students in rehabilitation counseling and special education. Fifteen (15) participants signed up for a semester-long course entitled, Applied Research in Special Education and Rehabilitation Counseling. The remaining eight students were enrolled in Instructional Designs Using Assistive Technology, a course that did not focus on research methods and utilization. Having gathered pretest data on the three dependent measures from all 23 participants, Schaller and Parker hypothesized that the course in applied research would result in lower levels of research anxiety, higher levels of perceived research utility, and greater confidence in using research skills among the 15 enrollees in comparison to the eight enrollees in the assistive technology course. Given that small sample sizes require larger between-group differences (i.e., larger treatment effects) for the researcher to infer statistical significance (see Chapter 3), it is not surprising that there were nonsignificant differences between the two groups on two of Schaller and Parker's three outcome measures (perceived utility and research confidence). Only research anxiety was significantly impacted by the applied research course; students in that course reported significantly lower levels of anxiety at posttest than did students who had taken the assistive technology course.

In another quasi-experiment, Bui, Schumaker, and Deshler (2006) investigated the efficacy of a comprehensive writing program called the Demand Writing Instructional Model (DWIM) for students with and without learning disabilities. The study involved five inclusive fifth-grade classrooms in two schools. Two classes in one school and one class in the other were randomly assigned to received the DWIM intervention once-daily from the researcher. Students in the comparison classrooms were given writing instruction by their usual teachers using a district-mandated writing curriculum. Assignment of individual students to treatment or comparison groups was not random. The school district would not allow students to be randomly divided and assigned to groups by the researchers. Instead, intact classes were randomly assigned to either receive or not receive the writing program. The DWIM intervention lasted for three months and included 30 lessons that lasted approximately 45 minutes to an hour. Each lesson typically involved the use of an advanced organizer, review, presentation of a new concept or strategy, guided practice for the whole group, and individual practice. Lessons were scripted to ensure consistent implementation across the experimental classes. Dependent variables included participant scores on several writing indicators (e.g., sentence writing, paragraph writing, text-structure, planning-time, knowledge of the writing process) and scores on a state test of writing competency.

One aspect of the investigation examined the outcomes of students with learning disabilities who attended the experimental ($n = 9$) and comparison ($n = 5$) classrooms. The students with learning disabilities who received the DWIM intervention made statistically significant gains from pretest to posttest across all of the writing indicators, but there was no difference in scores on the state test between students with learning disabilities in the experimental and comparison classrooms. Because there were only five students with learning disabilities in the comparison classrooms, the difference between their pretest and posttest scores could not be analyzed statistically. Descriptively, students with learning disabilities in the comparison classrooms appeared to make little to no progress in writing. The authors concluded that the DWIM can improve the writing skills of elementary-aged students with learning disabilities served in inclusive settings.

Analogue Studies

Researchers in special education and other social science fields have a long history of applying experimental and quasi-experimental techniques in what have come to be known as analogue studies (Heppner et al., 2015). The key distinguishing feature of analogue studies is that they approximate or mirror the processes involved in the teacher-student relationship or in the education-related interactions between children with disabilities and other individuals (e.g., other students, teachers, administrators, employers). Analogue studies involve laboratory or clinical simulations of particular instructional techniques, screenings of fictitious student files to gauge teachers' judgments and attitudes, and research to assess attitudes toward the inclusion of children with disabilities in educational and community settings. Typically, analogue studies involve exposing one group to a stimulus or intervention while withholding treatment (or providing a different stimulus/intervention) to another group. Analogue studies almost always fall into experimental or quasi-experimental classifications, depending upon whether groups are constituted using random assignment.

In one example of an analogue study, Bianco (2005) investigated the effect of student disability labels (learning disability and emotional and behavioral disorders) on the likelihood that general education and special education teachers would refer students to gifted programs. Two hundred and forty-seven teachers (52 special education teachers and 195 general education teachers) were randomly assigned to read one of three vignettes. All three vignettes provided a description of a student with gifted characteristics. In two of the vignettes, the student was also described as having either a learning disability or an emotional or behavioral disorder. In the third vignette, no disability label was mentioned. The dependent variable was teacher willingness to refer the student to a gifted program as measured by teacher ratings on a Likert scale. After reading one of the three vignettes, teachers completed a survey that included six questions. One question addressed the willingness of the teacher to refer the hypothetical student for gifted services. The remaining five questions were included to distract the participating teachers from the purpose of the study (thus reducing the possibility that teachers would provide what they thought was the "correct" response). Independent variables were disability label (learning disability, emotional or behavioral disorder, no disability) and teacher type (special education or general education).

A significant main level effect of disability label was found for teacher willingness to refer students to gifted programs. Teachers were more likely to agree to refer a hypothetical student without a disability than a student with a disability. Teachers were no more or less likely to refer a student if the disability label was a learning disability or an emotional or behavioral disorder. In addition, a significant main effect was found for teacher type. General education teachers were more likely than special education teachers to refer a student to a gifted program. Finally, no interaction was found between disability label and teacher type. In other words, different types of teachers were not more or less likely to be influenced by disability status in making a referral for gifted services. Based on these findings, the author recommended additional training for all teachers in recognizing gifted characteristics, particularly in populations that are underrepresented in gifted programs (e.g., students with disabilities).

The primary strength of analogue studies is that they provide important insights into the processes by which teachers and other stakeholders in special education form attitudes, develop relationships, and make instructional and policy-related decisions regarding students with disabilities. Analogue studies are especially useful when conducting research in which it is impossible for participants to naturally experience the intervention. However, analogue studies are typically limited by a lack of external validity. In other words, findings generated from a simulated situation do not necessarily generalize to students' or teachers' behaviors and attitudes in actual settings.

Quality Indicators for Group Experimental Research in Special Education

There is a wealth of research findings available for stakeholders in the education of students with disabilities, especially since the advent of the internet. Although ready access to multiple research studies can be beneficial, it can also be overwhelming and confusing (Landrum & Tankersley, 2004). Much of the considerable volume of available research is of less than high quality and studies sometimes yield findings that are contradictory, leading to considerable confusion as to what actually works.

To help determine which studies are of high quality and therefore trustworthy several organizations have attempted to create standards or indicators of research quality. In 2005, the Council for Exceptional Children's Division for Research commissioned a series of papers in which leaders in special education research established criteria for high quality research studies in special education. Gersten et al. (2005) prescribed quality indicators for group experimental research (true experiments and quasi-experiments) in special education. The authors delineated two levels of quality indicators: essential, which are critical for high quality studies to address, and desirable, which are important but not critical. Specifically, essential quality indicators of high quality research in special education include: (a) participants are described such that their disability is evident, (b) participants are shown to be comparable on relevant characteristics across conditions, (c) interventions/teachers are described and shown to be comparable across conditions, (d) the intervention is clearly described, (e) fidelity of implementation (e.g., observations indicating the intervention is implemented as intended) is shown to be adequate, (f) the services provided in the comparison or control condition are adequately described, (g) general outcome measures that are not closely tied to the intervention are included, (h) outcomes are measured at the appropriate time (e.g., including follow-up measures for interventions that claim to have longterm impacts), (i) data are analyzed appropriately, and (j) effect sizes as well as inferential statistics are reported.

The eight desirable quality indicators specified by Gersten et al. (2005) are: (a) attrition that is not severe (i.e., comparable across groups, less than 30% overall), (b) adequate reliability documented for outcome measures and individuals collecting and scoring unfamiliar with study conditions, (c) outcomes measured beyond an immediate posttest, (d) adequate validity documented for outcome measures, (e) quality (not just fidelity) of implementation is assessed, (f) nature of instruction in control or comparison group is documented, (g) audio- or videotaped excerpts are used to illustrate the intervention, and (h) results are reported clearly and coherently.

Research consumers can use these criteria to evaluate the quality of group experimental studies and determine to what degree study findings are trustworthy. Specifically, Gersten et al. (2005) recommended that high quality studies in special education must meet at least nine of ten essential quality indicators, but only four of the eight desirable quality indicators. Acceptable quality studies must also meet all but one of the essential quality indicators, but need only address one of the desirable quality indicators. The findings of studies that do not address two or more of the essential quality indicators, or fail to meet any of the desirable quality indicators, should be interpreted with great caution, as their methodological limitations may have rendered the findings inaccurate.

Over the last 15 years several other organizations have created their own standards for evaluating the quality of research. Most notably, What Works Clearinghouse (WWC), a publicly funded center for synthesis and communication of education research, has published a *Standards Handbook* that describes the benchmarks for quality used to evaluate the strength and extent of evidence in support of interventions, strategies, and programs. Now in its 4th edition, *The What Works Clearinghouse Standards Handbook* is now an important guide for intervention researchers as well as those seeking information on the quality of research that underlies many commonly used programs. Other organization such as the Best Evidence Encyclopedia and the National Center on Intensive Intervention provide similar mechanisms for evaluating research.

In any case, researchers themselves, as well as critical consumers of research, must be mindful of quality indicators as guideposts rather than an inflexible mechanism of gatekeeping. Research in all areas of social sciences must balance competing elements. The more tightly controlled an experiment is, the more likely it is that the results are legitimate to the exclusion of other potential factors. However, tightly controlled conditions may not be reflective of the reality of ecologically dynamic environments. Therefore, one must carefully consider the tradeoffs of each element in a research design in order to maximize the quality of the research as appropriate for the purpose of the research.

Single-Subject Designs

In the preceding discussions of experimental, quasi-experimental, and analogue studies, there is an underlying assumption that the effects of interventions or stimuli are best assessed by comparing groups of people. In those research designs, participants in an investigation are grouped depending on the level or type of treatment or information that they receive. Conversely, single-subject research (also known as small-N research) is designed to consider how an intervention might affect an individual or a small group of individuals. The term "single-subject" does not necessarily refer to the number of people who participate in this type of research but rather indicates the way comparisons are made. In single-subject research the analysis focuses on intra-subject, not inter-subject, comparisons (Kazdin, 2017). That is, the performance of one subject (whether constituted by one participant or one group of participants) is compared only with its own previous performance on the same measures. Measures of the subject's performance are not compared with measures of another person's or another group's performance. Because single-subject research is intended to focus on the change in behavior within the subject, the results are interpreted in terms of clinical rather than statistical significance. Changes in the dependent variable are evaluated in relation to the improved performance of the subject and whether the change in performance will benefit the subject rather than whether change in performance is statistically significant.

Single-subject designs evaluate changes in dependent variables across time in relation to the application, withdrawal, or modification of the independent variable. Typically, single-subject studies evaluate the progress of a subject before changing conditions in the environment—referred to as baseline—and then throughout the course of instituting the intervention. In single-subject designs, researchers apply, withdraw, or modify the intervention to verify that changes in the dependent variable are due to manipulations of the independent variable and not the result of chance factors or confounding variables in the environment. When systematic changes in the dependent variable are associated with manipulations of the independent variable, the research demonstrates a functional relationship between the variables (i.e., the dependent variable changes as a function of the independent variable; Alberto & Troutman, 2008). Special education researchers generally concur that the functional relationship established between variables in single-subject research can be used to infer whether an instructional intervention caused changes in outcomes for study participants (Tankersley, Harjusola-Webb, & Landrum, 2008).

Single-subject research designs have several requirements. First, the dependent variable must be one that can be measured repeatedly over time (Kazdin, 2017). Often, dependent variables in single-subject research are measured daily or even more frequently so that the performance of the subject can be well documented during the baseline and intervention phases. Research in special education that uses single-subject techniques often looks at performance of subjects on dependent variables associated with academic skills (e.g., proficiency, accuracy on assignments, attention-to-task), social behavior (e.g., initiating interactions, aggression, self-stimulation), work-related skills (e.g., productivity, job performance, reliability), and independent living skills (e.g., making a bed, preparing a meal, riding a bus). The dependent variables are behaviors that can be observed in the environment and defined in measurable terms so that more than one observer can agree on its occurrence. Such agreement on the occurrence of the dependent variable helps establish the trustworthiness of the research.

Single-subject research designs must first assess baseline performance of the subject. A baseline phase of the design provides information about the level of the dependent variable before the onset of treatment. Therefore, baseline data serve to describe the current extent of the behavior in question and to predict performance of this behavior if no intervention is implemented (Kazdin, 2017). Single-subject designs then require an active intervention phase, throughout which data are collected on the performance of the dependent variable. Comparisons of performance of behavior during baseline to performance during the intervention phase determine the effectiveness of the intervention.

Another requirement of most single-subject research designs is that at least one replication of these results (i.e., changes between baseline and intervention phases) is instituted within the design (Alberto & Troutman, 2008). For example, the reversal design (commonly referred to as the ABAB design) is one in which the intervention is sequentially applied and withdrawn in four phases: baseline performance of the dependent variable is collected first (the first A phase), followed by assessment of the dependent variable while intervention is in place (the first B phase), followed by the withdrawal of the intervention to return to baseline conditions (the second A phase), and finally the reinstatement of the intervention (the second B phase). This design is illustrated in Figure 6.1. A functional relationship between the dependent and independent variables is established by not only the dependent variable occurring more frequently in the first intervention phase compared with the first baseline phase but also by returning to a level close to the original baseline data (or the trend of the data appears in the opposite direction of the data in the first intervention phase) during the second baseline phase and again increasing during the second intervention phase.

Christensen, Young, and Marchant (2007) used an ABAB design to evaluate the effects of a behavior intervention plan on the socially appropriate classroom behavior of a socially withdrawn elementary school student with a learning disability. Jose, an eight-year-old boy in the third grade, was observed by school personnel to be timid, unassertive, and socially isolated.

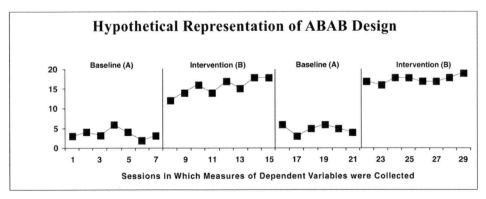

Figure 6.1.

Using national norms from the Systematic Screening for Behavioral Disorders (Walker & Severson, 1992), Jose was identified as at risk for an internalizing behavior disorder (e.g., depression, anxiety). The researchers defined a set of positive alternative behaviors that, as a group, formed the dependent variable for the study. Socially appropriate classroom behaviors included attending, being on-task, reading aloud, responding to classroom questions, asking for help or teacher attention appropriately, following directions, and following classroom rules and routines. The independent variable was the behavior intervention plan, which consisted of social skill training, peer mediation, self-management, and positive reinforcement. During baseline, Jose engaged in socially appropriate classroom behavior 48 percent of the time (range = 26–62%), which was well below the percentage of time Jose's classmates performed the same behavior. When the behavior plan was implemented during the first intervention phase, Jose displayed socially appropriate behavior an average of 94 percent of the time (range = 85–98%). Withdrawing the intervention during the second baseline resulted in a drop of 27 percent in Jose's mean performance of socially appropriate classroom behavior. When the behavior intervention plan was reintroduced, Jose's positive behavior returned to high levels and remained high even as the frequency of positive reinforcement for appropriate behavior was gradually and systematically reduced. On the basis of these findings, Christensen et al. concluded that assessment-based behavior intervention plans can be an effective way to address internalizing problems that, left untreated, could lead to negative developmental outcomes.

Another single-subject research design is the multiple baseline design. The multiple baseline design incorporates a baseline and an intervention phase (AB) for more than one subject (i.e., multiple baseline across subjects design), for more than one dependent variable (i.e., multiple baseline across behaviors design), or in more than one environment (i.e., multiple baseline across settings design). Once baseline levels of the dependent variable have been established for each subject, behavior, or setting, the intervention is sequentially introduced to the next subject, behavior, or setting (Alberto & Troutman, 2008). In this way, if the dependent variable(s) increases across individuals, settings, or behaviors at the various times when the intervention is introduced, the researcher has confidence that it is the functional relationship between the independent and dependent variable—rather than some other explanation—that has caused the change in the dependent variable(s). (See Figure 6.2 for an illustration of a multiple baseline design.) The multiple baseline design enables the researcher to establish a functional relationship without withdrawing the intervention (as is required in the reversal design). Therefore, this design is especially useful when the dependent variable is one that cannot be reversed because it has been learned (e.g., the

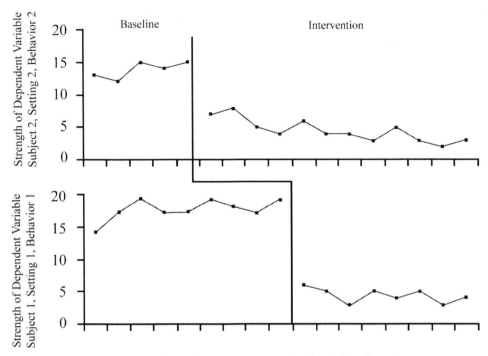

Figure 6.2. Hypothetical representation of multiple baseline design.

effects of an intervention that has taught the subject to read cannot be withdrawn) or should not be reversed because it is dangerous for the subject or others (e.g., self-injurious behaviors).

Schardt, Miller, and Bedesem (2019) used a multiple baseline across participants design to examine the effects of a technology-based mechanism for self-monitoring of engagement for elementary students during independent work time. During baseline, they evaluated students' on-task behaviors during 20-minute sessions using the Direct Behavior Rating–Single Item Scale. Students were observed with no intervention from researchers. For the intervention, students were given iPad minis equipped with the CellF-Monitoring app. The app prompted students at specified intervals to respond to the question "Are you on task?" Students then responded "yes" or "no" on screen and then continued with their assigned task. During the intervention phase, researchers observed students using the same procedures as during baseline. Implementation of the intervention was staggered for each participant in order to independently evaluate the effect of the treatment for each participant.

Researchers graphed the data for each phase in an ABC design (e.g., baseline, training, intervention). Visual analysis indicated that academic engagement improved in the intervention phase compared to the baseline condition. The timing of the change in behavior for all four participants was concurrent with the implementation of the intervention. Though data contained considerable variability in all phases, researchers were nonetheless able to conclude that there was a functional relation between the intervention and the change in students' observed engagement.

The results of single-subject research are typically graphed and then evaluated through visual inspection of the data (Kazdin, 2017). Data are graphed within phases of the design (i.e., baseline or intervention) for each session in which the dependent variable is measured. Changes in the dependent variable in relation to the presence or absence of the independent variable are assessed during each phase according to several criteria. For example, the mean level of the dependent variable is calculated (i.e., an average for all data within the phase is obtained) for each phase of the design, and then compared. If performance during the intervention phase(s) is better than performance during the baseline phase(s), the intervention may have clinical significance. Also important is the amount of overlap of data points between the intervention and baseline phases. Overlap refers to when data points in different phases fall within the same range of values. A basic interpretation is that the smaller the overlap of data points between intervention and baseline phases, the stronger the effect of the intervention. The immediacy of change must also be assessed. To be confident that the intervention caused a change in the dependent variable, the dependent variable must change immediately after the intervention is introduced or withdrawn. Delays in change raise questions about the strength of the relationship between the intervention and the dependent variable. Another aspect of determining the effectiveness of the intervention is assessment of the change in trend of the data. If the dependent variable is a behavior that the researcher wants to increase, for example, then an ascending trend during intervention phases would be important in determining the clinical significance of an intervention. The example above from Schardt, Miller, and Bedesem (2019) illustrates the ways in which each of these factors combine to influence researchers confidence in the findings of single-subject research.

Quality Indicators for Single-Subject
Research in Special Education

Just as Gersten et al. (2005) did for group experimental studies, Horner et al. (2005) established quality indicators for single-subject research studies in special education. Research consumers can use the quality indicators to evaluate studies and determine the degree to which they should trust the findings reported. Horner and colleagues delineated 21 quality indicators in seven broad areas. Related to describing participants and settings, Horner et al. (2005) recommended that (a) participants' characteristics (e.g., age, gender, disability), (b) the process of selecting participants, and (c) important aspects of the physical setting all be described in detail. With regard to the dependent variables, they suggested that the target behaviors investigated are (a) fully described and explained, (b) quantified, (c) measured in a valid manner that is well described, (d) measured multiple times, and (e) measured reliably (e.g., inter-observer reliability > 80%). The independent variable should be (a) described in detail, (b) manipulated (e.g., introduced, withdrawn) by the experimenter, and (c) implemented as designed (i.e., with documented fidelity of implementation). The baseline phase must include multiple data points that establish a pattern and baseline conditions must be described in detail. To meaningfully determine that a functional relationship exists between the independent and dependent variables (a) an experimental effect must be demonstrated three times (e.g., upon initial introduction of the intervention, withdrawal of the intervention, and the reintroduction of the intervention in reversal designs; upon introduction of the intervention across three different participants, settings, or behaviors in a multiple baseline design), (b) an appropriate single-subject research design is used (e.g., reversal, multiple baseline), and (c) results indicate a pattern of behavior indicating that the target behavior changes systematically with the presence of the intervention (as determined by visual inspection criteria). Finally, to be externally valid, a single-subject research study must (a) focus on a socially important target behavior, (b) result in a socially important degree of change in the target behavior, (c) use an intervention that is cost-effective, and (d) be implemented by typical people in typical settings.

NONMANIPULATION STUDIES

The very nature of the quantitative research paradigm continually reminds researchers that proving or demonstrating something new is a primary objective of scientific inquiry. Experimental designs exemplify the spirit of purposeful and active investigation in an effort to draw causal inferences concerning independent and dependent variables. By systematically manipulating the independent variable (usually an intervention or a stimulus) and randomly assigning participants to treatment and control groups, researchers using experimental techniques can claim the strongest warrants for new knowledge, that is, a causal link between an intervention or stimulus and realized outcomes. In many studies, however, it is not possible (or even desirable) to manipulate the independent variable in an effort to establish the warrant for causal connections. In these cases, researchers may test group differences or relationships among variables as they occur or as they have occurred. Nonmanipulation studies examine the strength or magnitude of association among variables, but no attempt is made to infer causality within an individual study. In this section, we describe nonmanipulation studies in two categories, correlational and group comparative designs.

Nonmanipulation Correlational Designs

One of the most common methods of establishing a relationship between variables is the correlation. A correlation coefficient is a statistic that describes the direction and magnitude of the linear relationship between two quantitatively coded variables. The independent variables in correlational studies must be continuous in nature, meaning that scores fall along a continuum from low to high levels of the variable. The dependent variable in correlational research is usually (but not always) continuous, as well. As discussed in Chapter 1, demonstrating that two variables covary is a necessary (though insufficient) condition for establishing that a causal relationship between the variables exists. The correlation coefficient provides empirical support for the strength of this relationship, and it serves as the initial condition for establishing that the variables are causally related.

It is important to keep in mind that the correlation is, first and foremost, a method for analyzing data. The procedure is undertaken to determine how much variation in the dependent variable (also known as the criterion variable) is shared with the independent variable (also known as the predictor variable). Although individual correlational studies are typically not able to establish strong warrants for causal relationships between variables, research consumers may draw causal inferences based on the total evidence generated in a number of related studies. Also, theory-based hypotheses used in correlational studies may provide a stronger warrant for causality when the proposed temporal sequence (i.e., the cause precedes the effect in time) of the variables is reflected in the data gathering phase, as is the case in longitudinal designs. Therefore, both covariation and temporal sequence may be established if the findings support the research hypothesis.

For example, a researcher wishing to determine the relationship between self-esteem and academic achievement among middle school students with learning disabilities conceptualizes self-esteem as the independent or predictor variable and academic achievement as the dependent or criterion variable. Because self-esteem is a precursory component of academic achievement according to the researcher's theory, self-esteem is hypothesized to predict academic achievement rather than vice versa. Therefore, if a positive correlation between the two variables is observed (meaning that, as self-esteem increases, so does academic achievement), it is assumed that variable

X (self-esteem) predicts variable Y (academic achievement). Even though the relationship between predictor and criterion variables cannot be considered causal (because there was no manipulation of the independent variable), a positive correlation between the variables permits readers to conclude that, in general (though not necessarily for every individual), higher self-esteem indicates a higher probability of academic achievement than does lower self-esteem.

The example presented above describes a simple, bivariate correlation, which involves one predictor variable and one criterion variable. Special education researchers also commonly use multiple correlations, which assess the additive relationship between a set of two or more predictor variables and one criterion (Cohen et al., 2003). These studies are usually conducted using multiple regression analysis, though there are several other related multivariate statistical techniques that allow researchers to test more sophisticated theoretical hypotheses pertaining to the interrelationships of multiple predictors and multiple criterion variables (Tacq, 1997). These related techniques are subsumed under what is known as the general linear model and include multiple discriminant analysis, canonical correlation analysis, path analysis, structural equation modeling, and multilevel modeling.

Correlational studies have long played a major part in special education research. For example, Osborne and Reed (2009) examined the association between parenting stress and the behavior problems of children (n= 65) with autism spectrum disorders (ASDs). Prior research had suggested that parent stress may be more strongly related to the severity of ASD symptoms than the child's behavior problems. Also, it is unclear whether behavioral problems tend to precede parenting stress, or vice versa. Thus, the researchers assessed the correlation between parenting stress and the behavior problems of children with ASD when controlling for other factors (such as severity of symptoms). In addition, they collected data at two different times (Time 1 and Time 2, approximately 10 months apart) to try to understand the temporal directionality of the relationship between parenting stress and behavior problems. The criterion variable in this investigation, parenting stress, was measured by a 52-item self-administered scale to measure "stress within the family, as the parents perceive and indicate it" (Osborne & Reed, 2009, p. 58). The rating scale included four subscales that assessed the impact of the child's disability on family activities and relationships; levels of parent depression; the effect of the child's specific problems on the family; and problems associated with the child's inability to care for him- or herself. The predictor variables included parent and/or primary caregiver ratings of ASD symptoms, behavior problems, cognitive abilities, and adaptive behavior. Results of a semipartial correlational analysis revealed that at Time 1, controlling for all of the other predictor variables, parenting stress was significantly related to ASD symptoms, but not behavior problems. However, at Time 2, parenting stress was significantly related to behavior problems, but not ASD symptoms. Also, the relationship between Time 1 and Time 2 factors suggested that parenting stress was much stronger in predicting future child behavior problems than child behavior problems were in predicting future parenting stress. Because of several limitations of their study, the researchers urged caution in interpreting their findings. The authors suggested that, in order to achieve the best outcomes for children with ASD, teaching programs should include interventions to reduce parenting stress, particularly in early stages when the child is first diagnosed.

In another example, Gage, Scott, Hirn, and MacSuga-Gage (2018) examined the relationship between teachers' implementation of classroom management strategies and students' behavior in elementary classrooms. Using the Multiple Option Observation System for Experimental Studies (MOOS-ES™; Tapp, Wehby, & Ellis, 1995). The sample contained 1,242 students across 65 schools. As a nonexperimental study, researchers were unable to randomly assign students or teachers to conditions. Students were *nested* within classes, within schools, which effectively creates a biased sample due to the nonrandomness of grouping. Nevertheless, researchers were able to make useful correlational inferences through the use of Latent Class Analysis (LCA) and Multilevel statistical modeling. LCA enabled researchers to parse the data from observations into homogeneous subgroups based on teachers' use of evidence-based practices. These groups (e.g., low-use, high-use) were then compared to observed behaviors of students (e.g., engagement, disruptions). Using multilevel modeling, researchers were able to account for the variance in outcomes potentially attributable to the nesting of students within classes, within schools, and estimate the relationship between teachers' use of evidence-based classroom management practices and students' behaviors. Results indicated that teachers' use of evidence-based practices was positively correlated with engagement and negatively correlated with instances of disruptive student behaviors.

Nonmanipulation Group Comparative Designs

Nonmanipulation group comparative designs (also known as causal comparative and case control designs) evaluate differences between derived or intact groups on theory driven dependent measures (Rumrill & Bellini, 2018). As with correlational studies, the warrant for causality in group comparative studies is limited because the independent variable (group membership or some other nominally coded characteristic) is not systematically manipulated. Instead, the purpose of these studies is to establish that variable relationships conform to theoretically or rationally derived expectations. Researchers typically use between group statistical methods (e.g., chi-square, t tests, analyses of variance, multivariate analyses of variance, discriminant analysis) to gauge whether the observed differences between groups on selected outcome measures are statistically significant.

Consider the example of a researcher who wants to examine differences in the self-esteem of boys and girls with behavior disorders in a large school district. She measures the self-esteem of 124 students with behavior disorders, 85 boys and 39 girls, using a popular standardized instrument. Statistical analysis indicates that boys with behavior disorders have, on average, higher self-esteem than girls with behavior disorders. On the basis of these results, can the researcher conclude that gender causes the level of self-esteem in students with behavior disorders? No, because there is obviously no systematic way to control and manipulate the independent variable in this example—the gender of students with behavior disorders. What she can conclude is that, in her sample, girls with behavior disorders have lower self-esteem than their male counterparts. The researcher may, then, rely on relevant theory to postulate explanations for the findings. For example, these results may be due to the tendency of schools to identify more boys than girls as having behavior disorders. Girls who are identified as such may, then, tend to have more severe problems and be likely to have lower self-esteem.

The conclusions that group comparative researchers are able to draw are limited by the passive nature of the between group design (i.e., the independent variable is not manipulated, nor is there random assignment to groups). However, many characteristics that we use to group and label special education students (and teachers) are not subject to manipulation or random assignment. Investigations of differences between intact or predetermined groups using group comparative designs are, therefore, frequently performed in special education research and provide valuable information about the impact of educational policies and instructional interventions on different groups of teachers and students.

As mentioned, nonmanipulation studies are particularly useful for studying the influence of participant characteristics that cannot be changed through experimental manipulation. In special education, such studies are particularly well suited for examining phenomena related to disability type. For example, a study from the *Journal of Pediatrics* (Levy et al., 2019) examined childhood rates of obesity among children ages 2–5 with developmental delays (DD; $n = 914$) or children with autism spectrum disorder (ASD; $n = 668$) compared to a general population comparison group ($n = 884$). Using a combination of statistical procedures to account for unbalanced groups and control for extraneous variables, researchers determined that children with ASD were 1.57 times more likely to be overweight than children in the comparison group. Children with DD were 1.38 times more likely to be overweight.

DESCRIPTIVE STUDIES

As noted in Chapter 1, one important purpose of scientific inquiry is to describe or explain observable phenomena in a manner that adds understanding or insight to a question or problem. The special education professional literature contains many examples of investigations whose primary goal is to describe events, experiences, attitudes, and observations regarding students with disabilities rather than to establish a causal or predictive relation between variables. Although the qualitative descriptive techniques presented in Chapter 7 have been used to describe various facets of special education with increasing frequency in recent years, researchers have also used a number of quantitative approaches in descriptive studies.

Descriptive research involves collecting data to test hypotheses or answer questions regarding the past or current status of selected variables. A descriptive study simply asks "what is" or "what was" at a point or several points in time. Researchers conducting descriptive studies examine such phenomena as achievement, attitudes, opinions, behaviors, and professional literature that are collected or observed from individuals or groups of participants. It is important to note that descriptive designs do not manipulate variables in an attempt to draw causal inferences, as is the case in intervention/stimulus studies—nor do they apply statistical tests to gauge relationships among variables or groups of participants, as is the case in nonmanipulation correlational and group comparative studies. By simply reporting what exists, descriptive studies help to amass evidence concerning a particular phenomenon and can make a valuable contribution to a discipline's knowledge base.

Researchers use a variety of sources to gather information for descriptive studies, including self-reports from research participants, reports from significant others, direct observations, and review of documents. As in other types of research, the techniques chosen are determined primarily by the research questions or hypotheses that are drawn from existing literature and theory. A number of descriptive methodologies exist in quantitative research, each of which has many possible iterations depending on the specific research question being asked and the resources available to the investigator(s). We have divided descriptive designs into seven categories: surveys, case studies, program evaluations, historical/archival research, longitudinal studies, empirical literature reviews, and meta-analyses. This section provides general overviews of these descriptive designs, illustrated with examples from professional journals in special education.

Surveys

Surveys have been a common type of descriptive research in recent special education literature. By use of self-report data that are collected in interviews with respondents (in which the researcher records data on the instrument) or by means of questionnaires (in which the respondent records his or her own answers on the instrument), surveys have become a part of virtually every aspect of life in contemporary American society. The primary purpose of survey research is to gauge the status of particular variables within a sample of respondents (e.g., attitudes of general educators toward inclusion) or to draw inferences regarding the constitution of a population of people on the basis of the characteristics of a sample of individuals drawn from that population (e.g., ethnic composition of students with learning disabilities). Surveys elicit relatively brief measures from relatively large numbers of people (Heppner et al., 2015; Rumrill & Bellini, 2018), in contrast to the more in-depth case study designs that involve collecting large amounts of information from smaller samples.

For example, Machek and Nelson (2007) devised an instrument to investigate school psychologists' perceptions of what criteria should be used to determine if a student has a reading disability and should receive special services. The survey was completed by a randomly selected national sample of 549 school psychologists. Traditionally, reading disabilities have been conceptualized as a significant discrepancy between expected and actual achievement in reading. To determine whether a reading disability is present, other explanations must be excluded (e.g., intellectual disability, poor instruction, sensory deficits). Over the past several years, there has been increasing criticism of the traditional discrepancy approach to defining reading disabilities, which has led to the development and implementation of an alternative approach called response to intervention, or RTI. Changes in federal law have permitted school districts to use RTI to identify students with reading disabilities.

Because school psychologists play a prominent role in reading disability evaluations, it is important to understand their beliefs about how reading disabilities should be operationalized in public school settings. The 25-item survey employed a five-point Likert scale (strongly agree, agree, disagree, strongly disagree, don't know) to assess the extent to which school psychologists agreed with different components of a reading disability definition. The survey respondents were also asked to indicate which component they thought was the most important, and whether exclusionary criteria (see above) are necessary, and if so, which ones. The researchers found that most school psychologists (81.1%) supported the RTI approach to identifying reading disabilities. A majority also agreed to strongly agreed that cognitive processing difficulties (77.6%) and a low score on phonemic processing (75.6%) were important components of operationalizing reading disabilities in school settings. A smaller majority (61.9%) supported the importance of a discrepancy between aptitude (IQ) and achievement. The researchers concluded that the continued support for the discrepancy component may be based on its practicality and usefulness while school personnel adapt to using RTI, or it may reflect the belief that RTI and discrepancy are not mutually exclusive and that both may contribute to a valid and meaningful assessment of reading disabilities.

Case Studies

Whereas survey research typically involves taking measures at one point or over a short period of time from a large number of participants, case studies typically involve an in-depth or prolonged examination of one person or a small group of people (Heppner et al., 2015). Rooted in epidemiological research in the medical field (particularly as a means of understanding uncommon conditions or illnesses), the quantitative case study design has been frequently applied in special education research to provide insights into many aspects of the education of students with disabilities. By reporting a large volume of data about a limited number of individuals, case studies can lend an understanding to a particular phenomenon that may not be obtainable using other quantitative designs. It is important to recognize, though, that attempts to generalize findings to the broader population from which participants were drawn are not warranted. Because case studies deal with only a small number of participants (who are typically not randomly selected from the population of interest), their external validity is severely limited. Nonetheless, preliminary information generated from a quantitative case study can be used to focus or guide more systematic inquiry in a particular area of research. The picture painted by a case study regarding an individual or group and their educational experience can be extremely useful in highlighting the potential effectiveness of an intervention method or the need for change in policy and practice in a given area.

For example, Haley, Allsopp, and Hoppey (2018) used a case-study method to examine the experience of a parent of a child with a learning disability who is also a teacher in the same district attended by the child. In this example, a structured case study methodology is useful because the primary goal of the study is to illuminate the complexity and difficulty parents face when attempting to navigate potentially conflicting experiences of being a district employee tasked with serving the needs of many children versus serving as the primary advocate for their own child. Case study methodology allows researchers to present an exceptionally rich portrayal of the participant's experience. In this case, researchers applied a predetermined heuristic for analysis based on data collected from questionnaires, interviews, and participant's journal entries. Results revealed several distinct themes and vignettes that may help teachers, administrators, and policymakers understand the situation itself as well as the ways in which teachers and parents in similar situations make decisions regarding their professional and personal responsibilities.

Program Evaluation

The primary goal of program evaluation research is to describe programs so that others may emulate their successes and learn from their shortcomings (Goodwin & Goodwin, 2012). A primary distinguishing feature of program evaluation research is that it does not purport to yield generalizable findings. Rather, the focus is placed on using a variety of measures to generate clear, concise descriptions of the methods by which the program was developed and delivered, specific parameters for evaluating the program's impact, and a measure of the program's cost-benefits in terms of fiscal and/or personnel resources relative to realized outcomes (McMillan & Schumacher, 2009). Program evaluations typically feature analyses of both processes and outcomes, also known as formative and summative evaluations. Program evaluations in special education may involve a wide range of programs, including those that educate students with disabilities or that train pre-service special education teachers and graduate-level special educators.

McMillan and Schumacher (2009) identified four criteria by which educational programs should be evaluated: utility, feasibility, propriety, and accuracy. In examining these criteria, program evaluators use a variety of methods and data sources. These include direct observations, documentary evidence, participant interviews, and end-user surveys (i.e., information solicited from participants after the program has concluded). Because the intent of program evaluation research is to describe rather than generalize, researchers typically report quantitative program evaluation data using descriptive (e.g., frequencies and means) rather than inferential (e.g., correlations and ANOVAs) statistics. The following paragraph summarizes the methods and findings of a program evaluation study.

In the past decade, there has been a rapid increase in programs at the college level to support students with ASD and other developmental disabilities. These programs typically provide a blend of academic, behavioral, social, and life skills training to support successful degree completion. To justify the human and financial resources necessary to sustain these programs, it is necessary to determine to what degree these programs meet their intended goals, and at what cost. For example, Ames, McMorris, Alli, and

Bebko (2016) published a program evaluation examining the success of a mentorship program to support students with ASD at a large university in Canada. Researchers were interested in a variety of important outcomes including (1) program enrollment and retention rates, (2) participants satisfaction with the services provided, (3) the degree to which the participants achieved their personal objectives, and (4) the degree to which the program itself met the explicitly stated objectives. Researchers were also interested in understanding who was using the program in terms of their social, academic, and behavioral intensity of needs. Researchers conducted systematic interviews, compiled basic demographic and participation data, examined enrollment trends, and administered a year-end anonymous survey.

Results indicated that enrollment increased by 200 percent in a 4-year period, with 95 percent of enrollees accessing one or more of the program services. Among participants, one-on-one meetings with program mentors constituted the most favored support (on a 5 point scale; $M = 4.25$, $SD = 0.97$) followed by group events ($M = 3.75$, $SD = 0.89$). Approximately 75 percent of participants had specific social skill goals as a part of the program's services. Participants also reported very high levels of satisfaction with the overall program ($M = 4.25$, $SD = 0.75$; max = 5). With these data and others, researchers were able to conclude that the mentorship program was in high demand, and highly valued by participants. Findings were generally consistent with those of previously published empirical research.

Historical/Archival Research

In many cases, the impact of a program, policy, or intervention is not readily apparent by observing phenomena as they occur or by conducting follow-up studies shortly after the program has been completed. Historical/archival studies are retrospective in nature and involve analysis of data that were previously collected. Primarily, historical/archival studies in special education have involved examinations of legislation, social trends, and large-scale programs designed to meet the needs of students with disabilities.

Fujiura and Yamaki (2000) used a historical/archival design to investigate their contention that as social and economic dynamics—as well as the numbers of individuals with disabilities—have changed in recent years, the relationship between poverty and disability status has also changed. The authors analyzed statistical summaries of the National Health Interview Surveys from 1983 to 1996. Independent variables were poverty (i.e., family above or below poverty level, living in a single-parent home) and being from a minority group. The dependent variable was being a child with a disability. The results of a regression analysis indicated that living in a single-parent home was significantly related to having a childhood disability in both 1983 and 1996. A child was 55 percent more likely to have a disability when being raised in a single-parent household (in comparison to a two-parent home) in 1983, and 88 percent more likely in 1996. After controlling for poverty and family status (being raised in a single- or two-parent household), minority status did not significantly relate to disability status in 1983 or 1996. Poverty did not significantly relate to disability status in 1983, but it did in 1996. A child was 86 percent more likely to have a disability when being raised in an impoverished household at this time. Results were interpreted to suggest "an exacerbation of the link between poverty and disability" (Fujiura & Yamaki, 2000, p. 196). The authors recommended that special education become less isolated and be considered in conjunction with related social health issues.

Longitudinal Studies

Whereas historical/archival investigations track participants over an extended period of time that has already elapsed, longitudinal studies actively track the sample by collecting data on participants at a point in time and then following them into the future, making periodic "checks" at specified intervals (McMillan & Schumacher, 2009). These studies typically involve large samples of participants with a set of common characteristics (e.g., a particular disability) and the researchers monitor participants' progress over time as a means of framing life activities, experiences, and outcomes in a developmental context. Longitudinal studies enable the researcher to make comparisons between participants' initial responses and the experiences that they record at each subsequent point of data collection. Longitudinal techniques are frequently used in educational research to gauge children's academic and intellectual development (McMillan & Schumacher, 2009).

Morgan et al., (2015) used a longitudinal design to investigate the degree to which students from minority demographic subgroups are represented in special education. Concerns regarding the overrepresentation of racial, ethnic, and language-minority students in the United States have led to considerable concerns over special education as a systematically discriminatory institution. The implications for systematic bias in special education are important on a number of levels ranging from national policy and law to diagnostic practices in schools. Morgan and colleagues used data from a nationally representative sample of students collected over many years. They began with a cohort of students ($n = 20,100$) beginning kindergarten in 1998–99 and included repeated measures of a variety of indices for the next nine years.

Because longitudinal data include multiple measures over time, analytic methods must account for changing conditions over time and the lack of independence of observations within subjects (e.g., scores from a single participant are correlated with one another). By applying analytic methods adapted from public health (e.g., discrete-time logit regression) researchers created separate predictive models for five disability categories. Rather than predict disability status at a singular point in time researchers measured duration until diagnosis, enabling a more effective method of analysis for longitudinal data. Among the specified models researchers found that students from minority backgrounds were underidentified relative to white children. After accounting for covariates, black children were 58–77 percent less likely to be identified for special education depending on the category of diagnosis. Similar results were found for other minority categories.

Forgan and Vaughn (2000) also used a longitudinal design to compare changes in outcomes over a two-year transition period (i.e., sixth and seventh grade) for seven included students with LD to outcome changes for seven nondisabled students. The transition from elementary to middle school can be problematic for all students, but can be particularly difficult for students with disabilities. Students in the two groups were from the same sixth-grade classroom and were matched on ethnicity and gender. The outcomes examined included reading performance, quality of students' friendships, and global and academic self-concept. Data on these outcomes were collected at the beginning and end of sixth grade (the last year of elementary school), and at the middle and end of the seventh grade (the first year of middle school).

Although students with LD made substantial progress in reading performance in the sixth grade, their reading performance actually decreased slightly from the middle to the end of the seventh grade. Nondisabled students made small gains in reading performance in both the sixth and seventh grades. Student with LD made very large gains in the quality of their friendships in the sixth grade. However, quality of friendships decreased slightly after entering middle school, and it increased only very slightly from the middle to the end of the seventh grade. Nondisabled students' quality of friendships increased slightly during the sixth grade, increased on attending junior high school, and then decreased slightly during the seventh grade. Reflective of their academic performance and quality of friendships, both the global and academic self-concept of students with LD increased during the sixth grade, was significantly lower after entering middle school, and increased slightly from the middle to the end of the seventh grade (although both aspects of self-concept remained lower at the end of the seventh grade than at the end of the sixth grade). The global self-concept of nondisabled students rose in the sixth grade, stayed relatively constant after entering middle school, and then declined slightly during the seventh grade. The academic self-concept of these students increased slightly during the sixth grade, remained the same after entering middle school, and then declined drastically from the middle to the end of the seventh grade. Forgan and Vaughn (2000) summarized that there were "no obvious differences regarding how students with LD and NLD [not learning disabled] students make the transition to middle school" (p. 38). Given that the only outcome on which students with LD decreased during the seventh grade was reading performance, it was suggested that academics be a focus of special concern for students with LD during this period of transition.

Empirical Literature Reviews

Empirical literature reviews involve the creation, codification, and analysis of numerical data on the basis of specific aspects (e.g., themes, topics, authors, and methods) of existing special education literature. It is the numerical expression of data that distinguishes the empirical literature review from the narrative literature reviews described in Chapter 8 (see Rumrill & Bellini, 2018). Special education researchers often use numerical expressions of data generated from the literature to answer questions such as "What institutions are most frequently represented in the professional literature?" and "What types of studies have been done in particular areas of inquiry?"

Mastropieri et al. (2009) used an empirical literature review to examine what had been published in 11 prominent special education journals over a 19-year time period (1988–2006). The authors classified each article according to type (research, review, position paper, editorial or commentary, program description, or practice paper). Research articles were further divided into discrete categories (intervention research with preschool to twelfth grade students, intervention research with other populations [e.g., teachers, parents], descriptive studies, survey research, or qualitative/case studies). Finally, intervention research with students was sorted by research design, participant demographics, and intervention focus. Longitudinal analyses were conducted to determine if proportions of different types of articles published in special education journals changed or remained stable over time.

The authors coded 6,724 articles in prominent special education journals and found that over half (58%) were research articles. The proportion of research articles increased slightly over time. The most common type of research article was descriptive (24.1%), followed by intervention research with students (15.9%), survey research (8.6%), qualitative/case study research (6.4%), and intervention research with nonstudent populations (3.1%). The most common research design used in intervention research with students was single-subject (50.5%), followed by experimental or quasi-experimental group designs (38.1%), and pre-post designs (11.4%). There has been a recent slight decline in the use of pre-post designs. Mastropieri and colleagues (2009) suggested that this may reflect increased emphasis on the use of high-quality designs in special education intervention research. Participants in this intervention research were most frequently identified as students with multiple disabilities (31.5%), followed by learning disabilities (21%), intellectual/ developmental disabilities (15.6%), emotional or behavioral disorders (9.6%), at risk (9.4%), autism (3.6%), other health impairments (3.5%), and attention deficit hyperactivity disorder (2%). Students with sensory, physical, or speech-language disabilities were each identified as participants in less than 1% of the intervention studies reviewed. Over time, the proportion of studies including students with learning disabilities decreased, whereas studies including at risk students and students with autism increased. The majority of intervention research focused on students in elementary and middle grades. Finally, most intervention research evaluated the effects of academic interventions (65%), followed by social/behavioral interventions (30%), and combined interventions (5%). The authors expressed concern regarding the low percentage of intervention research published in special education journals, and suggested that "future efforts might uncover ways to strengthen both the quality and quantity of intervention research in special education" (Mastropieri et al., 2009, p. 108).

Meta-Analyses

Rather than analyzing or interpreting the actual data contained in existing articles, the empirical literature review (as described earlier) creates data from the researcher's examination of the literature. This approach often yields important summary information, but it can also lead to readers drawing erroneous conclusions. Suppose that a researcher conducts an empirical literature review of 10 studies that examined the effects of intervention A and intervention B on behavior of students with autism. The researcher finds that six of the studies reported a greater impact on behavior with intervention A, whereas four studies indicated superior effects associated with Intervention B. On the basis of these findings, it may appear that intervention A is more effective and should be adopted in classrooms with students with autism. However, that conclusion cannot be reached with any real certainty without an examination of such factors as the relative effect sizes of the studies reviewed, the number of participants in each investigation, and the specific circumstances of each intervention trial. It is possible that most studies favoring intervention A involved very small samples of students and also frequently showed positive effects of intervention B. Alternatively, many of the investigations that reported that intervention B was more effective may have used very large samples and showed no positive effect for intervention A.

Despite the fact that intervention A was supported by more studies, intervention B may actually be more effective.

Meta-analyses go several steps further than empirical literature reviews in examining the aggregate findings of related studies. Meta-analyses involve the analysis of the actual findings of a number of published research studies. Essentially, meta-analyses calculate the average effect of an intervention or of group membership across a number of studies and participants. Meta-analyses can provide an in-depth description of research findings (Glass, 1976, 1977) and can also serve an explanatory function, because findings observed across numerous related investigations bring with them a deeper level of understanding that may explain the interrelationships of variables (Cook et al., 1992).

To conduct a meta-analysis, there must be a common measure for expressing results across many studies. This common measure is known as effect size, which expresses the strength or magnitude of a relationship between two variables (Cohen, 1988). It is a standard score that reflects the mean of one group or condition in relation to another group or condition. The basic formula for calculating an effect size for an intervention is as follows (Glass & Hopkins, 1996, p. 290):

$$ES = \frac{X_e - X_c}{SD_c}$$

where

X_e = the mean (arithmetic average) of the *experimental* group; X_c = the mean score for the *control* group; and
SD_c = the standard deviation of the scores for the *control* group.

Although this formula seems to imply that meta-analyses can only consider or include data from experimental designs, any studies in which two or more different treatment groups or conditions are observed can be included (Hunter & Schmidt, 1990; Lirgg, 1991).

The equation for calculating effect sizes indicates that a mean derived for one group or condition is compared with a standard or baseline (i.e., the other group or condition) to determine how much it deviates from that standard. The result is then evaluated in terms of the amount of variability present in the baseline condition or comparison group. The primary advantage of a meta-analysis is that a multitude of studies can be effectively summarized into a few relatively simple statistics. The effect size statistic, as calculated by the preceding formula, is expressed as a positive or negative number. A positive number indicates that the experimental or treatment group performed better than the control group or comparison condition. Alternatively, a negative number indicates that the comparison condition yielded higher performance on the outcome measure than did the treatment condition. Larger numbers, either positive or negative, represent greater between-group or between-condition differences. For example, an effect size of +1 indicates that the treatment group in a particular study outperformed the control group, on average, by one standard deviation. Meta-analyses are becoming increasingly common in the special education literature as researchers seek methods for objectively determining practices that are more effective than others (see Lloyd, Pullen, Tankersley, & Lloyd, 2005).

Singer, Ethridge, and Aldana (2007) used a meta-analysis to investigate the effectiveness of parenting and stress management interventions for parents of children with intellectual disabilities (ID). The authors identified 17 group treatment studies that met the researchers' criteria for inclusion in the analysis (e.g., participants included parents of children and youth with ID, the dependent variable was parental depressive symptoms or emotional stress as measured by a standardized self-report instrument, data reported were sufficient to compute an effect size). The mean weighted effect size for all of the studies was +.29, with the positive effect indicating that the treatment group experienced less emotional distress than the control group. The researchers sorted the studies by type of intervention to examine differences in effect sizes. Behavioral parent training (five studies) had a mean effect size of +.25; cognitive behavioral treatment (six studies) had a mean effect size of +.34; multiple component interventions (five studies) had a mean effect size of +.90; whereas the single study examining family systems interventions had an effect size of +.37. The average effect size for multiple component interventions was significantly higher than the average effect sizes for behavioral parent training or cognitive behavioral treatment alone. Results indicated that multiple component interventions that are implemented over a longer period of time lead to substantial reductions in the depressive symptoms and emotional distress of parents of children with ID.

In another example, Gilmour, Fuchs, and Wehby (2019) conducted a meta-analysis examining reading outcomes of students with and without disabilities as a function of access to the general education curriculum. After a comprehensive literature review researchers identified 23 studies that fit *a priori* inclusion criteria. Each study included (a) a sample of students with disabilities, (b) a comparison group of students without disabilities drawn from the same population, (c) a measure of reading comprehension, and (d) data necessary to calculate effect sizes. The included studies contained 180 effect sizes. Random-effects meta-analysis were performed with robust variance estimation to account for dependency of multiple effect sizes within a single study. Researchers found that the average gap for reading achievement was 1.17 standard deviations (approximately 3.3 years of reading growth) poorer for students with disabilities compared to students without disabilities.

SUMMARY

Researchers in special education apply a wide variety of quantitative techniques to answer a vast array of questions. Quantitative research has provided the foundation of scientific inquiry in the field of special education and has influenced policy and practice since the inception of our profession. Each type of study described in this chapter features distinct methods, analytical techniques, the use (or nonuse) of inferential statistics, levels and types of control or manipulation that are exerted on the independent variable, and strength of the warrant for new knowledge that is yielded. For all of the features that distinguish categories of quantitative designs, they all translate observations into numbers and focus on summarizing or aggregating these numbers to bring meaning to the research findings.

As readers move from this chapter and begin to examine qualitative research in Chapter 7, we caution against dichotomizing quantitative and qualitative methods. Although quantitative and qualitative modes of inquiry originated from different, sometimes competing, schools of thought, we believe that it is the researcher's questions, not his or her ideological persuasion, that should be the primary factor in determining the scientific methods that he or she selects. Despite them any specific differences between quantitative and qualitative research that will become apparent as readers examine the next chapter and compare it with the methods discussed here, effective quantitative and qualitative research can both generate new knowledge by answering the theory-based inquiries of special education researchers.

Chapter 7

QUALITATIVE RESEARCH DESIGNS

Tricia Niesz
Lynn C. Koch
Jennifer Davenport
Stuart Rumrill
Melissa Jones Wilkins

INTRODUCTION

Qualitative research is the inquiry into what people do, what people think, and the nature of social systems that contextualize their experiences through the use of nonnumerical sources of data. Typically through the use of interviews, observations, and the analysis of artifacts, qualitative researchers seek to understand how people engage with the world around them and make meaning of these engagements. Importantly, qualitative researchers typically seek to understand their participants on their own terms and in their own contexts. Unlike research approaches used to test broader theories or hypotheses, qualitative research is used to learn from participants how they experience particular phenomena or systems, and how they understand these experiences.

Special education researchers have engaged qualitative research methods for a range of purposes related to understanding the experiences, practices, and perspectives of students, teachers, and families involved in special education. A special education researcher might seek to understand how students with learning disabilities experience a new school program, how regular education and special education teachers learn to co-teach, how families understand the transition process their children will experience after high school, and so forth. Individuals' lives outside of schools and other institutional contexts are also of interest to many qualitative researchers in special education. A researcher may investigate how a particular youth group fosters relationships among a diverse group of teens, including those with emotional disabilities; how siblings of children with severe disabilities reflect on their family lives; or how members of the public understand, value, and support investments into community organizations serving youth and adults with developmental disabilities.

All of these kinds of studies take what Bos and Richardson (1993) refer to as a *contextualist* perspective. That is, qualitative researchers interested in the experiences, understandings, perspectives, and practices of those involved with special education attend holistically to the specific social and cultural contexts of their participants. In other words, qualitative researchers are not interested in decontextualized variables, but how social processes play out over time in the everyday lives of youth, educators, and families, as well as the meanings made of these processes. As Gersten and colleagues (2004) explained, this allows special education researchers to "shed light on unanticipated consequences of current practice and lead to a better conceptualization of interventions and reappraisal of practice" (pp. 330-331). Because of these features of qualitative research in special education, some have pointed to the importance of this approach in investigating the *social validity* of interventions and other special education practices (Kozleski, 2017; Leko, 2014). As Kozleski (2017) explained:

> Social validity, a hallmark of applied behavior analysis, has been a cornerstone of the degree to which what is studied offers real-time, applied value to the conduct of everyday life. The results of a study must demonstrate not only that the intervention worked with a specific group but that what was gained has social value in a specific context. (p. 21)

Descriptive qualitative data are important not only for novel phenomena in schools and communities, but also, as Kozleski (2017) suggested, for making "visible the everyday activities of life in classrooms that often go unexamined" but often have powerful impacts (p. 24). Moreover, the roles of culture, power, and unique features of specific social contexts are explored for the constraints and affordances they provide special educators, students, and families (Kozleski, 2017). In exploring the real-world implementation of programs and practices, special education qualitative researchers not only attend to contexts, but also often provide rich descriptions of practices, meanings, and contextual features of specific settings (Brantlinger et al., 2005).

Although the special education literature is replete with quantitative research that identifies factors important to all stakeholders in special education, many of these factors are surrounded by definitional ambiguity or are defined by experts in ways that stakeholders do not share. Definitional ambiguities make it difficult to study these constructs well (Hill, Noonan, Sakakibara, & Miller, 2010), and an overreliance on expert definitions may detract from the meaningfulness and usefulness of the research. Moreover, many of the subjective aspects of being a child or adolescent with a disability, a special educator, or parent may remain uncovered if researchers rely solely on quantitative methods (Shek & Lee, 2007). In light of these issues, qualitative researchers go directly to stakeholders to talk with them and spend time with them. In these ways, qualitative research is instrumental in helping special education researchers and teachers to learn from the perspectives of people with disabilities about the life roles that are important to them, what their experiences are in assuming these life roles, and how special educators can best assist them in addressing the difficulties they encounter in these life roles.

In addition to the practical purposes of qualitative research in special education, this kind of research is also used to develop and expand theory about phenomena of interest to special educators. Through using qualitative data to develop grounded theories of processes or practices, or to critique or expand upon current theories in the field, qualitative research has important roles to play in building bodies of scholarly knowledge. The data and findings from qualitative studies can also be used for social critique, to, in Trainor and Leko's (2014) words, "identify, describe, critique, and challenge current paradigms and practices that are inequitable or present enduring challenges to the field of special education" (p. 265). Indeed, on the topic of justice and equity, qualitative research is needed for amplifying the voices of people with disabilities and other stakeholders, as well as ensuring that their perspectives be central to decision-making processes in special education (Kozleski, 2017; Niesz, Koch, & Rumrill, 2008).

Even though in-depth knowledge of the experiences, understandings, and views held by those who influence special education practices and those who are served by them is important for the field, special education has been quite slow to embrace qualitative inquiry (Bos & Richardson, 1993; Pugach, 2001; Pugach, Mukhopadhyay, & Gomez-Najarro, 2014; Trainor & Leko, 2014). This is in contrast to many other fields of education research in which qualitative inquiry has a long history of prominence. A 2009 review of the special education literature indicated that only around 6 percent of research articles in major special education journals featured qualitative research (Mastropieri et al., 2009). Similar results were found in a review of five years (2014–2018) of articles in *The Journal of Special Education, Remedial and Special Education,* and *Exceptional Children* conducted specifically for this chapter. Only 7 percent of the articles published featured qualitative studies, although this count included a two-part special issue devoted entirely to qualitative research. If the special issue is removed from the count, only 5.3 percent of articles featured qualitative research. This paucity is despite the fact that, over the last quarter century, a number of prominent special educators have called for more qualitative research in the field (e.g., Bos & Richardson, 1993; Ferguson & Ferguson, 2000; Pugach, 2001).

Related to the underrepresentation of qualitative inquiry is a method-ologically conservative context in terms of the designs, approaches, and methods used in qualitative special education research (Brantlinger, 1997; Pugach, 2001). In the review conducted for this chapter, a strong majority of the qualitative research articles published were interview studies rather than more specialized designs, although grounded theory and phenomenology were also well-represented. Neither ethnography nor narrative inquiry was published in the five years of the three journals, and only one critical quali-tative study was identified. However, it is important to point out that quali-tative studies of special education are often published in non-special educa-tion specific journals, such as general education journals, rehabilitation jour-nals, and qualitative research journals.

Examining the factors that influence the education and development of youth as well as factors that impede and promote success, both inside schools and out, are critical lines of inquiry among special education researchers. Qualitative research is a valuable tool for gaining a better understanding of the practices, contexts, and understandings that contribute to successes and challenges. These understandings can lead to more powerful, appropriate, and effective school- and community-based interventions and programs.

The purpose of this chapter is to provide an overview of qualitative research approaches and methods, and to discuss their application to special education research. In the following sections, we examine (a) characteristics of qualitative research, (b) the researcher's role in qualitative inquiry, (c) issues in research design and methods, and (d) types of qualitative research designs illustrated with examples from the special education literature. Several of the sections that follow have been adapted from Koch, Niesz, and Jones Wilkins (2017) with the kind permission of the publisher, Charles C Thomas, Springfield, IL.

CHARACTERISTICS OF QUALITATIVE RESEARCH

Qualitative research is characterized by the use of interview, observation and artifacts to understand the experiences, practices, understandings, and views of people. Qualitative research has a number of additional character-istics as well, including the following (Creswell, 2007; Hagner & Helm, 1994; Hatch, 2002; Lincoln & Guba, 1985):

1. The research data generated from a qualitative study are reported in words or images rather than in numbers.

2. Qualitative research is *naturalistic* in that it is conducted in the settings in which people live, work, and play.

3. Qualitative researchers seek understanding, not prediction or control.

4. Participants' experiences, views, and practices are not judged or assessed by the researcher; researchers seek to understand people on their own terms and from their own points of view. Meanings and interpretations of research findings are developed and negotiated with the research participants because it is their perceptions or realities that the researcher seeks to understand and reconstruct.

5. Data analysis occurs through induction rather than deduction; hypotheses are not established a priori. Analytic categories thus emerge inductively from the data as opposed to being "overlaid like a template on the participants or their situation" (Hagner & Helm, 1994, p. 291).

6. Understanding occurs as a result of engaging in an in-depth—and often long-term—study of the phenomena of interest; researchers are as interested in the research process that is occurring as they are in the outcome.

7. Qualitative researchers make idiographic interpretations of the research findings; they are more interested in developing in-depth understanding of the particulars than they are in making generalizations. As Brantlinger and colleagues (2005) explained, "Qualitative research is not done for purposes of generalization but rather to produce *evidence* based on the exploration of specific contexts and particular individuals. It is expected that readers will see similarities to their situations and judge the relevance of the information produced to their own circumstances" (p. 203).

8. The criteria for judging the quality, rigor, and soundness of qualitative studies emphasize coherence, insight, instrumental utility, and trustworthiness rather than conventional notions of reliability and validity.

9. The researcher acts as the instrument of the research. In other words, the researcher typically generates, collects, analyzes, and interprets data without the use of any standardized instruments. Rew, Bechtel, and Sapp (1993) refer to the value of human beings' intersubjective experience in qualitative inquiry, explaining that researcher-as-instrument is important because "No other entity could fully capture the multidimensionality and intricacy of the human experience" (p. 301).

This final characteristic, researcher-as-instrument, is discussed in more depth in the next section about the researcher's role in qualitative inquiry.

RESEARCHER'S ROLE

Because of the focus on learning the perspectives and practices of others, the qualitative researcher's role is primarily that of a learner. Research participants teach the researcher through sharing experiences, stories, and the meanings that they make from them. Sometimes research participants even act as coresearchers to varied extents, which can make qualitative research a valuable tool for both understanding and empowering people with disabilities (Niesz, Koch, & Rumrill, 2008).

Because the qualitative researcher acts as the instrument of data generation, collection, analysis, and interpretation, the quality and credibility of the research findings depend on the decisions and actions of the researcher. Qualitative researchers have the responsibility to thoroughly and accurately represent participants' worlds and hold themselves accountable to participants' perspectives in every stage of the research. Fidelity to participants' lived experiences and meanings is the goal of any account of qualitative research. Achieving this goal takes many forms, from the accurate documentation of a child's spoken phrase during fieldwork to the production of theory that reflects teachers' experiences in a school. Specifically, the researcher must build rapport and appropriate relationships with research participants; take great care in being rigorous, careful, and ethical; and, perhaps most of all, be reflexive.

First, qualitative researchers thus must take care to be precise and accurate in the data they collect, in their analyses, and in their writing. When participants' words are presented, they must be presented verbatim. When observations of social activity are presented, they must accurately portray what happened. When participants' meanings are presented, they should not reflect the researcher's assumptions, but must be the meanings that participants actually report. In addition, to capture participants' worlds, qualitative researchers must move beyond surface observations and explanations to understand the phenomena in as much depth as possible. In most qualitative research studies, being thorough means striving to obtain multiple perspectives. Documenting and representing participants' worlds requires researchers to capture the complexity of social life in vivid detail. Some researchers refer to this as "thick description," description that is rich, detailed, nuanced. Qualities of precision, accuracy, thoroughness, depth, richness, and vividness in an effort to capture participants' worlds are hallmarks of a strong and rigorous qualitative study.

Because qualitative researchers interact directly with the research participants and their data sources, they must also be aware of their own experiences and personal characteristics and how these shape their interactions as well as the data collected, analyzed, and interpreted. As Corbin and Strauss

(2008) explained, qualitative researchers "don't separate who we are as persons from the research and data analysis that we do. Therefore, we must be self-reflective about how we influence the research process, and, in turn, how it influences us" (p. 11). Thus, in addition to taking care to be thorough, careful, and precise in all research processes, qualitative researchers must recognize their own influence on all aspects of the research, from their relationships during fieldwork to how their own thinking and life experiences predispose them to viewing and interpreting qualitative data in certain ways. Good qualitative researchers work to raise awareness of how their subjectivity could influence the research and take steps to avoid coloring their data and analyses with their own perspectives. This is called reflexivity.

Shwandt (2001) defined reflexivity as:

> the process of critical self-reflections on one's biases, theoretical predispositions, preferences, and so forth. . . . Reflexivity in a methodological sense can also signal more than inspection of potential sources of bias and their control. It can point to the fact that the inquirer is part of the setting, context, and social phenomenon he or she seeks to understand. Hence, reflexivity can be a means for critically inspecting the entire research process, including reflecting on the ways in which a field-worker establishes a social network of informants and participants in a study and examining one's personal and theoretical commitments to determine how they serve as resources for generating particular data, for behaving in particular ways vis-à-vis respondents and participants, and for developing particular interpretations. (p. 224)

The qualitative researcher's charge is to gain awareness of his or her subjectivity, address its influence in the design and practice of the research in ways that improve the research, and share this work with the reader of the study. Ultimately, qualitative researchers strive to follow the *participants'* lead in exploring issues, concerns, and feelings about the phenomenon, rather than ignoring what is not important to the researcher. Strategies for promoting a researcher's reflexivity are discussed in the trustworthiness section of the chapter.

Although a skillful qualitative researcher recognizes that the participants' views are most important to the study, he or she still develops his or her knowledge on the topic of interest in order to make quick decisions about what information to seek, what questions to ask, and what observations to make. He or she knows how to approach the problem in a manner that will yield the greatest detail and depth of information (Kvale, 1996). The qualitative researcher seeks to develop his or her skills in listening, interviewing, observing, and writing. In addition to these skills, the researcher must possess a keen understanding of human interactions as well as the ability to communicate effectively. Experiences with the phenomena under study can serve to enlighten and sensitize the researcher to the complexity of issues being explored. In fact, qualitative researchers sometimes even include their own experiences as data (Polkinghorne, 1991).

RESEARCH DESIGN AND METHODS

Designing and conducting qualitative studies requires thoughtful attention to a range of issues related to the collection, analysis, interpretation, and reporting of qualitative findings. Although agreement among qualitative researchers regarding specific procedures does not exist, there is reasonable consensus that consideration of the following are important in designing qualitative studies: (a) the literature review and theoretical framework, (b) research purpose and questions, (c) sampling, (d) data collection methods, (e) data management, (f) data analysis and interpretation, (g) trustworthiness and researcher reflexivity, (h) ethical considerations in qualitative research, and (i) the limitations of qualitative research.

The Literature Review and Theoretical Framework

In general, the literature review conducted for qualitative research is considered of secondary importance to the research participants' experiences, views, and meanings connected with the phenomena being investigated. Unlike literature reviews in quantitative research that establish a foundation for research questions and hypotheses, literature reviews in qualitative research are conducted to (a) identify gaps in the literature and limitations in methodological procedures used to investigate the phenomenon, (b) provide a basis for how qualitative research will close those gaps, and (c) fine tune the research design and methods being used by investigators (Glesne & Peshkin, 1992; Polkinghorne, 1991). Also, in qualitative research, the literature review continues beyond the outset of the project into the data collection and analysis phases of the study (Glesne & Peshkin, 1992; Strauss & Corbin, 1990). This continuous return to the literature occurs because emerging themes in data collection and analysis often require a review of previously unexamined literature (Creswell, 2007; Polkinghorne, 1991).

Because qualitative studies are exploratory, explanatory, descriptive or emancipatory in nature, the literature on the topic of interest is used inductively so that it does not direct researchers' questions, narrow their studies, or suppress the development of new theoretical formulations (Creswell, 2007; Strauss & Corbin, 1990). The amount of literature reviewed varies depending on the qualitative design. For example, in theoretically-oriented qualitative studies such as ethnographies, the literature review may be quite extensive; however, in grounded theory, case studies, and phenomenological studies, the literature review may be more restricted (Creswell, 2007).

The literature review in both quantitative and qualitative research informs readers about the results of related studies, provides a rationale for the current study, and relates the findings from the current study to prior studies (Creswell, 2007; Strauss & Corbin, 1990). In some written qualitative reports, a brief literature review is included in the introduction to the study to frame the problem of interest. In others, a more extensive literature review is provided in a separate section. In most studies, the literature is also compared and contrasted with the researcher's findings in the discussion section of their written reports (Creswell, 2007).

The use of theories in qualitative research is also more varied than it is in quantitative research. How or whether theory is used as a part of the investigation depends on the specific questions and qualitative design being used by the researchers (Creswell, 2007). For example, theory is typically included as part of a study's conceptual framework. For example, critical disability theory might be used in developing a critical ethnography. The development of theory may also be an endpoint of the study, as in grounded theory research. Some qualitative studies engage with prior theory, using their findings to contest, extend, or further contribute to theories in the field. Finally, existing theory may not be used at all in some qualitative studies. Some approaches to phenomenology and grounded theory eschew existing theory in order to focus the entire study on the participants' experiences, views, and meanings. When theory is used in qualitative research, its general purpose is to provide the researcher and research participants with a lens to promote understanding. Qualitative researchers do not seek to rigidly fit their data to existing theories or use their data to confirm or disconfirm existing theories as in more deductive approaches (Koch, Niesz, & McCarthy, 2014).

Research Purpose and Questions

In qualitative investigations, the purpose of the study and corresponding research questions can be classified as exploratory, explanatory, descriptive, or emancipatory (Marshall & Rossman, 2011). Exploratory questions are posed to study phenomena that are not well-understood and to generate questions for future inquiry. Explanatory questions are posed for the purpose of discerning patterns underlying the phenomena being investigated, or for identifying relationships that shape the phenomena. Descriptive questions call for documenting and detailing social processes and participants' experiences, views, practices, and meanings. Finally, emancipatory questions are posed when researchers want to actively engage participants, who are typically members of marginalized populations, in collaborative inquiry, social critique, and action.

Qualitative research questions are broad, open-ended, and generally few (usually limited to one to three questions). Open-endedness is especially important due to the inductive nature of qualitative studies. Initial research questions are formulated to provide a framework within which to focus the research topic and guide the selection of a qualitative research design with corresponding sampling, data collection, and analysis methods (Glesne & Peshkin, 1992). Research questions are not static, nor do they lead to hypotheses to be tested as in quantitative research (Strauss & Corbin, 1990). Rather, they are continuously refined throughout the data collection and analysis processes to reflect the researcher's increasing understanding of the phenomena under investigation. This flexibility enables the researcher to follow the lead of the research participants rather than impose his or her perspective on those of the participants. As qualitative researchers engage in data collection, it is not unusual for them to discover that their original research question(s) fail to uncover what the participants view as important to understand. In these cases, researchers will revise their research questions and follow the lead of their participants.

Sampling

Sampling techniques in qualitative research are quite different from those used in quantitative research. The most important considerations in qualitative sampling decisions are determining the research settings, times, and who will serve as the research participants. Decisions regarding these issues will have a significant impact on answering the research questions (Maxwell, 1996), and they must be carefully examined prior to the initiation of the inquiry. Each qualitative research design differs regarding the typical number of participants or research sites, and these can range from one (e.g., case study, autoethnography) to hundreds (e.g., large grounded theory investigations). However, as noted by Hunt (2011), the primary consideration in sampling is not number of participants, but the detail and insight into the phenomena that participants are able to provide.

Because it is impossible to interview everyone, or to observe everything, qualitative researchers employ a sampling strategy to determine which sites, times, and participants to include (Glesne & Peshkin, 1992). The sampling strategy used in qualitative research is referred to as "purposeful" (Maxwell, 1996, p. 70) and is defined differently than "purposeful" sampling in quantitative research. In qualitative research, purposeful sampling is used to identify participants who are best able to provide detailed information to answer the research questions. Purposeful sampling in qualitative research, also referred to as "criterion-based selection" (LeCompte & Preissle, 1993, p. 69), involves the deliberate selection of participants, not for their representativeness, but on the basis of their experiences with the phenomena of interest and their ability to help researchers answer their research questions. In other words, participants are selected on the basis of the *type* of information they can provide or provide access to. If the researcher is more interested in developing an in-depth understanding of the participants' practice and experience in context, extended periods of time will be spent with a small number of participants. If the researcher wants to gather a broader perspective, a larger number of participants will be interviewed in a less intensive manner (Creswell, 2007).

In some qualitative research, access to research participants may be difficult to achieve (e.g., accessing students with low incidence disabilities). Because of the potential stigma and discrimination that could occur, as well as other considerations such as protecting their identities, researchers may use a sampling technique known as snowball sampling (Patton, 2002) to access participants who otherwise would not be discovered. Snowball sampling involves asking study participants to recommend additional potential participants.

Although purposeful sampling typically refers to the selection of participants, it can also refer to the selection of sites of the study or timing of the research. Although many research questions and problems do not require an actual site or setting and focus entirely on the selection of individuals, other research questions/problems will require determination of the specific site of the research. According to Marshall and Rossman (1989), the following four issues require consideration in selecting the appropriate sampling site(s): "(a) physical access to the site; (b) variety of data sources; (c) access to the site, participants, and data will be granted for as long as is necessary; and (d) quality and credibility of the data can be reasonably assured" (p. 54).

Timing of the research project includes addressing site and participant availability and access, the approximate length of time required to access entry to data collection sites and recruit research participants, and the approximate amount of time during which data collection will take place. The researcher will need to consider each decision regarding timing by asking questions like: "What will be the effect of this particular decision?" "What will be gained?" "What could be missed?" The researcher must be thoughtful about the potential implications of each of these decisions (Bogdan & Biklen, 1998).

Data Collection Methods

In qualitative research, the data emerge from the interactions of researchers with their participants that typically take place in participants' local contexts. As noted earlier, interview, observation, and artifacts are the most prominent sources of data in qualitative inquiry. Ultimately, the researcher analyzes texts or images produced by these sources. For example, a qualitative researcher may work with hundreds of pages of transcripts from audio-recorded interviews, months of field notes detailing observations and other interactions, archival records, photographs and video recordings, physical artifacts, and documents.

Qualitative researchers sometimes spend time with potential participants in the settings they plan to study before data collection begins. For example, they may spend time in a classroom, give presentations to educators and administrators, and meet with gatekeepers to discuss their research. This early work enables potential participants to get to know the researcher and helps the researcher establish trust and credibility, which can help individuals decide whether or not to participate in the study.

Interviews

The most widely used form of data collection in qualitative research is the interview (Creswell, 2007). The qualitative research interview explores the views, experiences, understandings, beliefs, practices, descriptions, explanations, and motivations of participants. Interviews allow extensive communication between the researcher and participant to provide a wealth of information about participants' lives and the meanings they make from their experiences. In-depth interviews allow participants to reflect upon and elaborate the specifics of their experiences, and allow the researcher to probe for clarification, nuance, and detail (Bogdan & Biklen, 1992; Glesne & Peshkin, 1992; Marshall & Rossman, 1989).

Qualitative researchers are careful to avoid narrow, closed-ended questions that lead the participants in a direction that supports the researchers' assumptions about the phenomenon (Koch, Niesz, & McCarthy, 2014). In fact, asking one broad, open-ended prompt or question (e.g., "Tell me what it is like to teach students with severe disabilities at this school?") is often all that is required to collect rich, nuanced data from the participants. Researchers can then use probes and follow-up questions to obtain stories and specific examples of their experiences and in-depth elaborations. This approach ensures that the researcher follows the participants' lead rather than steering responses in the direction of what the researcher assumes is relevant.

In many qualitative investigations, interview protocols or guides are developed to initiate the data collection process. These protocols may be structured, semi-structured, or unstructured, although semi-structured approaches are most common. Semi-structured interview protocols are designed to be flexible enough to incorporate modifications and changes as the data collection process continues (Denzin & Lincoln, 2000; Glesne & Peshkin, 1992). Ensuring that guides or protocols are designed to uncover issues important to the research participants is often addressed by having focus groups or expert panels review the questions and make specific recommendations for changes or additional questions. Members of these focus groups or expert panels typically consist of individuals with characteristics similar to those of targeted research participants and experts in qualitative research design and the phenomena being investigated. Pilot interviews are another way in which researchers can prepare for their study. As with focus groups and expert panels, pilot interviews conducted with people similar to those to be recruited for the study can help the researcher reflect on and subsequently improve his or her protocol. In addition, interview guides may be developed on the basis of literature reviews, consultation with others who have investigated the topic being explored, the researchers' own (professional or personal) experiences with the phenomena, or using a combination of techniques. Interview protocols are often revised once researchers begin collecting data and find that the questions they are asking do not uncover what is important to the research participants or that additional questions are needed based on what has been learned in earlier interviews.

Interviews are conducted over a period of anywhere from 30 minutes to several hours, and in many studies, participants are interviewed more than once. In addition, recording devices (e.g., audio or videorecorders) are typically used to record the interview. Such devices must be used as unobtrusively as possible to minimize any influence on the data collection process (Marshall & Rossman, 1989). Recordings are then transcribed to produce a verbatim account of the interview. Qualitative researchers work closely with interview transcripts when analyzing their data.

Focus groups are used to interview several participants at one time (Frey & Fontanta, 1991) when the researcher wants to develop an understanding of the shared meaning of a phenomenon (Camic, Rhodes, & Yardley, 2003). Morgan (1988) explained that "The hallmark of focus groups is the explicit use of the group interaction to produce data and insights that would be less accessible without the interaction found in a group" (p. 12). Focus group interviews can be generative in the sense of eliciting topics through group dialogue that may not have emerged in a one-on-one interview.

As with any approach to research, focus groups are not without their limitations. One common problem is when a single member of the group or several group members dominate the conversation or intimidate other members of the focus group. When this happens, the discussion generates data that are more representative of vocal members; quiet or intimidated members' voices may not be heard. This problem can be alleviated by conducting both individual and focus group interviews or by providing members with an opportunity to respond to interview questions in writing. Confidentiality is also an important issue in focus group interviews, especially when participants are discussing sensitive topics. Therefore, it is critical that, at the outset of focus group meetings, researchers instruct participants that all information shared in these groups is to remain confidential. Ultimately, however, the researcher has little control over participants' willingness to adhere to confidentiality agreements. Another challenge of focus groups is the difficulty of identifying which participant is talking during the course of the discussion, particularly when parallel positions are being voiced (Flick, 2002). This problem may be reduced by use of video recording or having a note-taker in the room during the focus group.

With the growing diversity of research methods and the rise of technology over the last 50 years, there are now more possibilities than ever to gather interview data. Some contemporary approaches to interviewing include reciprocal peer interviews, Photovoice, and use of technology such as Skype. As an alternative to individual interviews and focus groups, Porter, Neysmith, Reitsma-Street, and Collins (2009) introduced reciprocal peer interviewing as a means to remove power inequities between the researcher and research participant by enabling participants to co-construct their own meanings of the phenomenon being studied without influence of the researcher. In traditional interview modes, the researcher/interviewer engages the participant/interviewee in an interrogatory dialogue. This places the interviewer in a position of control and power over the interview process. Reciprocal peer interviewing attempts to reduce this power differential by allowing participant pairs to perform both the roles of interviewer and interviewee. This allows the researcher to take on a secondary role as facilitator and observer. The resulting conversation is then one of shared authority. In reciprocal peer interviewing, participants undergo a brief training session on interviewing and then pair up with another research participant to alternate roles in interviewing each other. This approach to data collection gives participants greater freedom in their verbal expressions without the influence of the researcher.

Photovoice is an approach in which individuals photograph their everyday life experiences. Photovoice can be used as an alternative method to enhance the understanding of experiences that are difficult to capture through other qualitative methods. Wang and Burris first introduced a version of this approach in 1994, and, since that time, Photovoice has become a vital tool for community-based participatory research (CBPR) because of the authenticity of the information gathered (Graziano, 2004). In addition to taking photographs that represent their experiences, research participants write descriptions of the photographs' meanings. They also discuss the meanings they ascribe to their photos in interviews with the researchers. In line with emancipatory research, participants and researchers sometimes use these photographs to share findings and educate others.

Developments in technology and changes in communication have influenced interview techniques in qualitative research. Online interviewing using technology such as Skype can now facilitate access to research respondents who are geographically dispersed. Skype is a popular voice communication application that specializes in providing video chat and voice calls. There are benefits and drawbacks to the use of Skype in qualitative interviewing. For instance, using this platform helps overcome problems experienced with doing face-to-face interviews such as time and financial limits, geographical dispersion, and physical mobility limitations of research populations (Cater, 2011). By using a webcam, researchers are still able to see the presence of nonverbal and social cues (Stewart & Williams, 2005; Sullivan, 2012). On the other hand, seeing only a limited "head shot" provided by webcam can create obstacles building rapport and observing all of the individual's body language (Cater, 2011).

Many qualitative research questions can be answered with interview data alone. For this reason, many qualitative studies, especially those using grounded theory and phenomenological designs, rely solely on interviews as data sources. However, many studies also require observation and/or artifacts (especially documents) to generate the data needed to answer the research questions. Indeed, using multiple sources of data when appropriate is considered a good strategy for building a more thorough and trustworthy account of participants' experiences and meanings (Lincoln & Guba, 1985; Merriam, 2002; Schwandt, 2001).

Observation

Qualitative researchers observe social life in settings relevant to their studies in order to understand practices, social dynamics, and the role of specific contexts on phenomena of interest. Observation—particularly participant observation—brings researchers up close to participants, offering plenty of opportunity for interaction. Not only does observation allow learning through these informal interactions and researchers' direct views of practice-in-context, it also allows researchers to develop highly relevant questions for formal interviews. Even in a study that relies primarily on interview data to answer the research questions, observation can help the research ask the right questions in interviews.

Participant observation (often referred to as "fieldwork") in which the researcher not only observes in a social setting, but also participates in it, has a long history in qualitative research. Ethnographers, for example, have long participated in culture to learn about culture. However, some observation in qualitative research does not entail participation. Spradley (1980) discusses a range of researcher roles in fieldwork, including complete participation, active participation, moderate participation, passive participation, and non-participation. Decisions about the kind of observation to conduct depend on the study design, the research questions, and the specific characteristics of the social settings relevant to the study.

Observations are typically documented in detailed field notes that provide a chronological record of what the researcher saw, heard, and did throughout the observation. Although notes are often taken during the observation, these are typed up and fleshed out with significant detail immediately after the observation. Some researchers with more specific questions may use a protocol form to document what they observe in the field. Video recording may also be used if deemed unobtrusive enough for the activity in the setting. Even note-taking might be deemed inappropriate in some settings.

Researchers themselves must be relatively unobtrusive in conducting observations and fieldwork. At the beginning of most studies, a qualitative researcher's presence will be unusual for the setting and may change the activity that takes place. Yet, over time, participants return to more typical activity and the researcher becomes less obtrusive. For this reason, it is recommended that qualitative researchers spend a significant amount of time doing observation. This not only makes it more likely that the observations capture typical activity but also allows the researcher to *identify* what is typical and what is not in the setting or community of interest.

Artifacts

Artifacts are items made or used by participants in social settings. Qualitative researchers often collect artifacts to learn more about the participants and the setting. These may provide contextual information of interest or even data directly relevant to the research questions. Documents are the most commonly collected artifacts among qualitative researchers. Personal documents may include diaries, journals, personal letters, and poems. Official documents may include newsletters, policy documents, codes of ethics, minutes from meetings, and personnel files. In special education studies, IEPs, school records, curricular materials, and student assignments may be relevant artifacts.

Data Management

A great deal of data is generated during a qualitative research project—often hundreds of pages of transcripts and field notes. Data management and data analysis are integrally linked throughout the research process, and the data must be well-organized to facilitate systematic analysis. Researchers should keep logs of all research activities throughout the project. Data sources must be consistently stored and labeled with detailed contextual information.

Advances in technology have aided qualitative researchers in managing their data. Computer-assisted qualitative data analysis software (CAQDAS) systems are increasingly being used by qualitative researchers to organize, index, and retrieve their data throughout both data collection and analysis (Salmona & Kaczynski, 2016). A growing number of CAQDAS systems are available for Windows and Macintosh computers (Fielding, 2001) and are divided into three broad types of programs: text search, text code-and-retrieve, and code-based theory builder programs. A few examples of commonly used CAQDAS software packages include NVivo, Atlas.ti, MAXQDA, and HyperResearcher (Drisko, 2013). Some computer software companies have websites that offer a trial use of their software programs, and some CAQDAS systems are available at no cost to the researcher. Although CAQDAS programs can be valuable for storing and organizing data, they do not make analytic decisions for researchers (Drisko, 2013). As such, they should be viewed as tools for data management and analysis, but not as a program that will analyze the data.

Data Analysis and Interpretation

Qualitative data analysis involves making sense of volumes of data, determining what data to include and exclude in the analysis, and recursively interrogating data to learn from them and develop findings. Different qualitative approaches and designs have different approaches to and methods of data analysis. However, most qualitative studies involve analytic strategies for (a) organizing the data by category (often through coding) and studying the categorized/coded data to answer research questions and develop findings, or (b) analyzing the data by looking contextually or connectedly across data sources in a chronological manner (Creswell, 2007; Maxwell, 2012). Data are reviewed at the micro-level (i.e., each participant interview) and at the macro-level (i.e., across data sources) throughout the analytic process.

Qualitative designs are built on an iterative process (i.e., back-and-forth movement from data gathering to analysis back to more data gathering). Thus, data collection and analysis go hand-in-hand. Researchers begin their analyses while still collecting data rather than waiting until data collection is completed. In this manner, preliminary analyses may inform future data collection (i.e., going back to previously interviewed participants to ask them new interview questions), and ongoing data collection informs data analysis (i.e., returning to preliminary analyses and modifying or expanding on these analyses based on new data collected in the field).

When interviews are the dominant or only data sources in qualitative research, researchers often begin the data analysis process by first listening to or watching each interview and reading transcribed interviews in their entirety (often several times) to acquire a sense of the data before beginning to break them apart for the purpose of analysis and interpretation (Creswell, 2007). Field notes are often treated in a similar manner in studies featuring observation. In this initial stage of analysis, researchers often write down key ideas or topics that emerge in their reading of their data sources. These may be recorded as short phrases in the margins of transcripts and field notes, under photos, or on other documents collected. The emerging ideas are also discussed in researcher memos that document ongoing analysis. Memos are also used to record initial impressions, common topics that recur within and across data sources, insights about the data, and emerging patterns and themes. When multiple researchers are involved in the investigation, they discuss with each other their preliminary observations and thoughts and share their memos to obtain a broader picture of the data.

At some point in this work, qualitative researchers may identify initial categories, codes, or structures for organizing the data. They often identify variations and examples and then make comparisons of the data across codes, categories, or structures. Initially, researchers may develop a large number of categorical codes or structures; however, through the iterative process of comparison, these are often condensed into larger meaning units. Broader themes within the data are typically identified through contrasting and comparing categorized data. These broader themes and their interconnections are often explained and illustrated in a narrative description and sometimes supplemented by tables or matrices.

As noted earlier, qualitative researchers are increasingly using software programs, CAQDAS, as tools for data management and analysis. CAQDAS programs typically have tools that make coding and categorizing data easy. Retrieving data assigned to particular codes OR categories is also aided by CAQDAS programs, as is moving directly from coded data back into the original data source. Some programs have features to allow advanced queries of data and a range of data visualizations.

One aim of much qualitative data analysis is thick description. Thick description, a term introduced in ethnography by Geertz (1973), refers to acquiring an understanding of the participants' experiences with the phenomenon that goes beyond surface explanations to understand the participants' experiences in as much depth as possible. Thick description requires researchers to make explicit the patterns of cultural and social dynamics that shape the participants' experiences with the phenomenon. It also requires precision and depth in documenting and representing the participants' worlds (Koch, Niesz, & McCarthy, 2014).

As opposed to coding and categorizing methods for data analysis, some studies call for a connecting or contextualizing approach. These approaches do not separate excerpts from transcripts, field notes, and artifacts to categories for further study, but keep data sources whole and examine relationships among aspects of an interview, observation, artifact (e.g., letter, IEP, policy, etc.) holistically and, often, chronologically. As Maxwell (2005) explained, in these types of approaches, researchers "do not focus primarily on *similarities* that can be used to sort data independently of context, but instead look for relationships that *connect* statements and events within a context into a coherent whole" (p. 94).

Again, although many qualitative researchers use general categorizing or contextualizing approaches, specific research approaches and designs have their own approaches and methods of data analysis. Yet, most approaches also entail interpretation. Data interpretation answers the "so what?" question (Chang et al., 2013). It involves making meaning of the data in terms of how the findings advance understanding of the phenomena that was investigated, determining new insights or understandings gained from the study that add to the scholarly literature, and comparing the findings with those of related research on the phenomena to identify commonalities and discrepancies across studies. Data analyses and interpretations are sometimes shared with the research participants to ensure that they are truly representative of participants' experiences, understandings, and views, as we discuss in the next section.

In written reports, participant quotations and descriptions from observations are included as evidence of the findings (Creswell, 2008). Verbatim quotations or brief vignettes from observations are judiciously interwoven throughout the qualitative report to support researchers' arguments, descriptions, and explanations. Including data in the reports illustrates the findings, making them more powerful to readers, and also shows the reader that the findings represent participants' experiences and perspectives.

Trustworthiness and Researcher Reflexivity

Because the intent of qualitative research is to uncover meaning rather than verify causal relationships between variables or generalize the research findings to other settings and populations, the terms "reliability" and "validity" are not usually considered appropriate to the evaluation of the quality and rigor of qualitative research studies. In fact, following the work of Lincoln and Guba (1985), many qualitative researchers use terms such as "trustworthiness" and "credibility" instead of "reliability" and "validity."

Established techniques used to promote the trustworthiness of qualitative research findings are discussed next.

Audit Trail

Qualitative researchers keep detailed records and materials from their study. Often referred to as an audit trail, this documentation provides a basis for subsequent reviews of the process of the study by other researchers. An audit trail can include (a) raw data, including audio- and video-recordings, interview notes, field notes, artifacts, and so forth; (b) products related to data reduction and analysis, including memos, journals, and coding records; (c) products related data reconstruction and synthesis; and (d) process notes, including notes on trustworthiness (Lincoln & Guba, 1985).

Memos and Field Journals

Memos and researcher journals are used throughout the research process to document the researcher's reflections, perspectives, intuitions, and preliminary ideas regarding the ongoing investigation (Bogdan & Biklen, 1992). Memos and journals are also used to identify and record researcher subjectivity, assumptions, and feelings that may arise in the process of data gathering, analysis, and interpretation. As such, they are two of several tools the researcher uses to promote his or her reflexivity. In addition, recording the researcher's preliminary ideas safeguards against the forgetting of important ideas during the research process (Glesne & Peshkin, 1992). Finally, memos may be used by peer reviewers to gain additional perspectives on the data.

Triangulation

Triangulation is conceptualized as the comparison of information collected from different sources, different data collection methods, or by different researchers (Denzin, 1970). In order to ensure that their assertions are grounded in multiple sources of information, researchers compare what they learn from interviews to that from other data, like observations or artifacts. Multiple sources of data serve to ensure that data and findings hold up to close scrutiny. This type of triangulation also provides a means of cross-referencing interpretations arrived at during data analysis.

The active participation of multiple researchers in qualitative studies is another type of triangulation that provides several advantages. The first is the ability to evaluate multiple sites during the same timeframe. In addition, multiple researchers bring different skills, attributes, and perspectives to the evaluation process (Cassell, 1978; Wax, 1979). Such differences further serve to reduce the influence of researcher preconceptions or subjectivity on the findings (Hagner & Helm, 1994).

Discrepant Case Analysis

Another practice qualitative researchers use to ensure the trustworthiness of their analysis is to deliberately search for data that do not support their preliminary conclusions. Discrepant data must be rigorously examined, along with supporting data, to determine whether the research findings are to be retained or modified. The qualitative researcher must be diligent in the search for discrepant data to avoid prematurely dismissing relevant data that do not fit with existing conclusions (Maxwell, 1996).

Member Checks

Participant feedback is considered critically important in establishing the trustworthiness of qualitative research findings and interpretations (Creswell, 2003; Denzin & Lincoln, 2000). Through a process called member checking, research participants are given the opportunity to review interview transcripts and research findings and interpretations in order to provide feedback on the data generated and the conclusions reached by the researchers (Fielding & Fielding, 1986). Member checks provide an additional level of credibility by providing opportunities for participants to clarify their views or experiences and contest any inaccurate interpretations made by the researcher. Member checks also provide a checkpoint for protecting confidential information or the identities of research participants.

Peer Debriefing

Peer debriefing is used as a means of testing the researcher's ideas against those of peers who have not been involved in the research project. The use of peer debriefers provides an opportunity to obtain alternative perspectives regarding the analysis and interpretation of the data. Peer debriefers aid researcher reflexivity by raising the researcher's awareness of subjective interpretations of data (Lincoln & Guba, 1985). Peer debriefers may be used throughout all phases of the research process as a means for researchers to check their insights and interpretations with someone who may have expertise in the research topic or qualitative inquiry but who is not personally invested in the project or its outcomes.

Transparency

Transparency requires qualitative researchers to make the essential components of their investigations clear to readers of their qualitative reports (Moravcsik, 2014). Qualitative researchers are charged with providing readers with specific details regarding the choices they made in terms of research strategies, participant selection, data sources, data collection, analysis and interpretation of their findings. This allows readers to assess the relevance of the study to their own professional or personal lives. Moravcsik (2014) describes three kinds of transparency: data transparency, analytic transparency, and production transparency. Data transparency allows readers access to the data used by the researchers to make their analyses and interpretations. Analytic transparency requires researchers to precisely describe the analytic process they used to draw their conclusions. Production transparency involves explaining to readers why the researchers chose to use specific approaches and methods, and how their choices resulted in methodological coherence throughout the study. Moravcsik (2014) underscored the importance of transparency, stating that "academic discourse rests on the obligation of scholars to reveal to their colleagues the data, theory, and methodology on which their conclusions rest" (p. 48).

Researcher Reflexivity

As discussed above, researcher reflexivity refers to the researcher's continuous scrutiny of his or her preconceptions with respect to the research, as well as the influence of those preconceptions on all aspects of the study. Reflexivity requires a willingness to make changes when the study falls short of exhibiting fidelity to *participants'* views, perspectives, and experiences. Malterud (2001) conceptualized reflexivity as "an attitude of attending systematically to the context of knowledge construction, especially to the effect of the researcher, at every step of the research process" (p. 484).

Reflexivity can be promoted through a variety of strategies, some of which have already been discussed. For example, during an interview, the researcher's use of reflective statements, open-ended questions, avoidance of leading questions, and restatement of the participant's comments are effective tools in managing reactivity (Maxwell, 1996). Bracketing, a term that originates from the phenomenological tradition, can also be used to minimize researcher bias (Schwandt, 2001; Moustakas, 1994). This technique requires researchers to "bracket" or suspend their assumptions about social reality and focus on the research participant's experience of the world. Arguing that subjectivity is inevitable in any research, Peshkin (1988) recommended that qualitative researchers conduct a subjectivity audit whereby they systematically seek out their preconceptions while their research is actively in progress. This ongoing audit enables researchers to bring their subjectivity into conscious awareness so that they understand how it may be shaping their research and can employ strategies to manage it.

Other strategies to promote reflexivity include keeping a self-reflective journal during the research process to record thoughts and feelings about what is happening in order to provide the researcher some distance in the research process (Niesz, Koch, & Rumrill, 2008). Safeguards such as triangulation, member checking, and peer debriefing can be built into the design and methods of qualitative projects to help the researcher be more reflexive and enhance the trustworthiness of the findings. Researchers may also ask a colleague to interview them using the same or similar questions that will be asked of participants. The self-interview helps researchers initiate the data collection process, clarify their research, understand their perspectives and experiences with the phenomenon being investigated, and become more aware of preconceptions that may interfere with their ability to accurately represent the research participants' perspectives (Polkinghorne, 1991).

Beyond being aware of their subjectivity and addressing its effects on the study, qualitative researchers are sometimes encouraged to explicitly write about their subjectivity, positionality, and reflexivity when reporting research results (Creswell, 2003). Contemporary qualitative researchers sometimes include a section of their research manuscripts devoted to this, potentially describing how their professional and personal understandings or experiences with the phenomena being investigated inform their data collection and analysis, the strategies they have used to raise their awareness of and document their subjectivity, and how they have worked to ensure that their subjectivity does not unduly influence their understandings of the data and their analyses.

Ethical Considerations in Qualitative Research

While ethical standards are important to all research endeavors, qualitative research poses unique ethical challenges that are not present in quantitative research. The most important consideration for qualitative researchers is the "ethical obligations a researcher has toward a research participant in terms of interacting with him or her in a humane, nonexploitive way while at the same time being mindful of one's role as a researcher" (Guillemin & Gillam, 2004, p. 264). Ethical qualitative researchers interact with participants in a manner that is respectful of participants' autonomy, dignity, and privacy. In designing their research studies, qualitative researchers proactively anticipate potential ethical dilemmas that may arise and consider how they will respond to these dilemmas. However, because ethical issues in qualitative research tend to be subtle and context-driven, it is not possible to anticipate all of the potential dilemmas that may arise (Guillemin & Gillam, 2004; Orb, Eisenhauer, & Wynaden, 2001).

Qualitative researchers have an ethical obligation to protect their participants' confidentiality by maintaining data in a secure place and by excluding names and any other information that could lead to the identification of the participants (Guillemin & Gillam, 2004; Orb et al., 2001). However, even when using pseudonyms and leaving out other potentially identifying information, confidentiality may still be unintentionally violated (Orb et al., 2001). For example, lengthy quotations included in written reports could allow others to identify participants. Even demographic data (e.g., race, age, disability type, educational level), especially in small populations, could lead to the identification of participants. This potential ethical violation underscores the importance of negotiating with participants what information to include and exclude from written reports.

Because qualitative researchers interact with the research participants directly, ethical issues can arise as a result of the partnership that is formed in the study. For example, the practice of in-depth interviewing and prolonged engagement with the research participants may lead participants to view the researcher as a confidante and feel betrayed when the relationship is concluded and the information shared is made public (Guillemin & Gillam, 2004). Participants may also find the interactions with the researcher to be therapeutic. Thus, researchers have a responsibility to ensure that participants understand that the purpose of the relationship and the interactions is to conduct research and not to provide therapy. Potential harm may result when conducting in-depth interviews, particularly when the focus of the interview is on sensitive topics (e.g., trauma, psychosocial adaptation to disability, stigma, discrimination, etc.). Participants may experience emotional distress when discussing these issues or may later regret personal information that they revealed to the researcher (Orb et al., 2001).

Several strategies can be implemented by qualitative researchers in an attempt to address these potential sources of harm. First, the potential for emotional distress must be included as a risk of participation in consent forms. Researchers must also make decisions about how far to probe a participant who reveals information about distressing experiences (Orb et al., 2001). In these instances, researchers must make ethical decisions about whether to continue the interview, shift topics in the interview, or to stop and make referrals for treatment or counseling. They can then follow up with the participants to check on their well-being. Researchers can also make provisions in their investigations for counseling referrals or other forms of support if emotional distress arises such as including contact information for counseling referrals on consent forms. In addition, member checks to review transcripts provide an opportunity for participants to remove information they do not want included in the study. That noted, additional ethical issues arise when individuals report instances such as child or elder abuse (Orb et al., 2001). Participants must be clearly informed at the outset that such information may be excluded from confidentiality and anonymity, and researchers may be required by law to report these instances.

Researchers can unintentionally cause harm to participants when they probe too far in asking questions that participants feel uncomfortable answering or, conversely, when they do not show enough interest in participants' responses (Guillemin & Gillam, 2004). These experiences with the researcher can lead the participants to feel vulnerable, rejected, ignored, or invalidated. Such feelings are especially likely to arise when interviewing members of marginalized populations who have a lifetime of experiences of being silenced, invalidated, or not supported by others in their lives. Feelings of invalidation can also arise when researchers fail to let participants discuss what is important to them and instead focus the interview on what is important to the researcher. To avoid these potential sources of harm, qualitative researchers must be adequately educated in the goals and ethics of qualitative research and in appropriate interviewing techniques.

When sharing interpretations and written reports with research participants to obtain their feedback on the accuracy of the interpretations, participants may feel too intimidated to challenge the researchers' interpretations because of perceived power imbalances (Guillemin & Gillam, 2004). Also, when data are framed in a larger context, participants may think that what they shared has been left out, and this could lead to feelings of being used or betrayed. The potential for these ethical issues to arise can be minimized by continually emphasizing to the research participants that they are the experts and the researcher's role is to learn from them. Re-emphasizing the participants' and researchers' roles increases the likelihood that participants will feel empowered to challenge the researchers' interpretations and to confront the researchers when they think their voices have been excluded in final reports.

Finally, qualitative researchers have an ethical obligation to conduct rigorous qualitative research that is methodologically sound and coherent (Oberle, 2002). If the study is of low quality, then participants are expending time and effort and potentially encountering undue risk for a project that fails to meet the standards of the field.

Although unintentional ethical violations may occur in qualitative studies, researchers can minimize this risk by being well-informed of the professional codes of ethics of their fields and institutions, as well as relevant laws and expectations. New researchers can find many sources to learn about ethics in qualitative research and should read widely on this topic. These steps can help researchers anticipate potential ethical dilemmas and violations that they may encounter in the conduct of their studies. If and when these dilemmas arise, researchers should consult with mentors and other qualitative researchers to gain advice.

Limitations of Qualitative Research

In judging the empirical soundness of qualitative research studies, one must keep in mind that the objective of qualitative research is fundamentally different from that of quantitative research. In qualitative research, the emphasis is placed upon understanding the peoples' experiences, practices, views, and the subjective meanings that they give to their worlds. The purpose of this inquiry is not to make broad generalizations or verify causal relationships between variables (Maxwell, 1996). Thus, the notion of empirical soundness (reliability and validity) takes on a different meaning in qualitative research. Rigor and credibility are as important to qualitative researchers as they are to quantitative researchers, but, as explained in the preceding section, the expectations and strategies are different. The established methods for building trustworthiness discussed above should be considered, engaged as appropriate, and explained to readers.

Qualitative research (like all research) is not without its limitations. The data collected in qualitative studies, for example, are often in the form of self-reports. Self-reports can introduce error to a study because they require individuals to reconstruct their experiences with the phenomena of interest (Polkinghorne, 1991). To accomplish this, research participants often have to rely on their memories. Memories are clearly unreliable, and recollections of past experiences are often heavily influenced by many factors outside one's awareness. Additional limitations of qualitative research may include problems that occurred in data collection, unanswered questions by research participants, unexplored topics during data collection, or the need for better sampling of participants or sites for inclusion in the study (Creswell, 2012).

Qualitative researchers as the instruments of data collection and analysis can introduce additional limitations to a study. They must be cognizant of how their role is perceived by research participants and how they influence the manner in which participants communicate with the researcher (e.g., what information is shared and what information is withheld). In addition, as discussed above, the researcher's own subjective views have the potential to lead to misinterpretation of participants' words or actions (Creswell, 2003). If reflexivity is not practiced, the study's findings may be limited.

Finally, the intent of qualitative research is for the researchers to develop a unique interpretation rather than generalize findings, as is done in quantitative research. As Brantlinger and colleagues (2005) explain:

Qualitative research is not done for purposes of generalization but rather to produce *evidence* based on the exploration of specific contexts and particular individuals. It is expected that readers will see similarities to their situations and judge the relevance of the information produced to their own circumstances. (p. 203)

However, a study could have limitations with respect to transferability (the extent to which findings are applicable to other contexts and settings) if the researcher does not provide sufficient descriptive details that can be used by readers to determine the relevance of findings to their settings. If the researcher does not address the central assumptions, the selection of participants, and the detailed methods used in the study, its usefulness to readers will be in question.

QUALITATIVE RESEARCH DESIGNS

Qualitative research approaches and designs are numerous and continue to evolve. A researcher selects a particular approach or design based on the purpose of the study and the research questions he or she intends to answer. A researcher's education, experiences, and researcher identity also influence the selection of an approach to the study. There are more qualitative research designs and variations than we can describe here, but for the purpose of this chapter, we focus on several designs typically used by special education researchers. These include (a) ethnography, (b) case study, (c) phenomenology, (d) grounded theory, (e) narrative inquiry, (f) consensual qualitative research, (g) generic designs, and (h) qualitative meta-syntheses.

Ethnography

Ethnography is the study of culture and cultural processes through long-term participant observation. Ethnography has been a powerful tool for anthropologists and sociologists for generations (Bogdan & Biklen, 1998; Crowson, 1993), and has more recently been adopted and adapted by other disciplines and professional fields. Ethnography provides an approach to understand the cultural practices and meanings of people in communities and organizations. Like other qualitative researchers, ethnographers place emphasis on understanding from the point of view of the participants in their local contexts.

Ethnographic data are obtained primarily through participant observation; ethnographers spend extensive amounts of time in a community and learn through talking, listening, observing, and participating in everyday life in the community (Guba, 1978). In addition to informal conversations at the field site, ethnographers usually engage in formal interviews with partici-pants as well. Ethnographic data gathered through these means provide a mechanism for learning cultural symbols, meanings, practices, and process-es. Bogdan and Biklen (1992) explained:

> When culture is examined from this perspective, the ethnographer is faced with a series of interpretations of life, common-sense understandings that are complex and difficult to separate from each other. The ethnographer's goals are to share in the meanings that the cultural participants take for granted and then to depict the new understanding for the reader and for outsiders. (p. 39)

Data analysis in ethnographic research focuses on understanding and building descriptions of cultural practices and cultural meanings. Research questions are always addressed through a sociocultural lens. Because the focus is on cultural description and the primary method of data collection is participant observation, ethnographers work with months if not years of field notes documenting what they saw and heard at the field site. Findings are supported with vignettes that relate particular observations from the site of the study. Ethnographers seek to present their findings in a way that brings their reader into the cultural context at the center of the study.

Ethnographers use different methods to conduct ethnographic analysis. For many, analysis resembles that of other kinds of qualitative research in that coding and categorizing are initially used to fracture hundreds of pages of field notes and interview transcripts into manageable categories for fur-ther study. In fact, many ethnographers use methods adopted and adapted from grounded theorists (discussed below) to analyze their data (Emerson, Fretz, & Shaw, 2011; Hammersley & Atkinson, 2007). Other ethnographers, however, engage in different types of analyses to develop cultural descrip-tions and interpretations (e.g., Agar, 1996; Spradley, 1980). Memos, which are used in data analysis for most approaches to qualitative inquiry, are espe-cially important in ethnography, as they provide spaces for researchers to reflect on what they are learning through cultural immersion and, later, through the data analysis process.

What is important about ethnographic analysis is the focus on working to understand the phenomena at the center of the study from the cultural insiders' point of view. Ethnographers compare what is called an emic un-derstanding (or a cultural insider's understanding) with their own etic or out-sider's understanding in order to learn about the cultural scene and relate findings to broader audiences. Most ethnographers are also engaged with theory throughout their study and, especially, during data analysis. Ethno-graphic findings are often used to contest, extend, or further develop social theory. Critical ethnography and feminist ethnography use theory to understand how local cultural practice and meaning is situated in larger frameworks of power, such as patriarchy, institutional racism, social class hierarchies, ableism, and so forth.

Becker (2010) conducted a three-year ethnography an alternative high school that examined students' responses to competing school discourses regarding students that "have problems" and students who "are problems." Students enroll in alternative schools for a number of reasons, including trouble listening in class, misbehaving, truancy, breaking the law, refusing to speak, or having learning/behavioral disabilities. At the school at the center of her ethnography, Becker found that the "are problems" students were those who were there due to their behavior, and the "have problems" students were those viewed as having special needs, such as a severe learning disability.

Becker (2010) engaged in ethnographic fieldwork that included long-term participant observation and over 40 interviews (some informal some formal) with students, teachers, and the principal. She taught a class at the school and spent time talking with students on breaks, at lunch, and sometimes in their homes. Becker recorded written or audiotaped field notes during or immediately following the observations. She analyzed her data through close review of data sources, coding, theming, and negative case analysis.

Becker (2010) found that, generally, teachers at the school had sympathy for students that "have problems," and peers gave respect to those who "are problems." She found that it was unusual for students to have both respect and sympathy from their teachers, and both respect and acceptance from their peers at the same time. Relationships with teachers and social position among peers influenced students' success in navigating both the academic and social worlds of schooling. Becker found that the students often backed away from the special needs rhetoric or the "having a problem" label in order to preserve a sense of self and social status and to be perceived as "cool" by their peers. In most cases, those who were perceived as "bad" or "cool" were more respected by their peers, but reported less positive relationships with their teachers. Some, albeit very few, students (referred to as "shining stars") were able to successfully balance the demands and retain teacher sympathy, self-image, and peer respect (Becker, 2010). These students positioned themselves as past troublemakers who have "been there, done that" to establish credibility with their peers, yet used their turnaround stories as resources in order to gain teacher sympathy. Becker found that race and gender affected how successfully students could manipulate the tension: the "shining stars" were typically white female students and the "troublemakers" were typically nonwhite and male.

Autoethnography

Variations on ethnography include autoethnography and collective autoethnography. Autoethnography is a form of self-reflection and writing that strives to explain and examine an individual's experiences with investigated phenomena in the context of cultural norms, beliefs, and values (Ellis, 2004; Holman Jones, 2005). It uses both self-reference and reference to culture as a method to combine features of life history and ethnography. This qualitative research approach is not simply autobiographical story-telling; rather it is a form of critical inquiry embedded in theory and practice (McIlveen, 2008). Autoethnographic research findings may be reported in typical research reports or as "short stories, poetry, fiction, novels, photographic essays, personal essays, journals, fragmented and layered writing, and social science prose" (Ellis & Bochner, 2000, p. 739).

While autoethnography is defined as an individual or personal account, collective or collaborative autoethnography (CAE) is the means by which two or more people explore their experience in cultural context as a team. Chang, Wambura- Ngunjiri, and Hernandez (2013) explained that CAE is "a qualitative research method that is simultaneously collaborative, autobiographical, and ethnographic" (p. 17). Data collection and analysis in CAE involves "a group of researchers pooling their stories to find some commonalities and differences and then wrestling with these stories to discover the meanings of the stories in relation to their sociocultural contexts" (Chang et al., 2013, p. 7). Specific data analytic procedures are decided upon by the research team members, may be borrowed from other qualitative designs, and evolve and change as data collection proceeds. CAE requires both solo and team approaches to data collection and analysis. For example, research team members may independently collect data (e.g., diaries, journals, personal records), engage in solo writing about their experiences, and then come together in team meetings to share their data and written narratives with co-researchers, probe each other to delve deeper into describing their experiences, and identify commonalities and discrepancies in their experiences. Through this process, a collaborative narrative is eventually developed to describe the researchers' collective experiences with the phenomena within a cultural context.

There is no set number of participants for a CAE team. Previous studies have involved as few as two and as many as 11 researchers. If a group has already been formed, members must collaborate to develop the topic of the study. In other studies, the research topic is developed first, and appropriate team is built to pursue the study. Collaboration among close colleagues engaged in autoethnography begins with existing rapport, and can thus allow the research to proceed more quickly. However, this familiarity may also inhibit the participants from seeing new things about each other through the research. On the other hand, collaborating with new research partners may take more to build trust and rapport, but it can allow for fresh perspectives on the phenomena being collaboratively explored.

Although autoethnography is not a commonly used qualitative approach by special education researchers, Hughes (2012) used autoethnography to explore his awareness of and abilities to cope with Asperger's syndrome. Diagnosed with Asperger's syndrome at the age of 12, Hughes used personal journal narratives, reflexive memos, and experiences from his school communication classes to investigate various barriers he faced in social situations. Because the purpose of autoethnography is to "actively engage with one's own life story narratives" to aid the journey towards identity, this auto-ethnography engaged social interactionism to interpret social situations.

Hughes (2012) sought to construct a full examination of his Asperger's world during different development life stages. His study entailed reflecting on (and later sharing with the reader) biographic stories related to gaining awareness of Asperger's syndrome and the associated learning that he experienced over time. Hughes explained that this "work illustrates how actively engaging with one's own life story narratives can help the Asperger's learner come to terms with his or her Asperger's self" (p. 94).

Case Study

Qualitative case studies are used to explore an issue or problem using a specific case or multiple cases as exemplifiers (Creswell, 2007). Cases may comprise a single individual, a group, a program, an organization, an event, or some other concrete unit. Multiple case studies examine and compare several of these units. Cases are often studied because of their uniqueness; these are called intrinsic case studies (Merriam, 2002). Cases are also studied as specific examples of phenomena of interest; these are called instrumental case studies (Merriam, 2002).

In qualitative case studies, researchers collect extensive data from multiple sources to provide a holistic description of the case. Data sources may include interviews of various stakeholders, archival records, direct observations, participant-observations, archival records, and physical artifacts. In data analysis, case study researchers typically develop a detailed description of the case. They also identify key issues or themes to illustrate the complexity of the case. Coding and other categorization strategies, discussed earlier in the chapter, are often used to develop a thorough understanding of key findings related to the case. When multiple cases are studied, researchers provide detailed descriptions of each case and then proceed to a cross-case analysis, identifying themes across cases. Reports of case study research are often highly descriptive, presenting the reader a full picture of the case.

Bogdan and Biklen (1992) classified case studies as historical organizational, and observational. Historical organizational case studies focus on a specific organization, examining its development over a certain period of time. Sources of information may include interviewing people who were involved in the organization since its inception, reviewing written records and other types of documentation, and observing the present organization. Observational case studies focus on the contemporary status of a phenomenon within a small group of participants, a specific program, or an organization. Participant observation serves as the main technique employed for data collection.

An example of a qualitative case study in special education is Lindstrom, Doren, and Miesch's (2011) examination of the career development process and post-school employment outcomes for individuals with disabilities who were working in living wage occupations seven to 10 years after exiting high school. As the career development process for individuals with disabilities is often complex, nonlinear, and chaotic, these researchers were interested in the factors that influenced career decision-making and employment opportunities. They were also interested in examining the barriers that youth with disability face when making transitions from high school to stable, long-term employment. To pursue these goals, they conducted a multiple case study of eight participants, each of whom represented a 'case.'

The researchers first developed interview protocols based on a review of the transition, rehabilitation, and career development literature. The interviews conducted with the participants covered the following major topics: (a) individual characteristics and attributes; (b) family support; (c) services and supports from high school and post school; (d) workplace experiences; and (e) any other post school training or education. In addition to the interview data, researchers collected information via family background questionnaires, job history forms, and review of special education and vocational rehabilitation records for all participants. The researchers ultimately found that the key influences on post-high school placement were (a) participation in work experiences; (b) transition services and supports; and (c) family support. Ongoing career advancement, on the other hand, was supported by factors such as (a) participation in postsecondary education; (b) steady work experiences; and (c) the participants' personal attributes, specifically, self-efficacy and persistence (Lindstrom, Doren, & Miesch, 2011).

McLeskey, Waldron, and Redd (2014) also conducted a case study to determine what factors contribute to the success of a highly effective, inclusive elementary school. Arguing that there are only a limited number of schools that are successful in meeting the demands for excellence and equity, especially as related to the inclusion of students with disabilities, the researchers conducted this case study to generate better understandings of success.

The two criteria used to select the case—the school—were (a) students with disabilities are included in classrooms at a level well above the state average, and (b) achievement levels for students with disabilities are well above the state average (McLeskey, Waldron, & Redd, 2014). Data collection involved 22 individual interviews with teachers and administrators, all of which were transcribed. Observations were conducted in 10 inclusive classrooms. Data analysis resulted in themes related to the key qualities that supported student achievement in this inclusive elementary school. From this case study, the researchers identified these findings: the school met the needs of *all* of the students; provided high quality instruction for *all* students; immersed teachers in professional development opportunities; were efficient but flexible in the use of resources; engaged in shared decision-making; and used data to inform decision-making (McLeskey, Waldron, & Redd, 2014).

Phenomenology

Many have noted that phenomenology is as much a philosophy as it is a method of research (Creswell, 2007; Hatch, 2002; Merriam, 2002). Guided by phenomenological philosophy, which focuses on how phenomena are perceived in human consciousness, the goal of phenomenological qualitative research is to understand the subjective world of the research participants and how they experience particular phenomena. In phenomenological inquiry, the researcher strives to understand the meanings that individuals confer upon objects, people, situations, and events (Bogdan & Biklen, 1992). Phenomenologists seek to gain an interpretive understanding of the interactions between the person(s) and the environment while suspending their own assumptions (Douglas, 1976). In other words, phenomenologists do not ascribe their own meanings to events and circumstances in the research participant's life. Rather, they endeavor to learn about the conceptual and perceptual world of the people being studied (Geertz, 1983). The perceptual lens through which people view *their* world serves to define their reality. It is this reality that phenomenologists attempt to understand.

Typically, researchers engaged in phenomenological studies are interested in what participants have in common as they experience a phenomenon (e.g., learning to teach inclusive classrooms, entering high school with an IEP, caring for a child with Down's Syndrome, etc.). Researchers collect data from persons who have experienced the phenomenon and develop a composite description of the essence of the experience for all the individuals (i.e., what they experienced and how they make meaning of it).

As a qualitative research approach, phenomenology involves extensive interviewing to draw out narratives of experience among a small number of research participants (Creswell, 2003). Although many studies only include interview data, some include other data sources like observations, journals, art, poetry, and music. Findings are expressed through a descriptive narrative generated by a synthesis of participants' descriptions of the meanings they make of the phenomena being studied.

Although phenomenological approaches vary in terms of how data are analyzed, Moustakas (1994) has recommended using the data analysis procedures of horizontalization, identifying clusters of meaning, developing textural and structural descriptions, and creating a composite description of the essence of participants' experiences with the phenomenon under investigation. In the process of horizontalization, researchers go highlight significant statements within interview transcripts that provide understandings of how the participants experienced the phenomenon. They then develop clusters of meaning, or themes, from the significant statements. Significant statements and themes are used to write a textural description of what the participants experienced and a structural description of the context or setting that influenced how the participants experienced the phenomenon. From the structural and textural descriptions, the researcher writes a composite description that focuses on the essence of the experience of the phenomenon shared by the participants.

Roberts and Whiting (2011) used eidetic phenomenology, also known as descriptive phenomenology, to achieve two goals:

> (1) to identify the perceptions and experiences of the primary caregivers of young children with epilepsy regarding their interaction with the schools which impact both the child's and family's quality of life, and (2) to clarify how families think schools can best support, accommodate and prepare for these children and families. (p. 169)

Using open-ended semi-structured interviews, the authors focused their investigation on the perceptions and experiences of primary caregivers of children with epilepsy with regard to their interactions with the school and related impacts on the child and family's quality of life.

In this study, phenomenological interviews were conducted and transcribed. The transcriptions were reviewed for patterns and themes capturing shared experience. Analysis resulted in themes related to five categories of experience: health-related issues, family coping, academic experiences, social belonging, and awareness (Roberts & Whiting, 2011). Examples of these themes included feeling appreciated, respected, and heard by school faculty, feeling isolated from other parents in the school, and observing their children experience bullying and isolation from peers. The study detailed the caregivers' strong desire for their children to live a "balanced, normal life" despite the health adjustments that epilepsy required of their lives (Roberts & Whiting, 2011, p. 174).

Grounded Theory

The grounded theory approach was initially developed by Glaser and Strauss (1967) as a means of "closing the embarrassing gap between theory and empirical research" (p. vii). They wanted use empirical data to build theories that manifest faithfulness to the phenomena being studied (Strauss & Corbin, 1990). In other words, in their approach, the researcher does not begin with a specific theory and seek to prove it. Instead, the researcher begins with an area of interest, gathers relevant data, analyzes the data, and develops a theory or model as the end product (Strauss & Corbin, 1990). Interviews are the most prominent source of data in grounded theory studies, but any kind of qualitative (or quantitative) data can be used. Data collection and analysis happen simultaneously and continue to be until the theory developed can account for all data.

Grounded theory is considered rigorous in its approach to data analysis, known as the constant comparison method. A systematic set of procedures is used to code data through open, axial, and selective coding (Strauss & Corbin, 1990). Open coding involves fracturing data apart for the purpose of examining, comparing, conceptualizing, and categorizing the data. Conceptual labels are constructed for specific happenings, events, or other types of phenomena. As similarities are discovered within the various concepts, they are grouped together in a new, more abstract categories (Strauss & Corbin, 1990). Axial coding is used to integrate the data or emerging themes in new ways by making connections between categories. Causal conditions such as events, incidents, and happenings that lead to the occurrence or development of a specific type of situation or phenomenon are explored (Haworth & Conrad, 1997).

Selective coding provides a means of integrating information and produces a higher level of systematic analysis through a series of nonlinear steps. The first step involves the conceptualization of the "story line" (i.e., the core or primary category) identified in the previous stages of coding (open and axial). The next steps consist of relating similar categories to the core/primary category and validating those relationships by referring back to the data for corroboration (Strauss & Corbin, 1990). Emerging relationships among categories are tested by deliberately searching for contradictory evidence. If contradictory evidence is discovered, the initial categories are revised to incorporate the new evidence. This process is repeated until categories are sufficient to account for all of the various pieces of evidence; at such point, data collection is ceased. This point is referred to as theoretical saturation. Theoretical saturation occurs when new data emerging from interviews or other data sources no longer require a revision of the theory, when the categories have been well developed, and when the relationships among categories have been clearly established (Strauss & Corbin, 1990).

Glaser and Strauss (1967) identified the following criteria for determining the applicability of a grounded theory of a central phenomenon: fit, understanding, and generality. Fit is accomplished if the theory is considered to reflect the everyday reality of the area being studied. If the theory is carefully induced from diverse data, then the theory should be "understandable" to the individuals who participated in the research project and to others (Strauss & Corbin, 1990). In achieving generality, the interpretations must be conceptual in nature, broad enough to yield an abstractable quality, and include the various contexts related to the phenomenon being studied.

Yuknis (2014) used grounded theory to examine the essay revision process of middle school students who are deaf or hard-of-hearing. She aimed to develop a theory related to how these students approach the process of revising their own writing in school. Participants in the study included eight students and their English teachers, and data were collected through interviews, observations of the students engaged in essay writing, and the collection of writing samples.

Yuknis (2014) used the constant comparison method to analyze these data, which yielded two major themes related to the students' revision processes: interacting with language and interacting with instruction. Language was a major factor in how students approached the revision process, and the "interacting with language" theme captured the students' struggles with learning a language that is already difficult for them to access, while at the same time manipulating the language in a complex way in order to compose their essays. The participants showed an awareness of their struggles with writing, yet did now know what steps to take in order to improve or correct their writing errors. The second theme, "interacting with instruction," referred to how the students' experiences with revising their essays were shaped by their interactions with their teachers. The teachers did not necessarily provide feedback, but simply corrected the students' errors when the papers were finished. The students accepted and made the changes without asking questions. Ultimately, Yuknis argued that "students did not participate much in revising their texts and teachers assumed most of the cognitive burden of writing" (p. 307). Furthermore, she explained, method of instruction for deaf or hard-of-hearing students could lead them to becoming passive learners who are overly reliant on their teachers for success. Teachers have a significant role in the development of writing and revising skills, but these particular students were not afforded an opportunity to practice the skills that would lead to learning and quality writing.

In a second example of grounded theory in special education research, Bettini and colleagues (2017) utilized this approach to study how local special education administrators (LSEAs) conceptualize their roles in cultivating effective special education teachers (SETs) in a high performing, inclusive school district. Data for this study were collected via interviews with LSEAs. These interviews consisted of three groups of questions. The first group focused on how the LSEAs conceptualized special education along with their own roles and the SETs roles. The second group focused on how the LSEAs communicated with the SETs (for example "how do you convey your expectations?). The third group of questions asked LSEAs to report both a positive story of an interaction with an SET and a negative interaction with an SET (Bettini et al., 2017). Interviews were audio-recorded and transcribed verbatim for data analysis.

Constructing a grounded theory on the LSEAs' perspectives involved four sequences: initial coding; focused coding; theoretical coding; and theory development. Bettini et al. (2017) concluded that LSEAs conceptualize SET quality as an interaction between teachers and leaders, and that teachers are responsible for demonstrating characteristics such as professional knowledge and a willingness to work hard, and leaders are responsible for developing teachers' knowledge and providing them with necessary conditions in order to teach effectively (Bettini et al., 2017). The LSEAs enact their values through a series of actions including selecting SETs who share the same values, enculturating all teachers into the values of the district, supporting SETs in gaining and enacting instructional skill, formally and informally evaluating SETs' strengths and needs, and retaining high quality SETs and dismissing those who fail to meet expectations (Bettini et al., 2017). The researchers concluded their article by encouraging district leaders to review the results of this study and take into account this vision of the wide set of roles that LSEAs may fulfill in cultivating high quality SETs (Bettini et al., 2017).

Narrative Inquiry

Narrative inquiry refers to a broad collection of approaches to qualitative research that share a grounding in stories: How do people story their lives? What can be learned from stories of experience? Although classic approaches, including oral histories, life histories, and biographies, have been around for generations, the last couple of decades has seen considerable growth in narrative inquiry (sometimes called narrative analysis or narrative research) across disciplines. This is likely due to increasing recognition that stories both shape and communicate meaningful understandings of human experience (Connelly & Clandinin, 1990).

Polkinghorne (1995) wrote that, "In the context of narrative inquiry, narrative refers to a discourse form in which events and happenings are configured into a temporal unity by means of a plot" (p. 5). This conceptualization manifests in different ways through at least three distinct approaches to narrative inquiry: the collection of stories as qualitative data, the use of qualitative data to build a descriptive and explanatory narrative, and the analysis of how stories are constructed and told.

In the first type, which Polkinghorne (1995) called paradigmatic-type narrative inquiry, researchers' collect the stories from a number of participants and analyze them thematically or taxonomically, using typical qualitative analytic methods. This approach is often used to understand what participants' stories tell us about experiences related to the problem under investigation. In contrast, narrative-type narrative inquiry engages the researcher in collecting qualitative data about events and experiences (often from only a single participant) to synthesize them into a developmental account or, in Polkinghorne's (1995) words, "configure them by means of a plot into a story or stories" (p. 12). Instead of using categorizing or coding methods, the researcher builds narrative/story from a synthesis of the data. Oral histories, other histories, biographical studies, and some case studies of events or specific processes may be developed in this way (Polkinghorne, 1995).

Finally, some narrative inquirers are interested in *how* people tell stories of their lives and experiences. As Schram (2006) explained, "narrative researchers extend their focus beyond content to include how people 'package' that content and how they recount events with an audience in mind" (105). For example, after collecting one or many stories, researchers may focus on the types of stories told, the linguistic elements of the story-telling (similar to some forms of discourse analysis), or how stories change for different purposes, audiences, contexts, or times. Researchers sometimes examine the function that stories serve for the narrator. Skinner and colleagues (1999) took this approach in their study of Latina mothers' construction of identity in stories of their children with disabilities, ultimately arguing that "disability narratives are a crucial means whereby individuals construct agency. . ." (p. 492).

Although these three types of narrative inquiry often stand alone, some researchers combine two types into a single study. Because of the focus on narratives of experience, individual interviews are the dominant form of data collection across all three types of narrative inquiry. For oral histories, life histories, and biographies, several lengthy interviews with a single person may be required. In other types of narrative inquiry, a single interview with many participants may be preferable. Across all three types of narrative inquiry, the voice of the narrator(s) are generally preserved and shared with readers (Schram, 2006). In addition to interviews, narratives may also be elicited from participants in writing or obtained from existing sources. Some forms of narrative inquiry include the analysis of diaries, letters, and other artifacts, either exclusively or in combination with interviews. Finally, although less common, some approaches to narrative inquiry also use observation in order to generate descriptions of shared experience across participants (Connelly & Clandinin, 1990).

An example of a narrative inquiry in special education is Marsh, Warren, and Savage's (2018) study of narratives of becoming a father of a child with an intellectual disability in Ireland. This study combined paradigmatic narrative inquiry—with stories collected and analyzed for themes—with an analysis of how the stories were told. In response to the predominance of the voices of mothers of children with disabilities in the literature, the purpose of this study was to understand fathers' narratives of experience. Using a single semi-structured interview with each participant, the researchers asked 10 Irish fathers to share their stories, leading up to and beyond the diagnosis of their child's intellectual disability. Researchers then conducted a thematic analysis. They did so while attempting to preserve the narratives in a holistic way. That is, they sought to avoid the fragmentation of narratives that is characteristic of other approaches to qualitative inquiry. In addition to the thematic analysis, interviews were also analyzed for storylines and plots.

The findings of this study centered around the fathers being told that 'something was wrong' with their child. Fathers' stories differed with respect the nature of their child's disability—its visibility or invisibility at birth, for example. The researchers explored aspects of the fathers' stories that had in common initial experiences of shock and disappointment, grief and loss, and denial and blame. The researchers also pointed to features common across the narratives, such as the vividness and detail of the sequence of events recounted. In concluding their study and providing implications, the researchers argued that "healthcare professionals need to be cognizant of the emotional upheaval that such a diagnosis can have on fathers and be sensitive to their needs in supporting them through this process" (Marsh, Warren, & Savage, 2018, p. 216).

Consensual Qualitative Research

Hill, Thompson, and Williams (1997) developed consensual qualitative research (CQR) in response to frustrations with vague descriptions of qualitative research approaches that were difficult to comprehend and implement. Consensus, an integral part of the approach they developed, "relies on mutual respect, equal involvement, and shared power" (Hill et al., 1997, p. 523). The five essential components of CQR are: (a) the use of open-ended questions in semi-structured interviews; (b) the involvement of several judges throughout the data analysis process to bring about multiple perspectives; (c) consensus-building among judges regarding the meaning of the data; (d) the use of at least one auditor to minimize the effects of groupthink and to check the analysis of judges; and (e) data analysis that involves the development of domains, core ideas, and cross-analyses.

CQR sampling is unusual among qualitative research designs in that it employs random selection from a homogeneous population of research participants who are experts on the phenomenon under investigation. The recommended sample size in CQR is 8-15 participants. The primary source of data is semi-structured interviews, guided by protocols with questions developed from the literature related to the phenomena of study. The role of the interviewer in CQR is usually as a "trustworthy reporter trying to uncover what the participant truly believes" (Hill et al., 2005, p. 197). Hill and colleagues have recommended conducting at least two interviews with each participant to ensure that researchers are able to obtain a rich understanding of the participants' views and experiences.

Consensual qualitative research (CQR), like all qualitative research designs, is an inductive approach. It incorporates elements from phenomenology, grounded theory, and comprehensive process analysis. Researchers follow three steps when conducting CQR data analysis: developing and coding domains, constructing core ideas, and developing categories to describe consistencies across cases (Hill et al., 1997). An emphasis is placed on consensus among judges in the construction of research findings. When engaging in data analysis, CQR researchers search for commonalities among research participants' experiences and meanings. This constructivist approach to understanding reality recognizes that there are multiple realities or versions of what constitutes truth and that all are equally valid.

Rabren and Evans (2016) used a CQR design to examine the perceived issues of parents of children with disabilities in transition out of high school. The study also generated parents' input on suggestions for improving transition activities within the school. The researchers selected the CQR approach because it allowed for "free interactive discussion of ideas from multiple participants" (p. 311).

Rabren and Evans (2016) generated data through three focus group interviews with parents of students with disabilities. Starting with two uniform interview questions, the focus of the focus group discussions was the parents' concerns with transition services. Data analysis included review of the data and organization of domains by the researchers. Following the CQR methodology, the team members grouped the interview transcripts into domain lists, which were reviewed and revised until a consensus was reached. An auditor reviewed notes, transcripts, and other raw data from the interviews to "determine if data were appropriately assigned domains with representative corresponding core ideas" (p. 313). Data analysis yielded six domains of parental concerns: transition preparation, integration, adult services, parent support, advocacy, and professionals' roles. The findings in each of these domains can inform both families and schools in better preparing for the transition experience. Rabren & Evans (2016) concluded that that collaborative meetings are an opportunity for all stakeholders to discuss intentional planning for post-school transition for young people with disabilities.

Generic Qualitative Research

Most researchers whose articles are published in special education journals either (a) draw on various qualitative methods to answer their research questions or (b) do not identify the use of any specific qualitative design. Caelli, Ray, and Mill (2003) refer to these types of studies as generic qualitative designs. Generic qualitative research studies are described by these researchers as:

> Those that exhibit some or all of the characteristics of qualitative endeavor but rather than focusing the study through the lens of a known methodology they seek to do one of two things: either they combine several methodologies or approaches, or claim no particular methodological viewpoint at all. (p. 2)

Researchers understand that it is more important to design a study that can best answer the research questions than to be bound by specific requirements of traditional research approaches. This is perhaps why generic qualitative research is not only the most common approach to qualitative research in special education but also the most common approach to qualitative research across disciplines and fields.

In generic qualitative research, the purpose is to simply understand and describe a phenomenon from the perspectives of research participants rather than to, for example, generate a theory based on the data as in grounded theory research or understand culture as in ethnography (Caelli, et al., 2003). In generic qualitative research, the lenses used by researchers to analyze and interpret data are typically derived from the theories, models, and concepts in their disciplinary literature. Data analysis and interpretation involve the identification of recurring patterns, categories, or themes as well as clinical applications that help to further inform the field.

In using generic designs, researchers must still adhere to standards of methodological coherence. Establishing methodological coherence is more difficult when using generic designs than it is in using established designs. To address this problem, Caelli and colleagues (2003) recommended that researchers using generic approaches explicitly address (a) the theoretical positioning of the researchers, (b) the coherence of their methodological decisions with the research questions, methods, and conclusions drawn from their investigations, (c) the strategies used to ensure rigor of their investigations, and (d) the analytic lens through which they made sense of and interpreted the meaning of the data.

Kucharczyk et al. (2017) used a generic qualitative approach to "explore the contexts, considerations, and complexities associated with delivering interventions to meet the needs of high school students with ASD" (p. 331). These researchers used purposeful sampling to recruit participants who were key stakeholders in the education of high school students with ASD. A total of 152 participants (e.g., parents, people with ASD, educators, administrators, related service providers, community members) were recruited to attend one of 28 focus groups. Each participant was asked to respond to the focus group questions from their own personal and professional vantage point.

The researchers used the same set of questions for each focus group. However, each focus group was also asked specific questions about the intervention components (e.g., social competence, academic, transition, family, adaptive behavior) that they were responsible for developing. The researchers used constant comparative analysis to code and analyze their data. Their involvement of focus group participants with a range of perspectives, experiences, and geographic locales provided the researchers with opportunities to triangulate (compare and contrast) their findings within and across focus groups.

The overarching theme that emerged from their data analysis was the inadequacy of interventions being used in secondary education. Furthermore, concerns were discussed regarding the feasibility of implementing evidence-based interventions, along with tailoring these to the diverse needs of students with ASD. Finally, focus group members underscored the need for more extensive awareness and training about autism within schools. The researchers were able to use their findings to recommend comprehensive interventions to replace those that were viewed by stakeholders as ineffective.

Qualitative Meta-syntheses

Qualitative meta-syntheses are used to summarize, synthesize, and interpret the findings from a number of qualitative investigations of a specific phenomenon (Finfgeld-Connett, 2016). Hammel (2007) described the five phases of meta-syntheses as (a) determining the focus of the meta-synthesis, (b) identifying papers relevant to the focus, (c) evaluating the rigor and quality of identified papers, (d) identifying and summarizing key themes from each paper, and (e) comparing and synthesizing themes across studies into new concepts.

Meta-syntheses require researchers to carefully select a collection of articles that address the purpose of the meta-synthesis. Analytic techniques vary and are borrowed from those used in other qualitative research designs. Meta-syntheses enable researchers to develop new concepts, frameworks, and theories as well as to expand those that already exist. They offer an empirical foundation for guiding evidence-based practices and fine-tuning these practices to the realities of the research participants. Meta-syntheses also are also used to generate hypotheses and inform policy and practice guidelines.

Scruggs, Mastropieri, and McDuffie (2007) conducted a qualitative meta-synthesis to investigate co-teaching in inclusive environments. They analyzed the findings of 32 qualitative investigations of co-teaching to develop an integrated review. They explained that this process contributed a "higher order synthesis that promotes broad understanding of the entire body of research, while still respecting the integrity of the individual reports" (p. 395).

Using CAQDAS to aid in organizing and analyzing the studies, the researchers identified 69 categories related to the co-teaching process. The researchers then worked with the codes to develop four overlapping categories among the studies: *expressed benefits of co-teaching, expressed needs for success in co-teaching, special and general education teacher roles in co-teaching,* and *how instruction is delivered in co-taught classes* (Scruggs et al., 2007). Metasynthesis allowed the researchers to compare issues within and across various studies, which led to the conclusion that co-teaching has a generally positive perception in the eyes of teachers, administrators, and some special education students. Yet, the study found that special education teachers often play a subordinate role in co-taught classrooms. According to their metasynthesis, the most popular form of co-teaching—*one teach, one assist*—incorporates a general education teacher, who assumes the primary responsibility, and a special education teacher who "drifts" or assists individuals as needed (p. 392). This metasynthesis also suggested that for co-teaching to succeed, teachers need sufficient time for lesson planning, compatibility with partner teachers, professional development, and appropriate skill levels of students. Most of these needs are linked to administrative support at the school and district levels.

SUMMARY

Qualitative research is conducted with the purpose of exploring, explaining, or describing phenomena from the perspectives of research participants, and sometimes engages participants in emancipatory processes of social critique and action. The strength of qualitative inquiry in special education research is in its focus on the lived experiences of youth with disabilities, their teachers, and their families, inside and outside schools. Seeking to develop understandings of special education stakeholders on their own terms and in their own contexts, qualitative research contributes knowledge through inductive analyses of interview data, observational data, and artifacts. These analyses convey findings through the use of "rich" and "thick" descriptions, permitting a deeper understanding of participants' views, understandings, and practices in the everyday settings of their lives. In asking individuals to describe their worlds and their experiences with special education, researchers gain a deeper understanding of the perspectives and circumstances of the key stakeholders in special education. Administrators, special education teachers, and general education teachers can incorporate what has been learned from research participants into improving their practices and advocating for policy changes to better meet the needs of special education students. Qualitative research empowers young people with disabilities and their families by making their experiences and concerns heard by those charged with making decisions and developing policy for special education services.

The authors of this chapter and the previous chapter have endeavored to provide readers with an overview of a range of quantitative and qualitative research designs in the hopes that the merits of each will be given due consideration. The field stands to gain immensely from the thoughtful and appropriate application of various research designs to study the issues that matter to young people, educators, and families involved with special education.

Chapter 8

NARRATIVE LITERATURE REVIEWS

INTRODUCTION

Quantitative and qualitative studies using data collected with students, teachers, parents, and other research participants constitute the foundation of the special education research base. In addition to conducting original research, in which researchers collect their own data, researchers often review and synthesize findings across multiple studies to advance the field's knowledge base. In meta-analyses, researchers statistically synthesize findings across multiple studies (see chapter 6). Researchers can also summarize and analyze findings across multiple studies without statistical analyses using either systematic or nonsystematic approaches.

In systematic literature reviews, researchers use and clearly report systematic procedures to identify and analyze research from other studies in their review (Maggin, Talbott, Van Acker, & Kumm, 2017). For example, in systematic reviews, researchers specify search procedures such as what electronic data bases they searched, the specific search terms used, and whether and how other search procedures were used (e.g., hand searching prominent journals, contacting authors who frequently publish in the area of focus). Systematic reviewers apply (a) clearly defined inclusion and exclusion criteria to determine whether initially identified studies will be included in the review and (b) procedures for extracting specific information to be reviewed (e.g., regarding characteristics of study participants, effect sizes). Using a systematic approach to reviewing the literature allows research consumers to understand how the researchers identified the studies included in the review, and it minimizes the likelihood that researchers may have "cherry picked" certain studies or certain findings within studies to review.

In nonsystematic reviews, researchers do not attempt to be systematic or comprehensive in selecting research to review. Rather, in nonsystematic reviews, researchers selectively target particular studies or sources to review. Virtually all publications reporting research studies include an abbreviated nonsystematic review of relevant research and theory in the Introduction section of the paper to provide a context for the research being reported (see Chapter 9). In contrast, in nonsystematic literature reviews, the researchers' primary task is reviewing selected literature to advance the field's knowledge base. Researchers do not comprehensively or systematically select the literature they review in nonsystematic reviews, and research consumers should be aware that other literature likely exists that is not included in these reviews. Nonetheless, non-systematic literature reviews make important contributions to the field by postulating or advancing new theories and models, examining important and/or controversial topics in the lives of special education teachers and students, presenting "how to" tips and strategies to improve best practices, and explaining new developments in educational and disability policy (e.g., laws and their effects, administrative regulations).

To be clear, meta-analyses and narrative literature reviews are not the same thing. As described in this chapter, researchers can conduct a narrative literature review without meta-analyzing study findings. However, literature reviews, especially systematic reviews, are often conducted in combination with meta-analysis such that the findings from multiple research studies identified in a narrative literature review are statistically analyzed using meta-analysis. Although researchers can meta-analyze findings from multiple studies identified through conducting either systematic or nonsystematic literature reviews, meta-analyses are typically associated with systematic literature reviews. This is because meta-analysts generally want to be sure they have objectively and comprehensively identified all relevant research to include in their meta-analyses.

Narrative literature reviews, be they systematic or nonsystematic, describe the current state of both art (practice) and science (research) in focused areas of inquiry, add new insights and applications, and provide critical analyses of other published works. By including this chapter, we want to emphasize that scholarship encompasses much more than the numerous empirical designs described to this point in the book; scholarship also includes thoughtful, systematic examinations of the impact, implications, and applications that researchers derive from reading the work of others. As in the companion text on research in rehabilitation counseling (Rumrill & Bellini, 2018), we have organized this chapter around categories reflecting the overarching purposes of selected narrative literature reviews. Although narrative literature reviews can address virtually any topic, in this chapter we describe narrative literature reviews that address four important purposes in special education scholarship: theory or model-building articles, treatises on complicated or controversial issues, informational reports and "how-to" strategies to enhance professional practice, and explanations of emerging and important issues.

THEORY OR MODEL-BUILDING

A recurring and important theme of this book is that theory both prompts and results from scientific inquiry. Theory provides the conceptual basis on which investigators deduce the specific relationships among variables or propositions that are evaluated by use of empirical observations drawn from particular samples. In many cases, the results of scientific efforts to test theory-based propositions lead researchers to suggest modifications in existing theories, thereby adding new knowledge that transcends the findings of a particular investigation. Theory also serves to bridge the "qualitative vs. quantitative" dichotomy; theory is, by definition, grounded in a qualitative understanding of human phenomena. Theory evolves and advances based on empirical evaluation of theory-based predictions in research studies. Narrative literature reviews can be used to synthesize related research in order to develop and refine theory.

The field of special education, like the social sciences in general, does not have a unifying theoretical base on which student services, teachers' professional identities, and preservice training are founded. It is our impression that a range of social scientific theories provide a menu of sorts from which special educators choose when considering their individual practices in the context of broader explanations of human behavior. Indeed, we believe that there is no need for the field of special education to develop a single overarching explanatory framework for the profession. We do, however, believe that it is imperative for our field to become more aware of the use and application of theory as it applies to both practice and research. With that in mind, we highlight in the forthcoming paragraphs two recent literature reviews that advanced theories or models to explain phenomena bearing on the education of children with disabilities.

For example, Hornby (2015) conducted a non-systematic review of the literature to unify the approaches of inclusive and exclusive special education services under a single framework of inclusive special education. Beginning with a brief description of the current state of special education in Great Britain and the United States, Hornby carefully described opposing schools of thought related to inclusion while clarifying key terms along the way. By acclimating the reader to the purpose of the article and the terminology, Hornby focused the reader on the main problem before discussing the historical, political, and logistical underpinnings. Hornby described much of the contemporary research while addressing the many ways in which inclusive and exclusive services have been characterized in academic texts. Hornby addressed important concepts by quoting key texts and carefully contextualizing the ways in which opposing factions each make their case. Though Hornby was clearly arguing for a unified model of inclusion and special education as the solution to great divisions in the rights and services of individuals with disabilities, he was careful not to belittle or degrade either side as wrong, illfounded, or inappropriate. Hornby's unified model acknowledges the value in the arguments for each side and proposes an imperfect framework that addresses extant evidence, practice, and legal issues in special education.

In 2017, a team of scholars interested in self-determination for children and adults with disabilities introduced a novel theory to help frame supports and interventions that specifically target self-determination as both a goal and a skill (Shogren et al., 2017). Shogren and colleagues began by tracing the history of self-determination theory and research from the early 1970s through the present day. They described several landmark studies and government sponsored initiatives aimed at bolstering the ability of individuals with disabilities to exercise their own life choices and hard fought rights. The article draws specific attention to a series of studies leading to self-determination as a key aspect of special education in secondary schools and post-secondary transition planning. Throughout the review, Shogren and colleagues strongly reiterated the case for self-determination in special education and identified shortcomings in current theory. They went on to propose a "reconceptualized" model of self-determination they called, "Causal Agency Theory" (p. 255). Causal Agency Theory seeks to broaden both the functional and conceptual understanding of self-determination by explaining how one becomes self-determined and the mechanisms by which interventions and supports may support development of self-determination. As a reconceptualization, Causal Agency Theory is poised to refocus both practice and research surrounding self-determination as a specific skill through goal setting and strategic interventions.

TREATISES ON COMPLICATED OR CONTROVERSIAL TOPICS

Another important role of narrative literature reviews in special education research is to identify, explain, and provide perspectives on complicated or controversial issues in the lives of children with disabilities and special education professionals. Typically, these treatises begin by tracing the history of the issue, then proceed with a description of the issue's current status and its implications for policy and practice. Finally, authors often conclude with recommendations regarding how to best address the issue, sometimes accompanied by a "call to action" for policymakers, practitioners, parents, advocates, and/or people with disabilities themselves.

For example, Bottiani and colleagues (2017) conducted a systematic literature review to explore evidence regarding the use of culturally responsive practices in the context of teacher inservice training. With increased attention to issues of disproportionality and educational outcomes among historically marginalized groups (including students with disabilities), the literature base surrounding culturally responsive practices has grown dramatically. Bottiani and colleagues recognize the need to periodically take stock of the depth, breadth, and quality of evidence in order to draw attention to gaps in the literature and highlight any substantive methodological shortcomings. In the case of culturally responsive practices, the research team determined the evidence base to be considerably weaker than previously assumed. Of the 179 studies identified, only 10 studies met basic inclusion criteria, and all 10 of those studies failed to meet minimum standards for efficacy, effectiveness, and dissemination. Bottiani and colleagues found insufficient evidence to draw any causal inference between culturally responsive inservice training and any meaningful outcomes. Furthermore, the research team was able to pinpoint a, "lack of consistent, integrated, psychometrically sound measurement approaches," as a major barrier (Bottiani et al., 2017, p. 382). This information serves as a call to employ more rigorous research designs and build consensus around common definitions and research methods.

Bottiani and colleagues' work is particularly relevant in the area of special education given the recent attention drawn to the issue of representation of students from racial minority groups in special education. Over the last several years, this topic has been hotly debated in the pages of peer reviewed journals including a series of articles published from 2015 to 2017 in *Educational Researcher*. In hopes of settling the debate, Morgan and colleagues (2017) conducted a systematic review of the best available evidence on the topic (i.e., studies that analyzed individual-level data, involved a nationally representative sample, and controlled for individual-level academic achievement). After an exhaustive literature search, researchers identified 22 studies that met their inclusion criteria. Though a meta-analysis would typically be used in this scenario, the research team opted for a narrative synthesis because, "very few features of design, analysis, and type of covariate adjustment, and samples were common across studies" (Morgan et al., 2017, p. 185), essentially making any quantitative meta-analysis impossible with the given data. Using an integrative, best-evidence methodology, the research team (a) identified studies that fit a priori inclusion criteria, (b) reported effect sizes from reviewed studies, and (c) reported any substantive methodological issues with each study. The researchers carefully coded studies and reported each methodological step necessary for replication by independent researchers. Despite a long history of Black children being overrepresented in special education, results of the review overwhelmingly suggested that Black children were less likely to receive special education services when compared to *otherwise similar* White children. Though the study was well conceived and carefully executed from a scientific perspective, the publication of this study certainly did not close the debate on representation of minority students. Nevertheless, it is an important addition to the larger discussion and empirical study of the impact of race in special education services.

INFORMATIONAL REPORTS AND "HOW-TO" STRATEGIES

One of the most fundamental roles of the research literature in special education is to provide information that can assist educators and practitioners in advancing contemporary standards of best practice. To that end, many journals in our field contain a wealth of "how-to" strategies to improve educational programs and services for people with disabilities.

For instance, Stevenson and Reed (2017) conducted a nonsystematic review of the literature to synthesize evidence on the topic of intensive instruction to help teachers operationalize key factors associated with improved achievement. Though the concept of intensifying instruction is commonly understood as a means of increasing the likelihood of effectiveness, it is often unclear exactly what it means to intensify instruction. After examining the literature on intensifying instruction, Stevenson and Reed distilled the best available evidence into eight actionable variables teachers can use in the planning and delivery of intensive instruction: (a) altering dosage, (b) reducing size of instructional groups, (c) increasing engagement, (d) increasing frequency and specificity of feedback, (e) improving motivation, (f) optimizing the fit between instruction and student needs, (g) changing the instructional delivery, and (h) using culturally responsive instruction. Each variable is clearly defined and presented with examples, along with a comprehensive planning guide to help teachers change instruction in meaningful, systematic ways. Stevenson and Reed not only communicated critical information on the research surrounding intensive instruction, but also provided a guide for teachers to effectively intensify instruction. This is a prime example of how current research can be distilled into steps that are meaningful to teachers in the field.

Similarly, Powell and Fuchs (2018) conducted a nonsystematic review of research on mathematical reasoning in the context of word problems as the basis for their discussion of pitfalls and alternatives to teaching the classic keyword strategy for problem solving in mathematics. Beginning with a nonsystematic review of the typical use of keywords and mathematics instruction in elementary classrooms, Powell and Fuchs showed many ways in which instruction focused on keywords can often lead to incorrect answers and larger mathematical misconceptions, complete with detailed examples that are easily relateable to real world classrooms. By walking the reader through examples, Powell and Fuchs built a strong case for attack strategies (i.e., in which students apply a series of steps to solve word problems) and schema instruction (i.e., in which students categorize word problems within problem types or schemas and apply a solution strategy for each schema) as robust and effective alternatives to keyword approaches. The reader is not only left with clear, thorough recommendations of what to do and what not to do, but can easily follow the included citations for more detailed information on the supporting research.

Graham, Harris, and Santangelo (2015) conducted a nonsystematic literature review regarding teaching writing to struggling learners (they identified experimental and qualitative studies of writing instruction for struggling learners included in over 20 previous literature reviews). The purpose of their review was to describe how evidence on effective writing instruction can be operationalized to best help struggling learners meet writing objectives specified in Common Core State Standards. Evidence accumulated over more than 30 years of research suggests that learning to write involves a complex set of discrete skills, background knowledge, social/contextual information, and cognitive/motivational information. Using a combination of meta-analyses and meta-syntheses (i.e., syntheses of qualitative studies), the authors summarized the available evidence to create a set of evidence-based practices that can serve as a solid foundation for writing instruction in grades K-8. By summarizing each of the major subsets of writing research (by research design and method), the authors created a comprehensive set of recommendations that are broad enough to span multiple content areas and grade levels, yet narrow enough to yield specific action for teachers: create a writing environment that is positive and supportive; establish writing routines that create a pleasant and motivating writing environment; implement a process approach to writing, create routines that ensure students write frequently; design instructional routines where students compose together; establish goals for students' writing; use twenty-first century writing tools; provide feedback; ensure students acquire needed writing skills, knowledge, and strategies; teach foundational writing skills; increase students' knowledge about writing; teach students strategies for planning, drafting, revising, and editing; and use writing as a tool to support students' learning.

Many other articles have presented strategies and guidelines for special education practitioners to expand their assessment and intervention repertoires. Though the results of a given study may be interesting in and of themselves, the vast majority of special education research is driven by a desire to positively impact the lives of students, families, and teachers in meaningful ways. Synthesizing research into recommendations and actionable steps for practice ensures that researchers' efforts (a) stay connected with the realities of students and schools, and (b) help research consumers to better understand the implications of research studies that can often seem arcane, abstract, or excessively narrow. As the examples above clearly show, narrative literature reviews provide a useful mechanism for gaining a global understanding of the collective evidence, providing direction for future research, and translating research to practice.

EXPLANATIONS OF EMERGING AND IMPORTANT ISSUES

A final category of articles that synthesize existing literature and present new perspectives pertains to examining and explaining important and emerging issues facing the special education field. These articles address such issues as the roles and functions of special education professionals, new developments in the policies that govern special education, and the changing needs of people with disabilities in a technologically advanced information age.

Speaking of technology, Newman Thomas and colleagues (2019) conducted a review of literature to examine emerging issues in regard to special education technology, teacher preparation, law, and public policy. The authors described disjunctures among the services students require (and are afforded by federal law), policy, teacher training, and the pace of technological and political change. The breakneck pace of technological change in schools and many workplace environments, as well as in society at large, has placed enormous pressure on special educators to infuse technology into a system that already struggles to meet the basic legal and educational outcomes with which it is charged. As the authors pointed out, aside from a few key legal rulings, federal law governing special education has not been updated since 2004. And, given the speed of technological change and innovation, 15 years is an extraordinarily long time, particularly considering that technology companies regularly plan for hardware obsolescence after less than two years and routinely end software support after less than five years. Newman Thomas and colleagues noted that organizations such as the Council for Exceptional Children and the International Society for Technology in Education are in a nearly perpetual fight to keep guidelines for professional training in line with current technologies. And yet, the gap between federal law and the reality of modern classrooms continues to grow. The authors highlighted important issues and described reasonable steps that can be taken to better align the systems of teacher training, law, and service to students (e.g., comply with law and policy, access professional development, use data to address research limitations, and select evidence-based practices). Additionally, the authors directed readers to several resources to help teachers and policy makers make use of current evidence to make informed decisions on behalf of students. This article is an excellent example of the ways in which examination of current evidence can help distill extraordinarily complicated topics such as law, special education, and technology into a collection of streamlined tasks and resources with high potential for positive change.

Determining what is known about effective instruction in special education is neither straightforward nor simple. To better understand the development of criteria and procedures for identifying effective practices in special education, Cook, Tankersley, Cook, and Landrum (2015) conducted a nonsystematic review of the criteria and procedures for identifying evidence-based practices in three different but related fields (clinical psychology, school psychology, and general education). They found that, for the most part, all of these fields focused on similar areas when evaluating scientific support for a particular practice. Procedures and criteria from all of the disciplines addressed issues related to research design; methodological quality; magnitude of effects; and, with the exception of school psychology, quantity of studies. Cook and colleagues also documented the substantial controversy and criticism that has surrounded the development of criteria and procedures for determining evidence-based practices in these other fields. Criteria and procedures have been criticized for being either too stringent or too flexible; for overreliance on randomized clinical trials (which are difficult to conduct in applied settings); for being too difficult and confusing; and for failing to generate clear and useful information about what works. The authors suggested that many of these controversial issues do not have clear-cut answers. Consequently, developing procedures and criteria for evidence-based practices inevitably requires balancing the benefits of more stringent criteria (e.g., confidence in the effectiveness of an intervention, clear distinctions between effective and ineffective interventions) with the benefits of somewhat flexible criteria (e.g., not automatically excluding potentially useful research). The authors also pointed out the importance of recognizing that effectiveness is not dichotomous (yes/no), but continuous (more or less effective). Implementing evidence-based special education practices in schools also requires professional judgment, although that judgment must be constrained by findings from reliable research.

Because every issue in special education has a historical context, calling any issue "emerging" is potentially misleading. Indeed, special education's most fundamental issues—what it should be, where it should take place, how it should be done—have been described as perpetual (Bateman, 1994). Despite an enormous volume of research being conducted in special education, none of the afformentioned issues have been settled or are likely to be settled anytime soon. However, with each new scientific study, and with each review of the extant literature, another piece is added to the puzzle, enabling scholars and practitioners to make more informed decisions concerning the services, rights, and outcomes of students with disabilities.

SUMMARY

Narrative literature reviews, both systematic and nonsystematic, make significant contributions to the theory and practice of special education. Synthesizing findings from across multiple studies brings forth new perspectives from comprehensive analyses of existing research in areas such as those discussed in this chapter, and has helped the special education profession to:

1. Build theoretical models on which to base practices;
2. Analyze and, in some cases, reconcile controversial issues in the lives of children with disabilities;
3. Develop important skills related to the delivery of responsive, effective services; and
4. Stay abreast of emerging issues in our dynamic field.

Because literature reviews involve synthesizing findings from across multiple studies, they represent an efficient way to access empirically-based recommendations for policy and practice in special education.

Chapter 9

ANATOMY OF A RESEARCH ARTICLE AND GUIDELINES FOR CRITIQUE

INTRODUCTION

In this chapter, we examine the sections of a research article and provide guidelines for conducting critical analyses of published works. Drawn from the American Psychological Association's (2013) *Publication Manual* and related descriptions in other research design texts (Goodwin & Goodwin, 2012; Heppner et al., 2015; Kazdin, 2017; Rumrill, Cook, & Wiley, 2011), general descriptions of each component of a research article are followed (section-by-section) by a reprinted article from the special education literature. We conclude the chapter with a framework that university instructors, graduate students, and rehabilitation practitioners can use in critiquing research articles on the basis of their scientific merits and practical utility.

SECTIONS OF A RESEARCH ARTICLE

The American Psychological Association (APA, 2013) presents guidelines for authors to follow in composing manuscripts for publication in professional journals as well as detailed standards for quantitative (Applebaum et al., 2018), qualitative, meta-analytic, and mixed methods (Levitt et al., 2018) research. Most journals in education and disability studies adhere to those style and formatting guidelines. When crafting a research article, authors are encouraged to refer to these documents both as helpful style guides and as a mechanism for ensuring that scientific findings are clearly and thoroughly reported. In the paragraphs to follow, descriptions of each section of a standard research article are presented: Title, Abstract, Method, Results, Discussion, and References. Following our generalized descriptions of each section, we have reprinted verbatim sections of an empirical article by Stevenson and Mussalow (2018). This article is reprinted from a 2018 issue of the *Journal of Positive Behavior Interventions, Volume 21*(3), pages 171–180, with the kind permission of IOS Press.

Title

As with other kinds of literature, the title of a journal article is a very important feature. At the risk of contravening the "You can't judge a book by its cover" maxim, we believe that most articles in special education journals are either read or not read based upon the prospective reader's consideration of the title. Hence, a clear, concise title that provides the article's key concepts, hypotheses, methods, and variables under study is critical. A standard-length title for a journal article in the social sciences is 12-15 words, including a sub-title if appropriate. Social science indexing systems, which track and categorize journal articles by topic area, rely heavily on titles in their codification systems. Such information is key in modern online search tools and databases. Therefore, if authors want other scholars to be directed to their works, they must carefully compose a title that reflects the article without distractive or irrelevant descriptors. Stevenson and Mussalow (2018, p. 137) presented the following title, within the 12–15 word convention:

"The Effects of Planning, Goal Setting, and Performance Feedback
on Avoidance Behaviors for Struggling Readers"

Before we move into descriptions of the text of a research article, we want to briefly address the concept of technical writing as it applies to the composition of academic manuscripts. Journals adhering to the APA's (2013) publication guidelines favor manuscripts that are written in direct, uncomplicated sentences. Editors prefer that text be written in the "active voice" whenever possible. That is, sentences should begin with their subjects and follow with verbs and objects (e.g., "The researcher conducted an experiment" rather than "An experiment was conducted by the researcher"). In the name of concise communication, extraneous phrases and clauses that add words to the sentence without enhancing the overall statement should be avoided (e.g., "In order to . . . ," "For purposes of . . . ," "As far as . . . is concerned . . ."). Technical writing is also marked by the sparing use of adverbs (e.g., very, somewhat, strikingly) and adjectives that do not serve to further define or specify the terms that they are modifying (e.g., interesting, important, good, noteworthy).

Organization is another critical element of an effectively composed journal article, with multi-level headings serving to guide the flow of text and keep the reader on track. For authoritative information regarding the style and formatting guidelines for submitting manuscripts to most journals in social science fields, readers should consult the APA's (2013) *Publication Manual.*

For a more literary perspective on technical writing, readers should consider the following composition guidelines that were first presented in George Orwell's (1946, 1982) *Politics and the English Language:*

1. Never use a metaphor, simile, or other figure of speech which you are used to seeing in print.
2. Never use a long word where a short one will do.
3. If it is possible to cut a word out, always cut it out.
4. Never use the passive (voice) where you can use the active.
5. Never use a foreign phrase, a scientific word, or jargon word if you can think of an everyday English equivalent.
6. Break any of these rules sooner than say anything outright barbarous (p. 170).

Abstract

Next to the title, the abstract is the most widely read section of a journal article (Rumrill & Bellini, 2018). In an empirical article, the abstract should be a succinct, 100-150-word summary of the investigation's key features, including background, objective, methods, results, and conclusions. Results of the study should be summarized in full in the abstract; authors should describe both significant and nonsignificant findings, not only those that upheld their hypotheses or expectations. The abstract serves as an "advance organizer" for the article, and it should include every important premise, method, and finding of the investigation. Like the "Preface" that commonly introduces readers to full-length textbooks, the abstract provides a thorough, albeit summary, glimpse of the contents of the article. In most instances, the title is what determines whether a reader will read the abstract; the abstract determines whether the reader will read the body of the article. Stevenson and Mussalow (2018, p. 137) prefaced their article with the following abstract:

> To improve reading achievement, teachers must ensure students actively engage in productive and meaningful reading tasks. Students with an established history of reading difficulty—including those with reading disabilities—may, over time, develop behaviors for passive and active avoidance of reading tasks. The current study explored the effects of a behavioral intervention on the latency to engagement in reading tasks for middle school students with (n = 3) and without (n = 3) reading disabilities. A multicomponent intervention using planning, goal setting, and performance feedback

was examined using a multiple baseline across participants design. Results of visual analysis indicated a functional relation between changes in latency and implementation of the intervention. Quantitative analysis indicated a strong overall effect that is statistically significant, Tau-U = −0.85, 95% CI = [−1, −0.61], $p < .01$. Limitations and recommendations for future research are discussed.

Introduction

Immediately following the abstract, the introductory section of the article sets the stage for the study upon which the article was based. It orients the reader to the problem or issue being addressed, develops the logic and rationale for conducting the investigation, and expresses the empirical hypotheses or research questions. Heppner et al. (2015) suggested that the introduction should answer questions such as why the topic is an important one to study, what previous work bears on the topic, how existing work logically connects to the author's research questions and/or hypotheses, how the question will be researched, and what predictions can be made.

To answer these questions, authors typically address three major elements in the introductory section of an article: (1) The Research Problem, (2) The Framework for the Study, and (3) The Research Questions and/or Hypotheses (Goodwin & Goodwin, 2012; Heppner et al., 2015). Although we will describe each introductory element in discrete, linear fashion in this text, it is important to point out that many (if not most) authors blend these considerations to fit the flow and logic of their respective manuscripts. The standards for writing in social sciences are generally more concerned with the inclusion of necessary information than with the order of such information. This is one area in which study authors have a modest degree of creative freedom in writing and communication.

The Research Problem

The very first sentences of an empirical journal article should draw the reader's attention to the scope, impact, and current status of the problem or issue being investigated. This initial orientation is most effectively achieved by applying the broadest-possible perspective to the concern. A study of a literacy intervention for third-graders with learning disabilities might be introduced by citing national statistics concerning reading and writing achievement for children with learning disabilities in the primary grades. An article describing the effects of a summer job placement intervention for secondary students with visual impairments or blindness might begin with a review of existing literature regarding the employment-preparation concerns and experiences of transition-age Americans who are blind or visually impaired.

The Framework for the Study

The specific theoretical and empirical framework for the particular investigation is typically the second part of the Introduction. Authors summarize existing literature related to the identified problem, and build a logical "case" for a study that addresses gaps or inconsistencies in the literature. The author(s) should present the theoretical or conceptual model that informs the inquiry and provides enough background to enable the reader to appreciate the rationale of the current study. This framework elucidates the purpose of the current study (e.g., to evaluate the effectiveness of a social skills intervention for middle school students with attention deficit/hyperactivity disorder), which is then operationalized in the research questions or hypotheses.

The Research Questions and Hypotheses

The Introduction section of a research article typically (or, often) concludes with a statement of the research questions and/or hypotheses that served to guide the study. A more speculative research question tends to be used in descriptive research designs (e.g., surveys, program evaluations, empirical literature reviews; see Chapter 6) or in qualitative studies (see Chapter 7). Examples of research questions could include: "What concerns do parents of children with disabilities have regarding social inclusion?" "What are the barriers to community participation faced by secondary students with chronic illnesses as they transition into adulthood?" and "What information and technical assistance do general education teachers need to meet the needs of included children with autism spectrum disorder?"

The hypothesis, on the other hand, is predictive by design. Its specificity is dependent upon the theory underlying it or previous, relevant research, but it should include the direction of the anticipated results whenever possible. Independent and dependent variables need not be operationalized in theory-based hypotheses (because this is done in the Method section), but the expected relationship among study variables must be clearly articulated. Examples of directional hypotheses could include: "Participation in a cognitive-behavioral stress management program will decrease symptom onset and magnification for children with behavior disorders," "Anxiety, depression, and low self-esteem will be collectively, negatively, and significantly related to perceptions of social capital for children with Type I diabetes mellitus," and "school administrators will evaluate the behavior of children with disability labels more negatively than they evaluate the same behavior of children without disability labels."

The introduction presented by Stevenson and Mussalow (2018, p. 171–172)—which effectively blends discussions of the research problem, the conceptual framework of the study, and research questions—is as follows:

The connection between academic engagement and positive learning outcomes has been well established in the research literature across several disciplines and contexts. The more time students spend engaged in academic tasks, the more likely they are to improve academically (Carini, Kuh, & Klein, 2006; Codding & Smyth, 2008; Fredricks, Blumenfeld, & Paris, 2004; Good & Beckerman, 1978; Greenwood, Horton, & Utley, 2002; Kuh, 2009; Marks, 2000; National Research Council, 2004). Engagement is a critical component of improving academic outcomes, particularly among students with considerable academic deficits, including those with disabilities (Carini et al., 2006; Hollowood, Salisbury, Rainforth, & Palombaro, 1994).

Students with persistent academic deficits may actively and/or passively avoid engagement in academic tasks (Neff, Hsieh, & Dejitterat, 2005). For example, a student may refuse to participate, therefore actively avoiding engagement in the activity; while another student may passively avoid participation by choosing to sit quietly and draw instead of participating. As early as first grade, academic deficits may impact critical school behaviors including task engagement and self-control (Morgan, Farkas, Tufis, & Sperling, 2008). It is not uncommon for students to avoid or delay assigned tasks by engaging in nonacademic behaviors (Codding & Smyth, 2008). Avoidance behaviors may include, but are not limited to, (a) extended transitions between activities, (b) sudden need to address bodily needs (e.g., using the restroom, getting a drink), (c) gathering materials, and (d) engaging in nonacademic conversation. Such behaviors enable students to avoid engagement with tasks in which they have previously struggled and/or avoid potential opportunities for failure (Neff et al., 2005).

Although some avoidance behaviors for children and adults may be ordinary and even typical (e.g., procrastination; Ferrari & Tice, 2000), avoidance of academic tasks in school carries an opportunity cost. Each opportunity in which a student avoids engagement reduces the time spent doing meaningful learning activities (Codding & Smyth, 2008). Over time, academic avoidance may result in a widening performance gap between struggling students and their same age peers, thus creating a *negative reinforcement trap* in which poor performance enables further avoidance behaviors and vice versa (Maag, 2001; Patterson, 1975).

For example, students with difficulty learning to read may be hesitant to engage in reading tasks. Struggling readers may find such tasks laborious, difficult, and unpleasant. Engagement in reading tasks in a classroom setting may draw attention to a relative area of weakness, making the student vulnerable to ridicule and stigma among peers (Neff et al., 2005; Ryan, Pintrich, & Midgley, 2001). Adolescents who struggle with reading may be particularly impacted, as aversion to reading tasks may be compounded by years of struggle and an increased reliance on reading-to-learn in older grades (Roberts, Torgesen, Boardman, & Scammacca, 2008). Furthermore, avoidance behaviors undermine teachers' attempts at remediation. Students cannot benefit from tasks in which they do not engage. Teachers therefore need effective ways to help students initiate and sustain engagement in assigned learning tasks.

It is important to note that although compliance and engagement are distinctly different behaviors, they are in many ways inextricably linked. When the focus is engaging students in academic tasks they tend to avoid, engagement and compliance are functionally equivalent. Each time a teacher directs a student to complete a task that is academically beneficial, compliance with the teacher's directions and task engagement are one and the same.

There have been a number of studies examining novel uses of existing practices and interventions to help improve compliance and academic engagement. Interventions, such as precorrection and active supervision (De Pry & Sugai, 2002), high-probability (high-p) request sequences (Banda & Kubina, 2009; Wehby & Hollahan, 2000), and teacher greetings (Allday, Bush, Ticknor, & Walker, 2011), along with technologies such as sound field amplification (SFA) systems (Losinski, Sanders, Katsiyannis, & Wiseman, 2017; Maag & Anderson, 2007), have each been shown to generally improve compliance with teachers' directions and reduce delays in engagement. These strategies use verbal prompts as antecedents to desired behaviors, take little to no planning, and can integrate with other positive behavioral supports and classroom management practices (Lane, Menzies, Ennis, & Bezdek, 2013).

Effective behavioral supports not only reinforce immediate compliance with teacher directions but also may lead to the long-term development of prosocial skills, such as planning ahead and self-regulation. In the short term, teachers need strategies that will enable students to engage in assignments without delay. In the long term, students need to develop a set of skills and strategies they can use to engage in tasks that may be undesirable, but are nonetheless beneficial (Gettinger & Seibert, 2002). Unfortunately, there are few empirical studies that describe such interventions as they relate to classroom transitions and academic engagement.

One study conducted by Stevenson (2016) attempted to address the proximal and distal goals of behavioral interventions for transition time between activities by developing an intervention based on core elements of self-regulation and self-regulated learning (Lavik, 2014; Schunk, 1985, 1990; Zimmerman, 2000). Through a brief intervention in which students created a plan for classroom transitions and set goals for transition time, the research team attempted to reduce transition time between classroom activities. The study included four middle school students with a history of reading problems and employed a multiple-baseline design across participants. The researchers measured latency between the completion of teacher's directions and engagement in assigned tasks over several weeks.

Although Stevenson (2016) argued in favor of a functional relation between changes in transition time and the implementation of planning and goal setting, results are best characterized as inconclusive. Considerable instability in baseline and intervention phases, along with positive interven-

tion phase trends in two of four participants, make it difficult to confident-
ly conclude a functional relation exists. The questionable intervention effects may be attributable to elements of the intervention. Although planning
and goal setting are indeed key components in a variety of established behavioral and academic interventions (Cleary & Zimmerman, 2004; Meece,
Anderman, & Anderman, 2006; Page-Voth & Graham, 1999), it is rare to
see them used without a mechanism for feedback or reinforcement. Failure
to include a structured consequence (e.g., feedback or reinforcement) limits
the likelihood of control over the target behavior and leaves open the possibility for students to experience an aversive event that could ultimately
undermine the goals of limiting transition time and improving task engagement.

A more successful intervention would likely include a mechanism
whereby planning and goal setting are followed by specific feedback on students' engagement or duration of transitions. Specific feedback would
enable students to (a) self-evaluate performance relative to established goals,
(b) adjust behavior based on past performance, and (c) provide a mechanism by which students can adjust daily goals based on a nonarbitrary level
of performance.

The current study builds on the work of Stevenson (2016) by replicating the conditions of study (e.g., similar setting and participants) and ex-
tending the intervention to include planning + goal setting + performance
feedback. We hypothesized that adding a mechanism for performance feedback would improve students' awareness of their performance relative to
classroom expectations, provide a mechanism for students to adjust behavior to meet goals more readily, limit student avoidance behaviors, and ultimately result in students beginning assigned reading tasks more quickly.
The current study attempted to answer the following question: What is the
effect of an intervention comprised of planning + goal setting + performance feedback on the latency to engagement in reading tasks for students
with significant reading deficits?

Method

The Method section delineates how the research questions were addressed and/or how the hypotheses were tested. It should provide the reader with sufficient information so that another researcher could replicate the
investigation. Because the Method section is the primary source for determining the validity of the study (see Chapter 5), the quality and clarity of
this section is generally regarded as the strongest determinant of whether an
empirically-based manuscript will be accepted for publication (Heppner et
al., 2015).

Although the type and order of sub-sections found in the Method section of a research article vary depending upon the design of the study and
the author's judgment related to the flow of text, most articles include de-

scriptions of the study's subjects/participants, instruments/measures/variables, materials, design, and procedures.

Subjects/Participants

According to Heppner et al. (2015), the Method section should include (a) total number of subjects and numbers assigned to groups, if applicable, (b) how subjects were selected and/or assigned, and (c) demographic and other characteristics of the sample relevant to the study's purpose. Some authors also include a description of the population from which the study sample was drawn, an indication of the representativeness of the sample vis a vis the broader population, the circumstances under which subjects participated (e.g., whether they were compensated, what risks they assumed), statistical power analyses, and response rates (if applicable).

Instruments/Measures/Variables

The Method section must include a detailed description of how all study variables were operationalized, measured, scored, and interpreted. All instruments or measures that were used in sampling, conducting the study, and evaluating results must be specified in terms of content (number of items, response sets), how measures were administered, scoring procedures, relationship to study variables, and psychometric properties (reliability and validity). Authors should also include a rationale for selecting each instrument, i.e., why that instrument was the best choice for measuring a particular construct.

Materials

Researchers should also include a description of any materials that were used to carry out the investigation. Written guides for participants, instructional manuals, media or technology, and scientific apparatus or equipment should be noted in detail. Authors may also be asked to provide direct access to supplementary materials as a part of the manuscript submission. Many journals now embed links to access materials directly in digital publications. Some authors, especially those who conducted reliability and validity studies with psychometric instruments, include a description of the setting in which the study was executed and data were collected.

Design

One of the most important features of the Method section is a clear description of the design of the study. This is essential because the design serves as the link between (a) the research questions/hypotheses and the scientific procedures used in carrying out the study, and (b) the findings of the study and how these are interpreted. Authors typically label their designs in terms of how variables were manipulated, observed, and analyzed. Thereby, the design is the unifying force in connecting the research objectives to the results and to the knowledge claim that is made. To every extent possible, a direct reference to the hypotheses should be made when authors identify the design of a particular investigation. For example, Rumrill, Roessler, and Denny (1997, p. 7) described their design as follows: "The researchers selected a three-group, posttest-only (experimental) design to assess the intervention's univariate and multivariate effects on (a) self-reported attitudes (situational self-efficacy and acceptance of disability), and (b) participation in the accommodation request process."

Procedures

The most important component of the Method section is the easiest to describe. In chronological order, authors simply list every step they took in developing, administering, and evaluating the study. Beginning with initial recruitment of participants, following the study through collection of the last datum, and including everything in-between, the Procedures subsection should provide the reader with a step-by-step protocol that could serve as a guide for replicating the study. Descriptions of any interventions should be provided in detail, along with summaries of the qualifications of project personnel who were instrumental in executing the investigation. Procedures should also include how the investigation was concluded and a statement of any debriefing or follow-up services provided to participants.

In aggregate, the Method section comprises the most important information found in a research article. Stevenson and Mussalow (2018, p. 173-176) captured the essence of a thorough and detailed Method section. It follows below:

Participants

The participating teacher was one of two reading intervention teachers at the participating school. Of the two eligible teachers, one teacher volunteered to participate in the study. The participating teacher was a Caucasian 43-year-old female, with 10 years of experience and a master's degree in education.

All participants were selected through a combination of teacher recommendation and structured observations by researchers. The teacher initially identified 10 students for participation based on a history of excessive transition times between activities and difficulty "getting started" in daily activities. All students were native English speakers with a documented history of avoidance of academic tasks (e.g., discipline records indicating non-compliance). Examples of common avoidance behaviors included using the restroom at the start of independent work time, asking to go to their locker, spending excessive time gathering materials, sharpening a pencil, and talking to classmates. The classroom teacher stated she typically expected students to transition from whole-group instruction to independent work in 30 to 60 s. She further stated that 80% to 90% of students in class transitioned in less than 1 min each day.

After obtaining parental consent for seven participants, the researchers conducted baseline observations to verify each student exhibited delays in engagement with assigned reading tasks. To estimate conservatively, researchers tripled the teacher's recommended transition time, setting 3 min as a cut point for excessive delays. Researchers observed baseline transition times of greater than 3 min for six of the seven recommended participants. After six observations, researchers observed zero instances of excessive transition time for one participant. As researchers were unable to verify demonstration of the target behaviors, the student was excluded from the reminder of the study. Six participants were retained.

School staff selected students for the reading intervention class based on the school's regularly administered gated battery of reading assessments. All students demonstrated scores of *below proficient* on statewide reading assessments for the previous school year, scores at or below the 15th percentile in reading fluency as measured by AIMSweb® Reading-Curriculum Based Measure (R-CBM), and below a score of 850 Lexile® points as measured by Scholastic® Reading Inventory (SRI). A score or 850 or below indicates a student's reading level is at or below approximately a fifth-grade equivalent. Data from students' SRI (assessed monthly) and R-CBM assessments were used to monitor students' reading improvement and ensure instruction was appropriately fit to each students' reading level.

Ana was a 13-year-old African American female in seventh grade. She was diagnosed with a learning disability (LD) in reading comprehension. Ana scored 102 WPM (12th percentile) in reading fluency using R-CBM and a Lexile® score of 715 (early fourth grade) in reading comprehension on SRI.

Carmen was a 13-year-old Latina (female) student in seventh grade. She was diagnosed with a LD in reading comprehension. Carmen was assessed at 97 WPM (10th percentile) in reading fluency and a Lexile® score of 685 (late third grade) in reading comprehension on SRI.

Maya was a 13-year-old Latina (female) student in seventh grade with no diagnosed disability. She scored 98 WPM as assessed by R-CBM and a Lexile® score of 690 (late third grade) in reading comprehension on SRI.

Lara was a 12-year-old Caucasian female student in seventh grade with no diagnosed disability. Lara scored 92 WPM (8th percentile) in reading fluency and a Lexile® score of 655 (mid third grade) on SRI.

Nora was a 13-year-old multiracial female in seventh grade with a diagnosed LD in reading comprehension. She scored 90 WPM (7th percentile) in reading fluency and a Lexile® of 640 (mid third grade) on SRI.

Rachel was a 12-year-old Caucasian female student in seventh grade with no diagnosed LD. Rachel scored 108 WPM (14th percentile) in reading fluency and a Lexile® of 750 (mid fourth grade) on SRI.

Ana, Carmen, and Nora each received special education services in the form of resource room Language Arts instruction. All three were diagnosed for special education services prior to entering middle school. Detailed information regarding students' individualized education programs was not available to researchers as a part of the current study.

Setting

The setting for this study was a middle school in a suburban school district in the Midwest. At the time of the study, enrollment included 478 students in seventh and eighth grade. Student population included 37.0% Caucasian, 27.5% African American, 18.9% Hispanic/Latino, 4.4% Asian, and 11.8% of students classified as two or more races. Approximately 15.4% of students received special education services, and 55.7% of students resided in households qualifying for free or reduced-price school lunch.

Data collection and intervention took place across two daily class periods of a reading intervention class taught by one teacher. All reading instruction was conducted using the *READ180©* program from Scholastic Inc. The *READ180©* is a comprehensive reading program that implements a mix of whole-class instruction, small-group instruction, independent reading, and computer-based instruction. As is typical with *READ180©*, all class sessions began with a brief (10–15 min) whole-class lesson that included a shared reading passage and explicit instruction in a specific literacy skill. Students then split into groups (based on the daily objectives and students' progress toward goals within the *READ180©* program) and transitioned to one of three stations. Students remained at each station for approximately 20 min before rotating to the next stations (e.g., computer-based activities, independent reading, or small-group instruction). Each class lasted approximately 1 hr. The teacher kept time for each rotation and provided warnings when there was approximately 2 min remaining before the next rotation.

Target Behaviors and Definitions

The current study examined initiation of engagement in teacher assigned reading tasks. The following definitions and directions were derived from prior research on latency and engagement for struggling readers (Stevenson, 2016). Assigned reading tasks included engagement in independent reading, small-group reading instruction, and computer-based activities using interactive software. The time between the completion of directions given by the teacher and engagement in the assigned task (latency) was measured. The teachers' directions were defined as complete when the teacher showed the daily rotation schedule, said, "Get started," and gave no further group directions within the next 10 s. Directions were also considered complete if the teacher spoke to another individual during the 10-s period but was not directly addressing the full class. Students were considered engaged in assigned tasks when one of the following conditions was met. For computer assignments, the student was engaged after successfully logging on to the interactive software and looking at the computer screen for a minimum of 10 consecutive seconds. Students assigned to independent reading were considered engaged when seated with their selected book open and looking at the book for a minimum of 10 consecutive seconds. For students assigned to small-group instruction, engagement was defined as being seated at the center table with their workbook open to the assigned page and looking directly at the teacher or the workbook for 10 consecutive seconds. For the group instruction definition, the *or* provision was included to ensure latency times would be unaffected if the teacher were delayed in getting to the table to begin instruction.

All timings were completed using a multiple timer app for iPad. Timers were started simultaneously at the conclusion of teacher's directions. Timers were stopped individually as each student was observed engaging in the defined behaviors. Timers were also stopped if transition times exceeded 10 min, which equates to 50% or more of the time allotted for the assigned tasks.

Procedures

The study used a multiple baseline across participants design. This design was selected to replicate the design of prior research conducted by Stevenson (2016). Data were collected concurrently for all participants. Design included two phases: (a) baseline and (b) intervention, consisting of planning + goal setting + performance feedback.

Baseline Condition

During the baseline condition, latency between the conclusion of the teacher's directions and engagement in assigned reading tasks was observed without intervention or interference with existing instructional rules, routines, procedures, or instruction. All class sessions followed lessons from the *READ180©* program manual. Typical procedures included students entering the classroom; gathering their program workbook, independent reading book, pencil, any other necessary materials; and then completing a brief *bell-work* assignment. Bell-work assignments consisted of brief writing prompts or questions students were expected to respond to in writing immediately at the start of class. The teacher required students to be engaged in the bell-work by the time the bell sounded over the school audio system indicating the start of class. Students were typically given 3 to 5 min to complete bell-work. The teacher then began a 10 to 15 min whole-class lesson. Following the whole-class lesson, students were dismissed to an assigned station as described above. The classroom teacher predetermined the assignments, activities, and group composition each day and posted a schedule of groups and activities at the front of the room.

Planning + Goal Setting + Performance Feedback

To facilitate shorter latency between the teacher's directions and engagement in assigned tasks, the researchers used a three-part intervention consisting of planning + goal setting + performance feedback. The intervention was designed to be implemented in a classroom setting with one or more students at a time. To support transition times for multiple students, procedures were not individualized to be function-based, but nonetheless promoted robust, prosocial replacement behaviors.

Prior to the start of each class session, students entered the classroom and went directly to a table near the front of the room where they could easily see the schedule of activities and group assignments. Again, the classroom teacher predetermined the assignments, activities, and group composition. Each student was given a folder containing copies of a goal setting and planning template. Each time a student completed a template it was placed back into the same folder. A copy of the template used for planning + goal setting + performance feedback is included in Online Appendix A.

Using the posted schedule and the planning template, each student recorded the activity to which she assigned. Students then listed all the required materials they would need for the assigned activity (e.g., pencil, reading log, independent reading book). Next, students set a time goal for the duration of the transition. Each student set goals independently. Neither the classroom teacher nor researchers commented on or assisted students with goal setting. The teacher was present to ensure students completed all required parts of the intervention, but did not provide any judgment, evaluation, or comments related to the appropriateness of students' goals. The teacher's interaction with students during planning and goal setting were limited to verbal or visual prompts to ensure all parts were complete. If an intervention session required prompts from the teacher, it was recorded as a part of the assessment of fidelity of implementation.

To provide performance feedback to students, the classroom teacher recorded each student's latency to task engagement on a copy of the planning and goal setting form to be used in the next class session. Times were recorded in the section marked, "Previous Transition Timing" (Online Appendix A). Access to prior latency timings enabled students to view their performance from the previous day and consider such times in setting a new goal. Students were also required to compare their previous goal with the actual transition time recorded and circle "yes" or "no" indicating whether they had met their goal. The teacher and researchers did not comment on students' performance relative to goals.

All intervention sessions lasted less than 2 min. Most intervention sessions began prior to the start of class (as indicated by school-wide tardy bell) and extended into the beginning of class for less than 60 s. Intervention sessions began with a single participant. Additional participants were added to the intervention group, consistent with multiple-baseline design across participants.

Immediately before beginning their first intervention session, each participant engaged in a brief pre-intervention training session that lasted approximately 3 min. During pre-intervention training, the teacher explained the purpose and step-by-step procedures for the intervention. The teacher then asked the student to summarize the rationale and state the steps to the intervention. If the student made a mistake in the summary or retelling of steps, the teacher repeated the information in its correct form and asked the student to try again. All six participants were able to explain the rationale and recite the steps to completing the intervention in two or fewer attempts.

Teacher Training

Approximately 3 days prior to the start of the intervention phase for the first participant, the classroom teacher was trained to complete the intervention. Training included definition and explanation of target behaviors including examples and nonexamples, step-by-step explanation and demonstration of intervention procedures, and guided practice. The classroom teacher was also given a copy of the intervention fidelity checklist. Researchers had the classroom teacher explain and demonstrate the full intervention sequence. Researchers then provided explicit feedback regarding the correct sequence and procedures. The classroom teacher demonstrated the intervention procedures correctly, in full, on the second attempt.

Treatment Fidelity

To ensure the intervention was delivered as intended, fidelity of intervention implementation was assessed for 32% of randomly selected sessions using an intervention fidelity checklist designed specifically for the current investigation (see Online Appendix B). Researchers directly observed whether teachers and students (a) listed the destination and tasks assigned for each classroom transition, (b) viewed timing data on transitions from the previous session, (c) set a goal based on timings from the previous session, and (d) completed the entire planning + goal setting + performance feedback intervention in less than 2 min. Intervention fidelity was 100% across all observed sessions.

Interobserver Agreement (IOA)

IOA for direct observation data was assessed by two independent observers. Prior to observations at the research site, all members of the research team participated in training observations. Training included explanation of the target behavior and observation procedures, examination of examples versus nonexamples of target behaviors, use of a multiple timer app for iPad, and practice observations via video examples. All observers achieved a minimum of 95% IOA with the primary observer before observing at the research site.

IOA was calculated for 30.2% (range = 25%–37% across students) of all observations in baseline and 55.6% (range = 24%–100% across students) of observations in intervention phase. IOA was calculated for baseline and intervention sessions by dividing the shortest of the two independently observed times by the longest of the two independently observed times. During baseline, mean IOA was 95% (range = 88%–99%). During planning + goal setting + performance feedback, mean IOA was 91% (range = 86%–97%).

Analysis

Primary analyses of the data were conducted using visual analysis. Graphed data were analyzed for changes in level, trend, and variability from baseline to intervention. Secondary analyses were conducted using quantitative effect size estimates. As baseline data showed instability, Tau-U was computed to yield a quantitative effect size (Parker, Vannest, Davis, & Sauber, 2011). Tau-U has several advantages over other commonly used single-case research effect size estimates including (a) strong statistical power which is advantageous for small data sets, (b) it is "distribution free" therefore can be used with any shaped distribution, (c) it is based on nonoverlap of data between phases consistent with visual analysis, and (d) problematic trends in baseline can be controlled to limit potential confounds in analysis including baseline data that are "very bouncy and hence very unreliable" (Parker & Vannest, 2012, p. 261).

Results

The Results section of a research article should include a complete inventory of all relevant findings obtained by the investigators. In articles that report quantitative studies (see Chapter 6), results are typically presented in two parts: summary, or descriptive, statistics related to participants' performance on whatever measures were taken (e.g., means, standard deviations, frequencies, percentages; see Chapter 3), and statistical analyses related to the specific hypotheses of the study (e.g., analysis of variance, multiple regression, factor analysis; see Chapter 3). We believe that all analyses conducted as part of the investigation should be reported in full, not only those that yielded statistically significant results. The *Publication Manual* of the APA (2013) provides considerable guidance related to how statistics should be presented in the Results section, but it does not provide adequate guidelines regarding *what* statistical information should be included. Heppner et al. (2015) identified a pattern in recent social science literature whereby researchers tend to err on the side of providing too little statistical information. Rumrill et al. (2011) expressed the same concern regarding contemporary special education research. Both sets of authors advocated for more complete presentations of statistical analyses in Results sections, especially regarding effect sizes which permit other researchers to compare findings across studies within a particular content domain.

It is also important to report statistics necessary to appropriately interpret effects. Though rarely the main focus of research, information such as confidence intervals and fit statistics may be necessary to fully understand the meaning and context of correlations or factor scores. Failure to report such information can lead to gross misinterpretation of results.

A quantitative Results section should be limited to the findings obtained by the researcher(s) in the current investigation. Speculation concerning what those findings mean in a larger context is reserved for the Discussion section.

The Results sections of qualitatively oriented articles display much more variety in the content and manner of presentation than is found in quantitative studies. Because the researcher's subjective interpretations help to shape the processes and outcomes of qualitative investigations (see Chapter 7), results are often framed in broad, interpretive contexts. In that regard, the lines between the Results and Discussion sections are often blurred in qualitative research.

Researchers (qualitative and quantitative) commonly use tables and figures to summarize and/or graphically depict their results. There is wide variability in terms of the content and presentation of tables and figures, with the most important universal requirement being easy interpretability for the reader. It is also important to note the use of tables and figures is not a replacement for in-text description of results. Tables and figures should be limited to those that supplement the text and/or provide information that is too cumbersome to adequately describe in the article narrative.

Stevenson and Mussalow (2018, p. 176–177) presented their results as follows:

Results

Visual analysis indicates three of the six participants showed distinct changes in latency to engagement in academic tasks following implementation of the intervention, while one student showed no substantive change. Data for two students are indeterminate (see Figure 1). Five of six participants showed changes in trend, and stability in the planning + goal setting + performance feedback condition versus baseline condition. Changes in latency were evident beginning with the first data point during planning + goal setting + performance feedback condition. Five participants demonstrated sustained and stable latency during the intervention phase. One of the six participants showed a nonsignificant reduction in mean and trend latency. During the intervention phase, three of the six participants achieved mean transition times at or below the teacher's expected transition times for all students (<60 s).

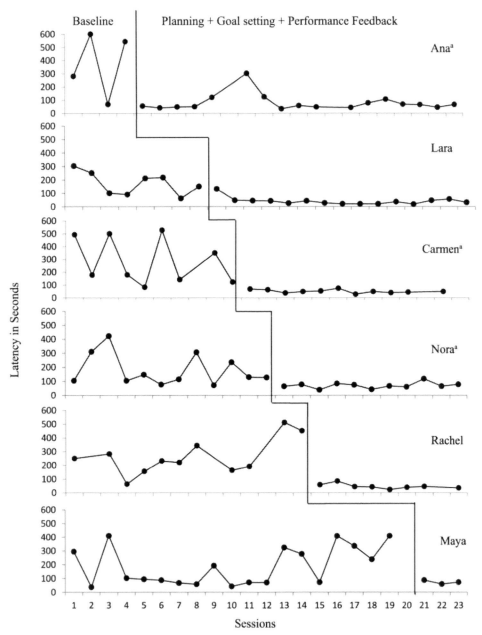

Figure 9.1. The observed latency between completion of teacher's directions and task engagement across students. [a]Students with diagnosed learning disabilities.

Baseline Tau-U contrasts were computed to examine baseline data for trend. Trend analysis showed no statistically significant trends ($p < .05$) in baseline for any of the six participants; therefore, no corrections for slope were included in analysis of baseline and intervention contrasts (Parker et al., 2011). Results for individual participants are as follows.

Ana demonstrated the greatest change between baseline and intervention conditions. Latency decreased from a mean of 373 s (range = 68–600 s) in baseline to a mean of 79 s (range = 34–302 s) in planning + goal setting + performance feedback. Effects were evident immediately, beginning with the first data point in intervention phase. Ana demonstrated a regression to baseline levels that was isolated to Sessions 9, 11, and 12, during intervention phase. Overall, Tau-U effect size for latency was –0.85, 95% CI = [–1, –0.61], demonstrating a strong effect that is statistically significant ($p < .01$).

Lara showed reduced mean latency from 174 s (range = 34–302 s) in baseline to 34 s (range = 62–303 s) in planning + goal setting + performance feedback. Lara had the lowest baseline mean and lowest intervention phase mean of all participants. Visual analysis indicates a slight downward trend in baseline and overall reduction in level and variability for planning + goal setting + performance feedback phase. Change was evident beginning with the second observation during intervention phase. Data remained stable through the end of data collection. However, baseline contrasts in Tau-U were nonsignificant ($p = .13$), therefore no correction was applied. Effect size for Lara was Tau-U = –0.95, 95% CI = [–1, –0.59], demonstrating a strong effect that is statistically significant ($p < .01$).

Results for Carmen showed a mean reduction in latency from 286 s (range = 82–527 s) in baseline to 50 s (range = 27–73 s) in planning + goal setting + performance feedback, which is below the classroom teacher's stated threshold for appropriate transition times. Visual analysis showed a reduction in level and variability corresponding with the implementation of the intervention. Effects were evident immediately, beginning with the first observation during intervention phase. Data remained stable through the remainder of the study. Quantitative analysis showed Tau-U = –1, 95% CI = [–1, –0.63], demonstrating a strong effect that is statistically significant ($p < .01$).

Results for Nora showed a reduction in mean latency from 179 s (range = 71–422 s) in baseline to 70 s (range = 39–117 s) in planning + goal setting + intervention. Nora showed a reduction in level, variability, and trend. Effects were evident with the first observation during baseline phase. Quantitative analysis for Nora was Tau-U = –0.82, 95% CI = [–1, –0.47], demonstrating a moderate effect that is statistically significant ($p < .01$).

Results for Rachel showed a reduction in mean latency from 260 s (range = 63–511 s) to a mean of 46 s (range = 23–84 s) in planning + goal setting + performance feedback, which is below the teachers' stated threshold for acceptable transition times. Visual analysis showed reductions in trend, level, and variability corresponding to the implementation of the intervention. Reduction in level was immediate, beginning with the first observation during the intervention phase. Latency remained stable for the remainder of the study. Quantitative analysis showed Tau-U = –0.97, 95% CI = [–1, –0.59], demonstrating a strong effect that is statistically significant ($p < .01$).

Maya's results showed reduction in mean latency from 189 s (range = 37–410 s) in baseline to a mean of 73 s (range = 59–87 s) in planning + goal setting + performance feedback. Given the limited data in intervention phase, visual analysis failed to confirm a functional relation between changes in latency and implementation of the intervention. Effects between baseline and intervention phase appear to be immediate, although considerable instability and overlap between baseline and intervention condition data do not provide sufficient evidence to confirm this finding. Quantitative analysis resulted in an effect that was not statistically significant, Tau-U = –0.39, 95% CI = [–0.89, 0.12], $p = .29$.

Discussion

The Discussion section serves as the researchers' forum to go beyond the current investigation and discuss the implications of the study findings to existing literature, theory, and professional practice. The first part of a thoughtful Discussion is typically an analysis of the study's results vis a vis the research questions and hypotheses. Researchers should begin with a discussion of whether the hypotheses were upheld, posit possible explanations for those outcomes, and draw implications from the findings back to the research problem that was identified in the Introduction. If the results provide a warrant for modifying or re-testing the conceptual framework upon which the investigation was based, the Discussion section is the place to suggest a reformulation of the underlying theory. Researchers should also include a statement of the scientific limitations of the current study, along with specific recommendations for future research. Finally, the researcher ends the article with a cogent summary of the conclusions, in the most general sense, that can be drawn from the methods and findings of the current study. Some authors use a separate Conclusion section for this purpose.

In their Discussion section, Stevenson and Mussalow (2018, p. 177–179) framed both the results of the study and the major discussion points within the context of the conceptual framework for the investigation and the literature review that were presented in the Introduction section:

Design features, data collection, and analysis of the current study are consistent with the What Works Clearinghouse criteria for *Meets WWC Pilot SCD Standards Without Reservations.* Data analyses provide *Moderate Evidence of a Causal Relation* as outlined in the What Works Clearinghouse Standard Handbook 4.0 (U.S. Department of Education, Institute of Education Sciences, National Center for Education Evaluation and Regional Assistance, 2018).

In this study, students' reading skills were closely monitored through regularly scheduled administrations of SRI and reading fluency assessments. These assessments enabled the teacher to ensure all assignments, computer-based activities, and small-group instruction were tailored to students' current levels of reading performance. Matching tasks to performance levels effectively controlled for potential effects of task difficulty during baseline and planning + goal setting + feedback phases. Progress monitoring procedures ensured there were no times during baseline or intervention phase in which students were asked to engage in tasks that were either too hard or too easy. The close match between students' reading ability and task difficulty makes it unlikely that assignment was a confound.

The implementation of planning + goal setting + performance feedback showed a functional relation between the intervention and changes in students' latency to task engagement for three participants. Changes in level and trend indicate students took less time transitioning between whole-group instruction and assigned reading tasks, thus increasing students' opportunities to benefit from assigned tasks. The change in trend and variability for five out of six participants during the intervention phase was more closely aligned with the classroom teacher's expected transition times for all students.

There were no clear indications that disability status was a factor in students' response to planning + goal setting + performance feedback. All six students responded favorably to the intervention in terms of transition time. Likewise, all six students demonstrated similar baseline levels of transition behavior and reading ability. Although only three participants have diagnosed LDs in reading, all six began the study with similar reading deficits. Results of visual and quantitative analyses do not provide evidence for significant differences in students' response to the intervention based on LD diagnoses.

Outcomes from the current study suggest that planning + goal setting + performance feedback may result in greater student improvements compared with planning + goal setting alone (Stevenson, 2016). Baseline means across participants were similar between the current study (range = 174–373 s) compared with Stevenson (2016; range = 194–370 s). During planning + goal setting condition (range = 105–194 s), latency contrasts sharply versus planning + goal setting + feedback (range = 34–79 s). The inclusion of a mechanism to help students track and evaluate their performance relative to goals may have enabled shorter transition times between activities, yielding greater opportunity to engage in meaningful academic tasks. A direct experimental comparison is needed to confirm this finding.

There was only one instance out of more than 130 observations in which an observation time reached the predetermined ceiling of 10 min. It is therefore unlikely that ceiling effects for data collection obscured the outcomes. This is a departure from work conducted by Stevenson (2016) in which all participants reached the 10-min timing ceiling 2 to 4 times each.

Finally, differences from prior research on similar transition time interventions (e.g., Stevenson, 2016), one must recognize the value of parsimony in intervention research. When the current study is contextualized with prior research, there is some evidence that feedback may have contributed to shorter transition times between activities and engagement in reading tasks for students that actively or passively avoid engagement in reading tasks. When taken together, the current study and extant research provide useful information regarding the effects of intervention components and ways such interventions could be modified to bolster the effects for specific populations and in-specific contexts.

A critical next step in this line of inquiry is to investigate generalization and maintenance of behaviors as a function of planning + goal setting + performance feedback. Data collection regarding generalization and maintenance was not possible in the current study due to the conclusion of schedule changes on the part of the participating school and the conclusion of the academic year. As previously mentioned, despite several extant strategies (e.g., greetings, high-p requests) with evidence of positive effects on compliance with teachers' directions, there are few interventions that address the proximal and distal goals of behavior management. Teachers require a variety of strategies to prevent and respond to problematic behavior in active classroom settings with lasting effects. It is critical that future research in this area address generalization and maintenance of prosocial behaviors in classroom settings and beyond.

Limitations

Although visual and quantitative analyses indicated some evidence of a functional relation between the change in latency and the intervention, there are several limitations that must be addressed. First, the intervention focused only on latency to initial engagement in assigned tasks. Researchers did not measure the duration of engagement nor the effects on academic achievement. Even though initial engagement improved for all participants, it is unclear to what extent students remained engaged. Students are unlikely to benefit from academic tasks unless they remain engaged in the task. Data collection on the duration of engagement was outside the scope of the current investigation but should be included in future research. Further research should also include assessments of academic progress to determine whether students experience any gains in reading achievement as a result of intervention.

Second, as the intervention was classroom based, and typically conducted in the minutes immediately preceding the start of class, it was neither feasible nor desirable to keep the students and teacher isolated from the rest of the class. To ensure the intervention was usable and feasible in a classroom setting, the teacher had to be able to complete the intervention with students and simultaneously monitor students coming into the classroom for the beginning of class. It is therefore reasonable to presume that participants in baseline phase could have potentially seen and heard what the students and teacher were doing in the intervention phase. This spillover effect may have impacted baseline data (i.e., reduced latency) for some participants. This may have been the case for Nora and Maya, who each demonstrated four or more consecutive latency timings in baseline phase that were within 60 s or less of the teacher's stated threshold for acceptable transition time. However, it is also important to note that any improvement in transition time as a result of spillover for Nora and Maya did not last. Data indicated that Nora and Maya both regressed to excessive levels of transition times in baseline condition following very brief periods of improvement. Although it may be useful to study the effects of exposure (e.g., spillover) versus isolation, conducting the intervention in isolation would likely reduce the feasibility and social validity of implementing the intervention in typical school settings.

Third, it is important to recognize the limitations of quantitative analysis in single-case experimental research. Among all the potential methods for calculating effect size estimates in single-case data, there is no agreed-upon standard. Estimates such as percentage of non-overlapping data are susceptible to floor and ceiling effects. Likewise, there is evidence that calculations for Tau-U may lead to increased risk of Type I error compared with other effect size estimates, particularly when data have been statistically corrected for trend in baseline (Tarlow, 2017). Although increased risk of Type I error is certainly possible in the current study, Tau-U remains the most appropriate effect size estimate given that no corrections for baseline trend were made and the variability and trend in baseline data were such that other single-case effect size estimates are ill fitted to the data. Furthermore, quantitative analysis in the current study was a secondary method of analysis that accompanied visual analysis as the primary method, therefore mitigating the risk of Type I error.

Finally, social validity of the intervention was not assessed. Future research should include assessment of social validity to ensure the intervention is meaningful and appropriate for students, teachers, and context in which it is used.

Conclusion

Feedback is a powerful mechanism for behavior change, as evidenced by research in a variety of applications including writing instruction (Codding & Smyth, 2008; Graham & Harris, 1992), self-regulated learning (Cleary, Platten, & Nelson, 2008; Cleary & Zimmerman, 2004), and behavior management (Lane, Menzies, Parks-Ennis, & Oakes, 2018). As predicted, the addition of performance feedback to a previously conceived intervention of planning + goal setting may have beneficial effects for students with a history of avoidance behaviors and reading difficulty. Performance feedback enables students to reflect on specific behaviors and make necessary improvements. Although, at the time of this study, it is unclear the extent to which planning **+** goal setting **+** performance feedback supports sustained engagement. Future research should continue to explore the ways in which the intervention described here, and each of its component parts, may be used to leverage effective behavioral and academic outcomes for students.

References

The final section of a research article is always a listing of the references that were cited in the body of the text. References are listed in alphabetical order, according to authors' last names. Most special education and related journals require adherence to the APA's (2013) guidelines regarding the composition of the References page. Whenever possible references to materials available via the internet or other digital resources should include the complete Digital Object Identifier (DOI), which provides a permanent unique link associated with each work. The works cited by Stevenson and Mussalow (2018) appear in the References section of this book.

GUIDELINES FOR CRITIQUING RESEARCH ARTICLES

It is our hope that understanding the components, organization, and composition of a research article, via the descriptions and examples provided to this point in the chapter, will make pre-service and practicing special educators better informed consumers as they read the professional literature. As readers digest the contents of research articles and apply them to their practices, the "anatomy" of empirical reports can serve as a useful rubric for critically analyzing the quality, content, and practical significance of published research. Table 9.1 presents guidelines and specific questions for conducting a section-by-section critique of a special education research article. Educators are encouraged to modify this framework to meet their students' specific needs in special education research utilization courses.

SUMMARY

As Chapters 6, 7, and 8 of this book attest, there are many ways to conduct scholarly research and make valuable contributions to the knowledge base of special education. When composing research reports, it is important for special education scholars to exercise creativity in their scientific endeavors within the context of prevailing publication guidelines set forth by the American Psychological Association (2013). Specifically, research articles published in most social science journals share in common clear and descriptive titles; 100–150 word abstracts; introductory sections including the research problem, the conceptual framework of the study, and research questions/hypotheses; Method sections including descriptions of the sample, instruments, materials, design, and procedures; full reports of relevant results; discussions of the limitations of the study and implications for future research; and references presented in accordance with the American Psychological Association's style guidelines.

Understanding the sections of a research article helps readers to make decisions regarding the quality and practical significance of research investigations published in the special education and disability studies literature. Familiarity with the components of a standard article facilitates the critical analyses that informed consumers of special education research make as they read reports in an effort to enhance their own practices. By delineating the "anatomy" of a research article and providing a framework for critiquing research reports, we hope that this chapter has prepared readers to assimilate contemporary special education literature into their professional development and continuing education activities.

Table 9.1
GUIDELINES FOR CRITIQUING RESEARCH ARTICLES

Instructions: Answer the following questions regarding the article, "Use examples from the article to support your analyses."

A. Title

1. Did the title describe the study?
2. Did the key words of the title serve as key elements of the article?
3. Was the title concise, i.e., free of distracting or extraneous phrases?

B. Abstract

4. Did the abstract summarize the study's purpose, methods, and findings?
5. Did the abstract reveal the independent and dependent variables under study?
6. Were there any major premises or findings presented in the article that were not mentioned in the abstract?
7. Did the abstract provide you with sufficient information to determine whether you would be interested in reading the entire article?

C. Introduction

8. Was the research problem clearly identified?
9. Is the problem significant enough to warrant the study that was conducted?
10. Did the authors present a theoretical rationale for the study?

continued

Table 9.1—*Continued*

11. Is the conceptual framework of the study appropriate in light of the research prob-
    lem?
12. Do the author's hypotheses and/or research questions seem logical in light of the con-
    ceptual framework and research problem?
13. Are hypotheses and research questions clearly stated? Are they directional?
14. Overall, does the literature review lead logically into the Method section?

D. Method

15. Is the sample clearly described, in terms of size, relevant characteristics, selection and
    assignment procedures, and whether any inducements were used to solicit subjects?
16. Do the instruments described seem appropriate as measures of the variables under
    study?
17. Have the authors included sufficient information about the psychometric properties
    (e.g., reliability and validity) of the instruments?
18. Are the materials used in conducting the study or in collecting data clearly de-
    scribed?
19. Are the study's scientific procedures thoroughly described in chronological order?
20. Is the design of the study identified (or made evident)?
21. Do the design and procedures seem appropriate in light of the research problem,
    conceptual framework, and research questions/hypotheses?
22. Overall, does the method section provide sufficient information to replicate the
    study?

E. Results

23. Is the Results section clearly written and well organized?
24. Are data coding and analysis appropriate in light of the study's design and hypothe-
    ses?
25. Are salient results connected directly to hypotheses?
26. Are tables and figures clearly labeled? Well organized? Necessary (non-duplicative of
    text)?

F. Discussion and Conclusion

27. Are the limitations of the study delineated?
28. Are findings discussed in terms of the research problem, conceptual framework, and
    hypotheses?
29. Are implications for future research and/or special education practice identified?
30. Are the author's general conclusions warranted in light of the results?

G. References

31. Is the reference list sufficiently current?
32. Do works cited reflect the breadth of existing literature regarding the topic of the
    study?
33. Are bibliographic citations used appropriately in the text?

Chapter 10

THE FUTURE OF SPECIAL EDUCATION RESEARCH

INTRODUCTION

Research plays a prominent role in the education of students with disabilities. One important function of research is to evaluate the impact of current trends in the field. That is, research can be used to determine whether policies and practices impact teacher behavior and student learning as desired. Perhaps more importantly, research findings can be used proactively to guide future policy directions and instructional decisions. Research, by virtue of its reliance on objective data, can provide trustworthy information regarding a host of educational issues, such as which instructional approaches are the most effective and should be prioritized by practitioners and policymakers. Using research to identify which practices are most likely to improve student outcomes is particularly important in special education. Although many students who do not have disabilities will perform adequately even when given less than optimal instruction, students with disabilities typically require highly effective (i.e., evidence-based) practices to be successful in school (Dammann & Vaughn, 2001).

Generally, special education researchers place a priority on investigating issues (a) that are likely to have a meaningful effect on important school outcomes, and (b) about which the field's knowledge base is insufficient. Thus, by examining current educational trends and identifying emerging topics on which more research is needed, we can make some reasonable deductions as to future areas of emphasis in special education research. Specifically, in this chapter we explore the emerging area of open science, which, we believe, will influence many aspects of special education research in the near future. Additionally, we will discuss what we see as likely areas of emphasis in the near future of special education research in relation to intervention and policies, student populations, and types of research studies.

OPEN SCIENCE AND THE FUTURE OF SPECIAL EDUCATION RESEARCH

Open science is a collection of practices intended to make research more trustworthy, efficient, and impactful by making every aspect of the research enterprise more open and transparent (see Cook, Lloyd, Mellor, Nosek, & Therrien, 2018). Open science is an umbrella term that encompasses many elements, one of which is open access—or making research reports (e.g., journal articles) freely accessible. However, open science involves more than just open access. In this section, we briefly discuss problems in the contemporary research culture and the research base that have given rise to the open-science movement, and then describe five specific areas of open science that we expect to see incorporated in future special education research (i.e., preregistration, Registered Reports, open data and materials, open review, and open access and preprints).

Need for Open Science

Although elements of open science have been around for a long time (indeed, some researchers consider open science to just be good science), they have coalesced into an identifiable reform movement in research only recently, largely in response to a replication crisis in science. As discussed in Chapter 1, replication plays a critical role in the larger scientific process, as the primary means to validate research findings. When multiple researchers report similar findings across multiple studies, research consumers can be confident that those findings are valid and should be used as the basis for policy and practice. Unfortunately, research conducted on the scientific research base (i.e., meta-research) has shown that replication studies are seldom conducted. For example, only 0.1 percent of published articles in the general education literature are identified as replication studies (Makel & Plucker, 2014). Moreover, when independent researchers have conducted replication studies, the findings reported in the original research are not consistently reproduced in subsequent replication studies (e.g., Camerer et al., 2018; R. A. Klein et al., 2018; Open Science Collaboration, 2015). This suggests that some research findings may not be trustworthy, and—because of the low rate of replication studies—research consumers will have a difficult time identifying which study findings merit their confidence, and which do not.

Many factors may explain why study findings fail to replicate. For one, even when researchers try their best to duplicate a previously conducted study as closely as possible, there are inevitable differences between an original study and a replication. For instance, even if participants are the same age, and gender, and have the same disability as in the original study, a replication study will involve different individuals who may respond differently to an intervention. Moreover, no study is perfect (which is why studies need to be replicated) and all studies contain error. The source of error in research that is the focus of open-science reforms is researcher bias. After all, researchers are human, with their own beliefs and value systems that influence their behaviors, often subconsciously. Although Merton (1973) suggested that researchers should be disinterested in their work, this is seldom the case. Researchers tend to investigate topics they are interested in and have studied extensively. Thus, they have typically formed beliefs about, for example, whether a practice is effective before they conduct a study. Indeed, many special education researchers are passionate advocates about the topics they research. These beliefs may influence how researchers, including those in special education, conduct, analyze, and report their research.

Additionally, many researchers work in jobs that require publishing in top-tier journals to earn promotions and obtain grant funding (see Nosek, Spies, & Motyl, 2012). Thus, some researchers may feel pressure to generate studies with findings that are most likely to be published in leading journals (e.g., studies showing that an instructional practice is effective; John, Loewenstein, & Prelec, 2012). The problem of researchers and journals tending to favor studies with positive findings is referred to as publication bias (sometimes also called the file-drawer problem because of the likelihood that studies showing a practice is ineffective often end up in a researcher's file drawer rather than being published in a journal; Rosenthal, 1979). In addition to simply not publishing studies showing that a practice didn't work (e.g., null findings), researchers may selectively report only the positive findings from a study or reanalyze data in different ways until positive findings are attained (sometimes called "p-hacking"; Cook et al., 2018).

Although the degree to which special education researchers engage in questionable research practices like p-hacking has not been investigated extensively, Shadish et al. (2016) did find that some single-case design researchers reported they would drop a case in which an intervention was not successful before submitting a study for publication. That is, a small proportion of single-case design researchers indicated that they would selectively report positive findings. Additionally, reviews of meta-analyses in special education have found that published studies tend to have larger effect sizes than unpublished studies (Chow & Ekholm, 2018; Gage, Cook, & Reichow, 2017; Sham & Smith, 2014), suggesting that selective reporting and publication bias may exist in the special education literature. Other reviews suggest that studies with null results are seldom published in the special education literature (Kittelman, Gion, Horner, Levin, & Kratochwill, 2018; Therrien & Cook, 2018). Finally, studies that explicitly replicate previous research comprise only 0.4 to 0.5 percent of the special education literature base (Lemons et al., 2016; Makel et al., 2016). These findings suggest that, like in other fields of research, efforts are needed to ensure the trustworthiness of research in special education.

Although researchers are beginning to conduct meta-research to examine the trustworthiness of the special education research base, such efforts are fairly new and incomplete. Thus, we expect to see more meta-research to be conducted in special education. For example, researchers might investigate more extensively the degree to which publication bias and selective reporting exists, the frequency and findings of replication research, and evidence of p-hacking and other questionable research practices. In addition to expecting more meta-research examining issues in the special education research base, we expect future researchers to increasingly implement and study the effects of open-science practices, as discussed in the following section, with the goal of improving the trustworthiness, accessibility, and impact of research in special education.

Open-Science Practices

Open science refers to an array of practices aiming to open up all aspects of science—including planning, conducting, analyzing, and disseminating research. Broadly speaking, advocates of open science hope to improve the use and impact of research by improving its accessibility and trustworthiness. In this section, we discuss five practices associated with open science (i.e., preregistration, Registered Reports, open data and materials, open review and preprints. and open access). We describe how we expect each practice to influence special education research and be the subject of future research.

Preregistration

Traditionally, researchers have had considerable flexibility in how they conduct, analyze, and report studies. That is, researchers can try different approaches for conducting, analyzing, and reporting studies to help achieve desired results. For example, a researcher might "p-hack" by conducting different statistical analyses until desired results are achieved, "cherry pick" by only reporting selected (e.g., statistically significant) findings, or contribute to the file-drawer problem (i.e., publication bias) by not writing up studies that did not yield desired results.

Preregistration involves researchers publicly posting specific and detailed plans for their study *before* the study is conducted (Nosek, Ebersole, DeHaven, & Mellor, 2018), typically in a public registry. In this way, any changes researchers make to how they conduct, analyze, or report a study are readily detectable by other researchers, journal editors and reviewers, and research consumers by comparing the preregistration to the published research. For example, if a researcher changes how she or he conducts a study (e.g., adding more participants), analyzes data (e.g., using additional covariates), or reports findings (e.g., write up only statistically significant findings) in order to generate desirable results, such changes are evident in comparison to the preregistration. Moreover, preregistration helps combat publication bias because a public record of research plans exists regardless of whether the study is published. Although researchers can still engage in questionable practices, preregistration discourages such practices by making them easily discoverable. Indeed, Kaplan and Irvin (2015) found that studies funded by the National Heart, Blood, and Lung Institute (NHBLI) after the NHBLI began to require preregistration were significantly more likely to report null findings.

Although special education researchers are beginning to preregister their studies, we expect this to occur with greater frequency in the future, hopefully becoming common practice. Researchers will likely conduct descriptive research in the future to examine the frequency with which special education researchers preregister their studies, and whether this changes over time. Researchers will also likely conduct relational research to examine whether certain groups of researchers (e.g., early career researchers) are more likely to preregister their studies, and whether preregistered studies in special education are more likely to report null findings. Finally, researchers may conduct experimental studies to determine if preregistration causes changes in research outcomes such as the reporting of null results.

Registered Reports

Registered Reports take preregistration a step further by applying study plans as the basis for making publication decisions. In the traditional publication process, reviewers and editors only read a research report after the study is completed and written up. Thus, reviewers and editors cannot provide proactive feedback to improve the article, and they have no way of knowing whether researchers p-hacked or reported only some of the analyses conducted. In Registered Reports, researchers submit detailed study plans to a journal *before* the study is conducted (Hardwicke & Ioannidis, 2018; Nosek & Lakens, 2014).

The registered Reports process involves two stages of review. In Stage 1 review, journal reviewers and editors provide feedback to a researcher's study plans. If, after negotiating potential changes to the study, the editor decides the study is important and methodologically sound, in-principle acceptance is granted, which guarantees that the study will be published regardless of the findings (even if null findings are reported), so long as the researcher conducts the study as it was proposed. At this point, the researcher preregisters the study plans that were accepted in principle. Stage 2 review occurs after the study has been conducted and written up. Stage 2 only involves reviewers checking to see that the study was conducted consistent with preregistered plans (with any exploratory analysis clearly identified and justified) and reported appropriately.

Registered Reports help make research more trustworthy by discouraging publication bias, selective reporting, and p-hacking. Because in-principle acceptance occurs before the study is conducted, decisions about whether a study will be published are made solely on the basis of the importance and quality of the study plans, not the direction or significance of study findings. Thus, possible bias against studies with null findings on the part of journal editors or reviewers is eliminated, because the publication decision is made before results are known. Additionally, the incentive for researchers to p-hack and selectively report findings in order to improve the likelihood that their study will be accepted for publication is removed. Indeed, the only way for researchers with in-principle acceptance to not get their study published is deviating from their preregistered plan. Given researchers' reduced flexibility when conducting and reporting Registered Reports, it is perhaps not surprising that greater than 60 percent of published Registered Reports have reported null findings, a rate many times higher than for traditional publications (Allen & Mehler, 2018).

We expect journals in special education and related disciplines to explore and adopt Registered Reports as an option for publication in the coming years. It appears to us to be a win-win situation, in that (a) reviewers and editors have the opportunity to proactively provide feedback and help improve studies, and (b) the format is designed to reduce p-hacking, selective reporting, and publication bias. As Registered Reports are implemented in special education, we expect that researchers will study them in different ways. For example, researchers will likely conduct qualitative research to explore different stakeholders' (e.g., researchers, reviewers, editors) perceptions and experiences using Registered Reports. Descriptive, quantitative research may be conducted to examine the frequency with which Registered Reports are conducted, and the journals and subfields of special education in which they are published. Finally, researchers may also conduct relational research examining whether null findings are more prevalent in Registered Reports than in traditional publications.

Open Data and Materials

Open data, sometimes called data sharing, involves researchers making available the actual data they used in a study, so that others can (a) reanalyze the data to confirm that reported findings are accurate, (b) use the data in research syntheses, and (c) explore new questions and analyses not examined in the study (O. Klein et al., 2018). Although data can be shared in many ways (e.g., responding to personal requests for data via email), O. Klein and colleagues recommended that researchers post data on public repositories that allow them to control when and with whom data is shared. It is important to note that some data may be redacted or may not be able to be shared at all in order to protect participants' confidentiality and accord with ethical requirements (see Levenstein & Lyle, 2018). To ensure that other researchers can use shared data meaningfully, researchers should also share the analytic codes they used when conducting statistical analyses to ensure that others can analyze the data in the same way. Researchers can also share other materials (e.g., surveys, data collection forms) used in a study to (a) enable other researchers to directly replicate the study, and (b) facilitate research consumers' understanding of the study.

Although researchers are not always able or willing to share data and materials for various reasons (e.g., concerns about others using one's data, protecting the confidentiality of study participants), doing so provides multiple benefits. For one, sharing data and analytic codes is critical for enabling other researchers to reproduce and verify the analyses reported in a study; without these data, research consumers have to trust the researchers that they have conducted and reported analyses correctly. Data sharing allows other researchers to analyze the original research questions in different ways. That is, published research studies typically examine only one of the many possible ways to defensibly analyze a research question. Allowing other researchers to explore different approaches to analyzing the same research question can provide a fuller and more nuanced understanding of the data. Finally, data sharing allows other researchers to analyze research questions not examined by the original researchers. Allowing other researchers to analyze a data set once the original researchers are finished with their analyses enables as much knowledge as possible to be garnered from the data. The original researchers are credited with collecting the original data in all subsequent analyses and publications.

We hope to see special education researchers sharing data, codes, and materials with greater frequency in special education. Researchers will likely conduct qualitative, observational, and relational research to examine questions such as (a) what are special education researchers' concerns about sharing data?, (b) how often do special education researchers share their data?, and (c) in which journals and in which sub-fields of special education are data and materials shared? Additionally, experimental research may be conducted to examine whether (a) data sharing increases outcomes such as perceived trustworthiness of study findings and number of citations, and (b) interventions such as recognizing authors with electronic badges (Kidwell et al., 2016) are effective in increasing data- and material-sharing.

Open Review

Having other scientists critically review research before it is accepted for publication is a hallmark of science. Peer review is intended to serve a gatekeeper function by identifying studies with significant flaws before they are published. Though peer review has and continues to play an important role in science, it is far from perfect. For example, in their classic study, Peters and Ceci (1982) found that when they resubmitted 12 studies that were rejected by a journal through peer review to the same journal, eight were then accepted by different peer reviewers. Moreover, Schroter et al. (2008) reported that peer reviewers typically identified fewer than three of nine major errors in studies they reviewed. Additionally, peer review typically involves a limited number of expert reviewers, usually no more than three, whose critical perspectives are not shared with research consumers. Open peer review intends to make the peer-review process more transparent and effective. Open peer review is an umbrella term that refers to a disparate collection of reforms (see Ross-Hellauer, 2017 for a review), including unmasking the identities of reviewers and/or authors so that reviewers and authors know each other's identities. Here, we focus on two open-review approaches: publishing peer reviews and ongoing, postpublication peer review.

Publishing peer reviews involves presenting reviews alongside published articles. Although this could be done in paper journals, reviews are typically published on journal websites with the electronic versions of articles. Publishing reviews allows all research consumers to consider the study in light of the comments and perspectives, both positive and critical, of the expert reviewers. Ongoing, postpublication peer review allows research consumers to comment on published articles on the article website. Researchers, practitioners, and even the authors themselves can engage in an ongoing discussion regarding the strengths, limitations, and implications of published studies. Ongoing peer reviews might involve reviewers rating different aspects of studies (e.g., from one to five stars) that can be averaged to provide a crowdsourced perspective on the strengths and weaknesses of a study. These approaches to making peer review open and accessible may help better inform research consumers as to the strengths and weaknesses of published research, and to more quickly identify fatally flawed studies that should be retracted.

Open review is relatively new and there is not strong consensus regarding whether and which open-review practices should be implemented. Accordingly, qualitative and survey research might be conducted to examine the perceptions of special education researchers and research consumers regarding the potential benefits and drawbacks of different open-review practices. Additionally, little research has been conducted on the effects of open-review reforms. Thus, researchers should conduct experimental studies examining whether published and ongoing reviews meaningfully improve research consumers' understanding of the strengths and weaknesses of a study.

Open Access and Preprints

The ultimate purpose of research in special education is for others to read the research; improve their understanding of an issue or practice; and use that understanding to inform and positively influence future practice, policy, and research. This purpose cannot be achieved if others cannot access and read published research. Unfortunately, most articles are hidden behind paywalls and only accessible to people (a) affiliated with institutions such as universities that subscribe to journal publishers (e.g., university faculty, university students), or (b) who are willing and able to pay a fee to download articles. Consequently, many teachers, administrators, parents, researchers in developing countries, and other special education stakeholders do not have access to relevant research.

Open access involves providing free access to publications to anyone on the internet. One approach for providing open access is for researchers to pay a fee to publish their articles in an open-access journal (e.g., *AERA Open*), in which all articles are open access, or to make their article open access in a traditional journal (in which most articles are not openly accessible). Fees, which typically range from $1,000 to $3,000, offset the loss of income for the publisher that is traditionally generated by charging for access to the article. A second, less expensive, approach for providing open access is for researchers to self-archive preprints of their articles. As the name suggests, preprints are typically the version of a manuscript before the researcher submits a paper for publication. The author retains the copyright to this version of a paper and can post a .pdf copy on an online, preprint repository such as https://www.preprints.org/ and osf.io/preprints for everyone to freely access. Although articles typically change as a result of peer review (e.g., by incorporating the recommendations of the reviewers), the basic research findings should be the same as in the published article. Preprints, sometimes simply referred to as papers, may also be manuscripts that the authors choose never to submit for publication, and can be posted after an article is published.

Providing open access to research findings allows for research to reach a considerably wider audience, and therefore increases its potential impact. Enhanced availability is likely the cause of the "open-access advantage," in which open-access articles are cited more frequently by other researchers than traditional publications (Piwowar et al., 2018). Preprints are not peer reviewed like journal publications, so they need to be read critically and interpreted cautiously. However, by removing the barrier of the paywall, preprints provide the benefits of open access without the cost. Additionally, researchers are free to post any of their research as preprints, regardless of the studies' outcomes. Thus, preprints provide a forum for making studies with null findings, which might not otherwise be published, available for all to read and consider (see Bourne, Polka, Vale, & Kiley, 2017).

OTHER AREAS OF FOCUS FOR FUTURE SPECIAL EDUCATION RESEARCH

In addition to open science, research in special education will evolve in a number of other ways, reflecting changes in the social, political, economic, and instructional climate. In particular, we propose that special education research will increase its focus on certain instructional interventions and policies (e.g., multitiered systems of supports [MTSS], data-based individualization), student populations (e.g., autism spectrum disorders, mental health disorders), and types of research (e.g., research syntheses, replication research) that reflect critical and emerging foci in special education.

Instructional Interventions and Policies

In the previous edition of this text (Rumrill, Cook, & Wiley, 2011), we predicted that Response to Intervention, or RTI, would be researched extensively (which it was, Google Scholar indicated approximately 19,000 hits for "response-to-intervention" in the scholarly literature from 2011 to 2018). Although we expect researchers in special education to continue to research RTI, we expect a stronger focus on the broader approach of **multitiered systems of supports**, or MTSS. RTI is a multitiered (typically three levels), schoolwide approach to intervention and support for meeting students' academic needs (most often in reading, but potentially in other areas such as mathematics; see Jimerson, Burns, & VanDerHeyden, 2015). As RTI grew in popularity, schoolwide positive behavioral interventions and supports (PBIS) model was also being implemented widely. Schoolwide PBIS draws on the same schoolwide approach of differentiating interventions and supports for learners using a three-tiered model that RTI does, but targets improving student behavioral outcomes rather than academic performance (see Horner & Sugai, 2015). After many years of conceptualizing and researching RTI and PBIS separately, special education researchers have now begun to think of RTI and PBIS as being encompassed under the broad model of MTSS.

MTSS, for all intents and purposes, utilizes the same three-tiered system of supports as RTI and PBIS, but it is conceptualized more broadly and is not specific to academics or behavior. In fact, MTSS is often portrayed as a two-part system consisting of RTI (for academic outcomes) and PBIS (for behavioral and social outcomes). As a recently developed schoolwide approach for instructional decision-making and student supports that incorporates two popular policies (RTI and PBIS), MTSS is a ripe topic for research. For example, although experimental researchers have shown that RTI and PBIS can be highly effective when implemented with fidelity in isolation (e.g., Bradshaw, Mitchell, & Leaf, 2010; Gersten et al., 2009), further experimental research is needed to examine the effects of RTI and PBIS being implemented together under MTSS. Similarly, experimental research is needed to investigate whether and the degree to which MTSS is effective for different types of schools (e.g., preschool, elementary, middle, and high schools), different types of learners (e.g., at-risk students, students with severe disabilities), and different outcomes (e.g., student-level academic, behavioral, social, and emotional outcomes; teacher-level outcomes such as efficacy and burnout; and school-level outcomes such as school climate).

Research has shown that, when implemented in the real world, schools frequently do not implement RTI and PBIS with fidelity (Balu et al., 2015), thereby compromising their effectiveness. Thus, additional descriptive, relational, and experimental research is needed to investigate whether and how MTSS can be implemented with fidelity at scale and over time. Qualitative researchers might, for example, explore how schools and educators adapt MTSS to fit the needs of school personnel without compromising effectiveness. Similarly, researchers might investigate which specific interventions reliably cause improved student outcomes at each MTSS tier, and how to efficiently and reliably monitor student outcomes across time. Another fruitful line of research may be to investigate how broadly MTSS can be applied effectively. For example, although MTSS is often conceptualized as targeting academic and behavioral outcomes, can it also incorporate social, emotional, and mental health supports? Similarly, future experimental research might investigate whether MTSS is an effective approach for providing professional development to support teachers' needs.

In MTSS models, Tier-1 (universal) supports are typically selected and applied across the whole school. In Tier 2 (targeted), interventions are delivered with greater intensity than in Tier 1 (greater dosage, in small groups), but the interventions are typically predetermined. In Tier 3 (individualized) interventions are both individualized and highly intensive (e.g., delivered 1:1). That is, because students in Tier 3 of MTSS models have not responded adequately to generally effective intervention even when delivered with heightened intensity in Tier 2, they appear to need intervention that is truly individualized and very intensive. However, that begs the question of how to individualize and intensify intervention for students in Tier 3? **Data-based individualization**, or DBI, is "an iterative, multistep approach to intensive intervention that involves the analysis of progress monitoring and diagnostic assessment data, followed by individualization of a validated academic or behavioral intervention program" (Danielson & Rosenquist, 2014, p. 7), which we expect will be researched frequently in the near future.

As described by Danielson and Rosenquist (2014, see Figure 1), DBI is based on a diagnostic assessment, which may include standardized assessments, error analysis of student work and formative assessments, and a functional behavioral assessment. The goal of the diagnostic assessment is to identify areas of difficulty for the individual student, and inform what intervention(s) will best meet her or his individualized needs. Additionally, the intervention may be adapted or individualized to maximize chances for effectiveness. For example, the targeted intervention may be delivered 1:1 rather than in a small group or delivered daily rather than twice per week. Additionally, the intervention content, student responding, and environment may be adapted. Whatever intervention is selected and however it is adapted, progress on targeted outcomes is frequently monitored through brief and regular (e.g., daily) assessments. Data from these assessments are analyzed to examine whether the student is making adequate progress toward meeting his or her goal. If the student is, the intervention is considered successful and continues to be implemented. If the student is not making adequate progress, the intervention should be further intensified and adapted; or discontinued and replaced with a new intervention if additional intensification and adaptation prove unsuccessful.

DBI appears to be a promising approach for individualizing interventions for students who are nonresponsive to typical instruction, with initial experimental research showing positive effects (e.g., Jung, McMaster, & delMas, 2017). However, more research needs to be done to better understand DBI. For example, descriptive and qualitative research should be conducted to examine and explore educators' beliefs and attitudes toward DBI, their extant knowledge and skills related to DBI, and their actual implementation of DBI. Similarly, descriptive and relational research might examine whether and how teacher preparation programs and professional development provide training in DBI; and experimental research should examine whether such training improves educators' beliefs, skills, and actual practice related to DBI. Further, descriptive case studies will be useful in illustrating for educators how DBI was used in specific instances to increase different outcomes for specific learners.

Future researchers should also conduct additional experimental research, including single-case design research, to examine the effectiveness of DBI for individual learners and groups of learners. A larger issue is how to examine the general effectiveness of data-based individualization, which is a process or framework that can vary in how it is applied. That is, there is not a single "right" way to implement DBI that can be researched. For example, two teachers might engage in the process of DBI, but use different diagnostic and progress-monitoring assessments, use different approaches for determining whether progress-monitoring data indicate the student is making inadequate progress, and adapt interventions differently. Thus, research on DBI will be complicated, and incorporate considerations of whether and to what degree the essential procedural components of DBI are being implemented with fidelity.

Student Populations

Researchers will need to conduct studies in the coming years to better understand existing and emerging student populations, and how educators can improve the experiences and outcomes of students with and at risk for all disabilities. Two particular student populations that we expect to be the focus of considerable research in the immediate future are autism spectrum disorder (ASD) and mental health disorders. The National Institute of Mental Health (2018) defined **ASD** as "a developmental disorder that affects communication and behavior" that can be diagnosed at any age but appears in the first two years of life. ASD is characterized by (a) difficulties communicating and interacting with others (e.g., making little or no eye contact with others), and (b) restricted interests and repetitive behaviors (e.g., having ongoing and intense interest in a particular topic; American Psychiatric Association, 2013). ASD is a heterogeneous disability, ranging from individuals who need minimal support related to repetitive and restrictive behavior, to those requiring very substantial support related to severe deficits in communication and behavior.

ASD has traditionally been considered a low-incidence disability. As recently as the early 1990s, rates of autism were estimated to be approximately 1 in 2,000 individuals (Rice et al., 2012), or 0.05 percent of the population, with little public awareness of the condition. Beginning in the mid-1990s, estimates of the prevalence of ASD began to rise; and have been increasing ever since. Indeed, Baio et al. (2018) reported that approximately 17 of every 1,000 (or 1.7%) 8-year-olds in the U.S. had ASD. And Kim et al. (2011) found that 1 in 38 (or 2.6%) of 7- to 12-year-old children in South Korea had ASD. Future researchers should conduct descriptive research to monitor whether these trends maintain and the prevalence of ASD continues to increase. Moreover, researchers will continue to conduct relational research to explore whether observed increases in ASD are due to environmental factors, or whether changes in awareness and diagnostic criteria explain increasing prevalence. Parents, educators, psychologists, and medical professionals are much more aware of ASD than they were decades ago; and ASD now includes individuals with less intensive needs, whereas it included almost exclusively individuals with intensive needs decades ago. As such, it is possible that the increasing prevalence of ASD is due primarily, or even exclusively, to changes in diagnosis and awareness.

Our understanding of factors underlying ASD has improved greatly since Kanner (1943) noted that ASD appeared to be associated with a lack of parental warmth, spawning misguided theories that "refrigerator moms" caused ASD. However, despite a growing research base, the causes of ASD are still not fully understood. Growing evidence suggests that genetics plays a role in ASD, though environmental factors, perhaps even in the womb, also appear to play a role (Gialloreti & Curatolo, 2018). Future relational research into the causes of ASD will help parent and educators better understand the condition and how to prevent and remediate it. Future relational research will also likely focus on developing reliable and valid screeners for identifying ASD at young ages, as research suggests that intervening early is critical for improving outcomes for individuals with ASD (Reichow, Barton, Boyd, & Hume, 2012).

Researchers have conducted a growing and robust body of studies investigating the effectiveness of educational interventions for students with ASD and have established many evidence-based practices for educators to implement (see Wong et al., 2015). However, continued experimental research is needed to identify more evidence-based practices, especially for groups of students with ASD for whom few evidence-based practices have been identified (e.g., adolescents with ASD). In addition to conducting research on effective instructional practices, future experimental research should also identify ineffective fads used for individuals with ASD. Perhaps because ASD is not fully understood, many unproven myths and fads related to ASD (e.g., facilitated communication, sensory integration training, special diets) have gained credence and influenced the behavior of parents and educators (see Travers, Ayres, Simpson, & Crutchfield, 2016).

Children with **mental health disorders** (commonly referred to as emotional and behavioral disorders [EBD] in schools) represent another student population that we expect will be the focus of increased research in coming years. The Centers for Disease Control and Prevention (2019) defined mental health disorders among children as "serious changes in the way children typically learn, behave, or handle their emotions, which cause distress and problems getting through the day" (paragraph 2). Common mental health disorders among children include attention deficit/hyperactivity disorder, behavior and conduct disorders, anxiety, and depression. Students with EBD experience some of the worst outcomes of any group of learners both in and out of school (e.g., poor health; low academic achievement and graduation rates; high expulsion and arrest rates; Mitchell, Kern, & Conroy, 2019). Despite these outcomes, students with mental health disorders appear to be severely underserved. For example, Whitney and Peterson (2019) reported that although about one in seven youth have a mental health disorder, only about half received needed treatment from a mental health professional. Moreover, less than 1 percent of school-age children receive special education under Emotional Disturbance, the IDEA disability category most closely aligned with mental health disorders. We expect increased research activity for this underserved group of students due to greater public awareness of mental health, as well as heightened concerns regarding school-safety issues such as bullying and school violence.

Given that students with mental health disorders appear to be underserved and underidentified in special education, we anticipate that researchers will continue to conduct relational research to validate approaches for efficiently screening all students for mental health risk in schools (see Miller et al., 2015). Under-identification appears to be especially common for children with internalizing disorders, such as anxiety and depression, for which symptoms are likely to be less obvious and disruptive than with externalizing disorders, such as behavioral and conduct disorders. Additionally, identifying risk for mental health disorders early is critical for effective prevention and treatment. Thus, researchers especially need to develop and validate universal screeners that identify children at risk for (a) internalizing disorders, and (b) mental health disorders at a young age. Although universal screening for mental health risk appears to align well with MTSS approaches, it is not regularly conducted in schools (Bruhn, Woods-Groves, & Huddle, 2014; Splett et al., 2018). As such, future researchers should also conduct qualitative, observational, and eventually experimental research to examine how to facilitate universal screening for mental health risk in schools.

We also expect future researchers to continue to investigate the effectiveness of intervention approaches for promoting positive outcomes for students with and at risk for mental health disorders. Considerable research supports the positive effects of multitiered schoolwide positive behavior supports (SWPBS) for school-level outcomes (e.g., Horner, Sugai, & Anderson, 2010; Mitchell, Hatton, & Lewis, 2018). However, more research is needed to examine the effects of SWPBS on students with more intensive needs, such as those with mental health disorders. We expect more single-case research, and potentially group experimental research, focusing on adapting and intensifying empirically validated interventions to meet the unique needs of this population. For example, Kilgus, Fallon, and Feinberg (2016) conducted a single-case design study to establish the effectiveness of modifying the Check-In/Check-Out intervention to address the identified function of students' behaviors. Finally, rigorous experimental research should also be conducted and synthesized to examine critically the effectiveness of emerging approaches for addressing the needs of students with mental health disorders such as trauma-informed teaching, social-emotional learning, and mindfulness.

Types of Research

In this final section of the chapter, we discuss two types of research we expect to see more of in special education: systematic research syntheses (or reviews) and replication studies. **Systematic research syntheses** are important because all individual studies involve some level of error. Therefore, findings from a single study might indicate that a practice is more or less effective than it actually is. Assuming error in studies is more or less random, error across studies should balance out when considering findings across many studies. The findings of research syntheses should, then, provide more trustworthy answers to research questions than individual studies. It is important that research reviews be systematic, or conducted according to "clearly articulated procedures that are selected to minimize subjectivity and maximize transparency, which increases the likelihood of providing reliable findings" (Maggin, Talbott, Van Acker, & Kumm, 2017, p. 53). In other words, systematic reviews follow objective rules for identifying studies and synthesizing findings across identified studies. If there were not clear and objective procedures for identifying which studies to review, researchers could subjectively select only those studies with findings that support their own beliefs to include in their review (i.e., cherry pick studies).

We expect systematic research reviews to be conducted frequently in the future because of the strong need for special education stakeholders to know which instructional practices are supported by multiple research studies as being generally effective (i.e., evidence-based practices). Systematic reviews that consider research findings across multiple experimental (including single-case designs) studies are an important and reliable way to identify which practices are evidence based and should be implemented. Additionally, the volume of research conducted in special education has continued to grow, with more and more studies conducted every year. Thus, it is difficult, if not impossible, for busy special education teachers to read all relevant research studies conducted on the interventions in which they may be interested. Reading research syntheses are an efficient way for research consumers to understand the collective findings of many relevant studies by only reading a single article (see Santangelo, Novosel, Cook & Gapsis, 2015). Although research reviews can take different forms (see Chapter 8), we expect future special education researchers to conduct meta-analyses, a popular type of research synthesis, with greater frequency in the coming years.

Meta-analyses involve statistically combining the effects from multiple studies into a single metric that estimates the average effect across all studies reviewed (Oh-Young, Filler, & Buchter, 2019). Meta-analyses have become a very popular method for synthesizing research findings in special education and estimating the general effectiveness of instructional practices. We expect them to grow even more in popularity because (a) single-case researchers have now developed effect sizes enabling single-case design studies to be meta-analyzed (Maggin, Cook, & Cook, in press), and (b) as new research is conducted older meta-analyses will have to be updated so that research consumers have up-to-date information on the effectiveness of instructional practices. Given that research indicates that studies with small effects are less likely to be published, we expect meta-analysis in special education to increasingly include unpublished studies (sometimes called grey literature; Gage et al., 2017). Additionally, the larger number of studies in the special education research base will enable meta-analysts to increasingly conduct moderator analyses to investigate whether and how effects differ across studies reviewed. Moderator analyses can examine, for example, whether an intervention was more or less effective across the studies reviewed in a meta-analysis for participants of different ages, for participants with different disabilities, and for different types of outcomes.

We also expect to see more **replication research** conducted in special education in the coming years. As previously discussed, replication is a critical part of the scientific process. Because all studies contain error, it is important that research findings be verified through replication. As in other fields, there have been relatively few replication studies conducted in special education (Lemons et al., 2016; Makel et al., 2016). The historic scarcity of replication studies may be due to researchers being worried that replications may be (a) perceived as an attack on the authors of the research being replicated, (b) considered unoriginal and not valued to the same extent as novel research, and (c) unlikely to be accepted for publication (Travers, Cook, & Therrien, 2016).

However, the importance of replication research has been highlighted in recent years in science generally (Ioannidis, 2018), in special education specifically (Cook, 2014; Cook et al., 2018), and in the popular media (Yong, 2018). Moreover, the National Science Foundation and the Institute for Education Sciences (2018), two major funders of research in education and special education in the United States, recently released a document with guidelines for conducting high-quality replication research, and are emphasizing replication research in their competitions for funding (e.g., Schneider, 2019). Indeed, special education researchers have already started to conduct more replication studies, which are being published in prominent journals in the field. For example, Coyne and colleagues (2013) replicated a previous study on the Early Reading Intervention, and Doabler and colleagues (2016) conducted a replication study investigating the effect of a kindergarten mathematics intervention. Given the increasing recognition (and funding) of replication research, we expect more studies like this in the near future.

Although researchers can and should replicate studies using all research designs, we expect replication studies to occur most frequently for experimental designs that examine the effectiveness of instructional interventions. We also hope to see more independent replication studies conducted in special education. Both of the replication studies cited in the previous paragraph, for example, were conducted by the same group of authors as the original study being replicated. Having independent researchers replicate previous studies may provide a more objective test of the original research. Finally, we hope to see more direct replications, in which researchers conduct a study exactly like the original study being replicated, conducted in special education. Most extant replication studies in special education are conceptual replications (Cook, Collins, Cook, & Cook, 2016), in which researchers replicate some aspects of a previous study (e.g., examine the same intervention), but differ some elements of the study (use a different outcome variable). Although conceptual replications are useful to determine, for example, whether the positive effects of an intervention reported in a previous study generalize to other groups of participants or to other outcome areas, they do not provide a direct test of the original effect.

SUMMARY

Although we believe that the areas discussed in this chapter will be the focus of considerable research activity in the coming years, prediction is a risky enterprise, and we may be wrong. Moreover, even if we are correct that researchers will conduct more research in these areas, this chapter is not intended to be exhaustive. High-quality research will be needed to inform special educators regarding other emerging policy initiatives, instructional approaches, and disability groupings. These caveats noted, we expect to see researchers focus increasingly on open science by preregistering their research, using Registered Reports to publish their studies, making data and materials openly available, engaging in open review, and providing open access to their work by posting uncopyrighted versions of articles as pre-prints. Additionally, we expect to see more research conducted on MTSS and DBI, studies examining students with ASD and mental health disorders, and research syntheses and replication studies. Whatever directions the future of special education research may take, we are confident that the future of special education policy and practice will continue to interact with and be informed by future special education research.

BIBLIOGRAPHY

Agar, M. H. (1996). *The professional stranger: An informal introduction to ethnography* (2nd ed.). New York, NY: Academic Press.

Al Otaiba, S., Puranik, C. S., Ziolkowski, R. A., & Montgomery, T. M. (2009). Effectiveness of early phonological awareness intervention for students with speech or language impairments. *Journal of Special Education, 43,* 107–128.

Alberto, P. A., & Troutman, A. C. (2008). *Applied behavior analysis for teachers* (8th ed.). Upper Saddle, NJ: Merrill.

Allday, A. R., Bush, M., Ticknor, N., & Walker, L. (2011). Using teacher greetings to increase speed to task engagement. *Journal of Applied Behavior Analysis, 44,* 393–396. doi:10.1901/jaba.2011.44-393

Allen, C. P. G., & Mehler, D. M. A. (2018, October 17). Open science challenges, benefits and tips in early career and beyond. https://doi.org/10.31234/osf.io/3czyt

Allen, M., & Yen, W. (2001). *Introduction to measurement theory.* Long Grove, IL: Waveland Press.

American Educational Research Association, American Psychological Association, & Council on Measurement in Education. (1985). Joint technical standards for educational and psychological testing. Washington, DC: American Psychological Association.

American Psychiatric Association. (2000). Pervasive developmental disorders. In *Diagnostic and statistical manual of mental disorders* (4th ed.–Text Revision; pp. 69–70). Washington, DC: Author.

American Psychiatric Association. (2013). *Diagnostic and statistical manual of mental disorders* (5th ed.). Arlington, VA: Author.

American Psychological Association. (1994). *Publication manual of the American Psychological Association* (4th ed.). Washington, DC: Author.

American Psychological Association. (2001). *Publication manual of the American Psychological Association* (5th ed.). Washington, DC: Author.

American Psychological Association. (2009). *Publication manual of the American Psychological Association* (6th ed.). Washington, DC: Author.

American Psychological Association. (2013). *Publication manual of the American Psychological Association* (6th ed.). Washington, DC: Author.

American Psychological Association Ethics Committee. (1983). *Authorship guidelines for dissertation supervision.* Washington, DC: Author.

Ames, M. E., McMorris, C. A., Alli, L. N., & Bebko, J. M. (2015). Overview and Evaluation of a Mentorship Program for University Students With ASD. *Focus on Autism and Other Developmental Disabilities, 31*(1), 27–36. doi:10.1177/1088357615583465

Anderson, J. A., Kutash, K., & Duchnowski, A. J. (2001). A comparison of the academic progress of students with EBD and students with LD. *Journal of Emotional and Behavioral Disorders, 9,* 106–111.

247

Anderson, N. H. (1961). Scales and statistics: Parametric and nonparametric. *Psychological Bulletin, 58*(4), 305–316.

Angoff, W. H. (1988). Validity: An evolving concept. In H. Wainer & H. I. Braun (Eds.), *Test validity* (pp. 19–32). Hillsdale, NJ: Erlbaum.

Anzul, M., Evans, J. F., King, R., & Tellier-Robinson, D. (2001). Moving beyond a deficit perspective with qualitative research methods. *Exceptional Children, 76*(2), 235–249.

Appelbaum, M., Cooper, H., Kline, R. B., Mayo-Wilson, E., Nezu, A. M., & Rao, S. M. (2018). Journal article reporting standards for quantitative research in psychology: The APA Publications and Communications Board task force report. *American Psychologist, 73*(1), 3–25. doi:10.1037/amp0000191

Artiles, A. J., Trent, S. C., & Palmer, J. D. (2004). Culturally diverse students in special education: Legacies and prospects. In J. A. & C. M. Banks (Eds.), *Handbook of research on multicultural education* (2nd ed., pp. 716–735). San Francisco: Jossey-Bass.

Ary, D., Jacobs, L., & Razavieh, A. (1985). *Introduction to research in education.* New York: CBS College Publishing.

Asher, S., Parkhurst, J., Hymel, S., & Williams, G. (1990). Peer rejection and loneliness in childhood. In S. Asher & J. Coie (Eds.), *Peer rejection in childhood* (pp. 253–273). New York: Cambridge University Press.

Autism and Developmental Disabilities Monitoring Network Surveillance. (2007). Prevalence of Autism Spectrum Disorders–Autism and Developmental Disabilities Monitoring Network, 14 Sites, United States, 2002. *Morbidity and Mortality Weekly Report, 56*(SS-1), 12–28. Retrieved on 9/2/09 from http://www.cdc.gov/mmwr/PDF/ss/ss5601.pdf

Babbie, E. (1995). *The practice of social research.* New York: Wadsworth.

Baio, J., Wiggins, L., Christensen, D. L., Maenner, M. J., Daniels, J., Warren, Z., & Dowling, N. (2018). Prevalence of autism spectrum disorder among children aged 8 years–autism and developmental disabilities monitoring network, 11 sites, United States, 2014. *MMWR Surveillance Summaries, 67*(6). Retrieved from https://www.ncbi.nlm.nih.gov/pmc/articles/PMC5919599/pdf/ss6706a1.pdf

Balu, R., Zhu, P., Doolittle, F., Schiller, E., Jenkins, J., & Gersten, R. (2015). *Evaluation of Response to Intervention Practices for Elementary School Reading (NCEE 2016-4000).* Washington, DC: National Center for Education Evaluation and Regional Assistance, Institute of Education Sciences, U.S. Department of Education.

Banda, D. R., & Kubina Jr., R. M. (2009). Increasing Academic Compliance with Mathematics Tasks Using the High Preference Strategy with a Student with Autism. *Preventing School Failure: Alternative Education for Children and Youth, 54*(2), 81–85. doi:10.1080/10459880903217564

Bateman, B. D. (1994). Who, how, and where: Special education's issues in perpetuity. *Journal of Special Education, 27,* 509–520.

Beauchamp, T. L., & Childress, J. F. (1979). *Principles in biomedical ethics.* Oxford: Oxford University Press.

Becker, S. (2010). Badder than "just a bunch of SPEDs": Alternative schooling and student resistance to special education rhetoric. *Journal of Contemporary Ethnography, 39*(1), 60–86.

Bellini, J., Bolton, B., & Neath, J. (1998). Rehabilitation counselor's assessments of applicant's functional limitations as predictors of rehabilitation services provided. *Rehabilitation Counseling Bulletin, 41*(4), 242–258.

Bellini, J. L., Fitzgerald, S., & Rumrill, P. (2000). Perspectives on scientific inquiry: The basics of measurement and statistics. *Journal of Vocational Rehabilitation, 14,* 131–143.

Bellini, J., & Rumrill, P. (2009). *Research in Rehabilitation Counseling* (2nd ed.). Springfield, IL: Charles C Thomas.

Benner, G. J., Allor, J. H., & Mooney, P. (2008). An investigation of the academic processing speed of students with emotional and behavioral disorders served in public school settings. *Education and Treatment of Children, 31,* 307–322.

Berliner, B. (2002). Helping homeless students keep up. *Education Digest, 68*(1), 49.

Bettini, E., Benedict, A., Thomas, R., Kimerling, J., Choi, N., & McLeskey, J. (2017). Cultivating a community of effective special education teachers: Local special education administrators' roles. *Remedial and Special Education, 38*(2), 111–126.

Bettini, E., Wang, J., Cumming, M., Kimerling, J., & Schutz, S. (2018). Special Educators' Experiences of Roles and Responsibilities in Self-Contained Classes for Students with Emotional/Behavioral Disorders. *Remedial and Special Education, 40*(3), 177–191. doi:10.1177/0741932518762470

Bianco, M. (2005). The effects of disability labels on special education and general education teachers' referrals for gifted programs. *Learning Disability Quarterly, 28,* 285–293.

Biklen, D. (1990). Communication unbound: Autism and praxis. *Harvard Educational Review, 60,* 291–314.

Boardman, A. G., Argüelles, M. E., Vaughn, S., Hughes, M. T., & Klingner, J. (2005). Special education teachers' views of research-based practices. *The Journal of Special Education, 39,* 168–180.

Bodfish, J. W. (2004). Treating the core features of autism: Are we there yet? *Mental Retardation and Developmental Disabilities Research Reviews, 10,* 318–326.

Bogdan, R. C., & Biklen, S. K. (1992). *Qualitative research for education.* Boston: Allyn and Bacon.

Bogdan, R. C., & Biklen, S. K. (1998). Foundations of qualitative research in education. Qualitative research in education: An introduction to theories and methods, 1–48. Ally & Bacon, Needham Heights, MA.

Bogdan, R. C., & Biklen, S. K. (1998). *Qualitative research for education: An introduction to theory and methods* (2nd ed.). Boston, MA: Allyn and Bacon.

Bogdan, R. C., & Biklen, S. K. (2006). *Qualitative research for education: An introduction to theories and methods* (4th ed.). Boston: Allyn & Bacon.

Bolton, B. (1979). *Rehabilitation counseling research.* Baltimore: University Park Press.

Bolton, B., & Parker, R. M. (1998). Research in rehabilitation counseling. In R. M. Parker & E. M. Szymanski (Eds.), *Research in rehabilitation counseling: Basics and beyond* (3rd ed., pp. 437–470). Austin, TX: Pro-Ed.

Borg, W. R., Gall, J. P., & Gall, M. D. (1993). *Applying educational research: A practical guide* (3rd ed.). New York: Longman.

Borg, W. R., & Gall, M. D. (1983). *Educational research.* New York: Longman.

Bos, C., & Richardson, V. (1993). Qualitative research and learning disabilities. In S. Vaughan & C. Bos (Eds.), *Research issues in learning disabilities* (pp. 178– 201). New York, NY: Springer-Verlag.

Bottge, B. A. (1999). Effects of contextualized math instruction on problem solving of average and below-average achieving students. *The Journal of Special Education, 33,* 81–92.

Bottiani, J. H., Larson, K. E., Debnam, K. J., Bischoff, C. M., & Bradshaw, C. P. (2017). Promoting Educators' Use of Culturally Responsive Practices: A Systematic Review of In-service Interventions. *Journal of Teacher Education, 69*(4), 367–385. doi:10.1177/0022487117722553

Bourne, P. E., Polka, J. K., Vale, R. D., & Kiley, R. (2017). Ten simple rules to consider regarding preprint submission. *PLoS Computer Biology, 13*(5), e1005473. https://doi.org/10.1371/journal.pcbi.1005473

Bradshaw, C. P., Mitchell, M. M., & Leaf, P. J. (2010). Examining the effects of schoolwide positive behavioral interventions and supports on student outcomes: Results from a randomized controlled effectiveness trial in elementary schools. *Journal of Positive Behavior Interventions, 12,* 133–148. doi: 10.1177/1098300709334798

Brantlinger, E. (1997). Using ideology: Cases of nonrecognition of the politics of research and practice in special education. *Review of Educational Research, 67*(4), 425–459.

Brantlinger, E., Jimenez, R., Klingner, J., Pugach, M., & Richardson, V. (2005). Qualitative studies in special education. *Exceptional Children, 71*(2), 195–207.

Brantlinger, E., Klingner, J., & Richardson, V. (2005). Importance of experimental as well as empirical qualitative studies in special education. *Mental Retardation, 43*(2), 92–119.

Brigham, F. J., & Kauffman, J. M. (1998). Creating supportive environments for students with emotional or behavioral disorders. *Effective School Practices, 17*(2), 5–35.

Brooks-Gunn, J., & Duncan, G. J. (1997). The effects of poverty on children. *The Future of Children, 7,* 55–71.

Browder, D., Ahlgrim-Delzell, L., Spooner, F., Mims, P. J., & Baker, J. N. (2009). Using time delay to teach literacy to students with severe developmental disabilities. *Exceptional Children, 75,* 343–364.

Brown, T. (2006). *Confirmatory factor analysis for applied research.* New York: Guilford Press.

Browne, T., Stotsky, B. A., & Eichorn, J. (1977). A selective comparison of psychological, developmental, social, and academic factors among emotionally disturbed children in three treatment settings. *Child Psychiatry and Human Development, 7,* 231–253.

Bruhn, A., McDaniel, S., & Kreigh, C. (2015). Self-Monitoring Interventions for Students with Behavior Problems: A Systematic Review of Current Research. *Behavioral Disorders, 40*(2), 102–121. doi:10.17988/bd-13-45.1

Bruhn, A., Woods-Groves, S., & Huddle, S. (2014). A preliminary investigation of emotional and behavioral screening practices in K–12 schools. *Education and Treatment of Children, 37,* 611–634. doi:10.1353/etc.2014.0039

Bui, Y. N., Schumaker, J. B., & Deshler, D. D. (2006). The effects of a strategic writing program for students with and without learning disabilities in inclusive fifth grade classes. *Learning Disabilities Research and Practice, 21,* 244–260.

Bullis, M., & Cheney, D. (1999). Vocational and transition interventions for adolescents and young adults with emotional and behavioral disorders. *Focus on Exceptional Children, 31*(1), 1–24.

Bullock, L. M., Gable, R. A., & Mohr, J. D. (2005). Technology mediated instruction in distance education and teacher preparation in special education. *Teacher Education and Special Education, 31,* 229–242.

Burns, M. K., Riley-Tillman, T. C., & Rathvon, N. (2017). *Effective school interventions: Evidence-based strategies for improving student outcomes* (3rd ed.). New York, NY: Guilford.

Burns, M. K., & Ysseldyke, J. E. (2009). Reported prevalence of evidence-based instructional practices in special education. *Journal of Special Education, 43,* 3–11.

Caelli, K., Ray, L., & Mill, J. (2003). 'Clear as mud': Toward greater clarity in generic qualitative research. *International journal of Qualitative Methods, 2*(2), 1–13.

Camerer, C. F., Dreber, A., Forsell, E., Ho, T.-H., Huber, J., Johannesson, M., & Wu, H. (2016). Evaluating replicability of laboratory experiments in economics. *Science, 351,* 1433–1436. doi:10.1126/science.aaf0918

Camerer, C. F., Dreber, A., Holzmeister, F., Ho, T.-H., Huber, J., Johannesson, M., ... Wu, H. (2018). Evaluating the replicability of social science experiments in Nature and Science between 2010 and 2015. *Nature Human Behaviour, 2*(9), 637–644. doi:10.1038/s41562-018-0399-z

Camic, P. M., Rhodes, J. E., & Yardley, L. (Eds.). (2003). Qualitative research in psychology: Expanding perspectives in methodology and design. American Psychological Association, Washington, D.C. doi:10.1037/10595-000

Campbell, D. T., & Fiske, D. W. (1959). Convergent and discriminant validation by the multitrait multimethod matrix. *Psychological Bulletin, 56*(2), 81–105.

Campbell, D. T., & Stanley, J. C. (1963). *Experimental and quasi-experimental designs for research.* Boston: Houghton-Mifflin.

Carini, R. M., Kuh, G. D., & Klein, S. P. (2006). Student engagement and student learning: Testing the linkages. *Research in Higher Education, 47,* 1–32. doi:10.1007/s11162-005-8150-9

Carnine, D. (1995). Trustworthiness, usability, and accessibility of educational research. *Journal of Behavioral Education, 5,* 251–258.

Carnine, D. (1997). Bridging the research-to-practice gap. *Exceptional Children, 63,* 513–521.

Cassell, J. (1978). *A fieldwork manual for studying desegregated schools.* Washington, DC: National Institute of Education.

Cassell, J. (1978). Risks and benefits to subjects of fieldwork. *American Sociologist, 13,* 134–143.

Cater, J. K. (2011). Skype a cost-effective method for qualitative research. *Rehabilitation Counselors & Educators Journal, 4*(2), 10–17.

Cavendish, W. (2017). The Role of Gender, Race/Ethnicity, and Disability Status on the Relationship Between Student Perceptions of School and Family Support and Self-Determination. *Career Development and Transition for Exceptional Individuals, 40*(2), 113–122. https://doi.org/10.1177/2165143416629359

Center for Education Evaluation and Regional Assistance, Institute of Education Sciences. U.S. Department of Education. (2018). Retrieved from https://ies.ed.gov/ncee

Centers for Disease Control and Prevention, (2007). *Prevalence of autism spectrum prevalence of autism spectrum disorders.* Autism and Developmental Disabilities Monitoring Network, Six Sites, United States, 2000. MMWR SS; 56 (No.SS–1).

Centers for Disease Control and Prevention. (2019). *What are childhood mental disorders?* Retrieved from https://www.cdc.gov/childrensmentalhealth/basics.html

Chang, H., Wambura-Ngunjiri, F. W., & Hernandez, K. A. C. (2012). *Collaborative autoethnography.* Walnut Creek, CA: Left Coast Press.

Chow, J., & Ekholm, E. (2018). Do published studies yield larger effect sizes than unpublished studies in education and special education? A meta-review. *Educational Psychology Review, 30,* 727–744. doi:10.1007/s10648-018-9437-7

Christenson, Young, & Marchant (2007). Behavioral intervention planning: Increasing the appropriate behavior of a socially withdrawn student. *Education and Treatment of Children, 30,* 81–103.

Christle, C. A., Nelson, C. M., & Jolivette, K. (2004). School characteristics related to the use of suspension. *Education and Treatment of Children, 27,* 509–526.

Cleary, T. J., Platten, P., & Nelson, A. (2008). Effectiveness of the self-regulation empowerment program with urban high school students. *Journal of Advanced Academics, 20,* 70–107. Retrieved from http://edci6325singlecasedesign.pbworks.com/f/Effectiveness+of+self +regulation+empowerement +program+with+urban+high+school+studens.pdf

Cleary, T. J., & Zimmerman, B. J. (2004). Self-regulation empowerment program: A school-based program to enhance self-regulated and self-motivated cycles of student learning. *Psychology in the Schools, 41,* 537–550. doi:10.1002/pits.10177

Codding, R. S., & Smyth, C. A. (2008). Using performance feedback to decrease classroom transition time and examine collateral effects on academic engagement. *Journal of Educational and Psychological Consultation, 18,* 325–345. doi:10.1080/10474410802463312

Cohen, J. (1969). *Statistical power analysis for the behavioral sciences.* New York: Academic Press.

Cohen, J. (1988). *Statistical power analysis for the behavioral sciences* (2nd ed.). Hillsdale, NJ: Lawrence Erlbaum Associates.

Cohen, J. (1990). Things I have learned (so far). *American Psychologist, 45,* 1304–1312.

Cohen, J. (1992). A power primer. *Psychological Bulletin, 112,* 155–159.

Cohen, J. (1994). The earth is round (p < .05). *American Psychologist, 47,* 997–1003.

Cohen, J., & Cohen, P. (1983). *Applied multiple regression/correlational analysis for the behavioral sciences* (2nd ed.). Hillsdale, NJ: Erlbaum.

Cohen, J., Cohen, P., West, S. G., & Aiken, L. S. (2003). *Applied multiple regression/correlation analysis for the behavioral sciences* (3rd ed.). Mahwah, NJ: Erlbaum.

Connelly, F. M., & Clandinin, D. J. (1990). Stories of experience and narrative inquiry. *Educational Researcher, 19*(5), 2–14.

Connelly, V. J., & Rosenberg, M. S. (2009). Special education teaching as a profession: Lessons learned from occupations that have achieved full professional standing. *Teacher Education and Special Education, 32,* 201–214.

Conrad, C., Neumann, A., Haworth, J. G., & Scott, P. (1993). *Qualitative research in higher education: Experiencing alternative perspective and approaches.* Needham Heights, MA: Ginn Press.

Cook, B. G. (2014). A call for examining replication and bias in special education research. *Remedial and Special Education, 35,* 233–246. doi: 10.1177/0741932514528995

Cook, B. G., & Cook, L. (2008). Nonexperimental quantitative research and its role in guiding instruction. *Intervention in School and Clinic, 44*(2), 98–104.

Cook, B. G., Collins, L. W., Cook, S. C., & Cook, L. H. (2016). A replication by any other name: A systematic review of replicative intervention studies. *Remedial and Special Education, 37,* 223–234. doi: 10.1177/0741932516637198

Cook, B. G., & Cook, S. C. (2013). Unraveling evidence-based practices in special education. *Journal of Special Education, 47,* 71–82. doi: 10.1177/0022466911420877

Cook, B. G., Cook, S. C., & Collins, L. W. (2016). Terminology and evidence-based practice for students with EBD: Exploring some devilish details. *Beyond Behavior, 25*(2), 4–13.

Cook, B. G., & Farley, C. (2019). The research-to-practice gap in special education. In D. F. Bateman, J. Cline, & M. L. Yell (Eds.), *Current trends and legal issues in special education.* Newbury Park, CA: Corwin.

Cook, L., & Friend, M. (1995). Co-teaching: Guidelines for creating effective practices. *Focus on Exceptional Children, 28*(3), 1–15.

Cook, B. G., Lloyd, J. W., Mellor, D., Nosek, B. A., & Therrien, W. J. (2018). Promoting open science to increase the trustworthiness of evidence in special education. *Exceptional Children, 85,* 104–118. doi: 10.1177/0014402918793138

Cook, B. G., McDuffie, K. A., Oshita, L., & Cook, S. C. (2017). Co-teaching and students with disabilities: A critical analysis of the empirical literature. In D. P. Hallahan & J. K. Kauffman (Eds.), *The handbook of special education* (2nd ed., pp. 233–248). New York: Routledge.

Cook, B. G., & Odom, S. L. (2013). Evidence-based practices and implementation science in special education. *Exceptional Children, 79,* 135–144. doi: 10.1177/001440291307900020

Cook, B. G., Smith, G. J., & Richards, C. (in press). Supporting evidence-based practice with practice-based evidence [special issue]. *Intervention in School and Clinic, 46*(2).

Cook, B. G., & Tankersley, M. (Eds.). (2013). *Research-based practices in special education.* Boston, MA: Pearson.

Cook, B. G., Tankersley, M., Cook, L., & Landrum, T. J. (2000). Teacher's attitudes toward their included students with disabilities. *Exceptional Children, 67,* 115–135.

Cook, B. G., Tankersley, M., Cook, L., & Landrum, T. J. (2008). Evidence-based practices in special education: Some practical considerations. *Intervention in School & Clinic, 44,* 69–75.

Cook, B. G., Tankersley, M., Cook, L., & Landrum, T. J. (2015). Republication of "Evidence-Based Practices in Special Education: Some Practical Considerations." *Intervention in School and Clinic, 50*(5), 310–315. https://doi.org/10.1177/1053451214532071

Cook, B. G., Tankersley, M., & Harjusola-Webb, S. (2008). Evidence-based practice and professional wisdom: Putting it all together. *Intervention in School & Clinic, 44*(2), 105–111.

Cook, B. G., Tankersley, M., & Landrum, T. J. (2009). Determining evidence-based practices in special education. *Exceptional Children, 75*(3), 365–383.

Cook, L., & Rumrill, P. (2005). Internal validity in rehabilitation research. *Work, 25,* 279–283.

Cook, T. D., & Campbell, D. T. (1979). *Quasi-experimentation: Design and analysis issues for field settings.* Chicago: Rand McNally.

Cook, T., Cooper, H., Cordray, D., Hartman, H., Hedges, L., Light R., Louis, T., & Mosteller, F. (1992). *Meta-analysis for explanation: A case book.* Newbury Park, CA: Sage Publications, Inc.

Corbin, A., & Strauss, A. (2008). *Basics of qualitative research: Techniques and procedures for developing grounded theory* (3rd ed.). Thousand Oaks, CA: Sage Publications, Inc.

Corey, G., Corey, M., & Callanan, P. (1998). *Issues and ethics in the helping professions* (5th ed.). Pacific Grove, CA: Brooks/Cole.

Corry, G., Corey, M. S., & Callanan, P. (2011). *Issues and ethics in the helping professions* (8th ed.). Belmont, CA: Brook/Cole.

Cortina, J., & Nouri, H. (2000). *Effect size for ANOVA designs.* Thousand Oaks, CA: Sage Publications, Inc.

Council for Exceptional Children. (1997, July 24). *CEC Standards for Professional Practice, professionals in relation to persons with exceptionalities and their families: Instructional responsibilities.* Reston, VA: Author. Retrieved September 2, 2000 from World Wide Web: http://www.cec.sped.org/ps/code.htm#3

Council for Exceptional Children. (2007). *Code of ethics for educators of persons with exceptionalities.* Retrieved April 9, 2009, from http://www.cec.sped.org/

Council for Exceptional Children. (2015). *What every special educator must know: Professional ethics and standards.* Arlington, VA: CEC.

Council for Exceptional Children. (n.d.). *CEC ethics and practice standards.* Retrieved on February 10, 2010 from http://www.cec.sped.org/Content/NavigationMenu/Professional Development/ProfessionalStandards/EthicsPracticeStandards/

Council for Exceptional Children. (n.d.). *Ethical principles and professional practice standards for special educators.* Retrieved from https://www.cec.sped.org/Standards/Ethical-Principles-and-Practice-Standard

Courtade, G. R., Test, D. W., & Cook, B. G. (2015). Evidence-based practices for learners with severe intellectual disability. *Research and Practice for Persons with Severe Disabilities, 39,* 301–318. doi: 10.1177/1540796914566711

Coyne, M. D., Little, M. E., Rawlinson, D. M., Simmons, D. C., Kwok, O., Kim, M., & Civetelli, C. (2013). Replicating the impact of a supplemental beginning reading intervention: The role of instructional context. *Journal of Research on Educational Effectiveness, 6,* 1–23. doi: 10.1080/19345747.2012.706694

Creswell, J. W. (2003). *Research design: Qualitative and quantitative approaches* (3rd ed). Thousand Oakes, CA: Sage.

Creswell, J. W. (2007). *Qualitative inquiry and research method: Choosing among five approaches* (2nd ed.). Thousand Oaks, CA: Sage.

Creswell, J. W. (2012). *Qualitative inquiry and research method: Choosing among five approaches* (3rd ed.). Thousand Oaks, CA: Sage.

Creswell, J. W. (2014). *Educational research: Planning, conducting, and evaluating quantitative and qualitative research* (5th ed.). Upper Saddle River, NJ: Pearson.

Crocker, L., & Algina, J. (2006). *Introduction to classical and modern test theory.* Wadsworth Publishing Company.

Cronbach, L. (1988). Five perspectives on the validity argument. In H. Wainer & H. I. Braun (Eds.), *Test validity*. Hillsdale, NJ: Erlbaum.

Cronbach, L. (1990). *Essentials of psychological testing* (5th ed.). New York: Harper & Row.

Cronbach, L., & Meehl, P. (1955). Construct validity in psychological tests. *Psychological Bulletin, 52*(4), 281–302.

Crowson, R. L. (1993). Qualitative research design methods in higher education. In C. Conrad, A. Neuman, J. G. Haworth, & P. Scott (Eds.), *Qualitative research in higher education: Experiencing alternative perspectives and approaches.* Ashe Reader Series. Needham Heights, MA: Ginn Press.

Dammann, J. E., & Vaughn, S. (2001). Science and sanity in special education. *Behavioral Disorders, 27,* 21–29.

Danielson, L., & Rosenquist, C. (2014). Introduction to the TEC special issue on data-based individualization. *Teaching Exceptional Children, 46*(4), 6–12. doi: 10.1177 /0040059914522965

Denzin, N. K. (1970). *The research act.* Chicago: Aldine.

Denzin, N. K., & Giardina, M. D. (2009). Introduction: Toward a politics of hope. In N. K. Denzin & M. D. Giardina (Eds.), *Qualitative inquiry and social justice* (pp. 11–50). Walnut Creek, CA: Left Coast Press, Inc.

Denzin, N. K., & Lincoln, Y. S. (1994). *Handbook of qualitative research.* Thousand Oaks, CA: Sage Publications, Inc.

Denzin, N. K. & Lincoln, Y. S. (2000). *Handbook of qualitative research* (2nd ed.). Thousand Oaks, CA: Sage.

Denzin, N. K., & Lincoln, Y. S. (2000). Strategies of inquiry. *Handbook of Qualitative Research, 2,* 367–378. Thousand Oaks, CA: Sage Publications.

De Pry, R. L., & Sugai, G. (2002). The effect of active supervision and pre-correction on minor behavioral incidents in a sixth grade general education classroom. *Journal of Behavioral Education, 11,* 255–267. doi:10.1023/A:1021162906622

Dexter, L. A. (1970). *Elite and specialized interviewing.* Evanston, IL: Northwestern University Press.

Diener, E., & Crandall, R. (1978). *Ethics in social and behavioral research.* Chicago: University of Chicago Press.

Dillman, D. (2007). *Mail and internet surveys* (2nd ed.). Hoboken, NJ: John Wiley.

Dimitrov, D. M. (2008). *Quantitative research in education: Intermediate and advanced methods.* Oceanside, NJ: Whittier.

Dimitrov, D., Fitzgerald, S., & Rumrill, P. (2000). Speaking of research: Multiple regression in rehabilitation research. *Work, 15,* 209–215.

Dimitrov, D., Fitzgerald, S., Rumrill, P., & Hennessey, M. (2001). Speaking of research: Reliability in rehabilitation research. *Work, 16,* 159–164.

Doabler, C. T., Clarke, B., Kosty, D. B., Kurtz-Nelson, E., Fien, H., Smolkowski, K., & Baker, S. K. (2016). Testing the efficacy of a tier 2 mathematics intervention: A conceptual replication study. *Exceptional Children, 83,* 92–110. doi: 10.1177/0014402916660084

Douglas, J. D. (1976). *Investigative social research: Individual and team field research.* Beverly Hills, CA: Sage.

Drew, C. F. (1980). *Introduction to designing and conducting research* (2nd ed.). St. Louis: C. V. Mosby.

Drisko, J. W. (2013). Qualitative data analysis software. In A.E. Fortune, W.J. Reid, & R. Miller (Eds.), *Qualitative Research in social work* (2nd ed.), (pp. 284–306). New York, NY: Columbia University Press.

Drummond, R. (2004). *Appraisal procedures for counselors and helping professionals* (5th ed.). Englewood Cliffs, NJ: Prentice-Hall, Inc.

Ducan, G. J. (1997). The promise and perils of alternative forms of date representation. *Education Researcher, 26*(6), 4–10.

Eisner, E. W. (1997). The promise and perils of alternative forms of data representation. *Educational Researcher, 26*(6), 4–10.

Ellis, C. (2004). *The ethnographic I: A methodological novel about autoethnography.* Walnut Creek, CA: AltaMira.

Emerson, R. M., Fretz, R. I., & Shaw, L. L. (2011). *Writing ethnographic fieldnotes* (2nd ed.). Chicago, IL: University of Chicago Press.

Ensminger, M. E., Forrest, C. B., Riley, A. W., Kang, M., Green, B. F., Starfield, B., & Ryan, S. A. (2000). The validity of measures of socio-economic status of adolescents. *Journal of Adolescent Research, 15,* 392–219.

Espin, C., Deno, S., & Albayrak, Kaymak, D. (1998). Individualized education programs in resource and inclusive settings: How "individualized" are they? *The Journal of Special Education, 32*(3), 164–174

Etscheidt, S. (2006). Issues in transition planning, *Career Development for Exceptional Individuals, 29*(1), 28–47.

Farmer, T. W., Farmer, E. M. Z., Estell, D. B., & Hutchins, B. C. (2007). The developmental dynamics of aggression and the prevention of school violence. *Journal of Emotional and Behavioral Disorders, 15,* 197–208.

Fassinger, R. (1987). Use of structural equation modeling in counseling psychology research. *Journal of Counseling Psychology, 34,* 425–436.

Ferguson, D. (1993). Something a little out of the ordinary: Reflections on becoming an interpretivist researcher in special education. *Remedial and Special Education, 14*(4), 35–43, 51.

Ferguson, D., & Halle, J. (1995). Considerations for readers of qualitative research (Editorial). *Journal of the Association for Persons with Severe Handicaps, 20*(1), 1–2.

Ferguson, D. L., & Ferguson, P. M. (2000). Qualitative research in special education: Notes toward an open inquiry instead of a new orthodoxy? *Journal of the Association for Persons with Severe Handicaps, 25*(3), 180–185.

Ferrari, J. R., & Tice, D. M. (2000). Procrastination as a selfhandicap for men and women: A task-avoidance strategy in a laboratory setting. *Journal of Research in Personality, 34,* 73–83. doi:10.1006/jrpe.1999.2261

Fielding, N. (2001). Computer applications in qualitative research. In W. P. Atkinson, A. Coffey, S. Delamont, J. Lofland, & L. Lofland (Eds.), *Handbook of ethnography* (pp. 453–467). London: Sage Publication.

Fielding, N., & Fielding, J. (1986). *Linking data.* Beverly Hills, CA: Sage Publications.

Fielding, N. G., & Fielding, J. L. (1986). *Linking data.* Newbury Park, CA: Sage Publications, Inc.

Finfgeld-Connett, D. (2016). The future of theory-generating meta-synthesis research. *Qualitative Health Research, 26*(3), 291–293.

Fitzgerald, S., Dimitrov, D., & Rumrill, P. (2001). Speaking of research: The basics of non-parametric statistics. *Work, 16,* 287–292.

Fitzgerald, S., Rumrill, P., & Hart, R. (2000). Speaking of research: Using analysis of variance (ANOVA) in rehabilitation research investigations. *Work, 14,* 61–65.

Fitzgerald, S., Rumrill, P., & Merchant, W. (2014). A response to Harris, Gould, and Fujiura: Beyond scoping reviews—a case for mixed-methods research reviews. *Work: A Journal of Prevention, Assessment, and Rehabilitation, 50*(2), 335–339.

Fitzgerald, S., Rumrill, P. D., & Schenker, J. D. (2004). Perspectives on scientific inquiry: Correlational designs in rehabilitation research. *Journal of Vocational Rehabilitation, 20,* 143–150.

Flick, U. (1998). *An introduction to qualitative research.* Thousand Oaks, CA: Sage.

Flick, U. (2002). Qualitative Research - State of the Art. Social Science Information, 41(1), 5–24. doi:10.1177/0539018402041001001

Forgan, J. W., & Vaughn, S. (2000). Adolescents with and without LD make the transition to middle school. *Journal of Learning Disabilities, 33,* 33–43.

Forness, S. R. (2005). The pursuit of evidence-based practice in special education for children with emotional and behavioral disorders. *Behavioral Disorders, 30,* 311–330.

Forness, S. R., Kavale, K., Blum, S., & Lloyd, J. W. (1997). Mega-analysis of meta-analyses: What works in special education and related services. *Teaching Exceptional Children, 24,* 4–9.

Forness, S. R., & Knitzer, J. A. (1992). A new proposed definition and terminology to replace "serious emotional disturbance" in the Individuals with Disabilities Act. *School Psychology Review, 21,* 12–20.

Fredricks, J. A., Blumenfeld, P. C., & Paris, A. H. (2004). School engagement: Potential of the concept, state of the 10 evidence. *Review of Educational Research, 74,* 59–109. doi:10.3102 /00346543074001059

Freedman, D. H. (2010). *Wrong: Why experts keep failing us—and how to know when not to trust them.* New York, NY: Little, Brown, and Company.

Freedman, R. I., & Fesko, S. L. (1996). The meaning of work in the lives of people with significant disabilities: Consumer and family perspectives. *Journal of Rehabilitation, 62,* 49–55.

Fuchs, D., & Fuchs, L. S. (2005). Responsiveness-to-intervention: A blueprint for practitioners, policymakers, and parents. *Teaching Exceptional Children, 38*(1), 57–61.

Fuchs, D., & Fuchs, L. S. (2006). Introduction to response to intervention: What, why, and how valid is it? *Reading Research Quarterly, 41,* 93–99.

Fujiura, G. T., & Yamaki, K. (2000). Trends in demography of childhood poverty and disability. *Exceptional Children, 66,* 187–199.

Gage, N. A., Cook, B. G., & Reichow, B. (2017). Publication bias in special education meta-analyses. *Exceptional Children, 83,* 428–445. doi: 10.1177/0014402917691016

Gage, N. A., Scott, T., Hirn, R., & MacSuga-Gage, A. S. (2018). The relationship between teachers' implementation of classroom management practices and student behavior in elementary school. *Behavioral Disorders, 43*(2), 302–315. https://doi.org/10.1177 /0198742917714809

Gaito, J. (1980). Measurement scales and statistics: Resurgence of an old misconception. *Psychological Bulletin, 87*(3), 564–567.

Gallagher, D. J. (2006). If not absolute objectivity, then what? A reply to Kauffman and Sasso. *Exceptionality, 14,* 91–107.

Gartin, B., Rumrill, P., & Serebreni, R. (1996). The higher education transition model: Guidelines for facilitating college transition among college-bound student with disabilities. *Teaching Exceptional Children 28*(5), 30–33.

Gaumer Erickson, A. S., Noonan, P. M., Zheng, C., & Brussow, J. A. (2015). The relationship between self-determination and academic achievement for adolescents with intellectual disabilities. *Research in Developmental Disabilities, 36,* 45–54. doi:10.1016/j.ridd.2014 .09.008

Gay, L., & Airasian, P. (2003). *Educational research: Competencies for analysis and applications* (7th ed.). Upper Saddle River, NJ: Pearson Education, Inc.

Geertz, C. (1973). *The interpretation of cultures.* New York, NY: Basic Books.

Geertz, C. (1983). Thick description: Toward an interpretive theory of culture. In *Contemporary field research: A collection of readings* (pp. 37–59). Boston: Little, Brown.

Geisinger, K., Spies, R., Carlson, J., & Plake, B. (2007). *The seventeenth mental measurements year-book.* University of Nebraska Press.

Gerber, M., & Semmel, M. (1984). Teacher as imperfect test: Reconceptualizing the referral process. *Educational Psychologist, 19,* 137–146.

Gersten, R., Baker, S. K., Smith-Johnson, J., Flojo, J. R., & Hagan-Burke, S. (2004). A tale of two decades: Trends in support for federally experimental research in special education. *Exceptional Children, 70*(3), 323–332.

Gersten, R., Beckmann, S., Clarke, B., Foegen, A., Marsh, L., Star, J., . . . Scott, L. (2009). Assisting students struggling with mathematics: Response to intervention (RtI) for elementary and middle schools (Institute of Education Sciences Practice Guide). Washington, DC:U.S. Department of Education

Gersten, R., Compton, D., Connor, C. M., Dimino, J., Santoro, L., Linan-Thompson, S., & Tilly, W. D. (2008). *Assisting students struggling with reading: Response to Intervention and multi-tier intervention for reading in the primary grades. A practice guide.* (NCEE 2009–4045). Washington, DC: National Center for Education Evaluation and Regional Assistance, Institute of Education Sciences, U.S. Department of Education. Retrieved from http://ies.ed.gov/ncee/wwc/ publications/practiceguides/

Gersten, R., Fuchs, L. S., Compton, D., Coyne, M., Greenwood, C., & Innocenti, M. S. (2005). Quality indicators for group experimental and quasi-experimental research in special education. *Exceptional Children, 71,* 149–164.

Gettinger, M., & Seibert, J. K. (2002). *Best practices in increasing academic learning time.* Retrieved from http://dal lasisd.schoolwires.net/cms/lib/TX01001475/Centricity/Domain/11206 /Best%20Practices%20In%20Increasing%20 Academic%20Learning%20Time.pdf

Gialloreti, L. E., & Curatolo, P. (2018). Autism spectrum disorder: Why do we know so little? *Frontiers in Neurology, 9,* 670. doi: 10.3389/fneur.2018.00670

Gilmour, A. F., Fuchs, D., & Wehby, J. H. (2018). Are students with disabilities accessing the curriculum? A meta-analysis of the reading achievement gap between students with and without disabilities. *Exceptional Children, 85*(3) 329–346. doi:10.1177/0014402918795830

Gilmour, A. F., Fuchs, D., & Wehby, J. H. (2019). Are Students With Disabilities Accessing the Curriculum? A Meta-Analysis of the Reading Achievement Gap Between Students With and Without Disabilities. *Exceptional Children, 85,* 329–346. doi:10.1177/0014402918795 830

Glaser, B., & Stauss, A. (1967). *The discovery of grounded theory: Strategies for qualitative research.* Chicago, IL: Aldine.

Glass, G. (1976). Primary, secondary, and meta-analysis of research. *Educational Researcher, 5,* 3–8.

Glass, G. (1977). Integrating findings: The meta-analysis of research. In L. Shulman (Ed.), *Review of research in education.* Itasca, IL: Peacock.

Glass, G., & Hopkins, K. (1996). *Statistical methods in education and psychology* (3rd ed.). Needham Heights, MA: Allyn & Bacon.

Glassberg, L. A. (1994). Students with behavioral disorders: Determinants of placement outcomes. *Behavioral Disorders, 19,* 181–191.

Glesne, C., & Peshkin, A. (1992). *Becoming qualitative researchers: An introduction.* White Plains, NY: Longman.

Goff, C., Martin, J. E., & Thomas, M. K. (2007). The burden of acting white: Implications in transition. *Career Development for Exceptional Individuals, 30*(3), 134–146.

Goldstein, H. (2003). *Multilevel statistical models* (3rd ed.). New York: Oxford University Press.

Good, T. L., & Beckerman, T. M. (1978). Time on task: A naturalistic study in sixth-grade classrooms. *The Elementary School Journal, 78,* 193–201. doi:10.1086/461101

Goodwin, C. J., & Goodwin, K. A. (2012). *Research in psychology: Methods and design* (7th ed.). Hoboken, NJ: Wiley Publications.

Graham, S., & Harris, K. R. (1992). Self-regulated strategy development: Programmatic research in writing. In B. Y. L. Wong (Ed.), *Contemporary intervention research in learning disabilities: An international perspective* (1st ed., pp. 47–64). New York, NY: Springer. doi:10 .1007/978-1-4612-2786-1_3

Graham, S., Harris, K., & Santangelo, T. (2015). Research-Based Writing Practices and the Common Core: Meta-analysis and Meta-synthesis. *The Elementary School Journal, 115*(4), 498–522. doi:10.1086/681964

Gravetter, F. J., Wallnau, L. B., & Forzano, L. B. (2017). *Essentials of statistics for the behavioral sciences* (9th ed.). Boston, MA: Cengage Learning.

Graziano, K. (2004). The power of teaching and learning with documentary photography and storytelling: A photovoice case study. In *Proceedings of World Conference on Educational Multimedia, Hypermedia and Telecommunications* (pp. 3881–3886).

Greenbaum, P. E., Dedrick, R. F., Friedman, R. M., Kutash, K., Brown, E. C., Lardieri, S. P., & Pugh, A. M. (1996). National Adolescent and Child Treatment Study (NACTS): Outcomes for children with serious emotional and behavioral disturbance. *Journal of Educational and Behavioral Disorders, 4,* 130–146.

Greenwood, C. R., Horton, B. T., & Utley, C. A. (2002). Academic engagement: Current perspectives on research and practice. *School Psychology Review, 31,* 328–349.

Gresham, F. M. (2005). Response to intervention: An alternative means of identifying students as emotionally disturbed. *Education and Treatment of Children, 28,* 328–344.

Gresham, F. M., MacMillian D. L., Beebe-Frankenberger, M. E., & Bocian, K. M. (2000). Treatment integrity in learning disabilities intervention research: Do we really know how treatments are implemented? *Learning Disabilities Research and Practice, 15,* 198–205.

Grimm, L., & Yarnold, P. (2000). *Reading and understanding multivariate statistics.* Washington, DC: American Psychological Association.

Guba, E. G. (1978). *Toward a methodology of naturalistic inquiry in educational evaluation.* CSE Monograph Series in Evaluation, 8. Los Angeles: Center for the Study of Evaluation, University of California.

Guba, E. G., & Lincoln, Y. (1981). *Effective evaluation: Improving the usefulness of evaluation results through responsive and naturalistic approaches.* San Francisco: Jossey-Bass.

Guillemin, M., & Gillam, L. (2004). Ethics, reflexivity, and "ethically important moments" in research. *Qualitative Inquiry, 10*(2), 261.

Gunter, P. L., & Reed, T. M. (1997). Academic instruction of children with emotional and behavioral disorders. *Preventing School Failure, 42,* 33–37.

Hagner, D. C., & Helm, D. T. (1994). Qualitative methods in rehabilitation research. *Rehabilitation Counseling Bulletin, 37,* 290–303.

Hair, J., Black, W., Babin, B., & Anderson, R. (2009). *Multivariate data analysis.* Englewood Cliffs, NJ: Pearson.

Haley, K., Allsopp, D., & Hoppey, D. (2018). When a Parent of a Student With a Learning Disability Is Also an Educator in the Same School District: A Heuristic Case Study. *Learning Disability Quarterly, 41*(1), 19–31. doi:10.1177/0731948717690114

Hallahan, D. P., Kauffman, J. M., & Pullen, P. C. (2009). *Exceptional Learners: Introduction to special education* (11th ed.). Needham Heights, MA: Allyn and Bacon.

Hammell, K. W. (2007). Quality of life after spinal cord injury: a meta-synthesis of qualitative findings. *Spinal Cord, 45*(2), 124–139.

Hammersley, M., & Atkinson, P. (2007). *Ethnography: Principles in practice.* New York, NY: Routledge.

Hardwicke, T. A., & Ioannidis, J. P. A. (2018). Mapping the universe of registered reports. *Nature: Human Behaviour, 2,* 793–796. doi: 10.1038/s41562-018-0444-y

Harris, K. R., & Graham, S. (2009). Almost 30 years of writing research: Making sense of it all with The Wrath of Khan. *Learning Disabilities Research and Practice, 24,* 58–68.

Hatch, J. A. (2002). *Doing qualitative research in education settings.* Albany: SUNY Press.

Hawken, L. S., Vincent, C. G., & Schumann, J. (2008). Response to intervention for social behavior: Challenges and opportunities. *Journal of Emotional and Behavioral Disorders, 16,* 213–225.

Haworth, J. G., & Conrad, C. F. (1997). *Emblems of quality in higher education: Developing and sustaining high-quality programs.* Boston: Allyn and Bacon.

Hays, W. (1988). Statistics (4th ed.). New York: Holt, Rinehart, & Winston.

Heck, R. H., & Thomas, S. L. (2009). *An introduction to multilevel modeling techniques* (2nd ed.). New York: Psychology Press.

Heiman, T., & Margalit, M. (1998). Loneliness, Depression, and Social Skills Among Students with Mild Mental Retardation in Different Educational Settings. *The Journal of Special Education, 32*(3), 154–163. doi:10.1177/002246699803200302

Helling, I. K. (1988). The life history method. In N. K. Denzin (Ed.), *Studies in symbolic interaction.* Greenwich, CT: JAI.

Heppner, P., Kivlighan, D., & Wampold, B. (1992). *Research design in counseling.* Pacific Grove, CA: Brooks/Cole.

Heppner, P., Kivlighan, D., & Wampold, B. (1999). *Research design in counseling* (2nd ed.). Pacific Grove, CA: Brooks/Cole.

Heppner, P., Wampold, B., & Kivlighan, D. (2008). *Research design in counseling* (3rd ed.). Pacific Grove, CA: Brooks/Cole.

Heppner, P., Wampold, B., Owen, J., Thompson, M., & Wang, K. (2015). *Research design in counseling* (4th ed.) Independence, KY: Cengage Learning.

Hill, C. E., Thompson, B. J., & Williams, E. N. (1997). A guide to conducting consensual qualitative research. *The Counseling Psychologist, 25*(4), 517–572.

Hill, M. R., Noonan, V. K., Sakakibara, B. M., & Miller, W. C. (2009). Quality of life instruments and definitions in individuals with spinal cord injury: A systematic review. *Spinal Cord, 48*(6), 438–450. doi:10.1038/sc.2009.164

Hinkle, D. E., Wiersma, W., & Jurs, S. G. (2003). *Applied statistics for the behavioral sciences* (5th ed.). Florence, KY: Cengage Learning Inc.

Hollenbeck, A. F. (2007). From IDEA to implementation: A discussion of foundational and future responsiveness-to-intervention research. *Learning Disabilities Research and Practice, 22,* 137–146.

Hollowood, T. M., Salisbury, C. L., Rainforth, B., & Palombaro, M. M. (1994). Use of instructional time in classrooms serving students with and without severe disabilities. *Exceptional Children, 61,* 242–253.

Holman Jones, S. (2005). Autoethnography: Making the personal political. In Norman K. Denzin & Yvonna S. Lincoln (Eds.), *Handbook of qualitative research* (pp. 763–791). Thousand Oaks, CA: Sage.

Hood, A., & Johnson, R. (1997). *Assessment in counseling: A guide to the use of psychological assessment procedures* (2nd ed.). Alexandria, VA: American Counseling Association.

Hood, A., & Johnson, R. (2002). *Assessment in counseling: A guide to the use of psychological assessment procedures* (3rd ed.). Alexandria, VA: American Counseling Association.

Hornby, G. (2015). Inclusive special education: development of a new theory for the education of children with special educational needs and disabilities. *British Journal of Special Education, 42*(3), 234–256. doi:10.1111/1467-8578.12101

Horner, R. H., Carr, E. G., Halle, J., McGee, G., Odom, S., & Wolery, M. (2005). The use of single-subject research to identify evidence-based practice in special education. *Exceptional Children, 71,* 165–179.

Horner, R. H., & Sugai, G. (2015). School-wide PBIS: An example of applied behavior analysis implemented at a scale of social importance. *Behavior Analysis in Practice, 8,* 80–85.

Horner, R. H., Sugai, G., & Anderson, C. M. (2010). Examining the evidence base for school-wide positive behavior support. *Focus on Exceptional Children, 42*(8), 1–14.

Hott, B. L., Dibbs, R. A., Naizer, G., Raymond, L., Reid, C. C., & Martin, A. (2018). Practitioner perceptions of algebra strategy and intervention use to support students with mathematics difficulty or disability in rural Texas. Advance online publication. *Rural Special Education Quarterly, 38*(1), 3–14. doi: 8756870518795494

Howie, J., Gatens-Robinson, E., & Rubin, S. (1992). Applying ethical principles in rehabilitation counseling. *Rehabilitation Education, 6,* 41–55.

Hughes, P. (2012). An autoethnographic approach to understanding Asperger's syndrome: A personal exploration of self-identity through reflexive narrative. *British Journal of Learning Disabilities, 40,* 94–100.

Hunt, B. (2011). Publishing Qualitative Research in Counseling Journals. *Journal of Counseling & Development, 89*(3), 296–300. doi:10.1002/j.1556-6678.2011.tb00092.x

Hunter, J., & Schmidt, F. (1990). *Methods of meta-analysis.* Newbury Park, CA: Sage Publications, Inc.

Ioannidis, J. P. (2018). Why replication has more scientific value than original discovery. *Behavioral and Brain Sciences, 41,* e137. doi: 10.1017/S0140525X18000729

Idol, L. (2006). Toward inclusion of special education students in general education: A program evaluation of eight schools. *Remedial and Special Education, 27,* 77–94.

Individuals with Disabilities Education Improvement Act of 2004, 31 U.S.C. (2006). Retrieved from https://www.govinfo.gov/content/pkg/PLAW-108publ446/html/PLAW-108publ446 .htm

Jimerson, S. R., Burns, M. K., & VanDerHeyden, A. M. (Eds.). (2015). *Handbook of response to intervention: The science and practice of multi-tiered systems of support* (2nd ed.). New York, NY: Springer Publishing Company.

John, L. K., Loewenstein, G., & Prelec, D. (2012). Measuring the prevalence of questionable research practices with incentives for truth telling. *Psychological Science, 23,* 524–532. doi:10.1177/0956797611430953

Jolivette, K., Wehby, J. H., & Hirsch, L. (1999). Academic strategy identification for students exhibiting inappropriate classroom behaviors. *Behavioral Disorders, 24,* 210–221.

Jung, P. G., McMaster, K. L., & delMas, R. C. (2017). Effects of early writing intervention delivered within a data-based instruction framework. *Exceptional Children, 83,* 281–297. doi: 10.1177/0014402916667586

Kalton, G. (1983). *Introduction to survey sampling.* Newbury Park, CA: Sage Publications, Inc.

Kanner, L. (1943). Autistic disturbances of affective contact. *Nervous Child, 2,* 217–250.

Kaplan, R. M., & Irvin, V. L. (2015). Likelihood of null effects of large NHLBI clinical trials has increased over time. *PLOS ONE, 10*(8), e0132382. doi:10.1371/journal.pone.013238

Kauffman, A. M., Conroy, M., Gardner, R., & Oswald, D. (2008). Cultural sensitivity in the application of behavioral principles to education. *Education and Treatment of Children, 31,* 239–262.

Kauffman, J. M. (2005). *Characteristics of emotional and behavioral disorders of children and youth* (8th ed.). Upper Saddle River, NJ: Merrill Prentice.

Kauffman, J. M. (1996). Research to practice issues. *Behavioral Disorders, 22,* 55–60.

Kauffman, J. M. (1999). The role of science in behavioral disorders. *Behavioral Disorders, 24,* 265–272.

Kauffman, J. M., & Badar, J. (2014). Instruction, not inclusion, should be the central issue in special education: An alternative view from the USA. *Journal of International Special Needs Education, 17*(1), 13–20.

Kauffman, J. M., Mock, D. R., & Simpson, R. L. (2007). Problems related to under-service of students with emotional or behavioral disorders. *Behavioral Disorders, 33,* 43–57.

Kavale, A., & Spaulding, L. S. (2008). Is response to intervention good policy for specific learning disability? *Learning Disabilities Research and Practice, 23,* 169–179.

Kazdin, A. (1982). *Single-case research designs.* New York: Oxford University Press.

Kazdin, A. (1992). *Research design in clinical psychology* (2nd ed.). Needham Heights, MA: Allyn & Bacon.

Kazdin, A. (2002). The State of Child and Adolescent Psychotherapy Research. *Child and Adolescent Mental Health, 7*(2), 53.

Kazdin, A. (2003). *Research design in clinical psychology* (4th ed.). Needham Heights, MA: Allyn & Bacon.

Kazdin, A. (2017). *Research design in clinical psychology* (5th ed.). Needham Heights, MA: Allyn & Bacon.

Kazdin, A. E. (1998). *Research design in clinical psychology.* Allyn and Bacon. Boston, MA.

Keith, T. Z. (2006). *Multiple regression and beyond.* New York: Pearson Education.

Keith, T. Z. (2014). *Multiple regression and beyond: An introduction to multiple regression and structural equation modeling.* Routledge. New York, NY.

Kercood, S., & Grskovic, J. A. (2009). The effects of highlighting on the math com_putation performance and off-task behavior of students with attention problems. *Education and Treatment of Children, 32,* 231–241.

Kidwell, M. C., Lazarevic, L. B., Baranski, E., Hardwicke, T. E., Piechowski, S., Falkenberg, L.-S., Nosek, B. A. (2016). Badges to acknowledge open practices: A simple, low cost effective method for increasing transparency. *PloS Biology, 14*(5), e1002456. doi:10.1371/journal.pbio.1002456

Kilgus, S. P., Fallon, L. M., & Feinberg, A. B. (2016). Function-based modification of Check-in/Check-Out to influence escape-maintained behavior. *Journal of Applied School Psychology, 32,* 24–45. doi:10.1080/15377903.2015.1084965

Kim, Y. S., Leventhal, B. L., Koh, Y. J., Fombonne, E., Laska, E., Lim, E. C., & Song, D. H. (2011). Prevalence of autism spectrum disorders in a total population sample. *American Journal of Psychiatry, 168,* 904–912.

King, M. T., Merrin, G. J., Espelage, D. L., Grant, N. J., & Bub, K. L. (2018). Suicidality and intersectionality among students identifying as nonheterosexual and with a disability. *Exceptional Children, 84*(2), 141–158. https://doi.org/10.1177/0014402917736261

Kitchner, K. (1984). Intuition, critical evaluation, and ethical principles: The foundation for ethical decision in counseling psychology. *The Counseling Psychologist, 12*(3), 43–55.

Kittelman, A., Gion, C., Horner, R. H., Levin, J. L., & Kratochwill, T. R. (2018). Establishing journalistic standards for the publication of negative results. *Remedial and Special Education, 39,* 171–176. doi:10.1177/0741932517745491

Klein, O., Hardwicke, T. E., Aust, F., Breuer, J., Danielsson, H., Mohr, A. H., & Frank, M. C. (2018). A practical guide for transparency in psychological science. *Collabra: Psychology, 4*(1): 20. doi:http://doi.org/10.1525/collabra.158

Klein, R. A., Vianello, M., Hasselman, F., Adams, B. G., Adams, R. B., Jr., Alper, S., & Nosek, B. A. (2018, November 19). *Many Labs 2: Investigating variation in replicability across sample and setting.* Retrieved from https://doi.org/10.31234/osf.io/9654g

Klem, L. (1995). Path analysis. In L. Grim & P. Yarnold (Eds.), *Reading and understanding multivariate statistics.* Washington, DC: American Psychological Association.

Kliewer, C., & Landis, D. (1999). Individualizing literacy instruction for young children with moderate to severe disabilities. *Exceptional Children, 66*(1), 85–100.

Klin, A. (2009). Subtyping the autism spectrum disorders: Theoretical, research, and clinical considerations. In S. Goldstein, J. A. Naglieri, & S. Ozonof (Eds.), *Assessments of autism spectrum disorders* (pp. 91–116). New York: Guilford

Klingner, J. K., & Bianco, M. (2006). What is special about special education for English language learners? In B. G. Cook & B. R. Schirmer (Eds.), *What is special about special education: The role of evidence-based practices* (pp. 37–53). Austin, TX: Pro-Ed.

Klingner, J. K., & Vaughn, S. (1999). Students' perceptions of instruction in inclusion classrooms: Implications for students with learning disabilities. *Exceptional Children, 66*(1), 23–37.

Koch, L., Niesz, T., & Jones Wilkins, M. (2017). Chapter 7: Qualitative research designs. In P. Rumrill & J. Bellini, *Research in rehabilitation counseling: A guide to design, methodology, and utilization* (3rd ed., pp. 186–227). Springfield, IL: Charles C Thomas.

Koch, L., Niesz, T., & McCarthy, H. (2014). Understanding and reporting qualitative research: An analytical review and recommendations for submitting authors. *Rehabilitation Counseling Bulletin, 57*(3), 131–143.

Koch, L., & Rumrill, P. (2017). *Rehabilitation counseling and emerging disabilities: Medical, psychosocial, and vocational aspects.* New York: Springer Publishing Company.

Kode, K. (2002). *Elizabeth Farrell and the history of special education.* Arlington, VA: Council for Exceptional Children.

Kortering, L. J., & Blackorby, J. (1992). High school dropout and students identified with behavioral disorders. *Behavioral Disorders, 18,* 24–32.

Kosciulek, J. F. (2007). The social context of coping. In E. Martz & H. Livneh (Eds.), *Coping with chronic illness and disability: Theoretical, empirical, and clinical aspects* (pp. 73–88). New York: NY: Springer Publishing Company.

Kosciulek, J. F., & Szymanski, E. M. (1993). Statistical power analysis of rehabilitation counseling research. *Rehabilitation Counseling Bulletin, 36,* 212–219.

Kozleski, E. B. (2017). The uses of qualitative research: Powerful methods to inform evidence-based practice in education. *Research and Practice for Persons with Severe Disabilities, 42*(1), 19–32.

Krathwohl, D. R. (1993). *Methods of educational and social science research: An integrated approach.* White Plains, NY: Longman.

Krathwohl, D. R. (1998). *Methods of educational and social science research: An integrated approach* (2nd ed.). White Plains, NY: Longman.

Kucharczyk, S., Reutebuch, C. K., Carter, E. W., Hedges, S., El Zein, F., Fan, H., & Gustafson, J. R. (2015). Addressing the needs of adolescents with autism spectrum disorder: Considerations and complexities for high school interventions. *Exceptional Children, 81*(3), 329–349.

Kuh, G. D. (2009). The national survey of student engagement: Conceptual and empirical foundations. *New Directions for Institutional Research, 2009,* 5–20. doi:10.1002/ir.283

Kvale, S. (1996). *InterViews—An Introduction to qualitative research interviewing.* Sage Thousand Oaks. CA.

Landrum, T. J., Cook, B. G., Tankersley, M., & Fitzgerald, S. F. (2007). Teacher perceptions of the usability of intervention information from personal versus data-based sources. *Education and Treatment of Children, 30*(4), 27–42.

Landrum, T. J., Cook, B. G., Tankersley, M., & Fitzgerald, S. F. (2002). Teachers' perceptions of the trustworthiness, usability, and accessibility of information from different sources. *Remedial and Special Education, 23,* 42–48.

Landrum, T. J., & Tankersley, M. (1999). Emotional and Behavioral Disorders in the New Millennium: The Future is Now. *Behavioral Disorders, 24*(4), 319–330. doi:10.1177 /019874299902400404

Landrum, T. J., & Tankersley, M. (2004). Science in the schoolhouse: An uninvited guest. *Journal of Learning Disabilities, 37,* 207–212.

Lane, H. (1979). *The wild boy of Aveyron* (Vol. 149). Harvard University Press.

Lane, K. L. (2004). Academic instruction and tutoring intervention for students with emotional and behavioral disorders: 1990 to the present. In R. B. Rutherford, M. M. Quinn, & S. R. Mathur (Eds.), *Handbook of research in emotional and behavioral disorders.* New York: Guilford.

Lane, K. L., Menzies, H. M., Ennis, R. P., & Bezdek, J. (2013). School-wide systems to promote positive behaviors and facilitate instruction. *Journal of Curriculum and Instruction, 7*(1), 6–31. doi:10.3776/joci.2013.v7n1pp6-31

Lane, K. L., Menzies, H. M., Ennis, R. P., & Oakes, W. P. (2018). Effective Low-Intensity Strategies to Enhance School Success: What Every Educator Needs to Know. *Beyond Behavior, 37*(3), 128–133. doi:10.1177/1074295618799044

Lane, K. L., Wehby, J. H., Little, M. A., & Cooley, C. (2005). Academic, social, and behavioral profiles of students with emotional and behavioral disorders educated in self-contained classrooms and self-contained schools: Part I–Are they more alike than different? *Behavioral Disorders, 30,* 349–361.

Lather, P. (1986). Research as praxis. *Harvard Educational Review, 56,* 257–277.

Lather, P. (2008). To appear other to itself anew: Response data. *Cultural Studies/ Critical Methodologies, 8*(3), 369–371.

Lavik, K. B. (2014). The effectiveness of a goal setting intervention that incorporates performance feedback, self-graphing, and reinforcement on improving the writing skills of high school students (Doctoral dissertation, Kent State University). Retrieved from https: //etd.ohiolink.edu/!etd.send_file?accessi on=kent1395826954&disposition=attachment

LeCompte, M. D., & Preissle, J. (1993). *Ethnography and qualitative design in education research* (2nd ed.). San Diego, CA: Academic Press.

Lee, S. W., Elliot, J., & Barbour, J. D. (1994). A comparison of cross-informant behavior ratings in diagnosis. *Behavioral Disorders, 19,* 87–97.

Leko, M. M. (2014). The value of qualitative methods in social validity research. *Remedial and Special Education, 35*(5), 275–286.

Lemons, C. J., King, S. A., Davidson, K. A., Berryessa, T. L., Gajjar, S. A., & Sacks, L. H. (2016). An inadvertent concurrent replication: Same roadmap, different journey. *Remedial and Special Education, 37,* 213–222. doi:10.1177/0741932516631116

Levenstein, M. C., & Lyle, J. A. (2018). Data: Sharing is caring. *Advances in Methods and Practices in Psychological Science, 1,* 95–103. doi:10.1177/2515245918758319

Levine, H. (1985). Principles of data storage and retrieval for use in qualitative evaluations. *Educational Evaluation and Policy Analysis, 7,* 169–186.

Levitt, H. M., Bamberg, M., Creswell, J. W., Frost, D. M., Josselson, R., & Suárez-Orozco, C. (2018). Journal article reporting standards for qualitative primary, qualitative meta-analytic, and mixed methods research in psychology: The APA publications and communications board task force report. *American Psychologist, 73*(1), 26–46. doi:10.1037 /amp0000151

Levy, S. E., Pinto-Martin, J. A., Bradley, C. B., Chittams, J., Johnson, S. L., Pandey, J., & Kral, T. V. E. (2019). Relationship of weight outcomes, co-occurring conditions, and severity of autism spectrum disorder in the study to explore early development. *The Journal of Pediatrics, 205,* 202–209. doi:10.1016/j.jpeds.2018.09.003

Lewins, & Silver (2007). *Using software in qualitative research: A step-by-step guide.* Thousand Oaks, CA: Sage Publications, Inc.

Lin, S. (2000). Coping and adaptation in families of children with cerebral palsy. *Exceptional Children, 66,* 201–218.

Linan-Thompson, S., & Oritz, A. (2009). Response to intervention and English-language learners: Instructional and assessment considerations. *Seminars in Speech and Language, 30,* 105–120.

Lincoln, Y., & Guba, E. (1985). *Naturalistic Inquiry.* Beverly Hills, CA: Sage Publications, Inc.

Lindstrom, J. H. (2007). Determining appropriate accommodations for postsec_ondary students with reading and written expression disorders. *Learning Disabilities Research and Practice, 22,* 229–236.

Lindstrom, L., Doren, B., & Miesch, J. (2011). Waging a living: Career development and long-term employment outcomes for young adults with disabilities. *Exceptional Children, 77*(4), 423–434.

Lirgg, C. (1991). Gender differences in self-confidence in physical activity: A meta-analysis of recent studies. *Journal of Sport and Exercise Psychology, 8,* 294–310.

Lloyd, J. W., Pullen, P. C., Tankersley, M., & Lloyd, P. A. (2006). Critical dimensions of experimental studies and research syntheses that help define effective practices. In B. G. Cook & B. R. Schirmer (Eds.), *What is special about special education: The role of evidence-based practices.* Austin, TX: Pro-Ed.

Lloyd, J. W., Pullen, P. C., Tankersley, M., & Lloyd, P. A. (2006). Critical dimensions of experimental studies and research syntheses that help define effective practices. In B. G. Cook & B. R. Schirmer (Eds.), *What is special about special education: The role of evidence-based practices* (pp. 136–153). Austin, TX: Pro-Ed.

Losinski, M., Sanders, S., Katsiyannis, A., & Wiseman, N. (2017). A meta-analysis of interventions to improve the compliance of students with disabilities. *Education and Treatment of Children, 40,* 435–463. doi:10.1353/etc.2017.0020

Maag, J. W. (2001). Rewarded by punishment: Reflections on the disuse of positive reinforcement in schools. *Exceptional Children, 67,* 173–186. doi:10.1177/001440290106700203

Maag, J. W., & Anderson, J. M. (2007). Sound-field amplification to increase compliance to directions in students with ADHD. *Behavioral Disorders, 32,* 238–253.

Machek, G. R., & Nelson, J. M. (2007). How should reading disabilities be operationalized? A survey of practicing school psychologists. *Learning Disabilities Research and Practice, 22,* 147–157.

MacMillan, D. L., & Siperstein, G. N. (2002). Learning disabilities as operationalized by the schools. In R. Bradley, L. Danielson, & D. P. Hallahan (Eds.), *Identification of Learning Disabilities: Research in Practice* (pp. 287–233). Mahwah, NJ: Lawrence Erlbaum.

MacSwan, J., & Rolstad, K., (2006). How language proficiency tests mislead us about ability: Implications for English language learner placement in special education. *Teacher College Record, 108,* 2304–2328.

Maddaus, J. W., Gerber, P. J., & Price, L. A. (2008). Adults with learning disabilities in the workforce: Lessons for secondary transition programs. *Learning Disabilities Research and Practice, 23,* 148–153.

Magasi, S., & Hammel, J. (2009). Women with disabilities' experiences in long-term care: A case for social justice. *American Journal of Occupational Therapy, 63*(1), 35–45.

Maggin, D. M., Cook, B. G., & Cook, L. (2019). Making sense of single-case design effect sizes. *Learning Disabilities Research & Practice.* doi:10.1111/ldrp.12204

Maggin, D. M., Talbott, E., Van Acker, E. Y., & Kumm, S. (2017). Quality indicators for systematic reviews in behavioral disorders. *Behavioral Disorders, 42,* 52–64. doi:10.1177/0198742916688653

Makel, M. C., & Plucker, J. A. (2014). Facts are more important than novelty: Replication in the education sciences. *Educational Researcher, 43,* 304–316. doi: 10.3102/0013189X14545513

Makel, M. C., Plucker, J. A., Freeman, J., Lombardi, A., Simonsen, B., & Coyne, M. (2016). Replication of special education research: Necessary but far too rare. *Remedial and Special Education, 37,* 205–212. doi:10.1177/0741932516646083

Malterud, K. (2001). Qualitative research: standards, challenges, and guidelines. *The Lancet, 358*(9280), 483–488.

Margalit, M. (1998). Loneliness and coherence among preschool children with learning disabilities. *Journal of Learning Disabilities, 31*(2), 173.

Marks, H. M. (2000). Student engagement in instructional activity: Patterns in the elementary, middle, and high school years. *American Educational Research Journal, 37,* 153–184. doi: 10.3102/00028312037001153

Marsh, L., Warren, P. L., & Savage, E. (2018). "Something was wrong": A narrative inquiry of becoming a father of a child with an intellectual disability in Ireland. *British Journal of Learning Disabilities, 46*(4), 216–224.

Marshall, C., & Rossman, G. B. (1989). *Designing qualitative research.* Newbury Park, CA: Sage Publications, Inc.

Marshall, C., & Rossman, G. B. (2006). *Designing qualitative research* (4th ed.). Thousand Oaks, CA: Sage Publications, Inc.

Marshall, C., & Rossman, G. B. (2014). *Designing qualitative research.* Thousand Oaks, CA: Sage Publications.

Mastropieri, M., Berkley, S., McDuffie, K., Graff, H., Marshak, L., Conners, N., & Cuenca-Sanchez, Y. (2009). What is published in the field of special education? Analysis of 11 prominent journals. *Exceptional Children, 76*(1), 95–109.

Mattison, R. E., Hooper, S. R., & Glassberg, L. A. (2002). Three-year course of learning disorders in children classified as behaviorally disordered. *Journal of the American Academy of Child and Adolescent Psychiatry, 41,* 1454–1461.

Maxwell, J. A. (1996). *Qualitative research design: An interactive approach.* Thousand Oaks, CA: Sage Publications, Inc.

Maxwell, J. A. (2005). *Qualitative research design: An interactive approach* (2nd ed.). Thousand Oaks, CA: Sage Publications, Inc.

Maxwell, J. A. (2012). *Qualitative research design: An interactive approach* (3rd. ed.). Thousand Oaks, CA: Sage.

Maxwell, L. (2005). The AD/HD book: Answers to parents' most pressing questions/attention deficit disorder: The unfocused mind in children and adults. *Library Journal, 130*(16), 96.

Mayer, R. E. (2000). What is the place of science in educational research? *Educational Researcher, 29,* 38–40.

McCardle, P., Mele-McCarthy, J., Cutting, L., Leos, K., & D'Emilio, T. (2005). Learning disabilities in English language learners: Identifying the issues. *Learning Disabilities Research & Practice, 20,* 1–5.

McDuffie, K., & Scruggs, T. (2008). The contributions of qualitative research to discussions of evidence-based practice in special education. *Intervention in School and Clinic, 44*(2), 91–97.

McGee, G. G., Morrier, M. F., & Daly, T. (1999). An incidental teaching approach to early intervention for toddlers with autism. *Journal of the Association for Persons with Severe Handicaps, 24,* 133–146.

McGrew, K. S., & Mather, N. (2001). *Woodcock Johnson III tests of achievement.* Itasca, IL: Riverside.

McIntosh, A. (2008). Current practice alerts: Functional behavioral assessments. *Division for Learning Disabilities & Division for Research.* Retrieved on February 14, 2010 from http://www.teachingld.org/pdf/alert16.pdf

McLeskey, J., Waldron, N. L., & Redd, L. (2014). A case study of a highly effective, inclusive elementary school. *The Journal of Special Education, 48*(1), 59–70.

McLoyd, V. C. (1998). Socioeconomic disadvantage and child development. *American Psychologist, 53,* 185–204.

McMahon, B., & Shaw, L. (1999). *Enabling lives.* Boca Raton, FL: CRC Press.

McMillan, M. (2000). Health care reforms in aged care in Australia. *Nursing and Health Sciences, 2*(2), A7.

McMillan, J. (2000). *Educational Research: Fundamentals for the Consumer.* New York: Longman.

McMillan, J., & Schumacher, S. (1997). *Research in education: A conceptual introduction* (4th ed.). New York: Longman.

McMillan, J. J., & Schumachers, S. (2009). *Research in education: Evidence based inquiry* (7th ed.). Upper Saddle River, NJ: Pearson.

McMillan, W. (2007). "Then you get a teacher"–Guidelines for excellence in teaching. *Medical Teacher, 29*(8), 209–218.

McPhail, J. (1995). Phenomenology as philosophy and method: Application to ways of doing special education. *Remedial and Special Education, 16*(3), 159–165.

McReynolds, C., & Koch, L. (1999). Qualitative research designs. In J. Bellini & P. Rumrill, *Research in rehabilitation counseling* (pp. 151–173). Springfield, IL: Charles C Thomas.

McReynolds, C. J., & Koch, L. C. (2009). Qualitative research designs. In J. Bellini & P. Rumrill (Eds.), *Research in rehabilitation counseling: A guide to design, methodology and utilization* (2nd ed., pp. 187–218). Springfield, IL: Charles C Thomas.

Meadows, N. B., Neel, R. S., Scott, C. M., & Parker, G. (1994). Academic perform_ance, social competence, and mainstream and nonmainstream students with behavioral disorders. *Behavioral Disorders, 19,* 170–180.

Meece, J. L., Anderman, E. M., & Anderman, L. H. (2006). Classroom goal structure, student motivation, and academic achievement. *Annual Review of Psychology, 57,* 487–503. doi:10.1146/annurev.psych.56.091103.070258

Merchant, W., Li, J., Karpinski, A., & Rumrill, P. (2013). A conceptual overview of structural equation modeling in rehabilitation research. *Work: A Journal of Prevention, Assessment, and Rehabilitation, 45,* 407–415.

Merriam, S. B. (1988). *The case study research in education.* San Francisco: Jossey-Bass.

Merriam, S. (Ed.) (2002). *Qualitative research in practice: Examples for discussion and analysis.* New York: Jossey-Bass.

Merton, R. K. (1968). *Social theory and social structure.* New York: Free Press.

Merton, R. K. (1973). The normative structure of science. In N. W. Storer (Ed.), *The sociology of science: Theoretical and empirical investigations* (pp. 267–280). Chicago, IL: University of Chicago Press. (Original work published 1942.)

Messick, S. (1980). Test validity and the ethics of assessment. *American Psychologist, 35,* 1012–1027.

Messick, S. (1988). The once and future issues in validity: Assessing the meaning and consequences of measurement. In H. Wainer & H. I. Braun (Eds.), *Test validity* (pp. 33–45). Hillsdale, NJ: Erlbaum.

Miles, J., & Shevlin. M. (2001). *Applying regression and correlation: A guide for students and practitioners.* London: Sage Publications, Inc.

Miles, M. B., & Huberman, A. M. (1994). *Qualitative data analysis* (2nd ed.). Thousand Oaks, CA: Sage Publications, Inc.

Miller, F. G., Cohen, D., Chafouleas, S. M., Riley-Tillman, T. C., Welsh, M. E., & Fabiano, G. A. (2015). A comparison of measures to screen for social, emotional, and behavioral risk. *School Psychology Quarterly, 30,* 184–196. doi:10.1037/spq0000085

Miller, S. P., & Hudson, P. J. (2007). Using evidence-based practices to build mathematics competence related to conceptual, procedural, and declarative knowledge. *Learning Disabilities Research and Practice, 22,* 47–57.

Miller, M. (1990). Ethnographic interviews for information about classrooms: An invitation. *Teacher Education and Special Education, 13*(3–4), 233–234.

Miller, M. D., Brownell, M. T., & Smith, S. W. (1999). Factors that predict teachers staying, leaving, or transferring from the special education classroom. *Exceptional Children, 65,* 201–218.

Milner, P., & Kelly B. (2009). Community participation and inclusion: People with disabilities defining their place. *Disability and Society, 24*(1), 47–75.

Mitchell, B. S., Hatton, H., & Lewis, T. J. (2018). An examination of the evidence-base of school-wide positive behavior interventions and supports through two quality appraisal processes. *Journal of Positive Behavior Interventions, 20,* 239–250. doi: 10.1177/10983 00718768217

Mitchell, B. S., Kern, L., & Conroy, M. A. (2019). Supporting students with emotional or behavioral disorders: State of the field. *Behavioral Disorders, 44,* 70–84. doi:10.1177 /0198742918816518

Montague, M. (2007). Self-regulation and mathematics instruction. *Learning Disabilities Research and Practice, 22,* 75–83.

Mooney, P., Denny, R. K., & Gunter, P. L. (2004). The impact of NCLB and the reauthorization of IDEA on academic instruction of students with emotional or behavioral disorders. *Behavioral Disorders, 29,* 237–246.

Mooney, P., Epstein, M. H., Reid, R., & Nelson, J. R. (2003). Status and trends in academic intervention research for students with emotional disturbance. *Remedial and Special Education, 24,* 273–287.

Moravcsik, A. (2014). Transparency: The revolution in qualitative research. *PS: Political Science & Politics, 47*(1), 48–53.

Morgan, P. L., Farkas, G., Hillemeier, M. M., Mattison, R., Maczuga, S., Li, H., & Cook, M. (2015). Minorities Are Disproportionately Underrepresented in Special Education: Longitudinal Evidence Across Five Disability Conditions. *Educational Researcher, 44*(5), 278–292. https://doi.org/10.3102/0013189X15591157

Morgan, P. L., Farkas, G., Cook, M., Strassfeld, N. M., Hillemeier, M. M., Pun, W. H., & Schussler, D. L. (2017). Are Black Children Disproportionately Overrepresented in Special Education? A Best-Evidence Synthesis. *Exceptional Children, 83*(2), 181–198. doi:10.1177/0014402916664042

Morgan, P. L., Farkas, G., Tufis, P. A., & Sperling, R. A. (2008). Are reading and behavior problems risk factors for each other? *Journal of Learning Disabilities, 41,* 417–436. doi: 10.1177/0022219408321123

Morocco, C., & Aguilar, C. (2002). Coteaching for content understanding: A schoolwide model. *Journal of Educational and Psychological Consultation, 13*(4), 315.

Mostert, M. P. (2001). Facilitated communication since 1995: A review of published studies. *Journal of Autism and Developmental Disorders, 31,* 287–313.

Moustakas, C. (1994). *Phenomenological research methods.* Thousand Oaks, CA: Sage Publications, Inc.

Munley, P., Sharkin, B., & Gelso, C. (1988). Reviewer ratings and agreement on manuscripts reviewed for the Journal of Counseling Psychology. *Journal of Counseling Psychology, 35,* 198–202.

Murawski, W. W., & Swanson, H. (2001). A meta-analysis of co-teaching research. *Remedial and Special Education, 22,* 258–267.

Murphy, L. L., Conoley, J. C., & Impara, J. C. (Eds.). (1994). *Tests in print. IV* (Vols. 1 and 2). Lincoln, NE: Buros Institute of the University of Nebraska. Buros Institute of Mental Measurements: University of Nebraska Press.

National Autism Center. (2015). *Findings and conclusions: National Standards Project, Phase 2.* Randolph, MA: Author.

National Center for Educational Statistics. (2007). *The Nation's Report Card: Reading 2007.* Washington, DC: U.S. Department of Education. Retrieved September 8, 2009 from http://nces.ed.gov/pubsearch/pubsinfo.asp?pubid=2007496

National Institute of Mental Health. (2018). *Autism spectrum disorder.* Retrieved from https://www.nimh.nih.gov/health/topics/autism-spectrum-disorders-asd/index.shtml

National Research Center on Learning Disabilities. (2007). *Responsiveness to intervention in the SLD determination process.* Retrieved on 8/30/09 from www.osepideasthatwork.org/toolkit/pdf/RTI_SLD.pdf

National Research Council. (2004). *Engaging schools: Fostering high school students' motivation to learn.* Washington, DC: The National Academies Press. doi:10.5860/ CHOICE.42–1079

National Science Foundation and Institute of Education Sciences, U.S. Department of Education. (2018). *Companion guidelines on replication & reproducibility in education research.* Retrieved from https://ies.ed.gov/pdf/CompanionGuidelinesReplicationReproducibility.pdf

Neff, K. D., Hsieh, Y. P., & Dejitterat, K. (2005). Self-compassion, achievement goals, and coping with academic failure. *Self and Identity, 4,* 263–287. doi:10.1080/13576500444000317

Nelson, J. R., Benner, G. J., Lane, K., & Smith, B. W. (2004). Academic achievement of K–12 students with emotional and behavioral disorders. *Exceptional Children, 71,* 59–63.

Nelson, J. R., Stage, S. A., Epstein, M. H., & Pierce, C. D. (2005). Effects of a pre-reading intervention on the literacy and social skills of children. *Exceptional Children, 72,* 29–45.

Nickerson, R. S. (1998). Confirmation bias: A ubiquitous phenomenon in many guises. *Review of General Psychology, 2,* 175–220.

Niesz, T., Koch, L., & Rumrill, P. D. (2008). The empowerment of people with disabilities through qualitative research. *Work: A Journal of Prevention, Assessment, and Rehabilitation, 31*(1), 113–125.

Nosek, B. A., Ebersole, C. R., DeHaven, A. C., & Mellor, D. T. (2018). The preregistration revolution. *Proceedings of the National Academy of Sciences, 115,* 2600–2606. doi:10.1073/pnas.1708274114

Nosek, B. A., & Lakens, D. (2014). Registered reports. *Social Psychology, 45,* 137–141. doi:10.1027/1864-9335/a000192

Nosek, B. A., Spies, J. R., & Motyl, M. (2012). Scientific utopia: II. Restructuring incentives and practices to promote truth over publishability. *Perspectives on Psychological Science, 7,* 615–631. doi:10.1177/1745691612459058

Oberle, K. M. (2002). Ethics in qualitative health research. *Annals (Royal College of Physicians and Surgeons of Canada), 35*(8 Suppl.), 563–566.

Oberman, L. M., & Ramachandran, V. S. (2007). The simulating social mind: The role of the mirror neuron system and simulation in the social and communicative deficits of autism spectrum disorders. *Psychological Bulletin, 133,* 310–327.

Odom, S. L., Brantlinger, E., Gersten, R., Horner, R. H., Thompson, B., & Harris, K. (2005). Research in special education: Scientific methods and evidence-based practices. *Exceptional Children, 71,* 137–148.

Oh-Young, C., Filler, J., & Buchter, J. (2019). *The Meta-analysis review: A valuable resource for special educators.* Intervention in School and Clinic. Advanced online publication. doi: 10.1177/1053451219842222

Open Science Collaboration. (2015). Estimating the reproducibility of psychological science. *Science, 349*(6251), aac4716. doi:10.1126/science.aac4716

Orb, A., Eisenhauer, L., & Wynaden, D. (2001). Ethics in qualitative research. *Journal of Nursing Scholarship, 33*(1), 93–96.

Orwell, G. (1946). Politics and the English language. In G. Orwell (Ed.), *A collection of essays* (pp. 157–171). San Diego: Harcourt, Brace, and Johanovich.

Osborne, L., & Reed, P. (2009). The relationship between parenting stress and behavior problems of children with autistic spectrum disorders. *Exceptional Children, 76*(1), 54–73.

Page-Voth, V., & Graham, S. (1999). Effects of goal setting and strategy use on the writing performance and self-efficacy of students with writing and learning problems. *Journal of Educational Psychology, 91,* 230–240. doi:10.1037/0022-0663.91.2.230

Palmer, L. (1998). Influence of students' global constructs of teaching effectiveness on summative evaluation. *Educational Assessment, 5*(2), 111.

Palsher, H., & Yantis, S. (Eds.). (2002). *Stevens' handbook of experimental psychology* (3rd ed.). New York, NY: John Wiley & Sons.

Parker, R. M., & Szymanski, E. M. (Eds.). (1998). *Rehabilitation counseling: Basics and beyond* (3rd ed.). Austin, TX: Pro-Ed.

Parker, R. I., & Vannest, K. J. (2012). Bottom-up analysis of single-case research designs. *Journal of Behavioral Education, 21,* 254–265. doi:10.1007/s10864-012-9153-1

Parker, R. I., Vannest, K. J., Davis, J. L., & Sauber, S. B. (2011). Combining nonoverlap and trend for single-case research: Tau-U. *Behavior Therapy, 42,* 284–299. doi:10.1016/j.beth.2010.08.006

Parker, R. M. (1990). Science, philosophy, and politics in the search for truth in rehabilitation research. *Rehabilitation Counseling Bulletin, 34,* 165–169.

Parker, R., & Szymanski, E. (1996). Editorial: Ethics and publication. *Rehabilitation Counseling Bulletin, 39*(3), 162–165.

Patterson, G. R. (1975). *Families: Applications of social learning to family life.* Champaign, IL: Research Press.

Patton, M. Q. (2002). *Qualitative research and evaluation methods* (3rd ed.). Thousand Oaks, CA: Sage Publications, Inc.

Pedhazur, E. (1982). *Multiple regression in behavioral research* (2nd ed.). New York: Harcourt College Publishers.

Pedhazur, E. (1997). *Multiple regression in behavioral research: Explanation and prediction* (3rd ed.). New York: Harcourt Brace.

Peters, D. P., & Ceci, S. J. (1982). The fate of published articles, submitted again. *Behavioral and Brain Sciences, 5*(2), 199–199.

Peterson, K. M. H., & Shinn, M. R. (2002). Severe discrepancy models: Which explains school identification practices for learning disabilities? *School Psychology Review, 31,* 459–476.

Piwowar, H., Priem, J., Larivière, V., Alperin, J. P., Matthias, L., Norlander, B., & Haustein, S. (2018). *The state of OA: A large-scale analysis of the prevalence and impact of Open Access articles.* PeerJ, 6, e4375. doi: 10.7717/peerj.4375

Polkinghorne, D. E. (1991). *Qualitative procedures for counseling research.* In C. E. Watkins & U. Schneider (Eds.), Research in counseling (pp. 163–204). Hillsdale, NJ: Erlbaum.

Polkinghorne, D. E. (1995). Narrative configuration in qualitative analysis. In J. A. Hatch & R. Wisniewski (Eds.), *Life history and narrative* (pp. 5–23). Abingdon, OX: Routledge Falmer.

Popper, K. (1959). *The logic of scientific discovery.* New York: Basic Books.

Porter, E., Neysmith, S. M., Reitsma-Street, M., & Collins, S. B. (2009). Reciprocal peer interviewing. *International Review of Qualitative Research, 2,* 291–312.

Powell, S. R., & Fuchs, L. S. (2018). Effective Word-Problem Instruction: Using Schemas to Facilitate Mathematical Reasoning. *Teaching Exceptional Children, 51*(1), 31–42. doi: 10.1177/0040059918777250

Power, P. (2013). *A guide to vocational assessment* (5th ed.). Austin, TX: Pro-Ed.

Pro-Ed. (2015). *Publications catalog.* Retrieved April 28, 2015 from www.proedinc.com/tests /catalog.html

Pugach, M. C. (2001). The stories we choose to tell: Fulfilling the promise of qualitative research for special education. *Exceptional Children, 67*(4), 439–453.

Pugach, M. C., Mukhopadhyay, A., & Gomez-Najarro, J. (2014). Finally making good on the promise of qualitative research in special education? A response to the special issue. *Remedial and Special Education, 35*(6), 340–343.

Pullen, P. C., & Lloyd, J. W. (2008). Current practice alerts: Phonics instruction. *Division for Learning Disabilities & Division for Research.* Retrieved on February 14, 2010 from http: //www.teachingld.org/pdf/alert14.pdf

Rabren, K., & Evans, A. M. (2016). A Consensual Qualitative analysis of parental concerns and strategies for transition. *Journal of Vocational Rehabilitation, 44*(3), 307–321.

Rafferty, Y., Piscitelli, V., & Boettcher, C. (2003). The impact of inclusion on language development and social competence among preschoolers with disabilities. *Exceptional Children, 69,* 467–479.

Raudenbush, S. W., & Bryk, A. S. (2002). *Hierarchical linear models: Applications and data analysis methods* (2nd ed.). Thousand Oaks, CA: Sage Publications, Inc.

Reichow, B., Barton, E. E., Boyd, B. A., & Hume, K. (2012). *Early intensive behavioral intervention (EIBI) for young children with autism spectrum disorders (ASD).* Cochrane Database of Systematic Reviews, 10, CD009260. Retrieved from https://www.cochranelibrary.com /cdsr/doi/10.1002/14651858.CD009260.pub2/full

Reid, R., Gonzalez, J. E., Nordness, P. D., Trout, A., & Epstein, M. H. (2004). A meta-analysis of the academic status of students with emotional/behavioral disturbance. *Journal of Special Education, 38,* 130–143.

Rew, L., Bechtel, D., & Sapp, A. (1993). Self-as-instrument in qualitative research. *Nursing Research, 42*(5), 300–301.

Rice, C. E., Rosanoff, M., Dawson, G., Durkin, M. S., Croen, L. A., Singer, A., & Yeargin-Allsopp, M. (2012). Evaluating changes in the prevalence of the autism spectrum disorders (ASDs). *Public Health Reviews, 34*(2), 1–22. doi: 10.1007/BF03391685

Roberts, G., Torgesen, J. K., Boardman, A., & Scammacca, N. (2008). Evidence-based strategies for reading instruction of older students with learning disabilities. *Learning Disabilities Research & Practice, 23*(2), 63–69. doi:10.1111/ j.1540-5826.2008.00264.x

Roberts, J., & Whiting, C. (2011). Caregivers of school children with epilepsy: findings of a phenomenological study. *British Journal of Special Education, 38*(4), 169–177. doi:10.1111 /j.1467-8578.2011.00519.x

Robinson, W. S. (1951). The logical structure of analytic induction. *American Sociological Review, 16,* 812–818.

Roessler, R., & Gottcent, J. (1994). The Work Experience Survey: A reasonable accommodation/career development strategy. *Journal of Applied Rehabilitation Counseling, 25*(3), 16–21.

Roessler, R., Reed, C., & Brown, P. (1998). Coping with chronic illness at work: Case studies of five successful employees. *Journal of Vocational Rehabilitation, 10*(3), 261–269.

Roessler, R., Rubin, S., & Rumrill, P. (2017). *Case Management in rehabilitation counseling: A systematic approach* (5th ed.). Austin, TX: Pro-Ed.

Rosenthal, R. (1979). The "file drawer problem" and tolerance for null results. *Psychological Bulletin, 86,* 638–641. doi:10.1037/0033-2909.86.3.638

Rosenthal, R., & Rosnow, R. L. (1969). The volunteer subject. In R. Rosenthal & R. L. Rosnow (Eds.), *Artifact in behavioral research* (pp. 61–118). New York: Academic Press.

Rosnow, R. L., & Rosenthal, R. (1989). Statistical procedures and the justification of knowledge in psychological science. *American Psychologist, 44,* 1276–1284.

Ross-Hellauer, T. (2017). What is open peer review? A systematic review. *F1000Research, 6,* 588. doi:10.12688/f1000research.11369.1

Rubin, H. J., & Rubin, I. S. (2005). *Qualitative interviewing: The art of hearing data* (2nd ed.). Thousand Oaks, CA: Sage Publications, Inc.

Rubin, S., & Roessler, R. (1995). *Foundations of the vocational rehabilitation process.* Austin, TX: Pro-Ed.

Rubin, S., & Roessler, R. (2008). *Foundations of the vocational rehabilitation process* (6th ed.). Austin, TX: Pro-Ed.

Rubin, S., Roessler, R., & Rumrill, P. (2016). *Foundations of the vocational rehabilitation process* (7th ed.). Austin, TX: Pro-Ed.

Ruhl, K. L., & Berlinghoff, D. H. (1992). Research on improving behaviorally disordered students' academic performance: A review of the literature. *Behavioral Disorders, 17,* 178–190.

Rumrill, P., & Cook, B. (2001). *Research in special education* (2nd ed.). Springfield, IL: Charles C Thomas.

Rumrill, P., & Bellini, J. (2018). *Research in rehabilitation counseling* (3rd ed.). Springfield, IL: Charles C Thomas.

Rumrill, P. R., Cook, B. G., & Wiley, A. L. (2011). *Research in special education: Designs, methods, and applications* (2nd ed.). Springfield, IL: Charles C Thomas.

Rumrill, P., Roessler, R., & Denny, G. (1997). Increasing confidence in the accommodation request process among persons with multiple sclerosis: A career maintenance self-efficacy intervention. *Journal of Job Placement, 13*(1), 5–9.

Ryan, A. M., Pintrich, P. R., & Midgley, C. (2001). Avoiding seeking help in the classroom: Who and why? *Educational Psychology Review, 13,* 93–114.

Ryan, S., & Ferguson, D. L. (2006). On, yet under, the radar: Students with fetal alcohol syndrome disorder. *Exceptional Children, 72*(3), 363–379.

Sabornie, E. J., Cullinan, D., Osborne, S. S., & Brock, L. B. (2005). Intellectual, academic, and behavioral functioning of students with high-incidence disabilities: A cross-categorical meta-analysis. *Exceptional Children, 72,* 47–63.

Sackett, D. L., Rosenberg, W. M. C., Gray, J. A. M., Haynes, R. B., & Richardson, W. S. (1996). Evidence based medicine: What it is and what it isn't. *British Medical Journal, 312,* 71–72.

Sagan, C. (1996). *The demon-haunted world: Science as a candle in the dark.* New York: Ballantine Books.

Salmona, M., & Kaczynski, D. (2016). Don't blame the software: Using qualitative data analysis software successfully in qualitative research. *Forum: Qualitative Social Research, 17*(3), Article 11.

Samson, J., & Lesaux, N. (2009). Language-minority learners in special education: Rates and predictors of identification for services. *Journal of Learning Disabilities, 42,* 148–162.

Santangelo, T., Novosel, L., Cook, B. G., & Gapsis, M. (2015). Using the 6S Pyramid to identify research-based instructional practices for students with learning disabilities. *Learning
Disabilities Research and Practice, 30,* 91–101. doi:10.1111/ldrp.12055

Satsangi, R., Hammer, R., & Hogan, C. D. (2018). Studying Virtual Manipulatives Paired With
Explicit Instruction to Teach Algebraic Equations to Students With Learning Disabilities.
Learning Disability Quarterly, 41(4), 227–242. https://doi.org/10.1177/0731948718769248

Schaller, J., & Parker, R. (1997). Effect of graduate research instruction on perceived research
anxiety, research utility, and confidence in research skills. *Rehabilitation Education, 11,*
273–287.

Schardt, A. A., Miller, F. G., & Bedesem, P. L. (2019). The Effects of CellF-Monitoring on
Students' Academic Engagement: A Technology-Based Self-Monitoring Intervention.
Journal of Positive Behavior Interventions, 21(1), 42–49. doi:10.1177/1098300718773462

Schneider, M. (2019, April 15). *List of proposed interventions for the systematic replication RFA.*
Retrieved from https://ies.ed.gov/director/remarks/4-15-2019.asp

Schram, T. H. (2006). *Conceptualizing and proposing qualitative research* (2nd ed.). Upper Saddle
River, NJ: Pearson Prentice Hall.

Schriner, K. F., Rumrill, P., & Parlin, R. (1995). Rethinking disability policy: Equity in the
ADA era and the meaning of specialized services for people with disabilities. *Journal of
Health and Human Resources Administration, 17,* 478–500.

Schroter, S., Black, N., Evans, S., Godlee, F., Osorio, L., & Smith, R. (2008). What errors do
peer reviewers detect, and does training improve their ability to detect them? *Journal of
the Royal Society of Medicine, 101,* 507–514. doi:10.1258/jrsm.2008.080062

Schultz, R. T. (2005). Developmental deficits in social perception in autism: The role of the
amygdala and fusiform face area. *International Journal of Developmental Neuroscience, 23,*
125–141.

Schumacker, R. E., & Lomax, R. G. (2015). *A beginner's guide to structural equation modeling* (4th
ed.). New York, NY: Routledge, Taylor & Francis Group.

Schunk, D. H. (1985). Participation in goal setting: Effects on self-efficacy and skills of learning disabled children. *The Journal of Special Education, 19,* 307–317. doi:10.1177
/002246698501900307

Schunk, D. H. (1990). Goal setting and self-efficacy during self-regulated learning. *Educational
Psychologist, 25,* 71–86. doi:10.1207/s15326985ep2501_6

Schwandt, T. A. (2001). *Dictionary of qualitative inquiry* (2nd ed.). Thousand Oaks, CA: Sage
Publications, Inc.

Scruggs, T. E., Mastropieri, M. A., & McDuffie, K. A. (2007). Co-teaching in inclusive classrooms: A metasynthesis of qualitative research. *Exceptional Children 73*(4), 392–416.

Seethaler, P. M., & Fuchs L. S. (2005). A drop in the bucket: Randomized controlled trials
testing reading and math interventions. *Learning Disabilities Research & Practice, 20,* 98–
102.

Semmel, M. I., Gottlieb, J., & Robinson, N. (1979). Mainstreaming: Perspectives in educating
handicapped children in the public schools. In D. Berliner (Ed.), *Review of research in education* (pp. 223–279). Itasca, IL: Peacock.

Serlin, R. C. (1987). Hypothesis testing, theory building, and the philosophy of science.
Journal of Counseling Psychology, 34, 265–371.

Shadish, W. R., Zelinsky, N. A., Vevea, J. L., & Kratochwill, T. R. (2016). A survey of publication practices of single-case design researchers when treatments have small or large
effects. *Journal of Applied Behavior Analysis, 49,* 656–673. doi:10.1002/jaba.308

Sham, E., & Smith, T. (2014). Publication bias in studies of an applied behavior-analytic intervention: An initial analysis. *Journal of Applied Behavior Analysis, 47,* 663–678. doi:10.1002
/jaba.146

Shek, D. T., & Lee, B. M. (2007). A comprehensive review of quality of life (QOL) research in Hong Kong. *The Scientific World Journal, 7,* 1222–1229.

Shermer, M. (2002). *Why people believe weird things.* New York: Henry Holt and Company.

Shogren, K. A., Wehmeyer, M. L., & Palmer, S. B. (2017). *Causal agency theory. Development of self-determination through the life-course,* 55–67. doi:10.1007/978-94-024-1042-6_5

Siegel, S. (1956). *Nonparametric statistics for the behavioral sciences.* New York: McGraw-Hill.

Simons, D. J., & Chabris, C. F. (1999). Gorillas in our midst: Sustained inattentional blindness for dynamic events. *Perception, 28,* 1059–1074.

Simons, H., Kushner, S., Jones, K., & James, D. (2003). From evidence-based practice to practice-based evidence: The idea of situated generalization. *Research Papers in Education, 18,* 347–364. doi:10.1080/0267152032000176855

Sinclair, M. F., Christenson, S. L., & Thurlow, M. L. (2005). Promoting school completion of urban secondary youth with emotional or behavioral disabilities. *Exceptional Children, 71,* 465–481.

Singer, G. H., Ethridge, B. L., & Aldana, S. I. (2007). Primary and secondary effects of parenting and stress management interventions for parents of children with developmental disabilities: A meta-analysis. *Mental Retardation and Developmental Disabilities Research Reviews, 13,* 357–369.

Sirin, S. R. (2005). Socioeconomic status and academic achievement: A meta-analytic review of research. *Review of Educational Research, 75,* 417–453.

Skinner, D., Bailey Jr., D. B., Correa, V., & Rodriguez, P. (1999). Narrating self and disability: Latino mothers' construction of identities vis-à-vis their child with special needs. *Exceptional Children, 65*(4), 481–495.

Slavin, R. E (2008). What works? Issues in synthesizing educational program evaluations. *Educational Researcher, 37*(1), 5–14.

Smith, G. J., Schmidt, M. M., Edelen-Smith, P., & Cook, B. G. (2013). Pasteur's quadrant as the bridge linking rigor and relevance. *Exceptional Children, 79,* 147–161. doi:10.1177/001440291307900202

Smith, S. W., Daunic, A. P., & Taylor, G. G. (2007). Treatment fidelity in applied educational research: Expanding the adoption and application of measures to ensure evidence-based practice. *Education and Treatment of Children, 30,* 121–134.

Snijders, T., & Bosker, R. (1999). *Multilevel analysis.* London: Sage Publications, Inc.

Snyder, P., & Lawson, S. (1993). Evaluating results using corrected and uncorrected effect size estimates. *Journal of Experimental Education, 61,* 334–349.

Spicer, J. (2005). *Making sense of multivariate data analysis.* Thousand Oaks, CA: Sage Publications, Inc.

Splett, J. W., Trainor, K. M., Raborn, A., Halliday-Boykins, C. A., Garzona, M. E., Dongo, M. D., & Weist, M. D. (2018). Comparison of universal mental health screening to students already receiving intervention in a multitiered system of support. *Behavioral Disorders, 43,* 344–356. doi: 10.1177/0198742918761339

Spradley, J. P. (1980). *Participant observation.* Fort Worth, TX: Holt, Rinehart, & Winston, Inc.

Stenhoff, D. M., & Lignugaris-Kraft, B. (2007). A review of the effects of peer tutoring on students with mild disabilities in secondary settings. *Exceptional Children, 74,* 8–30.

Stevens, J. (2002). *Applied multivariate statistics for the social sciences* (2nd ed.). Hillsdale, NJ: Erlbaum.

Stevens, J. (2007). *Intermediate statistics.* New York: Lawrence Erlbaum Associates.

Stevens, J. P. (2012). *Applied multivariate statistics for the social sciences.* Routledge. New York, NY.

Stevens, S. S. (1946). On the theory of scales of measurement. *Science, 103,* 677–680.

Stevens, S. S. (1951). Mathematics, measurement, and psychophysics. In S. S. Stevens (Ed.), *Handbook of experimental psychology* (pp. 1–49). Oxford, England: Wiley.

Stevenson, N. (2016). Effects of planning and goal setting on reducing latency to task engagement for struggling readers in middle school. *Journal of Behavioral Education, 25,* 206– 222. doi:10.1007/s10864-015-9238-8

Stevenson, N. A., & Mussalow, P. R. (2018). The Effects of Planning, Goal Setting, and Performance Feedback on Avoidance Behaviors for Struggling Readers. *Journal of Positive Behavior Interventions,* 109830071880456. doi:10.1177/1098300718804566

Stevenson, N. A., & Reed, D. K. (2017). To Change the Things I Can: Making Instruction More Intensive. *Intervention in School and Clinic, 53*(2), 74–80. doi:10.1177/10534512176 93365

Stewart, K., & Williams, M. (2005). Researching online populations: the use of online focus groups for social research. *Qualitative Research, 5*(4), 395–416.

Strauser, D. (2014). *Career development, employment, and disability in rehabilitation.* New York: Springer Publishing Company.

Strauss, A., & Corbin, J. (1990). *Basics of qualitative research: Grounded theory procedures and techniques.* Newbury Park, CA: Sage Publications, Inc.

Sullivan J. R. (2012) Skype: An appropriate method of data collection for qualitative interviews? *The Hilltop Review, 6,* 54–60.

Sutherland, K. S., Lewis-Palmer, T., Stichter, J., & Morgan, P. L. (2008). Examining the influence of teacher behavior and classroom context on the academic and behavioral outcomes for students with emotional and behavioral disorders. *Journal of Special Education, 41,* 223–233.

Swanson, H. L., & Hoskyn, M. (1998). Experimental intervention research on students with learning disabilities: A meta-analysis of treatment outcomes. *Review of Educational Research, 68,* 277–321.

Swanson, H. L., Hoskyn, M., & Lee, C. (1999). *Interventions for students with learning disabilities: A meta-analysis of treatment outcomes.* New York: Guilford Press.

Tacq, J. J., & Tacq, J. (1997). *Multivariate analysis techniques in social science research: From problem to analysis.* Sage. Thousand Oaks, CA.

Tankersley, M., & Cook, B. G. (in press). *Research-based practices in special education.* Upper Saddle River, NJ: Pearson.

Tankersley, M., Harjusola-Webb, S., & Landrum, T. (2008). Using single-subject research to establish the evidence base of special education. *Intervention in School and Clinic, 44*(2), 83–90.

Tapp, J., Wehby, J., & Ellis, D. (1995). A multiple option observation system for experimental studies: MOOSES. *Behavior Research Methods, Instruments, & Computers, 27*(1), 25–31.

Tarlow, K. R. (2017). An improved rank correlation effect size statistic for single-case designs: Baseline corrected Tau. *Behavior Modification, 41,* 427–467. doi:10.1177/01454455166 76750

Taylor, R. (1999). *Assessment of exceptional children.* Needham Heights, MA: Allyn & Bacon.

Templeton, T. N., Neel, R. S., & Blood, E. (2008). Meta-analysis of math interventions for students with emotional and behavioral disorders. *Journal of Emotional and Behavioral Disorders, 16,* 226–239.

Therrien, W. J., & Cook, B. G. (2018). Null effects and publication bias in learning disabilities research. *Learning Disabilities Research & Practice, 33,* 5–10. doi: 10.1111/ldrp.12163

Thomas, C. N., Peeples, K. N., Kennedy, M. J., & Decker, M. (2019). Riding the Special Education Technology Wave: Policy, Obstacles, Recommendations, Actionable Ideas, and Resources. *Intervention in School and Clinic, 54*(5), 295–303. doi:10.1177 /1053451218819201

Thompson, B. (1986, November). *Two reasons why multivariate methods are unusually vital.* Paper presented at the annual meeting of the Mid-South Educational Research Association, Memphis, TN.

Thorndike, R. (2005). *Measurement and evaluation in psychology and education* (7th ed.). Upper Saddle River, NJ: Pearson Education, Inc.

Tracey, T. (1991). Counseling research as an applied science. In C. E. Watkins & L. J. Schneider (Eds.), *Research in counseling* (pp. 3–31). Hillsdale, NJ: Lawrence Erlbaum

Trainor, A. A. (2005). Self-determination perceptions and behaviors of diverse students with LD during the transition planning process. *Journal of Learning Disabilities, 38*(3), 233–249.

Trainor, A. A. (2008). Using cultural and social capital to improve postsecondary outcomes and expand transition models for youth with disabilities. *Journal of Special Education, 42,*148–162.

Trainor, A. A., & Leko, M. M. (2014). Qualitative special education research: Purpose, rigor, and contribution. *Remedial and Special Education, 35*(5), 263–266.

Travers, J. C., Ayers, K., Simpson, R. L., & Crutchfield, S. (2016). Fad, pseudoscientific, and controversial interventions. In R. Lang, T. Hancock, & N. Singh (Eds.), *Early intervention for young children with autism spectrum disorder* (pp. 257–293). Switzerland: Springer.

Travers, J. C., Cook, B. G., Therrien, W. J., & Coyne, M. D. (2016). Replication research and special education. *Remedial and Special Education, 37,* 195–204. doi:10.1177 /0741932516648462

Trent, S. C., Kea, C. D., & Oh, K. (2008). Preparing preservice educators for cultural diversity: How far have we come? *Exceptional Children, 76,* 328–350.

Trochim, W. M. K. (2006). The regression-discontinuity design. *Web Center for Social Research Methods.* Retrieved on 9/2/09 from http://www.socialresearchmethods.net/kb/quasird .htm

Trout, A. L., Nordness, P. D., Pierce, C. D., & Epstein, M. H. (2003). Research on the academic status of children with emotional and behavioral disorders: A review of the literature from 1961 to 2000. *Journal of Emotional and Behavioral Disorders, 11,* 198–210.

U. S. Census Bureau. (2003). *Language use, English ability, and linguistic isolation for the population 5 to 17 years by state: 2000.* Retrieved on 9/10/09 from http://www.census.gov /population/www/cen2000/briefs/phc-t20/tables/tab02.pdf

U. S. Department of Education. (2009). *28th annual report to Congress on the implementation of the Individuals with Disabilities Education Act, 2006.* Washington, D.C.: Author.

U.S. Department of Education. (2018, January). *39th annual report to Congress on the implementation of the Individuals with Disabilities Education Act,* 2017 (ED-OSE-12-C-0031). Retrieved from https://www2.ed.gov/about/reports/annual/osep/index.html

U.S. Department of Education, Institute of Education Sciences, National Center for Education Evaluation and Regional Assistance. (2018). *What Works Clearinghouse: Procedures handbook* (Version 4.0). Retrieved from https://ies.ed.gov/ncee/wwc/Docs /referenceresources/wwc_procedures_handbook_v4.pdf

Vacha-Haase, T., & Thompson, B. (2004). How to estimate and interpret various effect sizes. *Journal of Counseling Psychology, 51,* 473–481.

Vaughn, S., Mathes, P., Linan-Thompson, S., & Francis, D. (2005). Teaching English language learners at risk for reading disabilities to read: Putting research into practice. *Learning Disabilities Research and Practice, 20,* 58–67.

Vaughn, S., Roberts, G., Wexler, J., Vaughn, M. G., Fall, A. M., & Schnakenberg, J. B. (2015). High School Students with Reading Comprehension Difficulties: Results of a Randomized Control Trial of a Two-Year Reading Intervention. *Journal of Learning Disabilities, 48*(5), 546–558. https://doi.org/10.1177/0022219413515511

Vaughn, S., Wanzek, J., Murray, C. S., Scammacca, N., Linan-Thompson, S., & Woodruff, A. L. (2009). Response to early reading intervention: Examining higher and lower responders. *Exceptional Children, 75,* 165–183.

Volkmar, F. (2009). Autism and autism spectrum disorders: Diagnostic issues for the coming decade. *Journal of Child Psychology and Psychiatry and Allied Disciplines, 50,* 108–115.

Wagner, M. M. (1995). Outcomes for youth with serious emotional disturbance in secondary school and early adulthood. *The Future of Children, 5*(2), 90–111.

Wagner, M., Kutash, K., Duchnowski, A. J., Epstein, M. H., & Sumi, W. C. (2005). The children and youth we serve: A national picture of the characteristics of students with emotional disturbances receiving special education. *Journal of Emotional and Behavioral Disorders, 13,* 79–96.

Walker, H. M., & Severson, H. H. (1992). *Systematic screening for behavior disorders.* Longmont, CO: Sopris West.

Walker, H. M., Ramsey, E., & Gresham, F. M. (2004). *Antisocial behavior in school: Strategies and best practices* (2nd ed.). Pacific Grove, CA: Brooks-Cole.

Walker, M. L. (1993). Participatory action research. *Rehabilitation Counseling Bulletin, 37,* 2–5.

Wanzek, J., & Vaughn, S. (2006). Bridging the research-to-practice gap: Maintaining the consistent implementation of research-based practices. In B. G. Cook & B. R. Schirmer (Eds.), *What is special about special education: The role of evidence-based practices* (pp. 165–174). Austin, TX: PRO-ED.

Wax, R. (1979). Gender and age in fieldwork and fieldwork education: No good thing is done by any man alone. *Social Problems, 26,* 509–523.

Wehby, J. H., & Hollahan, M. S. (2000). Effects of high-probability requests on the latency to initiate academic tasks. *Journal of Applied Behavior Analysis, 33,* 259–262. doi:10.1901/jaba.2000.33-259

Wehman, P. (2013). *Life beyond the classroom.* Baltimore, MD: Paul Brookes.

Wehmeyer, M., & Schwartz, M. (1997). Self-Determination and Positive Adult Outcomes: A Follow-up Study of Youth with Mental Retardation or Learning Disabilities. *Exceptional Children, 63*(2), 245–255. doi:10.1177/001440299706300207

Weiss, M. P. (2004). Co-teaching as science in the schoolhouse: More questions than answers. *Journal of Learning Disabilities, 37*(3), 218–223.

White, K. R. (1982). The relationship between socioeconomic status and academic achievement. *Psychological Bulletin, 91,* 461–481.

Whitney, D. G., & Peterson, M. D. (2019). US national and state-level prevalence of mental health disorders and disparities of mental health care use in children. *JAMA Pediatrics, 173,* 389–391. doi: 10.1001/jamapediatrics.2018.5399

Wiener, J., & Sunohara, G. (1998). Parents' perceptions of the quality of friendship of their children with learning disabilities. *Learning Disabilities Research and Practice, 13,* 242–257.

Wiley, A., Siperstein, D., Bountress, K., Forness, S., & Brigham, F. (2008). Social context and the academic achievement of students with emotional disturbance. *Behavioral Disorders, 33*(4), 198–210.

Williams-Diehm, K., Wehmeyer, M. L., Palmer, S. B., Soukup, J. H., & Garner, N. W. (2008). Self-determination and student involvement in transition planning: A multivariate analysis. *Journal on Developmental Disabilities, 14,* 27–39.

Wing, L., & Potter, D. (2009). The epidemiology of autism spectrum disorders: Is the prevalence rising? In S. Goldstein, J. A. Naglieri, & S. Ozonoff (Eds.), *Assessments of autism spectrum disorders* (pp. 18–54). New York: Guilford.

Winston, R. B. (1985). A suggested procedure for determining order of authorship in research publications. *Journal of Counseling and Development, 63,* 515–519.

Wolgemuth, J., Cobb, R., & Alwell, M. (2008). The effects of mnemonic interven_tions on academic outcomes for youth with disabilities: A systematic review. *Learning Disabilities Research and Practice, 23*(1), 1–10.

Wong, C., Odom, S. L., Hume, K. A., Cox, A. W., Fettig, A., Kucharczyk, S., & Schultz, T. R. (2015). Evidence-based practices for children, youth, and young adults with autism spectrum disorder: A comprehensive review. *Journal of Autism and Developmental Disorders, 45,* 1951–1966.

Woodcock, R. W., McGrew, K. S., & Mather, N. (2001). *Woodcock Johnson III tests of achievement.* Itasca, IL: Riverside.

Woodcock, R.W., McGrew, K.S., Mather, & N. (2007). Woodcock-Johnson III Tests of Achievement. Riverside Publishing, Rolling Meadows, IL.

Wright, B. A. (1983). *Physical disability: A psychosocial approach* (2nd ed.). New York: Harper Collins.

Yell, M. L., Rogers, D., & Rogers, E. L. (1998). The legal history of special education: What a long, strange trip it's been! *Remedial and Special Education, 19,* 219–228.

Yin, R. K. (1989). *Case study research: Design and methods.* Newbury Park, CA: Sage Publications, Inc.

Yin, R. K. (2009). *Case study research: Designs and methods* (4th ed.). Thousand Oaks, CA: Sage Publications, Inc.

Yong, E. (2018, November 19). Psychology's replication crisis is running out of excuses. *The Atlantic.* Retrieved from https://www.theatlantic.com/science/archive/2018/11/psychologys-replication-crisis-real/576223/

Yuknis, C. (2014). A grounded theory of text revision processes used by young adolescents who are deaf. *Exceptional Children, 80*(3), 307–322.

Zigmond, N., Kloo, A., & Volonino, V. (2009). What, where, and how? Special education in the climate of full inclusion. *Exceptionality, 17,* 189–204.

Zimmerman, B. J. (2000). Attaining self-regulation. In M. Boekaerts, P. R. Pintrich, & M. Zeidner (Eds.), *Handbook of self-regulation* (2nd ed., pp. 13–39). Burlington, MA: Elsevier. doi:10.1016/b978-012109890-2/50031-7

INDEX

ABOUT THE AUTHORS

Phillip D. Rumrill, Jr., Ph.D., CRC, is a Professor of Rehabilitation Counseling and Director of Research and Training in the Human Development Institute at the University of Kentucky, Lexington. Dr. Rumrill received his bachelor's and master's degrees from Keene State College in New Hampshire and his doctorate from the University of Arkansas. His professional work experience includes residential services for people with developmental disabilities, substance abuse counseling, and assistive technology training for college students with disabilities. Dr. Rumrill's research interests include the career development implications of disability, cognitive support technology, chronic illness, transition services for adolescents with disabilities, and disability issues in higher education. He has authored or co-authored more than 350 professional publications, including books entitled *Employment Issues and Multiple Sclerosis, Research in Rehabilitation Counseling, Foundations of the Vocational Rehabilitation Process,* and *Case Management and Rehabilitation Counseling.*

Bryan G. Cook, Ph.D., is a Professor of Special Education at the University of Virginia, Charlottesville. Dr. Cook received his bachelor's, master's, and doctoral degrees—as well as general and special education teaching licenses—from the University of California, Santa Barbara. His professional work experience includes teaching youth and adolescents with a variety of disabilities in educational and residential settings. Dr. Cook's research interests include open science, evidence-based practice in special education, and physical activity of students with disabilities. Dr. Cook currently co-edits the journal *Behavioral Disorders* and the annual volume *Advances in Learning and Behavioral Disabilities;* and is associate editor for *Exceptional Children and Remedial and Special Education.* He is past-president of the Council for Exceptional Children's Division for Research and chaired the workgroup that developed the Council for Exceptional Children's *Standards for Evidence-Based Practices in Special Education.* Dr. Cook co-directs the Consortium for the Advancement of Special Education Research (CASPER).

Nathan A. Stevenson, Ph.D., is an Assistant Professor of Special Education at Kent State University. Dr. Stevenson received his bachelor's and doctoral degrees from Michigan State University. His professional work experience includes direct care for adults in residential settings and teaching students with disabilities in inclusive settings in elementary and middle school. Dr. Stevenson's research interests include the development of academic and behavioral supports to improve the quality of inclusive education and school-wide systems of support. He has presented nationally and internationally on the topics of classroom management, Positive Behavior Interventions and Supports, and Assessment. Dr. Stevenson has published numerous articles related to special education research and currently serves on the editorial boards for *Education and Treatment of Children and Assessment for Effective Intervention.* In 2016, Dr. Stevenson was co-recipient of the Early Career Research Award from the Society for the Study of School Psychology.